The ICSA Handbook of

Good Boardroom Practice

Second Edition

The ICSA Handbook of

Good Boardroom Practice

Second Edition

BARBARA COOPER

BA, MSc, FCIS

ICSA

PUBLISHING

Published by ICSA Publishing Limited
16 Park Crescent
London W1B 1AH

Typeset in Minion with Gill Sans by Hands Fotoset, Nottingham

Printed and bound in Great Britain by TJ International, Padstow, Cornwall

British Library Cataloguing in Publication Data
A catalogue record for this book is available from the British Library

ISBN 10: 1 86072 343 8
ISBN 13: 978 1860 723 438

Contents

Introduction *viii*

Abbreviations *xi*

Part 1: Listed companies and their operating environment *1*

1   Legal framework *2*
2   Codes of corporate governance *18*
3   The international dimension *28*
4   Emerging expectations *40*

Part 2: Application of the Combined Code *49*

5   Collective role of the board *51*
6   Composition of the board *64*
7   Board effectiveness *81*
8   Appointment of directors *96*
9   Directors' remuneration *107*
10   Reporting to shareholders *127*
11   Audit committee and auditors *143*
12   Internal control and risk management *160*
13   Relations with institutional investors *174*
14   Constructive use of the AGM *190*

Part 3: Source materials *205*

Appendix 1
Combined Code of Corporate Governance (July 2003) *207*

Appendix 2
Association of British Insurers: Disclosure Guidelines on Socially Responsible Investment
(October 2001) *225*

v

CONTENTS

Appendix 3
ICSA Guidance Note: Matters Reserved for the Board (November 2003) *229*

Appendix 4
ICSA Guidance Note: Terms of Reference – Executive Committees
(September 2004) *232*

Appendix 5
ICSA Guidance Note: Directors' and Officers' Insurance (April 2005) *237*

Appendix 6
ICSA Guidance Note: Due Diligence for Directors (July 2003) *245*

Appendix 7
ICSA Guidance Note: Induction of Directors (February 2003) *248*

Appendix 8
ICSA Code of Good Boardroom Practice *252*

Appendix 9
ICSA Guidance Note: Terms of Reference – Nomination Committee
(October 2003) *254*

Appendix 10
Association of British Insurers: Principles and Guidelines on Remuneration
(December 2005) *259*

Appendix 11
ICSA Guidance Note: Terms of Reference – Remuneration Committee
(October 2003) *273*

Appendix 12
Association of British Insurers and National Association of Pension Funds: Joint Statement
on Best Practice on Executive Contracts and Severance (December 2005) *278*

Appendix 13
ICSA Guidance Note: Terms of Reference – Audit Committee (October 2003) *283*

Appendix 14
Combined Code of Corporate Governance: Smith Guidance on Audit Committees
(July 2003) *289*

Appendix 15
Smith Report: Outline Report to Shareholders on the Activities of the Audit
Committee *300*

Appendix 16

Financial Reporting Council: Internal Control – Revised Guidance for Directors on the Combined Code (October 2005) *301*

Appendix 17

Institutional Shareholders' Committee: The Responsibilities of Institutional Shareholders and Agents – Statement of Principles (September 2005) *310*

Appendix 18

ICSA Guidance Note: Disclosing Proxy Votes (August 2004) *314*

Glossary *317*
Bibliography *331*
Index *335*

Introduction

This Handbook is intended to help directors and those who advise them to explore how the principles of good governance can be translated into sustainable good practice in the boardroom. Although it focuses on UK listed companies, it is now widely accepted that organisations of all kinds face similar challenges and can learn from each other. As a result, there is growing evidence that good practice is readily transferable between different sectors of the economy. Examples are the now wide-spread use in the public and not-for-profit sectors of the audit committee concept first developed in the corporate sector, and the increasing emphasis on the need for governing bodies of all kinds to include a strong independent element. Conversely, there is growing recognition that management skills developed in running large public and charitable bodies may be equally valuable on company boards. While it is expected that this Handbook will find much of its audience amongst the directors and secretaries of listed companies, it is hoped that it will also be of use to those involved in the management of public bodies, charities and non-listed companies.

For more than a decade, standards of boardroom practice in UK listed companies have attracted intense political, regulatory and public scrutiny. In part, this reflects the enormous economic and social significance of such companies. In his report *Institutional Investment in the United Kingdom*, published in March 2001, Paul Myners estimated that around 80 per cent of shares in UK listed companies are held on behalf of individual savers and investors by insurance companies, pension funds and other financial institutions. UK listed companies thus represent a pool of assets comprising the savings and pensions investments of millions of individuals, and their management and control is therefore a matter of the highest relevance for public policy. In part, however, the continuing high level of debate has been fuelled by corporate failures and scandals – from Maxwell to Enron and beyond – which have undermined investor and wider public confidence in the quality, integrity and effectiveness of company boards.

As in any other kind of organisation, the function of the board in a listed company is to take responsibility for managing the company's business on behalf of its members or shareholders. Separation between membership and management has many advantages, not least that decision-making can be entrusted to those with the necessary skills and capacities, leaving the members to enjoy the benefits of their association with the organisation without needing to involve themselves in matters of detail. In a listed company, the separation of membership and management facilitates efficient aggregation and use of capital, by enabling the possessors of capital to invest in enterprise without requiring them to become involved in its operation. At the same time, it allows responsibility for the strategic direction and control of business to be delegated to professional managers who (it is assumed) possess the required entrepreneurial skills and management expertise.

However, separation between membership and management may also create tensions between the interests of the parties. In listed companies, these tensions are known collectively as the 'problem of agency' – essentially, the special potential for conflicts of interest between shareholders, as the company's owners, and its directors, as their agents. According to agency theory, the managers of the company, as rational beings, will seek to maximise their own well-being through their control of the company's resources. As a result, they are likely to pursue self-serving objectives, which will not necessarily be in the best interests of the shareholders.

The problem of agency is not a new phenomenon. In *The Wealth of Nations*, published in 1776, Adam Smith famously warned that 'negligence and profusion' were inevitable where owners did not themselves attend to the needs of the business, but instead appointed managers as their agents. In contemporary terms, the problem of agency may manifest itself in board decisions that promote the interests of the directors, but do not necessarily enhance the value of the company for the shareholders. Examples of such decisions might include:

> pursuit of short-term share price growth, where sustained investment in the company's asset base might produce greater long-term benefits for share-holders;

> inappropriate expansion or diversification of the company's activities into areas which involve unwarranted risks to shareholders' investments; or

> resistance by managers to mergers or takeovers which might threaten their own job security, but which may be in the best interests of the company's shareholders.

In some cases, the potential for conflict of interest between owners and managers may be exacerbated by the company's executive remuneration arrangements. As shown by highly publicised events in companies such GlaxoSmithKline, Tesco and Barclays, remuneration and incentive arrangements may be intended to align the interests of directors and shareholders but may, in practice, reward the pursuit of inappropriate objectives, while failing to punish poor management performance.

The problem of agency in listed companies can be exacerbated by the board's ability to control the supply of information to shareholders about the company's position and performance. In extreme cases, this may result in shareholders and others being seriously misled. A recent notorious example concerns the US energy corporation Enron, whose directors systematically overstated profits, failed to inform shareholders about risky financing arrangements and continued to declare the corporation's financial soundness until days before its filing for bankruptcy protection.

In any organisation in which the management of activities is separated from the membership, the governing body must be provided with the powers and authorities needed to enable it to manage the organisation's activities effectively. At the same time, however, there must be sufficient checks and balances on the governing body's actions to assure the members that the organisation will be run in their interests. In any organisation, therefore, a system of good boardroom practice is essential, comprising as its generic components:

> ❭ a definition of the role and responsibilities of the governing body, including its membership, the limits on its powers of management and rules for the proper conduct of its business;
> ❭ a requirement for the governing body to account for its actions through timely reporting of complete and accurate information; and
> ❭ the retention by the organisation's members of powers to appoint and remove the governing body and to ratify key decisions affecting their interests.

Good boardroom practice in any organisation is therefore concerned with the relationship between managers and owners – in other words, it relates essentially to the *internal* governance of the organisation. But many organisations, including listed companies, also exist and operate within an external framework of laws, regulations and public expectations.

Abbreviations

ABI	Association of British Insurers
AGM	annual general meeting
APB	Auditing Practices Board
ASB	Accounting Standards Board
CA 1985	Companies Act 1985
CA 1989	Companies Act 1989
CBI	Confederation of British Industry
CDDA 1986	Company Directors Disqualification Act 1986
CEO	chief executive officer
CFO	chief financial officer
CGAA	Co-ordinating Group on Accounting and Auditing Issues
CLR	Company Law Review
DTI	Department of Trade and Industry
EC	European Commission
EEA	European Economic Area
EGM	extraordinary general meeting
EU	European Union
FRC	Financial Reporting Council
FRRP	Financial Reporting Review Panel
FSA	Financial Services Authority
FSMA 2000	Financial Services and Markets Act 2000
IA 1986	Insolvency Act 1986
ICAEW	Institute of Chartered Accountants in England and Wales
ICSA	Institute of Chartered Secretaries and Administrators
IoD	Institute of Directors
ISC	Institutional Shareholders Committee
NAPF	National Association of Pension Funds
NED	non-executive director
NYSE	New York Stock Exchange
OECD	Organisation for Economic Co-operation and Development
OFR	Operating and Financial Review
PIDA 1998	Public Interest Disclosure Act 1998
PIRC	Pensions Investments Research Consultants Ltd
SEC	Securities and Exchange Commission
SFS	Summary Financial Statement
SOX	Sarbanes-Oxley Act (the US Public Company Accounting Reform and Investor Protection Act of 2002)
TSR	Total Shareholder Return
UKLA	United Kingdom Listing Authority

Listed companies and their operating environment

Part 1 of this Handbook examines the external environment in which listed companies operate, taking into account legal and regulatory requirements, international developments and changing public attitudes to the way in which companies conduct their activities and account to society for their impacts. To this end:

- Chapter 1 briefly describes the framework of current company law in the UK and considers the extent to which this provides an appropriate context for good boardroom practice.

- Chapter 2 traces the development of non-statutory codes of corporate governance in the UK, from the Cadbury Report of 1992 up to and including the 2003 Combined Code of Corporate Governance.

- Chapter 3 examines issues of good boardroom practice in other economies worldwide and assesses the evidence for an emerging international consensus on key issues of corporate governance.

- Chapter 4 discusses contemporary challenges to traditional ideas about corporate purpose and accountability and describes the growing need for companies to demonstrate high standards of social, ethical and environmental responsibility.

Legal framework

This chapter explores the legal environment within which UK listed companies are established and operated, with particular reference to those statutory and regulatory provisions which impact on their governance. As such, it considers:

> why and how companies are formed;
> the principal legal provisions currently governing the operation of companies in the UK;
> current proposals for fundamental legislative change arising, in particular, from the recommendations of the Company Law Review; and
> the relationship between existing and prospective provisions of company law and good boardroom practice.

It is not possible within the scope of this chapter to provide a comprehensive guide to the detailed technical requirements of UK companies legislation in respect of registration, filing and other administrative obligations. For suggested sources of information on these matters, see the selected bibliography at the end of this Handbook.

Why and how companies are formed

When a company is formed, a legal distinction is created between the existence and identity (or 'personality') of the company itself and those of its members or shareholders. This distinction gives incorporated form significant advantages as a means of establishing and carrying on business:

> As a legal person in its own right, a company can possess rights and privileges not available to its shareholders, and can take action to enforce these rights.
> Conversely, only the company, and not its shareholders, can be sued for breach of its legal duties.
> Property owned by the company is distinct from the property of its shareholders, with the result that shareholders' property is unaffected by the claims of creditors in the event that the company becomes insolvent.
> Unless a fixed lifetime is specified in its constitution, the company can continue in business indefinitely, undisturbed by changes in its shareholder base.

Under UK law, there are three basic forms of company:

> *Registered companies* are formed under the Companies Acts and are the most numerous type of company, with an estimated 1.5 million registered companies

currently active in Great Britain. As discussed below, registered company form is extremely versatile and is capable of adaptation to a wide range of commercial and other purposes.

> *Statutory corporations* are formed under specific statutory provisions. There are currently fewer than 10,000 statutory corporations, of which the majority are co-operative societies formed under the Industrial and Provident Societies Acts.

> *Chartered companies* are formed pursuant to letters patent issued under Royal Prerogative or special statutory powers. There are currently approximately 750 chartered companies, consisting mainly of organisations established for charitable or quasi-charitable purposes, but also including a small number of long-established trading companies.

While all three types of company provide the benefits of separate legal personality, registered company form has the additional advantage that members are able to limit their potential liability for the company's debts. Limitation of liability is achievable in two ways, by guarantee or by shares:

> In *guarantee companies*, the liability of members to subscribe to the company's debts in the event of liquidation is limited to an amount agreed in advance, but there is no provision for the distribution of any profits to members. For this reason, guarantee company form is generally used for social or charitable purposes only.

> In *companies with liability limited by shares*, profits can be distributed to shareholders in proportion to their holdings in the company. At the same time, the potential liability of each shareholder to contribute towards the company's debts in the event of insolvency is limited to the nominal value of their shares. Registration with liability limited by shares thus provides a convenient way of allocating profit amongst the shareholders of a commercial enterprise, while enabling them to know in advance the extent of the risk to their investment.

Registration with liability limited by shares is the most commonly used method of incorporation: according to the Department of Trade and Industry (DTI), companies of this type represent approximately 95 per cent of all companies currently constituted in Great Britain.

Registration with liability limited by shares is available to both private companies, in which shares cannot be offered for sale to the general public, and public companies, in which shares can be offered for sale to the general public under closely regulated conditions. Public companies account for less than 1 per cent of all registered companies in Great Britain, while fewer than 2,000 public companies have their shares listed for trading on the main market of the London Stock Exchange. Despite their relative small number, however, UK listed companies are of major economic significance: the total market value in December 2005 of UK shares listed on the London Stock Exchange (including Techmark) was more than £1,780 billion, of which 80 per cent was represented by fewer than 100 companies.

A key objective of company law is to ensure that the advantages of incorporation are readily available, by ensuring that companies can be formed quickly, easily and relatively cheaply. At the same time, it seeks to manage the consequences of separate personality and limited liability by:

> establishing minimum standards for the proper conduct of business by companies, in particular by establishing model constitutional arrangements;
> providing for the appointment of directors and obliging them to deal fairly with the company;
> requiring the disclosure of key information; and
> creating enforceable rights for shareholders and (to a lesser extent) creditors of the company.

Principal UK legal provisions

Current legislation

Until comparatively recently, all the main legal provisions relevant to the formation and operation of companies were contained in single Acts of Parliament. From the mid-1980s onwards, however, separate branches of specialised legislation have been established to deal with different aspects of company operation, such that currently:

> the Companies Act 1985, the Companies Act 1989 and associated secondary legislation set out requirements for the formation and operation of companies;
> the Financial Services and Markets Act 2000 provides for the regulation of the securities markets;
> the Company Directors Disqualification Act 1986 makes arrangements for the disqualification of delinquent directors;
> the Insolvency Act 1986 (as modified by the Enterprise Act 2002) establishes a legislative regime for corporate insolvency and personal bankruptcy; and
> the Companies (Audit, Investigations and Community Enterprise) Act 2004 strengthens company accounting requirements, independent regulation of the accounting and audit profession and the DTI investigation regime.

In addition to these statutory provisions, there is a large body of sometimes difficult and obscure case law, particularly in the areas of directors' duties and the rights and legal remedies available to shareholders.

Companies Act 1985

The Companies Act 1985 (CA 1985) sets out the basic statutory provisions governing the formation and registration of companies, including the requirement for key documents relating to the purpose, ownership and management of the company to be lodged with the Registrar of Companies and regularly updated. Provisions of particular relevance to the governance of the company and the protection of shareholders' interests are as follows:

> *Directors*: disclosure of directors' interests in the company's shares (CA 1985, Part VI); the qualifications, duties and responsibilities of directors (Part IX);

and the enforcement of fair dealing by directors, in particular to restrict the ability of directors to take unfair financial advantage of their position (Part X).

> *Accountability*: the requirements for preparation of annual accounts (Part VII) and the appointment of external auditors (Part XI).
> *Shareholders' powers and entitlements*: arrangements for the allotment of shares (Part IV) and limitations on the company's ability to vary the voting rights attaching to shares (Part V); shareholders' entitlements to participate in distributions of profits and other assets (Part VIII); and the requirements for general meetings of shareholders (Part XI).

In addition, regulations made under CA 1985 set out, in a series of tables, model Memoranda of Association and Articles of Association for companies of different types.

Taken together, a company's Memorandum and Articles of Association comprise its constitution and define the relationship between the shareholders and the directors. Broadly speaking, the Memorandum of Association defines the company's identity, in terms of its name, the jurisdiction in which it is registered, the amount of its authorised share capital and its division into shares of a fixed amount and, in the 'objects clause', the purpose and scope of the company's intended activities.

The Articles of Association give further details of the company's share capital, including the transferability of shares, shareholders' pre-emptive rights to purchase shares offered in a rights issue and arrangements for the declaration and payment of dividends. The Articles also set out internal aspects of the company's constitution, including arrangements for appointment, retirement and removal of directors.

Model Articles for public and private companies limited by shares are set out in Table A to CA 1985. While it is for the company itself to decide whether to adopt a model Memorandum or model Articles, in whole or in part, its Memorandum (and its Articles unless it adopts the format prescribed in Table A) must be delivered to the Registrar of Companies and appear on the public register.

Companies Act 1989

The main purpose of the Companies Act 1989 (CA 1989) was to take account of the UK's membership of the European Union (EU) by implementing the requirements of the Seventh Company Law Directive (Directive 83/349/EEC), dealing with consolidated accounts, and the Eighth Company Law Directive (Directive 84/253/EEC), dealing with audit. In addition, the opportunity was taken to introduce many new and reformed domestic provisions, including the establishment of the Financial Reporting Council (FRC), the Accounting Standards Board (ASB) and the Financial Reporting Review Panel (FRRP) to monitor standards of financial reporting by UK companies and to make, amend and withdraw accounting standards as necessary.

Financial Services and Markets Act 2000

The provisions of company law are supplemented for listed companies by the requirements of the Financial Services and Markets Act 2000 (FSMA 2000). This appoints the Financial Services Authority (FSA), in its capacity as the United Kingdom Listing

Authority (UKLA), as the competent authority in the UK for the listing of company shares and other securities for trading on public stock exchanges.

As the competent authority for listing, the UKLA promulgates Listing Rules intended to ensure that investors have access to relevant and accurate financial information to enable them to make informed investment decisions. To this end, the Listing Rules require that, as a condition of access to the markets for listed securities, companies must prepare detailed prospectuses or listing particulars setting out the nature of their businesses, their management and financing arrangements and potential material risks to potential investors. Once a company's securities have been listed for trading, it is required by the Listing Rules to fulfil a number of ongoing obligations, which in many cases amplify existing duties under the Companies Acts. These include:

> financial reporting in accordance with the accounting standards set and monitored by the FRC;
> full and timely disclosure of other information relevant to the interests of existing shareholders, such as related party transactions, directors' dealings in the company's shares and changes in major shareholdings; and
> the provision of adequate opportunity for shareholders to consider and vote on proposals for major changes in the business operations of the company and other matters of importance concerning the company's management and constitution.

In addition, the Listing Rules require the directors of listed companies to report to shareholders on whether they comply with recommendations of the Combined Code of Corporate Governance appended to the Listing Rules and to explain their reasons for any departures from the Code. In this way, the Listing Rules give effect to the 'comply or explain' regime for corporate governance, discussed in more detail in *Chapter 2*.

The Listing Rules also give effect to the Model Code, the purpose of which is to regulate share dealing and other activities by directors, key officers and employees of a listed company, especially during the periods leading up to the announcement of the company's financial results or other significant announcements of price-sensitive information.

More broadly, FSMA 2000 gives the FSA power to impose penalties for market abuse, defined as the use of information not generally available to market users to give a false or misleading impression about the price or availability of listed securities. The market abuse provisions create a new civil offence, additional to the criminal offence of insider dealing under the Criminal Justice Act 1993, and are of special relevance to company directors and senior managers who have access to 'inside' information about their company's performance and prospects.

Company Directors Disqualification Act 1986

The Company Directors Disqualification Act 1986 (CDDA 1986) aims to protect shareholders and the general public by preventing the involvement in company management of persons who are considered by the courts to be unfit for such involvement because of their previous conduct.

CDDA 1986 applies to both solvent and insolvent companies and empowers the courts to disqualify individuals, for periods of between two and 15 years, from acting as directors or being concerned in the management of companies. It therefore regulates who may act as a director, and applies to all persons directly or indirectly involved in the promotion, formation and management of a company.

Insolvency regime

Under the Insolvency Act 1986 (IA 1986), directors and other officers of an insolvent company may be required to contribute to the assets of the company if they have acted negligently or in breach of their fiduciary duties, which include a duty to consider the interests of the company's creditors. In addition, a director who knew or should have known that there was no reasonable prospect of avoiding insolvent liquidation may be liable for wrongful trading if he or she failed to take every step which could have been taken to minimise losses to creditors.

Measures introduced by the Enterprise Act 2002 are intended to streamline corporate insolvency procedures, in particular to facilitate the rescue of viable companies.

Companies (Audit, Investigations and Community Enterprise) Act 2004

The Companies (Audit, Investigations and Community Enterprise) Act 2004 introduced a package of measures designed to strengthen investor confidence in company accounting and auditing practices and improve the reliability of financial reporting and the independence of auditors and auditor regulation in the wake of the Enron and WorldCom scandals. Measures introduced by the Act include:

> ❯ a new requirement for directors to make a statement in the directors' report about the disclosure of relevant information to their auditors;
> ❯ a requirement for the professional accountancy bodies which supervise auditors to adopt independent auditing standards, monitoring and disciplinary procedures;
> ❯ broadening the scope of the FRRP and giving it new powers to require documents; and
> ❯ strengthening the DTI company investigations regime by improving investigators' access to relevant information, reducing the scope for delay or obstruction and introducing more effective sanctions.

In addition, the Act establishes a new statutory framework to give community interest companies (CICs) access to incorporated form and to provide for their conduct and supervision.

The Act also made it easier for companies to indemnify directors against liability. Prior to the Act, companies were not permitted to undertake to indemnify or exempt directors against any liability arising from negligence, default, breach of duty or breach of trust relating to the company, other than in limited circumstances (for example, where an application for relief from liability is granted by the courts on the grounds that the director has acted honestly and reasonably). However, CA 1989 allowed companies to purchase liability insurance for directors and to pay their legal costs if they were successful in defending themselves in legal proceedings.

The Act restated the core prohibition on companies exempting directors from and indemnifying them against liability to the company, but has introduced two important relaxations of the prohibition by permitting companies to:

> indemnify directors in respect of proceedings brought by third parties and applications for relief from liability; and

> pay directors' costs of defence proceedings as they are incurred, even if the action is brought by the company itself or is a derivative action. However, directors are still liable to pay damages and to repay their defence costs to the company if their defence is unsuccessful.

Further discussion on directors' personal liabilities and their mitigation is set out in *Chapter 6*.

Proposed legislative changes

UK company law in its current form relies on a mixture of statute, regulation and common law, reflecting a piecemeal approach to company law reform over many decades. More recently, amendments to UK domestic law have been required to take account of European Council Directives designed to harmonise company law and the securities market.

The resulting position is widely regarded as unsatisfactory, in particular because the structure and complexity of the current provisions can make it difficult for companies and their directors to identify and understand their legal responsibilities. In addition, there is concern that the essentially backward-looking nature of company law is inhibiting desirable innovation, including the wider use of electronic communications.

In the light of these and other concerns, the Government initiated a fundamental review of company law in 1998, under the direction of the Company Law Review (CLR). The aim of the Review was to improve the consistency, transparency and predictability of company law, taking into account the increasing globalisation of business, contemporary developments in information technology and the need for a more sophisticated approach to corporate governance.

The final CLR report, published in mid-2001, made a large number of wide-ranging recommendations for legislative change, including proposals designed to:

> simplify and modernise the law for small companies, for example by making it easier for private companies to take decisions by written resolution, without the need for a general meeting;

> clarify and update the law relating to directors' duties through a new, definitive statement of directors' duties to replace the existing loose assembly of common law duties;

> promulgate the concept of 'enlightened shareholder value' by making clear that, in promoting the success of the company, directors must take account of long-term as well as short-term consequences, and recognise the importance of relations with employees, suppliers, customers and other stakeholders; and

> facilitate the exercise of shareholder rights through measures designed to improve access to company disclosure, make it easier for shareholders to put forward resolutions and provide greater transparency about the way in which institutional investors exercise their voting powers.

Following publication of the final CLR report, the Government indicated that it had accepted the bulk of the recommendations, and in 2002 it issued the White Paper *Modernising Company Law* for consultation. However, the Enron crisis led to a reassessment of legislative priorities, including the introduction of the Companies (Audit, Investigations and Community Enterprise) Act 2004, described above.

As a result, it was not until March 2005 that detailed proposals for new primary legislation were published, in the form of the White Paper *Company Law Reform*. The revised legislative proposals set out in the Company Law Reform Bill represent a complete overhaul of UK company law and will have significant implications for the directors, shareholders and auditors of companies of all kinds, whether private, public or quoted. Although large parts of CA 1985 will be repealed it will not be completely replaced by the new Act, as originally envisaged. Instead, about one-quarter of the 1985 Act will remain in force, while the new Company Law Reform Act will set out new provisions and make amendments to the 1985 Act. As a result, UK company law will in future be contained in both CA 1985 and the new Act.

Key proposals brought forward in the Company Law Reform Bill include:

> simpler, more accessible arrangements for private companies;
> a new statutory statement of directors' duties, including a specific duty to promote the success of the company;
> enhanced ownership rights for investors who hold their shares indirectly through an intermediary;
> greater use of e-communications;
> extended rights for shareholders to sue directors for negligence;
> encouragement for institutional investors to disclose how they exercise their votes, with a reserve power for government to require disclosure if necessary;
> provision for external auditors to limit their liability with the consent of client companies and their shareholders;
> a new criminal offence of recklessly or knowingly including misleading detail in audit reports; and
> new powers to enable Ministers to amend company law more easily and quickly in future.

A summary of the principal differences between existing company law and the provisions of the Company Law Reform Bill is given on pages 10 and 11.

The legislative proposals set out in the Bill will be subject to detailed debate and amendment during the Parliamentary approvals process, and numerous textual changes are inevitable. The Government has itself already identified a significant area of change following its unexpected decision, announced by the Chancellor of the Exchequer in November 2005, to repeal the Companies Act 1985 (Operating and Financial Review and Directors' Report etc) Regulations 2005. As a result of this

PRINCIPAL DIFFERENCES BETWEEN EXISTING COMPANY LAW AND PROVISIONS OF COMPANY LAW REFORM BILL

	Current law	Proposed new law
Directors	Directors' duties derived from case law	New statutory statement of directors' duties
	Conflicts of interest contained in Part X of CA 1985	Simplified provisions on transactions between directors and companies requiring shareholder approval
	All legal persons, including other companies, may be directors	Corporate directors permitted, but at least one director must be natural person
Resolutions	Written resolution requires unanimous agreement of shareholders	In private companies, written ordinary resolutions passed by simple majority (75% majority for written special resolutions)
Shareholder communications	All companies must hold AGM once a year	Private companies need not hold AGM (but public companies must hold AGM within 6 months of financial year-end)
	Companies must communicate with shareholders in paper form	With shareholder consent, all companies may use electronic communications
Shareholder rights	Limited common law right to sue directors for wrongs done to company	Extended statutory right to sue directors for broader range of conduct
	Beneficial owners with shares held through intermediaries have no statutory right to receive information or vote	Provision for beneficial owners to be nominated by registered shareholder and exercise registered shareholder's rights
Auditor liability, audit quality and accounts	Unlimited auditor liability	Auditors may negotiate limit on liability subject to shareholder approval
	No requirement to publish auditors' terms of appointment	Ministers may order publication of terms of appointment

decision, quoted companies will not, as previously intended, be required by law to prepare an Operating and Financial Review (OFR): instead, the Company Law Reform Bill will be amended to require such companies to produce an annual Business Review in compliance with the EU Accounts Modernisation Directive. Further discussion on the OFR concept and the new statutory requirement for a Business Review can be found in *Chapter 10*.

Current law	Proposed new law
Auditors need only give reasons for resignation where circumstances must be reported to shareholders or creditors	Quoted company auditors must always publish statement of reasons for resignation
	New criminal offence of knowingly or recklessly including materially misleading information in audit report
Filing of private company annual report required within 10 months of year-end (7 months for public companies)	Deadlines shortened to 9 months for private companies and 6 months for public companies

Company formation and constitution

Table A sets out default articles for all companies limited by shares	Simplified default articles for private companies. Separate default articles for public companies, similar to current Table A
Public company requires at least two members	One person may form public company

Capital maintenance and share provisions

Companies may not give financial assistance for the purchase of their own shares	Financial assistance provisions for private companies abolished, provided they are not subsidiaries of public companies
Capital reductions require court approval	Simpler solvency-based procedure for private companies to reduce their capital
Aveling Barford Ltd v *Perion Ltd* case (1989) cast doubt on validity of intra-group transfers of assets by reference to book	Clarifies that where transferring company has distributable profits, it may transfer assets to group members at book value rather than market value

Source: Extracted from a briefing written by Rita Dattani, Norton Rose. A full copy of the briefing can be read at: www.nortonrose.com/publications/companylaw

Subject to Parliamentary approval, the Company Law Reform Act is expected to become law by late 2006, with most of its provisions coming into force not earlier than April 2007. However, provisions which implement the EU Takeover Directive will need to be introduced earlier in order to meet the May 2006 deadline for implementation of the Directive by Member States.

Company law and good boardroom practice

Role of directors

There is no formal legal definition of a director, but the term is generally understood to mean one of a group of individuals at the top of the company who have been duly appointed by the shareholders to direct and control the business, formulate its strategy and supervise its management. Despite the emphasis in corporate governance on the need for a balance of executive and non-executive directors (NEDs) on the board, no such distinction is made in law. Consequently, all directors who have been formally appointed are considered to have the same duties, powers, obligations and liabilities as set out in statute, regulation and common law.

Directors' duties – current position

There is currently no definitive statement in law of the duties owed by directors to the company. Although some statutory guidance is available (for example in Part X of CA 1985), the principles on which directors' duties are currently based derive mainly from common law. In this context, the directors are agents of the company, to which they owe the fiduciary duties of loyalty and good faith expected of trustees. Unlike trustees, however, directors are expected to take entrepreneurial risks on behalf of the company, and in doing so are expected to exercise care and skill.

The fiduciary duties of directors entail the obligation to:

> behave loyally towards the company and obey its constitution, as laid down in its Memorandum and Articles;
> act in good faith in the company's best interests, where necessary by balancing long-term objectives against the short-term interests of present shareholders;
> maintain independence of judgment and avoid conflicts, actual and potential, between duties to the company and personal interests; and
> act fairly as between shareholders.

Directors must not use their powers under the company's constitution for purposes for which they were not intended: where the directors use their powers for an improper purpose (for example to issue additional shares in order to defeat a possible takeover bid), it is not enough that they honestly and reasonably believed that their actions were in the best interests of company.

In addition to their fiduciary duties, directors are expected to apply reasonable care and skill in the exercise of their functions. The standards of care and skill expected of directors have been developed through case law, such that directors' performance is expected to meet both:

> an objective test applicable to directors generally (did the director concerned have, and exercise, the general knowledge, skill and experience reasonably to be expected of a person carrying out the functions carried out by that director in relation to the company?); and
> a more demanding subjective test applicable to each director personally (did the director concerned exercise the particular knowledge, skill and experience that he or she actually possessed?).

Directors' duties – proposed legislative changes

The Company Law Reform Bill sets out, for the first time, a statutory statement of directors' general duties. This codifies the existing duties derived from common law rules and equitable principles and will thus continue to require directors to:

> act within the company's powers;
> exercise independent judgment;
> exercise reasonable care, skill and diligence;
> avoid conflicts of interest;
> refrain from accepting benefits from third parties;
> declare any interest in a proposed transaction or arrangement with the company; and
> act fairly as between members.

The most radical element of the new statement is the new duty to act in a way which a director considers, in good faith, will be most likely to promote the success of the company for the benefit of its members as a whole, having regard (so far as reasonably practicable) to the principle of enlightened shareholder value. This will involve consideration of:

> the long-term consequences of a decision;
> employee interests;
> relationships with the company's trading partners;
> the effect of the company's operations on the community and the environment; and
> the desirability of maintaining the company's reputation for high standards of business conduct.

Directors' powers

A company's Articles will usually entrust the directors to manage the business of the company and exercise all of the company's legal powers.

In exercising these powers, the directors must have regard to the current limits on the company's corporate capacity, as set out in the objects clause of its Memorandum. In principle, any transaction outside the objects clause is void, although CA 1985 provides that the validity of a transaction cannot be called into question on the grounds that the company lacks capacity because of a gap in its objects clause.

Nonetheless, it is currently possible in principle for shareholders to bring proceedings to stop any transaction not specifically permitted by the objects clause, provided that they obtain an injunction before the transaction becomes legally binding. Moreover, the directors may be personally liable if they exceed their powers under the Memorandum, unless the shareholders have approved a special resolution relieving the directors of liability.

This position will be reversed by the provisions of the Company Law Reform Bill, whereby all companies will have unlimited capacity, subject to any explicit contrary provision in the Articles. Unless a company's Articles specifically restrict its objects, there will be no limitation on either the company's capacity or the authority of the directors to bind the company.

Further, the Bill provides that new companies will have a single constitutional document, consisting of the Articles of Association, which will set out the internal workings of the company. The Memorandum will state only that the subscribers wish to form a company and agree to become members of it. Any other provisions in the Memorandum of an existing company will be treated as if they were provisions of its Articles.

Currently, directors must observe limits placed on their authority by provisions of CA 1985 which either prohibit certain transactions or require them to be approved in advance by shareholders in general meeting. The transactions affected include the following:

> *Substantial property transactions*: except in limited circumstances, a director is not permitted to enter into an arrangement to acquire from the company or transfer to the company any non-cash asset without first obtaining the approval of shareholders in general meeting – a provision which is intended to ensure that directors cannot sell property to the company at an inflated price or acquire property from the company at less than its full value.

> *Loans to directors*: subject to specific exemptions, a company is not permitted to: make loans to directors or connected persons; provide guarantees or security for such loans; or assume responsibility to a third party for a loan entered into by a director or a connected person.

> *Service contracts*: while the board has general authority to negotiate the terms and conditions of directors' service contracts, it must seek shareholders' approval in certain circumstances, for example where the proposed contract is for a term of more than five years.

> *Takeovers and mergers*: when considering or recommending to shareholders an offer for a takeover or merger, the directors must observe their fiduciary duties and act honestly in the interests of the company and its shareholders as a whole. Accordingly, any payment receivable by a director in compensation for loss of office as a consequence of the transaction must be disclosed to and approved by the shareholders. In addition, the directors of listed companies must observe the requirements of the Listing Rules and the Takeover Code in respect of the information to be provided to shareholders, the equal treatment of shareholders and the protection of minority interests.

The Company Law Reform Bill seeks to simplify the current provisions regulating transactions between directors and the company. It brings together the existing provisions relating to substantial property transactions, loans, long-term service contracts and *ex gratia* payments to directors for loss of office. In addition, it permits companies, with shareholder consent, to make loans, give guarantees or provide security in connection with a loan to a director, thereby reversing the current prohibition on such transactions.

Currently, directors must observe complex capital maintenance rules intended to ensure that the company receives full value on the initial issue of its shares and thereafter maintains its paid-up share capital as a fund available to creditors in event of a winding-up. The rules specify the conditions on which the directors are permitted to take actions, which might involve: the diminution of its paid-up share capital, including the allotment and issue of shares at less than nominal value; distributions to shareholders in the form of dividends or returns of capital; the purchase and redemption of the company's own shares; and the provision of financial assistance for the purchase of the company's shares.

The Bill will simplify the current law by removing unnecessary and burdensome requirements for private companies, although the current requirements will remain in force for public companies and their subsidiaries.

Directors' obligations

In keeping with the obligation on directors not to put themselves in a position where there is a conflict between their personal interests and their duty to the company, current and prospective company law requires directors to disclose certain information both to the company and to the shareholders, including the following:

> *Interests in contracts and transactions*: a director who has a direct or indirect material interest in a contract or proposed contract, transaction or other arrangement with the company must disclose it at a board meeting at the earliest opportunity. The director's interest must be formally recorded by the company and must be disclosed to shareholders in the annual report and accounts.
> *Interests in shares*: directors must notify the company of their own and connected persons' interests in the company's shares or debentures. A listed company must record directors' interests in shares and share options in its register of directors' interests, disclose them to shareholders in the annual report and accounts and promptly announce any changes in directors' interests in accordance with the Listing Rules.

Accountability to shareholders

As noted above, directors of listed companies are required to disclose information on such matters as the company's financial position and performance, proposed transactions affecting the future of the company, and the interests of directors and connected persons in the company's shares. Although disclosure is required in the interests of prospective investors and the general public, its primary purpose is to enable existing shareholders to understand the company's position and performance and to facilitate the exercise of their authority.

The principal means by which information must be disclosed include the following:

> *Circulation to shareholders*: directors of listed companies are required to prepare and approve annual reports and accounts (discussed further in *Chapter 10*) and to lay them before the shareholders in general meeting, of which appropriate notice must be given to shareholders and other entitled parties in accordance with prescribed notice periods (discussed further in *Chapter 14*).

> ❯ *Filing of returns with the Registrar of Companies*: the directors are responsible for notifying to the Registrar of Companies key information relating to the company's location, structure and management, and for updating this information as necessary.
> ❯ *Availability of statutory records for inspection*: the directors are responsible for making sure that the statutory books and records of the company (including details of the company's shareholders, directors' interests in the company's shares and debentures, other significant interests in the company's securities and any changes in such interests, and details of any mortgages and charges over the company's assets) are complete and up to date, and for making them available for inspection at the company's registered office or any other place as notified to the Registrar of Companies.

Retained powers of shareholders

The retained powers of shareholders to control and influence the actions of the directors are of two main types, known as 'voice' and 'exit'.

The power of 'voice' consists of the shareholders' ability to exercise the voting powers attaching to shares. As explained above, significant decisions of the company, including the appointment and reappointment of directors, proposed dividend payments and other substantial transactions, must be disclosed to shareholders and considered at general meetings. The shareholders have the power, in principle at least, to give or withhold approval for any of the resolutions proposed by the directors, or ultimately to dismiss the directors themselves. The shareholders' power of 'voice' is preserved in UK law by the disclosure obligations outlined above, by the requirement for listed companies to hold general meetings of all shareholders and by the limits imposed by CA 1985 on the ability of companies to vary the voting and other rights attaching to shares.

The power of 'exit' consists of the choice available to the shareholders to maintain, increase or dispose of their shares in the company according to their opinion of the performance of the business and the quality of the directors. Widespread dissatisfaction with the company's performance, particularly on the part of large institutional shareholders, could potentially result in the disposal of large numbers of the company's shares, adversely impacting on its share price and ultimately on the bonuses and career prospects of the directors. The power of 'exit' is safeguarded principally through the provisions of FSMA 2000, which ensure the maintenance of transparent markets in listed companies' shares.

Beyond their powers of 'exit' and 'voice', individual shareholders, as distinct from the company as a whole, currently have only limited ability to seek legal remedies against careless, delinquent or underperforming directors.

In most circumstances, there is a general presumption that, where directors' performance or conduct is considered to be unsatisfactory, it is for the company as a whole, rather than for shareholders individually, to take action, for example by bringing legal action against directors who are considered to be in breach of their duties. However, there are currently four main routes available to aggrieved individual shareholders, namely:

> a claim for breach of the statutory contract formed by the company's Memorandum and Articles of Association (although this is rarely used in practice);

> a claim under IA 1986 for the company to be wound up on the grounds that it is just and equitable to do so (which is of little benefit to shareholders in a company with a large shareholder base);

> a claim by a minority shareholder on his or her own behalf under CA 1985 for unfair prejudice (the most widely used remedy, but involving lengthy court proceedings and substantial costs); and

> the common law right of a shareholder to bring a derivative action seeking relief on the company's behalf, rather than that of the shareholder bringing the action.

The Company Law Reform Bill seeks to extend the existing derivative action and place it on a statutory footing in order to make it easier for shareholders to sue directors or others for a broad range of misconduct. Under the new statutory procedure, it will be possible for shareholders to bring a claim in a wider range of circumstances than is currently the case, for example in respect of an actual or proposed act or omission involving negligence, default, breach of trust or breach of duty (including breach of the new statutory statement of directors' duties). A shareholder will still need to apply to court for permission to continue the claim, which may be refused if its continuation would not promote the success of the company for the benefit of its members or if the conduct complained of has been authorised or ratified by the company's shareholders.

Conclusions

Existing UK company law and current proposals for fundamental reform address outward-facing aspects of corporate governance, particularly in respect of accountability and the reserved powers of shareholders. However, the law does not attempt to regulate matters of internal governance, such as the composition, conduct and effectiveness of the board of directors, reflecting a traditional assumption that these are essentially private issues for resolution at the company's own discretion. As *Chapter 2* explains, however, company failures and continuing controversy over issues such as executive remuneration have challenged the concept of companies as self-regulating entities and have prompted the development of voluntary codes of corporate governance designed to raise standards of boardroom practice.

2

Codes of corporate governance

This chapter:

> explains the 'comply or explain' approach to corporate governance adopted in the UK;
> traces the evolution of successive UK codes of corporate governance; and
> examines the UK's response to the corporate governance issues raised by the Enron scandal.

Introduction

It has long been recognised that the separation of ownership and control in all but the most closely held companies entails a risk that the directors, as the managers of the business, will exploit the powers delegated to them to serve their own interests at the expense of the shareholders. As a result, the interests of shareholders and directors may diverge on a wide range of issues, including the strategic direction of the company, its response to takeover and merger proposals, the composition of the board and the remuneration of directors.

In these and other areas, the ability of the shareholders to detect and censure unsatisfactory performance or improper conduct may be severely curtailed by the directors' control over information. The legal provisions described in *Chapter 1* seek to redress the imbalance between directors and shareholders by requiring companies to report externally on their ownership, financing arrangements and performance and by reserving to shareholders powers to appoint and dismiss the company's directors and to ratify key decisions affecting their interests.

In addition, there is widespread debate about issues of corporate governance and standards of boardroom conduct which are not regulated by law. In the UK, this debate was initially prompted by a series of unexpected company failures and other corporate scandals in the late 1980s and early 1990s, including BCCI, Polly Peck and the Maxwell Communications Group. These events aroused widespread public concerns about the standards of business conduct and the credibility of company reporting. In addition, they highlighted the difficulties experienced by boards, external auditors and shareholders in controlling the actions of dominant chairmen and chief executives.

These concerns led to the adoption in 1993 of the UK's first code of corporate governance, the Cadbury Code of Best Practice. Through a continuing process of revision and amendment, successor Codes have addressed the structure and numerical balance of the board, focusing in particular on the role of non-executive directors (NEDs) in ensuring that executive directors were unable to exercise unfettered power over critical decisions. Although the Cadbury Code and its successors were addressed to listed companies, they were widely influential on other types of company and on organisations outside the corporate sector.

The collapse of Enron in late 2001, followed by other major corporate crises in the US and elsewhere, has called into question the effectiveness of many of the established concepts of corporate governance. As a result, the adequacy of corporate governance arrangements in the US, the UK and internationally have come under close scrutiny. In the UK, this process has involved wide-ranging review, focusing in particular on the role and effectiveness of NEDs and the arrangements for audit committees, and leading to the introduction of a revised Combined Code of Corporate Governance in July 2003.

'Comply or explain' regime

A key feature of the UK's approach to corporate governance, from the Cadbury Code onwards, has been the avoidance of prescriptive rules, reflecting the view that different governance approaches will be appropriate for different companies depending on their size, business activity, operating environment and ownership structure. Similarly, successive Codes have had no statutory force, but have been appended to the Listing Rules, with a requirement on listed companies to disclose in their annual reports whether or not they have complied with Code recommendations and, to the extent that they have not, to give reasons for the areas of non-compliance. Companies' statements of compliance are reviewed by their external auditors, who are required to report their findings to shareholders.

Under the resulting 'comply or explain' regime, a company is under no formal obligation to comply with the best practice recommendations enshrined in the Code. However, the disclosure obligation ensures that the company's shareholders are able to monitor the extent of its compliance, consider the explanations provided by the directors for any areas of non-compliance and, if dissatisfied, express their concerns through their voting behaviour at the AGM. At the same time, shareholders are urged to avoid a 'box-ticking' approach when evaluating companies' corporate governance arrangements, by showing flexibility in the interpretation of Code recommendations and judging directors' explanations on their merits.

From Cadbury to the Combined Code of 1998

Cadbury Committee on the Financial Aspects of Corporate Governance

In response to concerns about the low level of public confidence in financial reporting and in the safeguards provided by external auditors, the Cadbury Committee on the Financial Aspects of Corporate Governance was set up in 1991 by the Financial Reporting Council (FRC), the London Stock Exchange (then the listing authority in the UK) and the accountancy profession.

At the time of the Committee's establishment, it was commonplace for the offices of chairman and chief executive officer (CEO) to be combined in one powerful individual (as, for example, in the case of Robert Maxwell). Some company boards had no NEDs at all and, where NEDs were appointed, they were usually outnumbered by executive directors. Further, in many cases, the independence of NEDs was in doubt because of their status as former executive directors of the same company, close connections with major shareholders or external advisers, or personal relationships with the chairman. Reflecting developments in the US, about 75 per cent of the top 250 companies in the UK had audit committees, but formally constituted remuneration and nomination committees were the exception rather than the rule.

The Code of Best Practice resulting from the Cadbury Committee's investigations was appended to the Listing Rules in 1993. The Cadbury Code identified generic themes of abiding concern and has had a major impact on thinking about corporate governance across the corporate, public and not-for-profit sectors within and beyond the UK.

The key recommendations of the Cadbury Code were in four main areas.

Board of directors

To ensure that the board functions as an authoritative decision-making body, rather than as a formal rubber stamp for executive decisions, the Cadbury Code recommended that the full board should meet regularly. In addition, it should establish a formal schedule of matters (including material acquisitions and disposals, capital projects and treasury and risk-management policies) specifically reserved for its collective decision. The board should monitor the performance of executive management and should agree formal procedures for the taking of material decisions between meetings of the full board.

The board should have access to professional advice, both from independent external sources and internally from the company secretary. Importantly, the responsibilities of the company secretary for procedural and corporate governance matters were explicitly recognised by the Code, which recommended that any proposals for the removal of the company secretary should be a matter for the full board.

The Code contained a number of recommendations on the composition and balance of the board. It expressed a clear preference for a formal separation between the roles of chairman and CEO. Recognising, however, that some companies would be reluctant to abandon this practice, it recommended that, where the posts were combined, there should be strong and independent NEDs, including a recognised senior NED. The Code made no formal recommendation on the number of NEDs required, but suggested that in most cases a minimum of three NEDS would be needed, one of whom might also be the non-executive chairman.

Non-executive directors

The Cadbury Code provided the first formal definition of the role of NEDs, suggesting that, in addition to their share in the strategic responsibilities of the board, they should have explicit control and monitoring functions which are distinct from the day-to-day managerial responsibilities of their executive colleagues. Accordingly, a majority of the NEDs on the board should be 'independent of management and free from any business or other relationship which could materially interfere with the exercise of their independent judgement, apart from their fees and shareholding'. In addition, the Code recommended that the interests of NEDs should be disclosed in the annual report and accounts to enable shareholders to make informed judgments on their independence.

To preserve their independent status, the Code recommended that NEDs should be appointed for specified terms by means of a formal selection and appointment process and that their reappointment to the board should not be automatic. Although the Code contained no absolute requirement for the establishment of nomination committees, it commended this as good practice and suggested that, where nomination committees were set up, they should have a majority of NEDs and be chaired by the chairman or an NED.

Executive directors

The Cadbury Code's treatment of executive remuneration issues was sparse by later standards, but did acknowledge the potential for conflicts of interest between shareholders and directors on matters of pay, performance and job security. Accordingly, it recommended that shareholder approval should be obtained for new service contracts in excess of three years (compared with the five-year contracts permitted by statute) and stated that executive pay should be subject to the recommendations of a remuneration committee made up wholly or mainly of NEDs. In addition, the annual report and accounts should contain full and clear disclosure on directors' remuneration, including basic salary, performance-related pay, pension contributions and share options.

Reporting and controls

The Cadbury Code emphasised the board's obligation to present to shareholders a balanced and understandable assessment of the company's position. This should include a coherent narrative explanation of its performance and prospects, with details of setbacks as well as successes. In order to discourage incomplete and potentially misleading reporting, the Code recommended that the directors should acknowledge publicly their responsibilities for preparing the accounts and should report to shareholders that the business is a going concern, with supporting assumptions and qualifications as necessary.

Recognising the need for independent validation of the company's disclosures, the Code also recommended the establishment of audit committees of at least three NEDs, the majority of whom should be independent. Further, it emphasised the need for the board to ensure that an objective and professional relationship was maintained with the external auditors, who should review the company's compliance with Code recommendations and report to shareholders on their findings.

The Cadbury Committee recommended that the directors should report to shareholders on the effectiveness of the company's system of internal control. Although it made clear in its report that it intended that the directors' responsibilities should encompass a systematic approach to risks of all kinds, this proposition was not generally accepted in consultation. As a result, the guidance for directors eventually produced by the accounting profession (in the form of the Rutteman Report issued in 1994) concluded that directors should limit their review to internal financial controls. Further, they should report only that they have carried out such a review, giving no opinion on whether or not the controls are effective.

Greenbury Study Group on Directors' Remuneration

The Greenbury Study Group on Directors' Remuneration was established in 1995 in response to public concern over apparently unjustified increases in the level of directors' remuneration, particularly in recently privatised utilities. The Study Group's remit was to establish good practice in determining directors' remuneration, particularly in the hitherto neglected area of performance-related pay. The resulting Code of Best Practice for directors' remuneration was appended to the Listing Rules in October 1995.

The Greenbury Code had as its principal objectives to:

> *Prevent executive directors from setting or influencing their own remuneration.* To this end, it recommended that responsibility for determining executive remuneration should be formally delegated to a remuneration committee, rather than merely inviting the remuneration committee to make recommendations to the board, as envisaged by Cadbury. To ensure their objectivity, the Greenbury Code recommended that remuneration committees should consist exclusively of NEDs with no personal financial interests other than as shareholders, no cross-directorships and no day-to-day involvement in running the business;

> *Introduce greater rigour into the design of executive remuneration packages,* particularly in respect of performance incentives and rewards. To this end, the Greenbury Code contained an explicit recommendation that executive rewards should be linked to the performance of the company and of the individual director. In addition, it established as recognised good practice that executive directors' service contracts should not contain notice periods in excess of one year or provide for termination payments in excess of one year's salary and benefits.

> *Improve accountability to shareholders.* For this purpose, The Code recommended that explicit statements should be included in the annual report and accounts on the remuneration of each director and on the company's remuneration policy, including performance criteria and measurement and compensation commitments for early termination of executive directors' service contracts.

The recommendations of the Greenbury Code were reflected, largely unchanged, in the Combined Code introduced in 1998. However, executive remuneration, and in particular the link between company and individual performance and pay, have remained highly contentious. In 2002, the UK Government introduced secondary legislation, in the form of the Directors' Remuneration Report Regulations 2002, to enforce improved accountability to shareholders by quoted companies. A more detailed discussion on remuneration issues is set out in *Chapter 9.*

Hampel Committee and Combined Code of 1998

The Cadbury and Greenbury Codes operated concurrently until June 1998, when a new Combined Code of Best Practice was appended to the Listing Rules. The Combined Code was based on the recommendations of a Committee on Corporate Governance established in 1995 under the chairmanship of Sir Ronald Hampel.

Although intended primarily as an updating and consolidation of the two earlier Codes, the Combined Code represented a considerable broadening of the scope and detail of directors' obligations, particularly in the areas of internal control and risk management, accountability to shareholders and the company's relations with institutional investors.

The 1998 Combined Code consisted of 17 Principles of Good Governance – 14 addressed to listed companies and the remainder to institutional investors. Each principle was amplified by a number of more detailed provisions, and the Code also contained schedules on the design of executive remuneration packages and their disclosure to shareholders. The principles and provisions applicable to companies were divided into the following broad areas:

> *Directors*: the Combined Code confirmed the principle first established in the Cadbury Code that listed companies should be led by an effective board, with a balance of executive directors and NEDs and a clear division of responsibilities between the chairman and CEO. However, it placed much greater emphasis on the personal competencies of the directors, through a recommendation that directors should receive appropriate training on first appointment and subsequently as necessary. In addition, the Code recommended that the board should establish a formal and transparent procedure for appointing new directors, and that all directors should stand for re-election by the shareholders at least every three years.

> *Directors' remuneration*: the Combined Code broadly endorsed the principles established in the Greenbury Code. It emphasised that directors' remuneration should not be higher than necessary to recruit and retain directors of the right calibre. Further, it recommended that some element of executive pay should be performance-related so as to encourage the achievement of corporate objectives and to reward individual performance. No director should be involved in determining his or her own remuneration, and details of the company's remuneration policy and the remuneration of each director should be stated in the annual report and accounts.

> *Relations with shareholders*: the Combined Code emphasised the need for companies to be prepared to enter into a dialogue with institutional investors and to encourage the active participation of private investors in the annual general meeting.

> *Accountability and audit*: the Combined Code endorsed the Cadbury Code's recommendations in respect of the board's responsibility for presenting a balanced and understandable assessment of the company's financial position and prospects. In addition, it emphasised the central role of the audit committee in considering how to apply the principles of financial reporting and internal

control, and in safeguarding the independence and objectivity of internal and external auditors.

Turnbull Guidance on internal control

Perhaps the most significant innovation introduced by the 1998 Combined Code was the extension of directors' responsibilities not merely for financial control, but for the effectiveness of all internal controls, including financial, operational and compliance controls and risk management. Responsibility for producing formal guidance for directors on the interpretation and implementation of this recommendation was given to a working party appointed by the Institute of Chartered Accountants in England and Wales (ICAEW) and chaired by Nigel Turnbull. The final report of the working party was published in September 1999.

The Turnbull Guidance encouraged companies to embed their internal control systems in the day-to-day management of the business to ensure that the control measures were able to evolve over time to meet changes in the company's business environment. To this end, it advocated the development of a risk-based approach to internal control and the review of its effectiveness. In addition, it provided guidance on the respective roles of the board, the audit and other committees and the management in designing and maintaining effective internal controls, and set out questions to assist the board in its ongoing and annual review of the effectiveness of the company's system of internal controls.

In July 2004, the FRC established a Turnbull Review Group chaired by Douglas Flint, Group Financial Director of HSBC Holdings plc, to review the guidance and make recommendations for updating where necessary to take account of experience with its implementation and to reflect developments in the UK and internationally since 1999. The Review Group confirmed that the Turnbull Guidance had contributed to improvements in internal control in UK listed companies, and concluded on this basis that it should continue to cover all internal controls, rather than being limited to internal controls over financial reporting. Some updating was required to reflect changes in the Combined Code and the Listing Rules since 1999 and to take account of the proposed statement of directors' duties in the Company Law Reform Bill, but otherwise no significant changes were needed.

Accordingly, an updated version of the Turnbull Guidance was issued by the FRC in October 2005 for application to financial years beginning on or after 1 January 2006. A more detailed discussion on internal control and risk management and the influence of the Turnbull Guidance is set out in *Chapter 12*.

Corporate governance after Enron

Despite increasing levels of compliance with the recommendations of the Combined Code, investor and public confidence in standards of corporate governance, in the UK and worldwide, were severely shaken by the collapse in late 2001 of the US energy trader Enron, at that time one of the largest companies in the world.

Briefly, Enron announced in October 2001 that it was taking a $544 million charge to its reported earnings after tax in respect of transactions with an off-balance sheet entity owned by Enron, but created and controlled by its chief financial officer (CFO); in addition, shareholders' equity was to be reduced by $1.2 billion.

Less than one month later, the company announced that it was restating its accounts for the years 1997–2001 because of accounting errors in relation to off-balance sheet entities controlled by the CFO and other senior managers. The restatements involved reductions of between 10 per cent and 28 per cent in reported net income in each of the years affected, with substantial reductions in shareholders' equity and increases in the reported levels of indebtedness. The company also revealed for the first time that the CFO had received personal payments from off-balance sheet entities he controlled: these were originally estimated at $30 million, but were subsequently shown to be much larger.

Following these announcements, investor confidence in Enron's ability to recover its position collapsed and the company filed for bankruptcy in December 2001.

Subsequent investigations by independent consultants, regulators and the US courts indicated that the destruction of Enron had been brought about by a complex series of events in which individual officers, the board of directors and its sub-committees and the company's external auditors were all implicated. Specific findings of failures and weaknesses in corporate governance included:

> the waiver by Enron's board of directors of the company's rules on conflict of interest: this permitted the CFO and other senior managers to set up and control limited partnerships whose purpose was to hold assets and liabilities separate from the balance sheet;

> the subsequent failure of both the board and the audit committee to demand information about transactions between Enron and the off-balance sheet part-nerships, despite the explicit recognition that these transactions involved very high levels of risk;

> the lack of independence of Enron's external directors, some of whom had financial and other ties with the company, for example through consultancy fees;

> the failure of the board and the audit committee to prevent the exploitation of accounting rules to present a better picture of the company's financial position and performance than was justified: as a result, very large energy trading losses were systematically hidden from investors and the capital market through improper reporting of transactions with off-balance sheet entities, creating a false impression that Enron's exposures were hedged through contracts with third parties; and

> the failure of Enron's external auditors, Arthur Andersen, to provide the objective and professional scrutiny required to ensure that shareholders received an accurate account of the company's financial position.

The collapse of Enron was the catalyst for increased scrutiny of other major companies in the US, the UK and internationally, leading to further corporate bankruptcies, notably that of the US telecommunications company WorldCom. While the initial concerns related to the credibility of financial reporting, the events surrounding Enron triggered wide-ranging debate on issues including the operation of the capital markets, the adequacy of auditing standards and regulatory arrangements, and the quality and integrity of those involved in the governance of major companies. In response to these concerns, governments and regulators around the world have undertaken urgent reviews of their accounting, auditing and corporate governance arrangements. *Chapter 3* provides a brief survey of the international response to the issues raised by Enron.

In the UK, the Government established a Co-ordinating Group on Audit and Accounting Issues (CGAA) with responsibility for review of the existing arrangements for regulation of the accounting and auditing profession and oversight of financial reporting. Statutory and other reforms implemented as a result of this work are described in *Chapter 11*.

In addition, the UK's corporate governance arrangements were the subject of two major independent reviews, namely the Higgs Report on the role and effectiveness of NEDs and the Smith Report on audit committees, both published in January 2003. Following a period of consultation with listed companies and major investors, the revised Combined Code of Corporate Governance was published in July 2003 for application by UK listed companies in reporting years beginning on or after 1 November 2003.

For most listed companies, 2005 was the first full year of reporting on how they had applied the recommendations of the 2003 Combined Code. In July 2005, the FRC initiated a review of progress made by companies and investors in implementing the Code, which also considered whether any practical issues had emerged which required amendments to the Code.

The review concluded that there has been an improvement in the quality of corporate governance among listed companies since the introduction of the revised Combined Code and that most companies are choosing to apply the majority of Code provisions. In the view of both companies and investors, the dialogue between boards and shareholders is more constructive than previously – a measure of the success of the 'comply or explain' approach to corporate governance, which depends on constructive engagement between boards and investors.

In the light of the progress that has been made since 2003, the review concluded that significant changes to the Code are not necessary. Accordingly, only two detailed changes are intended: these relate to the composition of the remuneration committee and the conduct of proxy voting at AGMs, and are further discussed in *Chapter 9* and *Chapter 14* respectively.

Proposals for the necessary detailed amendments to the Combined Code were issued for consultation in January 2006, with the intention that the changes will have effect for financial years beginning on or after 1 November 2006. Beyond this, the FRC has indicated that it will continue to monitor the way in which the Combined Code is being implemented and will also keep under review the need for further changes to the Code arising from the Company Law Reform Bill and new EU requirements under the revised Fourth and Eighth Company Law Directives. In addition, the FRC will consider the implications of the Government's decision to remove the statutory requirement for quoted companies to publish an OFR and the outcome of the resulting DTI consultation on the statutory Business Review.

The text of the Combined Code is set out in full in *Appendix 1*. Its detailed recommendations and their implications for good boardroom practice are discussed in *Chapters 5 –14.*

3

The international dimension

> ... there is no single model of good corporate governance. Different legal systems, institutional frameworks and traditions mean that a range of different approaches have developed around the world. Common to all good corporate governance regimes, however, is a high degree of priority placed on the interests of shareholders, who place their trust in corporations to use their investment funds wisely and effectively. In addition, the best-run corporations recognise that business ethics and corporate awareness of the environmental and societal interest of the communities in which they operate can have an impact on the reputation and long-term performance of corporations.
>
> OECD (1999) *Principles of Corporate Governance*

This chapter describes:

> ❭ the main models of company ownership and control and their implications for corporate governance;
> ❭ the development of national codes of corporate governance, taking into account the impact of Enron and other major corporate failures; and
> ❭ the evidence for international convergence on key corporate governance principles.

Introduction

Within the legal and regulatory environment of the UK, ownership of listed companies is typically widely dispersed among numerous shareholders, who delegate to professional managers responsibility for the day-to-day conduct of the business. In this respect, the UK's legal and regulatory environment is similar to those of the US, the Republic of Ireland and certain Commonwealth countries, notably Australia, Canada and New Zealand. While no two countries have identical patterns of company ownership and control, these environments are, for the purposes of this discussion, broadly characterised as 'outsider' systems, because shareholders, as the owners of the company, are generally excluded from direct involvement in the management of the business.

In other legal and regulatory environments worldwide, including those of continental Europe, most Asian and South American countries and the emerging economies of the former Soviet bloc, the ownership of companies is typically more concentrated. As a result, the majority of shares may be held by one owner, or by a small number of connected owners. Again, no two countries are identical, but such environments are here described as 'insider' systems, because majority shareholders typically have direct involvement in or influence over the conduct of the business.

The factors leading to the development of the outsider and insider systems are not well understood, but may be related to underlying differences in legal system, history and culture. Importantly, there is no evidence to suggest that either system favours superior company performance: of the world's leading economies over the past half-century, the US is perceived as having an outsider environment, while Germany and Japan have historically been dominated by companies of the insider model.

Equally, neither system is immune from failure at the company or market level. Scandals such as Enron, WorldCom and Equitable Life in companies in the outsider environment of the US and UK have had their counterparts in the insider model: recent examples include the Dutch food retailer Ahold (which revealed in 2003 that it had overstated the pre-tax earnings of its US subsidiary by some US$880 million); and the Italian diary products conglomerate Parmalat (which filed for bankruptcy protection in December 2003 and subsequently disclosed more than €14 billion of debt, around eight times the amount reported by its former management).

Outsider systems

Common features

Certain generic features characterise outsider systems of company ownership and control. These include:

> *dispersal of ownership*: company ownership is widely dispersed amongst numerous shareholders, including both investment institutions and private individuals;

> *separation of ownership and control*: shareholders, as the owners of the company, generally do not participate in the management of the business, but delegate responsibility to professional managers who act as their agents; and

> *cash flow and voting rights*: all shareholders have rights, strictly protected in law, to receive part of the cash flows of the company in proportion to their shareholdings and to vote on major corporate decisions on a 'one-share-one-vote' basis.

Outsider systems of company ownership and control have typically evolved where there are liquid stock markets on which company shares can readily be traded, with strict disclosure requirements in respect of price-sensitive and other information of relevance to investment decisions. In most cases, there are active markets for corporate control, but mergers and takeovers are subject to tight regulatory controls which effectively prevent the accumulation of controlling interests in listed companies.

National variations between outsider systems

Alongside their shared characteristics, some significant differences exist between outsider systems in different countries. These are most apparent in the contrasting legal and regulatory approaches of the two most influential outsider systems, namely those of the UK and the US:

> In the UK, the preferred approach to company law and matters of internal governance has been to avoid prescriptive rules, relying instead on the definition of general principles and outcomes which require companies and individuals to assume wide responsibilities and exercise professional judgment.
> In the US, legislators and regulators have typically adopted a more legalistic, rules-based approach, which seeks to define clear boundaries within which companies and individuals are free to act.

The contrast between the two approaches is visible in the case of accounting standards. US accounting standards typically prescribe detailed accounting treatment according to the legal form of transactions, while UK standards generally permit the exercise of discretion to enable a 'true and fair' view of the substance of a transaction to be reflected.

Although a Model Business Corporation Act is maintained by a committee of the American Bar Association, the US has no nationally applicable company law: instead, it is left to individual states to produce their own legislation. Companies are able to incorporate in the state jurisdiction of their choice, leading to inter-state competition for company incorporation. The development of the outsider system in the US has been greatly influenced by this competition, which has led to a trend towards company laws which are, on balance, attractive to company management and unfavourable to shareholders. A key example is the relative tolerance in US law for 'poison pill' defences and similar measures designed to enable managers to protect their own positions by resisting takeover. As result, the managers of US companies typically have a greater degree of security than their counterparts in the UK (where such measures are illegal), while legal protections for shareholders are arguably less robust in the US than in the UK.

So far as other outsider systems are concerned, the framework of company law and corporate governance in the Republic of Ireland is broadly similar to that of the UK. Commonwealth countries such as Australia, Canada and New Zealand initially adopted UK-style legal and regulatory systems, but are now increasingly influenced by the US pattern.

Corporate governance in outsider systems

In outsider systems, the separation of ownership and control of listed companies means that conflicts of interest can arise between the directors, as the managers of the business, and the shareholders, as its owners. The development of codes of corporate governance in outsider systems has therefore been driven primarily by share-holder concerns about the perceived lack of effective board oversight of company performance. Key examples are the UK Cadbury Code and the Dey Report in Canada, both of which were developed in the early 1990s and have been widely influential as sources for the development of guidelines and codes in other countries.

In many outsider systems, notably the UK, Ireland, Canada and Australia, codes of corporate governance are in principle voluntary, but compliance is promoted through 'comply or explain' regimes whereby listed companies need not follow code recommendations, but must disclose whether they do so and provide an explanation of any divergent practices. The main exception to this is the US. Codes of best practice have been issued by organisations such as the Business Roundtable, the Council of Institutional Investors and the National Association of Corporate Directors, but have purely advisory status, while disclosure and other requirements are specified in legislation by the Securities and Exchange Commission and enforced through compulsory rules promulgated by, for example, the New York Stock Exchange (NYSE) and Nasdaq.

Insider systems

Common features

Insider systems of company ownership and control are typically characterised by:

> *Concentration of ownership*: company ownership is often concentrated in the hands of controlling shareholders (who may be individuals, family members, banks, other corporations or governments) or a group of connected shareholders.

> *Use of group structures*: cross-shareholdings may be used to create complex group and 'pyramid' structures, reinforcing the influence of large shareholders by enabling them to exercise a degree of control which is disproportionate to their actual investment in the company.

> *Involvement of controlling shareholders in management*: controlling shareholders may be directly involved in company direction and management, for example through their own membership of the board or through the power to appoint directors.

> *Cash flow and voting rights*: although all shareholders (including minority shareholders) are generally entitled to receive dividends in proportion to their shareholdings, the exercise of minority voting rights may be limited in insider systems through the issue of dual-class shares or through voting caps, proxy voting mechanisms and ownership chains which enable controlling shareholders to exercise disproportionate voting rights.

> *Participation in governance*: the rights of minority shareholders to attend, ask questions and table resolutions at company meetings may be limited and/or difficult to exercise in insider systems.

In insider systems, bank lending has historically been more important than shareholders' equity as a source of company financing. In some cases, stock markets may be relatively illiquid, making it difficult for dissatisfied shareholders to dispose of their holdings. In some jurisdictions, legal provisions make takeovers very difficult, rendering takeover ineffective as a means of disciplining underperforming managers. Reflecting their relative lack of importance, equity markets and associated disclosure requirements may be lightly regulated compared to those in outsider systems.

National variations between insider systems

Despite these generic similarities, there are marked differences between different insider systems, most noticeably in the identity of controlling shareholders:

> *Family control* is prevalent in many developing economies, particularly in Asia, where the company may be affiliated with a business group also controlled by the same family. However, family control is also found in more developed economies such as Sweden and Italy.
> *Other corporations* are the predominant shareholders in economies as diverse as Germany, Korea, Taiwan and Brazil.
> *Banks and other financial institutions* are the most important shareholders in Japan, typically exercising control through the *keiretsu* system whereby networks of companies are connected by cross-holdings around a major bank. Banks are also significant shareholders in Israel, while German banks have historically exercised voting powers in excess of their investments through their control of proxies on behalf of individual shareholders.
> *Governments* are still significant shareholders in some countries, ranging from transitional economies, such as China, to developed economies, such as Singapore and Austria.

In addition, significant differences exist in the company law and corporate governance of different insider economies. The most frequently cited examples of insider systems are those in mature economies, such as Japan and the countries of continental Europe. In these countries, the legal and regulatory environments relating to the operation of companies are sophisticated and well-established. However, insider systems also include examples of emerging economies, including some – notably China and the republics of the former Soviet bloc – where the company concept is itself relatively new. Understandably in such systems, concentration of ownership may be a defence against weakly entrenched property rights and relatively undeveloped systems of company law and corporate governance.

'Two-tier' boards

Perhaps the most striking variation between insider systems relates to the organisational structure of the board, as reflected by the use in certain developed economies of a 'two-tier' structure. In such structures, the supervisory and management functions of the board are formally separated between:

> a *supervisory board*, composed of outside directors, with responsibility for advising and supervising management and monitoring the performance of the company; and

> *a management or executive board*, composed entirely of executives, with delegated authority for the day-to-day operation of the business.

The two-tier board structure is required by law, for certain types of company or for companies of specified size, in four European countries: Germany, the Netherlands, Denmark and Austria. In France, Finland and Portugal, listed companies are able to choose between a unitary and a two-tier board structure. In France, the optional two-tier structure is similar to that used in Germany and provides scope for employee representation. However, the two-tier option is relatively little used, and most French companies have unitary boards.

The two-tier board model, particularly in its German manifestation, is frequently invoked as a solution to many of the corporate governance problems discussed elsewhere in this Handbook, primarily because it creates a clear separation between the management and monitoring functions of the board. The independence of the supervisory board is assured by excluding executive managers from membership, so conferring on the members of the supervisory board some of the characteristics of independent non-executive directors (NEDs) in the unitary board structure.

It is important to note, therefore, that the two-tier board structure is currently confined to a small number of mature continental European economies and has not been adopted elsewhere. Moreover, the two-tier structure is not without its disadvantages. In particular, members of the supervisory board may have more limited access to information than do NEDs in a unitary board, reducing both their understanding of the business and their ability to contribute effectively to its strategic direction.

Corporate governance in insider systems

In insider systems, conflicts of interest can arise between controlling shareholders and minority shareholders, and the aim of corporate governance is therefore to reinforce the position of minority shareholders and to ensure that controlling shareholders are not able to exercise a disproportionate influence over management. The development of codes of corporate governance has also been driven by the need for companies in insider economies to demonstrate acceptable standards of corporate governance in order to access the equity markets located in outsider economies, particularly those in the US and the UK.

In insider economies as diverse as Malaysia, Hong Kong, South Africa, Germany and the Netherlands, codes of corporate governance have been implemented as part of stock exchange listing rules, with mandatory disclosure enforced through 'comply or explain' reporting requirements. By contrast, codes of best practice promulgated in some developing economies, such as Brazil, Mexico, India and Thailand, have been designed to build awareness of governance best practice but have not been formally linked to listing requirements.

Impact of Enron

The collapse of Enron in 2001, followed by other major corporate crises, had a devastating impact on investor and public confidence in the quality of corporate governance around the world, affecting both outsider and insider systems. As a result, countries with existing codes of corporate governance have revised their provisions, while many countries have adopted codes for the first time.

In the US itself, radical reforms have been implemented under the terms of the Sarbanes-Oxley Act (formally the Public Company Accounting Reform and Investor Protection Act of 2002). Significant provisions of the Act include the following:

> *Integrity and completeness of company financial reports*: the chief executive officer (CEO) and chief financial officer (CFO) of a listed company are required to assume personal responsibility for the accuracy and completeness of its financial reports.

> *Non-interference in the audit process*: company directors and officers are explicitly prohibited from interfering with accounting firms in the performance of an audit. Civil penalties are provided against directors and officers, and anyone acting at their direction, who attempt to influence an audit for the purpose of rendering the company's financial statements materially misleading.

> *Audit regulation*: the Act establishes a new regulatory board, the Public Company Accounting Oversight Board (PCAOB), with responsibility for the registration and inspection of accounting firms and for promulgating auditing standards.

> *Audit independence*: the Act requires regular rotation of audit partners and other key personnel involved in the audit of a company and makes it unlawful for an accounting firm to provide specified non-audit services to an audit client.

> *Company records*: the Act makes it a criminal offence for anyone knowingly to alter, destroy or falsify a document or to shred, hide or alter a document or other object in order to impede or attempt to impede an official investigation.

> *Whistleblower protection*: audit committees are required to establish procedures for the investigation of concerns regarding accounting, internal accounting controls or auditing matters, while employees who raise such concerns are protected against dismissal, demotion, suspension, harassment and other forms of discrimination.

> *Codes of ethics*: companies are required to disclose whether they have adopted a code of ethics for senior financial officers and, if not, to explain their reasons.

In addition, changes to the listing rules of the NYSE and Nasdaq have introduced a number of recommendations which are new to the US environment, including a mandatory vote on remuneration policy, a requirement for the majority of the board to be independent, and formal separation of the positions of the chairman and CEO.

Although the provisions of the Sarbanes-Oxley Act have been widely influential in the context of revised and new codes of corporate governance outside the US, the prescriptive approach adopted by US legislators has been largely avoided. In most countries, new and revised codes rely for their effectiveness on 'comply or explain' regimes of the type already established in the UK. A comprehensive index of all current national and international codes of corporate governance, with electronic links to the full text of each code, is maintained by the European Corporate Governance Institute and can be accessed via its website at www.ecgi.org/codes/all_codes.php

International principles of corporate governance

The international nature of the response to the Enron crisis, in combination with the increasingly global nature of business activity, provide some evidence of a widening consensus, across outsider and insider systems, on a range of key corporate governance principles. These include the following:

> ❯ *Obligations owed to the generality of shareholders*: it is increasingly accepted that the board's duty to protect and enhance shareholders' investment is owed to all shareholders, not just to controlling shareholders.
> ❯ *Board responsibilities*: the responsibility of the board for the stewardship of the company is recognised, with emphasis on the board's financial reporting obligations and responsibility for oversight of the audit function.
> ❯ *Directors' qualifications*: while codes of corporate governance vary in the extent to which they specify the qualifications of directors, most now emphasise the need for appropriate experience, personal independence and the ability to make an adequate time commitment.
> ❯ *Directors' appointments*: there is increased emphasis on formal and transparent processes for appointing new directors, with some codes recommending the use of nomination committees.
> ❯ *Independent directors*: most codes agree that the ability to exercise objective judgment is necessary to enable boards to monitor management performance effectively, with many codes now specifying that boards should include at least some independent NEDs who are free of significant family and business relationships with management.
> ❯ *Independent board leadership*: many codes recommend a clear division of responsibilities between the chairman and the CEO, in particular where the board does not contain a majority of independent directors.
> ❯ *Board committees*: there is general agreement across codes about the need for an audit committee, with many codes also recommending that boards should establish nomination and remuneration committees in which independent NEDs have a key role.
> ❯ *Disclosure of information*: most codes of corporate governance augment existing legal requirements for disclosure by placing an obligation on directors to ensure that timely, accurate and meaningful information is made available to all shareholders.

OECD Principles of Corporate Governance

The emergence of a broad international consensus on key corporate governance issues is reflected in the Principles of Corporate Governance developed by the Organisation for Economic Cooperation and Development (OECD) to assist governments in their efforts to evaluate and improve the legal, institutional and regulatory framework for corporate governance in their countries, and to provide guidance and suggestions for stock exchanges, investors, companies and other interested parties. Originally issued in 1999, the Principles have been reviewed to take account of recent developments and experiences. The revised Principles, published in 2004, recommend that Member States should include in their national corporate governance frameworks the following key principles:

Principle I: *Ensuring the basis for an effective corporate governance framework*: the corporate governance frameworks developed in OECD and non-OECD countries should promote transparent and efficient markets, be consistent with the rule of law and clearly articulate the division of responsibilities among different supervisory, regulatory and enforcement authorities.

Principle II: *Rights of shareholders and key ownership functions*: corporate governance frameworks should protect and facilitate the exercise of shareholders' rights, including the rights to: secure methods of ownership registration; convey or transfer shares; obtain relevant and material information on the company on a timely and regular basis; participate and vote in general shareholder meetings; elect and remove members of the board; and share in the profits of the company.

Principle III: *Equitable treatment of shareholders*: corporate governance frameworks should ensure the equitable treatment of all shareholders, including minority and foreign shareholders, and should provide all shareholders with the opportunity to obtain effective redress for violation of their rights. Insider trading and abusive self-dealing should be prohibited, and directors should be required to disclose material interests in transactions or other matters directly affecting the company.

Principle IV: *Role of stakeholders*: corporate governance frameworks should recognise the rights of stakeholders established by law or through mutual agreements, and encourage active co-operation between companies and their stakeholders. In particular, employee participation in share ownership should be permitted to develop and employees should be able to communicate concerns about illegal or unethical practices without fear of reprisal. The corporate governance framework should be complemented by effective enforcement of creditor rights and an efficient insolvency framework.

Principle V: *Disclosure and transparency*: corporate governance frameworks should ensure that timely and accurate disclosure is made on all material matters regarding the company, including its financial situation, performance, ownership, governance and executive remuneration policy. The company's financial statements should be subject to independent annual audit by external auditors who are accountable to the shareholders and owe a duty to the company to exercise due professional care in the conduct of the audit.

Principle VI: *Responsibilities of the board*: corporate governance frameworks should ensure the strategic guidance of the company, the effective monitoring of management by the board and the board's accountability to the company and the shareholders. Directors should act in good faith, with due diligence and care, and in the best interest of the company and the shareholders. Boards should exercise objective independent judgment on corporate affairs and (where this is not already established practice) should consider assigning to NEDs tasks where there is a potential for conflict of interest, such as ensuring the integrity of financial and non-financial reporting, the review of related party transactions, nomination of directors and determining executive remuneration.

The full text of the revised OECD Principles of Corporate Governance can be found at www.oecd.org

ICGN Statement on Global Corporate Governance Principles

A more radical, and in some respects more prescriptive, approach to the codification of internal principles of corporate governance is represented by the revised Statement on Global Corporate Governance Principles, issued by the International Corporate Governance Network (ICGN) in July 2005.

The ICGN's membership is principally made up of 'activist' institutional investors and advisers, including UK bodies such as the Association of British Insurers (ABI), Hermes, and Pensions Investment Research Consultants Ltd (PIRC). Reflecting this, the Statement on Global Corporate Governance Principles is intended to provide guidance for investee companies on the principles of corporate governance which will influence the conduct of ICGN members as investors.

The Statement endorses the revised OECD Principles of Corporate Governance as a minimum acceptable standard of corporate governance, but identifies additional principles of particular concern to the ICGN members which, in some cases, go well beyond the OECD Principles and many national frameworks, particularly those applicable to insider systems of ownership and control. Examples include the following:

> *Disclosure of ownership and voting rights*: in addition to their financial and operating results, companies should provide information on ownership and voting rights, including details of controlling shareholders, significant cross-shareholding relationships and differential voting rights.
> *Appointment and removal of directors and auditors*: jurisdictions which do not have laws enabling the appointment and removal of a director or an external auditor by shareholders holding a majority of votes should enact those laws. In the meantime, companies incorporated in such jurisdictions should strive to provide such rights to shareholders.
> *Shareholder remedies*: jurisdictions which do not currently afford shareholders accessible remedies for inequitable treatment by a company should facilitate the development of alternative mechanisms for the resolution of disputes.
> *Election of directors*: each director should stand for election on a regular basis and, in any event, at least once every three years, and shareholders should be entitled to vote on the election of each director separately.

The full text of the ICGN Statement can be found at www.icgn.org.

EC Company Law Action Plan

Within the EU, the objective of creating a single market creates a need for harmon-
isation of company law and corporate governance practices across a range of different
systems of company ownership and control. To this end, the EC adopted a Company
Law Action Plan in 2003 which outlined a series of short-, medium- and long-term
measures intended to promote the integration of European capital markets and to take
account of the lessons arising from Enron and other financial scandals.

Some of the measures set out in the Action Plan are formal legislative initiatives
which will take the form of EC Regulations directly applicable in all Member States, or
EC Directives which must be incorporated into Member States' national laws. Other
measures are non-legislative, including Recommendations and the establishment of a
European Corporate Governance Forum. A number of measures relevant to corporate
governance have already been completed or are well advanced. These are as follows:

> *Independent NEDs*: a Recommendation regarding the role of independent
> NEDs was published by the EC in February 2005. This establishes the basic
> principle of board balance and independence, and urges Member States to
> ensure a strong role for independent NEDs in key areas such as audit, executive
> remuneration and the appointment of directors.

> *Directors' remuneration*: a Recommendation on directors' remuneration was
> published in December 2004 and invites Member States to adopt measures in
> four key areas, namely: the disclosure of remuneration policy in the annual
> accounts; an advisory vote of shareholders on remuneration policy; disclosure
> of the remuneration of individual directors; and prior approval of share and
> share option schemes by shareholders.

> *European Corporate Governance Forum*: the European Corporate Governance
> Forum was established by the EC in October 2004 with responsibility for
> examining best practice in EU Member States, facilitating convergence of
> national corporate governance codes and providing strategic advice to the
> Commission.

> *Proposed amendments to the Fourth and Seventh Company Law (Accounting)
> Directives*: the EC intends to amend the Company Law Directives in order to
> confirm at EU level the collective responsibility of directors for financial
> statements and key non-financial information and to introduce a requirement
> for a separate corporate governance statement in annual reports. In addition,
> the amendments will set out new requirements for disclosures regarding off-
> balance sheet arrangements and related party transactions.

Further measures relevant to corporate governance are expected in the medium term
(that is, before the end of 2008). These are as follows:

> *Shareholders' rights*: a Directive on shareholders' rights is intended to help facili-
> tate the exercise by shareholders of basic rights and to address current problems
> in exercise of such rights, particularly in relation to cross-border voting.

> *Enhanced disclosure by institutional investors*: a Directive is proposed to enhance
> disclosure by institutional investors of their investment and voting policies.

> *Choice of board structures*: a Directive is proposed to allow all listed companies within the EU to choose between unitary or two-tier board structures.
> *Enhanced responsibilities of board members*: a proposed Directive will enhance the responsibilities of board members and introduce a special investigation right, a wrongful trading rule and directors' disqualification.
> *Shareholder democracy*: a study will take place on the implications of an approach aimed at achieving full shareholder democracy for listed companies on a one-share, one-vote basis.

Other measures set out in the Company Law Action Plan will address areas of divergence between outsider and insider systems of company ownership and control, including: capital maintenance; groups of companies and pyramids; corporate restructuring and mobility; European legal forms of enterprises; and transparency of national legal forms of enterprises.

Outside the Company Law Action Plan, proposed revisions to the Eighth Directive are intended to clarify the duties of statutory auditors and to ensure their objectivity so that investors and other interested parties can rely on the accuracy of audited accounts. The aim of the revisions is to restore confidence in statutory audit and to enhance protection against the type of problems that arose in the Ahold and Parmalat cases by clarifying the duties, independence and ethics of statutory auditors, requiring the application of international standards on auditing, and setting criteria for public oversight of the audit profession.

4

Emerging expectations

> ... corporate social responsibility is a serious business issue, with serious implications for shareholders.
>
> Association of British Insurers (2001) *Investing in Social Responsibility*

This chapter considers the growing expectation that companies will behave responsibly and ethically in relation to non-shareholder stakeholders, including employees, suppliers, local communities and the environment, focusing on:

> ❯ the contrasting definitions of corporate purpose, from profit maximisation to social welfare, evaluated by the Company Law Review (CLR);
> ❯ current proposals for statutory reform to clarify directors' duties;
> ❯ the growing market demand for the disclosure by companies of information on their social, environmental and ethical practices; and
> ❯ the implications of Enron and other company failures for corporate culture, values and ethical practices.

Corporate purpose and accountability

Profit maximisation objective

The traditional view of corporate purpose and accountability, particularly in the outsider economies described in *Chapter 3*, can be described as a 'profit maximisation' model. This assumes that the objective of the company is to maximise financial returns to its owners. Company success can therefore be measured in terms of increased profitability, enabling larger dividends to be paid to shareholders and leading, in principle at least, to share price growth.

Consistent with this view, the directors of the company have overriding obligations to the shareholders to maximise the company's profits. As such, they should not take any actions which might reduce returns to shareholders, other than to the extent needed to comply with external laws and regulations in areas such as employment, health and safety, product safety and the environment.

The assumption that shareholders have overriding claims is based on the view that, as the ultimate owners of the business, they are uniquely exposed to the risk of financial losses if the company's business fails. While it is now generally acknowledged that other stakeholders, such as employees and suppliers, may invest in developing skills and processes in connection with the company's business, proponents of the profit maximisation model argue that because their skills and processes might well be transferable in the market in the event of the company's failure, these stakeholders are not exposed to the same degree of risk as shareholders.

Supporters of the profit maximisation model argue that, while the claims of the shareholders are paramount, this does not require directors to take a short-term view of the shareholders' interests or to act irresponsibly or unethically in the pursuit of profits. Accordingly, it may be permissible for the directors to risk or forgo profits at the margin in the interests of, for example, product safety, pollution control and fair dealing with other parties, even where there are no explicit external requirements.

Similarly, it is argued that profit maximisation is consistent with social welfare objectives, on the grounds that the returns generated by companies on behalf of their shareholders contribute to an overall increase in wealth. From this perspective, it is unnecessary – and indeed undesirable – for companies to acknowledge broader social responsibilities. As stated by the American economist Milton Friedman:

> '*In [a free] economy there is one and only one social responsibility of business – to use its resources and engage in activities designed to increase its profits so long as it stays within the rules of the game, which is to say, engages in open and free competition without deception or fraud.*'

The profit maximisation model is, on a strict interpretation, consistent with directors' duties as currently formulated in UK company law. However, it is increasingly criticised from a broad range of economic, social and political perspectives on the grounds that it fails to maximise overall prosperity and welfare. Specific challenges to the profit maximisation model include the following:

> ❯ *Short-termism*: despite the argument, noted above, that UK company law as currently formulated does not oblige directors to take a short-term view of their responsibilities, there is concern that a narrow focus on dividends and share price appreciation may discourage investment in longer-term projects, even though these might well ultimately be in the best interests of shareholders.
> ❯ *Claims of non-shareholder stakeholders*: the traditional view that shareholders' claims are overriding ignores the value to the company of the contributions made by other stakeholders, and inhibits the development of co-operative long-term relationships which would benefit the company as a whole.
> ❯ *Externalisation of costs and impacts*: reliance on external laws and regulations, which are slow to adapt to changing circumstances, may allow profit-maximising companies to evade responsibility for the adverse impacts of their activities by exploiting gaps and loopholes in legal provision.
> ❯ *Social injustice*: unmodified profit-maximising behaviour by companies may result in environmental damage and/or violations of human rights, especially in

the context of emerging economies where legal and regulatory frameworks may be relatively undeveloped.

Social welfare objective

In contrast to the profit maximisation model, the social welfare or 'pluralist' model proposes that a company's business should be managed so as to advance the interests of all participants, without the interests of any single group such as shareholders having overriding priority.

The social welfare model assumes that parties other than shareholders, including employees, suppliers of goods and services, customers and local communities, make commitments which contribute to the value of the company and represent part of its assets. Accordingly, these parties have a stake in the business and thus have claims, equivalent to those of owners, to have their interests taken into account in the formulation of business strategies. From this perspective, the company cannot be regarded as synonymous with its shareholders, but includes all other stakeholders who make commitments to it. By recognising that the commitments of such stakeholders are assets of the company and deserve consideration alongside shareholders' investments, it is argued that the company's ability to develop and maintain long-term co-operative relationships will be enhanced, to the benefit of all participants.

The main problem with the social welfare model is that it replaces the single goal of profit maximisation – with its clear channel of accountability to shareholders – with a broader but unspecific requirement to achieve a balance between the interests of shareholders and other stakeholders, and indeed between the interests of different stakeholder groups. In practical terms, this would require the company's directors to trade off competing claims (for example, between economic and social goals, the interests of shareholders and the interests of the wider community) without providing them with objective and consistent criteria against which corporate decisions could be made and company performance measured.

In the course of its fundamental review of UK company law, completed in mid-2001, the CLR concluded that (except where their Articles so provided) UK companies could not adopt an explicit social welfare objective in the context of company law as currently formulated. As a minimum, directors' duties would need to be revised to permit or, more radically, to require the directors to promote the success of the company in the interests of all stakeholders, with none of the participants, including the shareholders, being regarded as having overriding claims. In order to provide the directors with the necessary wide range of discretion, directors' duties would need to be expressed subjectively, involving a risk that there would then be no enforceable remedy for abuse of the directors' powers.

In addition to the reformulation of directors' duties, the CLR suggested that the implementation of the social welfare model in the UK might require changes to the existing rights of shareholders, particularly to appoint and dismiss directors, in order to enable constituencies other than shareholders to nominate directors to represent their interests.

Enlightened shareholder value

Unlike the social welfare model, the enlightened shareholder value model assumes that corporate purpose and accountability as currently envisaged in UK company law – that is, the generation of value for shareholders – is correct and, moreover, is the best means of securing overall prosperity and welfare. It differs from the profit maximisation model, however, in that it acknowledges the duty of the directors to take proper account of wider objectives, including the company's health and safety, employment and contracting practices and its impact on the environment. It argues further that well-managed companies with long-term strategic objectives will recognise that the acceptance of wider responsibilities is in their own enlightened self-interest. This recognition will be reinforced by external influences, including increased scrutiny by governments, regulators, the media, pressure groups and local communities, and the growing importance of corporate reputation.

Within this perspective, the recognition by the company of social responsibilities is consistent with its obligations to shareholders and may help it to discharge these obligations. Thus, it is argued that a business case can be made for corporate social responsibility, based on:

> the management of downside risks, particularly to corporate reputation, arising from, for example, poor management of supply chain issues, inadequate environmental standards, human rights abuses, and poor treatment of workers, customers and suppliers; and

> the creation of potential competitive advantage through the alignment of business practices with stakeholder expectations, resulting in, for example, reduced regulatory interventions, higher sales and increased customer loyalty, more supportive communities, the ability to attract and retain more talented employees, and better productivity, quality and innovation.

The CLR concluded that the enlightened shareholder value model was fully compatible with the existing formulation of directors' duties, which in no way required directors to take an unduly narrow or short-term view of their functions. It commented, however, that the existing law is widely misunderstood. In particular, directors often fail to recognise their obligation to have regard to the need to build long-term and trusting relationships with employees, suppliers, customers and others, as appropriate, in order to secure the success of the enterprise over time.

The CLR noted in addition that proper and meaningful company reporting was essential to enable shareholders, other stakeholders and the general public to evaluate performance and, where necessary, to bring pressure on the company to satisfy broader social requirements. It found, however, that current statutory reporting requirements paid little regard to the need to account for 'soft' assets and resources, such as the level of skills and the stability of the company's workforce, its relationships with its key suppliers or the value of its reputation and brands.

Proposals for statutory change

Statement of directors' duties

As explained in *Chapter 1*, the CLR recommended the incorporation into law of a new statutory statement of directors' duties embodying the concept of enlightened shareholder value. In the CLR's view, this should make clear that, in promoting the success of the company, directors must take account of long-term as well as short-term consequences and recognise the importance of relations with employees, suppliers, customers and other stakeholders.

In accordance with the CLR's recommendations, the Company Law Reform Bill sets out, for the first time, a statutory statement of directors' general duties. This contains a new duty to act in a way which a director considers, in good faith, will be most likely to promote the success of the company for the benefit of its members as a whole, having regard (so far as reasonably practicable) to the principle of enlightened shareholder value. This will involve consideration of:

> the long-term consequences of a decision;
> employee interests;
> relationships with the company's trading partners;
> the effect of the company's operations on the community and the environment; and
> the desirability of maintaining the company's reputation for high standards of business conduct.

Statutory reporting

The CLR also recommended that economically significant companies should be placed under a new statutory obligation to publish an annual Operating and Financial Review (OFR). In addition to a description of the company's business, objectives and development, this would require an account of the dynamics of the business, including risks and uncertainties arising from factors such as: dependencies on customers and suppliers; health, safety and environmental costs and liabilities; and programmes to maintain and enhance tangible and intellectual capital, including employee training. The CLR recommended in addition that companies covered by the OFR obligation should be required to report on key relationships with employees, customers, suppliers and others and on their environmental, community, social, ethical and reputation policies.

The CLR's recommendations were reflected in the Companies Act 1985 (Operating and Financial Review and Directors' Report etc) Regulations 2005 which, amongst other provisions, required quoted companies to prepare an annual OFR that presented a balanced and comprehensive analysis of the strategies adopted by the company and the likelihood of their success. Under the Regulations, the review must include information about the company's environmental, employment, social and community policies and their implementation, supported by key performance indicators where appropriate.

In November 2005, the Chancellor of the Exchequer announced that the Government had decided to repeal the Regulations and to replace the requirement for quoted companies to prepare an OFR with a new requirement for such companies to produce an annual Business Review in compliance with the EU Accounts Modernisation Directive. Further discussion on the OFR concept and the proposed statutory requirement for a Business Review can be found in *Chapter 10*.

Disclosure on social, environmental and ethical issues

Investor expectations

In practice, it appears likely that many companies will voluntarily adopt the OFR format in order to meet the requirements of institutional investors for increased disclosure on non-financial matters. An example is the publication by the Association of British Insurers (ABI) of guidelines on socially responsible investment. This aligns companies' social, environmental and ethical (SEE) policies closely to their management of risk and indicates that institutions expect the annual reports of listed companies to include information on whether the board of the company:

> takes regular account of the significance of social, environmental and ethical matters to the business of the company;
> has identified and assessed the significant risks to the company's short- and long-term value arising from SEE matters, as well as the opportunities to enhance value that may arise from an appropriate response;
> has received adequate information to make this assessment and that account is taken of SEE matters in the training of directors; and
> has ensured that the company has in place effective systems for managing significant risks, which, where relevant, incorporate performance management systems and appropriate remuneration incentives.

In addition, the ABI guidelines recommended that the annual report should include information on:

> SEE-related risks and opportunities that may significantly affect the company's short- and long-term value, and how they might impact on the business;
> the company's policies and procedures for managing risks to short- and long-term value arising from SEE matters;
> the extent to which the company has complied with its policies and procedures for managing risks arising from SEE matters; and
> the procedures for verification of SEE disclosures.

The full text of the ABI guidelines is given in *Appendix 2*, while further discussion on relations with institutional shareholders is contained in *Chapter 13*.

Non-statutory reporting frameworks

In addition to investor demands for a wider range of disclosure on social, environmental and ethical issues, governments, non-governmental organisations (NGOs) and other stakeholders are increasingly calling for companies to publish information on their approach to corporate responsibility. This concept encompasses the management of the company's external risks and impacts, its social, environmental and ethical policies and performance, and the quality of its relationships with key stakeholders.

There is now a large number of competing performance standards and reporting frameworks for corporate responsibility. These differ widely in the issues and impacts covered, the extent to which external auditing, validation or verification are required and the expectations placed on companies in terms of direct dialogue with stakeholders. Brief details of some of the main global and sectoral reporting frameworks now in use are set out below.

Corporate culture, values and ethics

The above discussion demonstrates that there is increasing focus on the responsibility of companies for managing the external impacts of their activities and for fostering positive long-term relationships with external stakeholders. Until relatively recently, however, less attention has been paid to the internal culture of the company, as represented by the values, ethical principles and standards of business conduct practised by employees at all levels. The significance of these issues was vividly demonstrated by the

SOCIAL RESPONSIBILITY REPORTING FRAMEWORKS

The following are some of the main standards for social, ethical and environmental reporting currently in use:

- *AA1000* (www.accountability.org.uk) The AA1000 framework developed by the Institute of Social and Ethical Accountability provides a standard for social and ethical accounting, auditing and reporting, including external verification and stakeholder engagement.
- *Sustainability Reporting Guidelines* (www.globalreporting.org) developed by the Global Reporting Initiative (GRI), a permanent institution of the UN. The Guidelines cover economic, environmental and social performance and aim to provide a universal structure for 'triple bottom line' reporting. Consultations are currently in progress on revised sustainability reporting guidelines, known as G3, which will cover economic, environmental, human rights, labour, product responsibility and social issues.
- *Social Accountability SA 8000* standard (www.sa-intl.org) developed by an international coalition of businesses, trades unions and NGOs on the basis of International Labour Organisation (ILO) conventions, the Universal Declaration of Human Rights and the UN Convention on the Rights of the Child. SA 8000 seeks to provide transparent, measurable and verifiable performance standards in the areas of: child labour; forced labour; health and safety; compensation; working hours; discrimination; discipline; free association and collective bargaining; and management systems.

collapse of Enron and other major US corporations amidst allegations of unethical practices on the part of corporate managers, independent auditors and other market participants.

As discussed in *Chapter 3*, the Enron scandal has caused governments and regulators, in the US and worldwide, to re-examine their legal frameworks, accounting and auditing standards and codes of corporate governance with the aim of restoring investor confidence in the integrity of company management and the wider financial markets. Reforms introduced in the US under the provisions of the Sarbanes-Oxley Act have been widely influential and include measures specifically intended to raise standards of business conduct within listed companies. These include:

> ❯ the requirement for listed companies to disclose in their annual reports whether they have adopted codes of ethics applicable to the chief executive officer (CEO), the chief financial officer (CFO) and other senior managers with accounting and financial functions and, if not, to explain their reasons; and
> ❯ the obligation of audit committees to establish procedures for the receipt, retention and treatment of 'whistleblower' reports regarding accounting, internal accounting controls and auditing matters.

While these and related measures reflect an understandable determination to avoid any repetition of the events at Enron, there is no evidence that those events were

- *UN Global Compact* (www.unglobalcompact. org) developed in partnership between the UN, multinationals and NGOs on the basis of the Universal Declaration of Human Rights, the ILO conventions and the Earth Summit Agenda 21 environmental principles. The Compact covers 10 universal principles in the areas of human rights, labour, the environment and anti-corruption. The Compact is not a regulatory instrument and there is no requirement for external verification. However, members of the Compact must publicly state their support for these principles and report annually on their performance.
- *Ethical Trading Initiative* (www.ethicaltrade.org) Base Code developed by an alliance of retailers, trades unions and NGOs to promote ethical sourcing of products. The Base Code is aligned to the ILO conventions, the Universal Declaration of Human Rights and the UN Convention on the Rights of the Child. The Code includes a reporting template for companies and an assessment framework for company disclosures.

In addition, there are several sector-specific standards which address issues relevant to particular business activities. Examples include:

- the *Responsible Care Scheme* for the chemicals industry (www.cia.org.uk);
- the *Green Globe 21* (www.greenglobe21.org) benchmarking and certification programme for the travel and tourism industry; and
- the *Green Alliance* (www.green-alliance. org.uk) environmental performance indicators for the waste management industry.

attributable to a lack of formal rules. Enron had a published statement of corporate values and maintained a confidential helpline for internal whistleblowers. Further, it required new employees to sign a written code of ethics, in line with the US Federal Sentencing Guidelines, which provide for mitigation of sentence for corporate defendants if it can be demonstrated that reasonable steps were taken by the company to prevent unethical conduct on the part of employees. This approach is designed to protect the company's legal position in the event that something goes wrong. As the example of Enron suggests, however, it does little to prevent ethical failures from occurring in the first place.

If Enron did not lack ethical rules, the evidence suggests that it did lack a corporate culture in which such rules were respected. At best, Enron appears to have had a compliance-based culture, in which it was considered sufficient to obey rules and regulations to the letter, while ignoring their intention. At worst, rules appear to have been regarded as an obstacle to creativity and enterprise, to be sidestepped or changed as necessary. This disrespect for rules was reinforced by the cultivation of aggressive business practices and by the prioritisation of profitability and share price performance, to the exclusion of almost any other consideration.

The collapse of Enron and subsequent major corporate failures led to an overall decline in public trust in business, characterised by concerns about the quality of corporate governance, the credibility of financial and auditing standards, the effectiveness of regulatory arrangements and the integrity of capital markets. In the task of restoring confidence, formal requirements for companies to have codes of ethics and to establish processes for the receipt and investigation of whistleblower reports have a useful, if limited, part to play.

On the positive side, written codes of ethics can provide helpful guidance, triggering reflection about appropriate standards of business conduct and prompting employees to modify their behaviour. Similarly, provided that confidentiality is assured and protection is provided against retaliation, whistleblower helplines can help to demonstrate that the company is serious in its commitment to ethical principles. The collective responsibility of the board of directors for standards of conduct within the company is outlined in *Chapter 5*, while *Chapter 12* discusses the need for whistleblower protection in the context of the company's system of internal control and reputational risk management.

PART

2

Application of the Combined Code

Part 2 is devoted to a detailed examination of the origins, content and practical implications of the main provisions of the 2003 Combined Code of Corporate Governance. This is the longest and most detailed such code promulgated in the UK to date, comprising some 16 Main Principles, 24 Supporting Principles and nearly 50 detailed provisions. It introduces a number of new concepts and principles, including the recommendation that boards should undertake formal and rigorous evaluation of their own performance. At the same time, it introduces a new clarity into previously nebulous areas, such as the independence of non-executive directors (NEDs) and the composition of board committees.

The increased length and specificity of the revised Combined Code was initially greeted with dismay in some boardrooms. It is important to bear in mind, however, that, like its predecessors, the Combined Code is not mandatory and has no statutory force. Listed companies are not required to comply with its provisions, but are required by the Listing Rules to disclose in their annual reports whether or not they have complied with Code recommendations and, to the extent that they have not, to give their reasons for non-compliance.

At the same time, it should be noted that the increasing degree of detail in the Combined Code's provisions is not a reflection of regulatory ambition. Rather, it is a response to *real* events and their consequences – that is, to scandals, failures and unprincipled actions which have undermined investor and public confidence in the quality, integrity and effectiveness of boardroom conduct.

The four main themes of the Combined Code are addressed in Part 2 as follows:

A Directors

- Chapter 5 considers the collective role of the board of directors in UK listed companies.
- Chapter 6 addresses the composition of the board, including the role of NEDs and the division of power and authority at the top of the company.
- Chapter 7 examines the new emphasis on the effectiveness of the board of directors, with particular reference to the need for the board to evaluate its own performance and that of its committees.
- Chapter 8 describes the processes for the selection and appointment of directors.

B Remuneration

- Chapter 9 outlines the role and composition of the remuneration committee and considers ongoing issues of regulatory and public concern, including the perceived problem of 'rewards for failure'.

C Accountability and audit

- Chapter 10 describes the current formal requirements for reporting to shareholders and explores current concerns about the adequacy of both financial and non-financial reporting by listed companies.
- Chapter 11 examines the measures taken to clarify and improve the effectiveness of the audit committee and the external auditors following the collapse of Enron and other corporate scandals.
- Chapter 12 outlines the board's responsibility for the establishment of an effective system of internal control and risk management.

D Relations with shareholders

- Chapter 13 considers the responsibilities of companies and their boards for fostering positive relationships with institutional shareholders and the reciprocal obligations of institutional shareholders to make considered use of their powers of ownership.
- Chapter 14 describes current best practice for the open and constructive conduct of business at the AGM.

5

Collective role of the board

> Every company should be headed by an effective board, which is collectively responsible for the success of the company.
>
> Combined Code (2003) Main Principle A.1

This chapter examines the key responsibilities of the board as defined in the 2003 Combined Code, taking into account:

> the need for the board to define its collective role and to reserve certain important matters for its collective decision;

> the conditions on which the board can properly delegate its decision-making powers;

> the board's responsibility for ensuring that the company's strategic objectives, policies and values are clearly communicated to employees, shareholders and other key stakeholders.

Introduction

In principle, the supreme decision-making body in a listed company is the general meeting of shareholders: the Companies Act, the Articles of Association and the Listing Rules all specify particular circumstances in which the approval of shareholders must be obtained for decisions affecting their interests. In practice, however, the company's Articles generally entrust the directors, as the agents of the shareholders, to manage the company and its activities. Thus, Table A, Regulation 70 provides that 'the business of the company shall be managed by the directors who may exercise all the powers of the company'.

In the UK's unitary board system, authority to act on behalf of the company is conferred on the whole board, consisting of both executive directors directly involved in management of company's activities and non-executive directors (NEDs) who have no such involvement. Equally, the board as a whole is responsible for monitoring management performance, safeguarding shareholders' assets and ensuring that the company's business is conducted in a manner which complies with legal and regulatory requirements and meets acceptable standards of business conduct.

Corporate failures, such as Marconi in the UK and Enron in the US, have demonstrated that boards are not always clear about their collective responsibilities, and in particular about the extent to which the board as a whole – not just its non-executive contingent – has a duty to monitor management performance and to intervene where necessary to control the actions of the chief executive officer (CEO) and other executive directors. A key issue for good boardroom practice is therefore to define the collective role of the board so as to strike an appropriate balance between its supervisory function and its responsibility for driving the business forward.

Even where the role of the board is clearly defined and understood, however, it will clearly be impractical for the board to have hands-on involvement in every area of the company's business. It is therefore essential for the board to determine the terms on which it can properly delegate authority in such a way as to ensure that it retains the ability to control the business and account to shareholders for its stewardship.

Key responsibilities of the board

In the absence of a definitive statutory summary of the role of the board, successive codes of corporate governance have offered their own definitions. The most recent of these, set out in Supporting Principle A.1 of the 2003 Combined Code, states that:

'The board's role is to provide entrepreneurial leadership of the company within a framework of prudent and effective controls which enables risk to be assessed and managed. The board should set the company's strategic aims, ensure that the necessary financial and human resources are in place for the company to meet its objectives and review management performance. The board should set the company's values and standards and ensure that its obligations to its shareholders and others are understood and met.'

According to this definition, the key responsibilities of the board are therefore:

- *Strategy*: setting the company's strategic aims, determining its strategic objectives and policies and providing clear definitions of responsibility.
- *Resources:* ensuring that the necessary financial and human resources, including key appointments, are in place to enable the company to meet its objectives.
- *Performance:* reviewing management performance and monitoring progress towards objectives.
- *Values and standards:* setting the company's values and standards and ensuring that all employees know what standards of conduct are expected of them, in particular by drawing up codes of ethics or statements of business practice and publishing them internally and externally.
- *Communication:* ensuring that the company's strategic objectives and obligations to shareholders and other stakeholders are clearly understood within the organisation and that all employees know what targets and standards are to be met.

The Combined Code makes clear that the board has active responsibility for the conduct of the company's business. Although the board, and in particular its NEDs, may fulfil a valuable advisory role, the collective purpose of the board is not to advise management, but to account directly to shareholders for the performance of the company.

The board derives its collective authority by direct delegation from the shareholders and must therefore exercise its authority in interests of shareholders. If the board fails to exercise its delegated authority effectively, the interests of shareholders will be unrepresented in the governance of the company and may become subordinated to the interests of other parties, including those of current company management.

Within the context of the unitary board structure, this means that the role of the board as a whole, including NEDs, is to lead and direct the company's activities. Conversely, the whole board, including the CEO and other executive directors, is responsible for monitoring the conduct and performance of management.

Matters reserved to the board

In order to discharge its collective duties of management and supervision of the company's business effectively, the board must determine the scope of its activities and the areas of the business to which it will assign high priority.

The Cadbury Code recommended that, in order to ensure that the direction and control of the company remained firmly in its hands, the board should specifically reserve for its collective decision matters such as material acquisitions and disposals. As a safeguard against misjudgments and possible illegal or unethical practices, the matters reserved to the board should be set out in a formal written schedule, thus making it more difficult for the company's executive management to usurp the authority of the board.

The requirement for a formal schedule of matters specifically reserved for the collective decision of the board has been confirmed in subsequent codes of corporate governance, with the additional recommendation, in the 2003 Combined Code, that the company should state in its annual report how the board operates, with a high level description of the types of decisions to be taken by the board or delegated to management.

In its Guidance Note, *Matters Reserved for the Board* (set out in full in *Appendix 3*), the ICSA recognises that the precise content of the schedule will vary from company to company according to the size and nature of the company's activities, its operating and regulatory environment and the board's assessment of the risks and opportunities faced by the business. Further, every board will need to establish its own view on the materiality of particular categories of decision, including, for example, the financial limits for transactions which should be referred to the board for approval.

With this proviso, it is likely that the boards of most listed companies will wish to reserve the following matters for their collective decision:

Companies Act and other legal requirements

> approval of interim and final financial statements;
> approval of the annual report and accounts;
> approval of the interim dividend and recommendation of the final dividend;

> approval of any significant changes in accounting policies or practices;
> appointment or removal of the company secretary;
> remuneration of the auditors and recommendations for the appointment or removal of auditors (subject in each case to the recommendations of the audit committee);
> the calling of any meeting of shareholders;
> resolutions and corresponding documentation to be put forward to shareholders at a general meeting;
> policy regarding charitable and political donations;
> environmental policy.

Listing requirements

> approval of all circulars and listing particulars requiring to be submitted to the London Stock Exchange prior to despatch to shareholders;
> approval of regulatory announcements and press releases concerning matters decided by the board;
> major changes in employee share schemes and the allocation of executive share options;
> application of the Model Code on share dealing.

Board membership and board committees

> approval of all board appointments and removals (subject to the recommendations of the nomination committee);
> approval of any recommendation to shareholders to re-elect a director on retirement by rotation (subject to the recommendations of the nomination committee);
> terms and conditions of directors and senior executives (subject to the recommendations of the remuneration committee);
> approval of any special terms and conditions attached to the proposed appointment of a director (subject to the recommendations of the remuneration committee);
> terms of reference of chairman, chief executive and other executive directors;
> terms of reference and membership of board committees;
> minutes, reports and referrals from committees of the board;
> appointments to the boards of subsidiary companies.

Management

> approval of the group's long-term objectives and commercial strategy;
> approval of the annual operating and capital expenditure budgets;
> changes relating to the group's capital structure or its status as a plc;
> changes to the group's management and control structure.

Corporate governance

> review of the company's overall corporate governance arrangements;

> internal control arrangements, including changes to the company's/group's management and control structure;
> risk management strategy;
> appointment or removal of the head of internal audit;
> amendments to the schedule of matters reserved for board decisions;
> directors' and officers' insurance.

Employment

> pay and human resource policy;
> major changes in the rules of the company pension scheme, or changes of trustees or (where this is subject to the approval of the company) changes in the fund management arrangements;
> health and safety policy and reports on significant incidents and 'near-misses'.

Financial

> delegations of authority to executive directors;
> subject to delegations of authority approved and in force:
> – major capital projects;
> – contracts of the company (or, where relevant, of any subsidiary) in the ordinary course of business, e.g. bank borrowings and acquisition or disposal of fixed assets which are material; contracts of the company (or, where relevant, of any subsidiary) not in the ordinary course of business, e.g. loans and repayments; foreign currency transactions; major acquisitions or disposals; in each case where the value exceeds the level predetermined by the board;
> – major investments, including the acquisition or disposal of material interests in the voting shares of any company or the making of any takeover bid;
> treasury policies, including foreign currency exposure and the use of derivatives and similar financial instruments;
> any significant change in accounting policies or practices.

Miscellaneous

> approval of the company's principal professional advisers;
> prosecution, defence or settlement of litigation which is material by reason of size or strategic significance.

The schedule of matters reserved to the board effectively constitutes the board's 'job description', reflecting its priorities and determining the extent of its intended direct involvement in particular areas of the business. Conversely, the schedule delineates the areas in which the board considers it appropriate to delegate authority to others, including board committees, the CEO and other executive directors. It is therefore of fundamental importance to the board's ability to control and direct the activities of the company in the interests of the shareholders, and demands both careful analysis and regular review. Some key points to bear in mind when preparing and reviewing the statement of matters reserved to the board are set out on page 56.

GOOD PRACTICE POINT

Preparing the schedule of matters reserved for the board

The preparation of the schedule of matters reserved to the board is too important to be regarded as a purely administrative exercise. The content of the schedule reflects the board's priorities and the matters in which it intends to be actively involved, and thus represents the board's collective 'job description' and the perpetual agenda for its meetings. The following issues are therefore of critical significance to the board's ability to lead and control the company in the interests of shareholders:

Ownership of schedule

- The board must 'own' the schedule of matters reserved for its collective decision and must be fully involved in and responsible for defining and controlling its own job.
- The company secretary has a key role in assisting the board in the preparation of the schedule, but should not be left with sole responsibility.
- The contents of the schedule must be determined by the board collectively, not by any individual or group of directors – whether the chairman, the CEO, the senior independent director, the executive directors or the NEDs.

Strategic content of schedule

- The schedule of matters reserved to the board must be an accurate reflection of the strategic issues of most importance to the company, having regard to its business activities, current position and performance, operating and regulatory environment, risk profile and long-term objectives.
- As the board's 'job description', the schedule must not focus exclusively on what is going on in the organisation, but must reflect the board's primary responsibility for determining the strategic direction of the company.
- The schedule must therefore distinguish clearly between the role of the board for defining the direction and objectives of the company and the responsibilities of management for realising the outcomes identified by the board.

Relevance of schedule

- The schedule must be reviewed regularly in the light of business developments to ensure that the board is devoting its attention to the strategic issues of most significance to the interests of shareholders.

Board's commitment

- The board as a whole must commit itself to active involvement in the matters it reserves to itself, taking into account its accountability to shareholders for its own actions and omissions.
- However, if particular matters so reserved prove to be an inappropriate use of the board's time and attention, the schedule must be amended promptly, and responsibility for the matters concerned must be delegated elsewhere, subject to appropriate reporting arrangements and other guidance as necessary.

Setting values and standards

The emphasis in the 2003 Combined Code on the board's responsibility for setting values and standards reflects growing recognition that the company's reputation is an important asset of the business. Good reputation contributes to confidence in the quality of the board's leadership and can enhance the company's credibility in the eyes of investors, with a positive influence on value and share price. Conversely, a poor or damaged reputation may reduce the company's market value and can threaten or even destroy its business: a key example is the accounting firm Arthur Andersen, which was destroyed by its perceived complicity in the Enron scandal.

The preparation by the board of an explicit statement of the values and standards of conduct expected of all employees can play a key role in upholding and enhancing the company's reputation. Key elements of such a statement include:

> openness and transparency of information, including the provision to shareholders and other stakeholders of timely, accurate and meaningful information about the company's position and significant developments in its affairs;
> compliance with the spirit, rather than the letter, of all applicable laws, regulations and corporate governance requirements;
> conduct of the company's relationships with shareholders and other stake-holders; and
> the ethical conduct of business.

The company's statement of values will often incorporate or be supported by an employee code of conduct or code of ethics. As a result of regulatory changes in the US following the Enron scandal, such codes are now mandatory in the US for certain employees of listed corporations. Although there is no equivalent formal requirement in the UK, it is increasingly the practice of well-regarded companies to produce written codes for the guidance of all employees.

Employee codes of conduct typically emphasise the personal responsibilities of individual employees for:

> honest and ethical conduct, including the avoidance of real or apparent conflicts of interest between personal and professional relationships;
> mutual respect in dealings with colleagues at all levels;
> full, fair, accurate, timely and understandable disclosure of information in company reports, documents and other public communications;
> fair dealing with customers, suppliers, employees and competitors;
> compliance with laws, regulations and other applicable requirements; and
> reporting illegal and unethical behaviour through the company's established whistleblower protection procedure (for further explanation, see *Chapter 12*).

The key stages in developing and implementing a code of conduct, based on guidance prepared by the Institute of Business Ethics, are outlined below. Further information can be found on the Institute's website at www.ibe.org.uk.

Written codes of conduct can provide guidance, trigger reflection about appropriate standards of business conduct and prompt individuals to modify their behaviour. However, they cannot in isolation have a decisive influence on business behaviour, but must be supported by a corporate culture in which ethical conduct is expected from all employees, irrespective of position or seniority, and in which ethical decision-making is seen to be practised at all levels, from the board down. To this end:

> Directors and senior managers must give leadership by demonstrating commitment to the company's ethical standards through their own behaviour and values, and by upholding compliance with the intention – as well as the letter – of internal rules and external laws and regulations.

> The company's performance management system must reward ethical behaviour and punish unethical behaviour by reflecting not just results, but the manner in which results have been achieved.

> Employee training programmes must include focus on realistic ethical dilemmas likely to be encountered in the workplace and promote open discussion of controversial ethical issues.

GOOD PRACTICE POINT ⊘

Developing and implementing a code of ethical business practice

Outline content of the code

Introduction
- the purpose of the code and the values that are important to the conduct of the business, including integrity, responsibility and reputation;
- the board's commitment to maintaining high standards, both within the organisation and in its dealings with others;
- the role of the company in the community;
- personal endorsement of the code by the chairman and/or CEO, setting out the expectation that the standards it contains will be maintained by all involved in the organisation.

Purpose and values of business
- the company's activities in terms of

its products and services, financial objectives and role in society as seen by the board.

Employees
- how the business values employees, including its policies on working conditions; recruitment; development and training; rewards; health, safety and security; equal opportunities; retirement and redundancy; discrimination and harassment;
- use of company assets by employees.

Customer relations
- the importance of customer satisfaction and good faith in all agreements;
- quality, fair pricing and after-sales service.

continued

GOOD PRACTICE POINT

Developing and implementing a code of ethical business practice *continued*

Shareholders or other providers of money
- the protection of investments made in the company and proper return on money lent;
- commitment to accurate and timely communication on achievements and prospects.

Suppliers
- prompt settling of bills;
- co-operation to achieve quality and efficiency;
- no bribery or excess hospitality accepted or given.

Society and the wider community
- compliance with the spirit of laws as well as the letter;
- the company's obligations to protect and preserve the environment;
- the involvement of the company and its staff in local affairs;
- corporate policy on giving to education and charities.

Implementing the code

- *Endorsement*: Make sure that the code is endorsed by the chairman and CEO.
- *Integration*: Produce a strategy for integrating the code into the running of the business at the time it is issued.
- *Circulation*: Send the code to all employees in a readable and portable form and give it to all employees joining the company.
- *Personal response*: Give all staff the personal opportunity to respond to the content of the code. An employee should know how to react

if he or she is faced with a potential breach of the code or is in doubt about a course of action involving an ethical choice.
- *Affirmation*: Have a procedure for managers and supervisors regularly to state that they and their staff understand and apply the provisions of the code and raise matters not covered by it.
- *Contracts*: Consider making adherence to the code obligatory by including reference to it in all contracts of employment and linking it with disciplinary procedures.
- *Regular review*: Have a procedure for regular review and updating of the code.
- *Enforcement*: Ensure that employees and others are aware of the consequences of breaching the code.
- *Training*: Ask those responsible for company training programmes at all levels to include issues raised by the code in their programmes.
- *Translation*: Ensure that the code is translated for use in overseas subsidiaries or other places where English is not the principal language.
- *Distribution*: Make copies of the code available to business partners (suppliers, customers, etc) and expect their compliance.
- *Reporting*: Reproduce or insert a copy of the code in the annual report and/or on the company's website so that shareholders and the wider public know about the company's position on ethical matters.

Source: Institute of Business Ethics, www.ibe.org.uk

Delegation of authority

No board, however effective, can have hands-on involvement in every area of the company's business. Some further degree of delegation of the authorities granted to the board by the shareholders is therefore inevitable.

Having defined its own role and responsibilities through the preparation of the schedule of matters reserved for its collective decision, the board must decide what authority and accountability it is appropriate to delegate to others. At the board's discretion, authority may be delegated to committees or to individuals, including the CEO and other executive directors. In either case, however, the board as a whole remains fully responsible for the exercise of the powers granted to it by the shareholders. Shareholders should therefore be able to assess the actions of the board, its committees and others to whom it has delegated authority, and should have the opportunity at the AGM to question the directors about the processes adopted and the decisions reached.

Delegation to committees

In most companies, the board is empowered under the Articles (Table A, Regulation 72) to delegate its powers to committees consisting of one or more directors. The board can impose regulations by which such committees operate and can also revoke any delegation of authority, whether to a committee to or an individual, at any time by recording its decision in the board minutes.

Under the terms of the 2003 Combined Code, the board of a listed company is required to establish:

> ❭ a nomination committee, a majority of the members of which should be independent NEDs, to lead the process for board appointments and to make recommendations to the board (see also *Chapter 8*);
> ❭ a remuneration committee of at least three (or, in the case of smaller companies, two) independent NEDs with delegated responsibility for developing policy on executive remuneration and for setting remuneration for all executive directors and the chairman (see also *Chapter 9*); and
> ❭ an audit committee of at least three (or, in the case of smaller companies, two) independent NEDs to monitor the integrity of the company's financial statements, oversee its relationships with its external auditors and monitor the effectiveness of the internal audit function (see also *Chapter 11*).

The board may set up further committees as necessary to deal with specific issues or to assist it with defined aspects of its own responsibilities. These may include:

> ❭ an executive committee, consisting of the CEO and other executive directors, with defined powers to take decisions between scheduled meetings of the full board: the ICSA Guidance Note, *Terms of Reference – Executive Committees*, is reproduced in *Appendix 4*;

> board committees, often consisting wholly or mainly of independent NEDs, with responsibility for advising the board as a whole on matters such as risk management, environmental and community responsibility and corporate ethics; and

> temporary committees, with membership drawn from the board and appropriate members of the company's senior management team, with delegated authority to deal with specific matters such as major acquisitions and mergers or to give final approval for the annual report and accounts and similar documents.

Whatever the purpose or expected lifetime of a committee, its powers to act are derived from those of the board, and its activities must therefore always remain under the board's control. For this reason, the board as a whole is responsible for ensuring that each committee's status and functions are clearly specified in advance in its terms of reference, which should set out:

> the committee's membership;

> the committee's key tasks, including, where appropriate, the timescale within which it is required to complete its activities;

> the powers delegated to the committee by the board and the limits of its delegated authority; and

> the committee's accountability, including the frequency with which it is required to report to the board on its activities.

Where appropriate, the minutes of committees should be circulated to all directors prior to the next board meeting to give them an opportunity to raise questions about the committee's activities at that meeting.

Delegation to individuals

The Articles of most companies permit the board to delegate such of their powers as they see fit and desirable to the CEO or any other director holding executive office (Table A, Regulations 84 and 72). Executive directors can therefore be given authority to take decisions on behalf of the board and to enter into contracts or agreements on behalf of the company. Such delegated authorities may be general or may be limited to certain types of transactions or to transactions up to a specified financial value. In addition, authority may be delegated, either directly by the board or indirectly by executive directors, to other members of the company's senior management team, including the company secretary.

As with the delegation of authority to committees, the board retains ultimate responsibility to shareholders for the activities of individual directors and officers to whom it has delegated authority. The board must therefore ensure that individuals to whom it delegates powers are fully accountable for their decisions and actions, for example by requiring them to report periodically to the full board on decisions taken.

Communicating strategic objectives and policies

Need for written statements

Important and demanding as these processes are, it is not enough for the board to define its own job description and agenda and determine the arrangements for the delegation of authority. It must also ensure that its decisions are clearly communicated inside and outside the company and that the organisation as a whole is aligned around the strategic objectives, policies and values determined by the board.

In many cases, boards will find it helpful, in the interests of internal and external accountability, transparency and auditability, to document their strategic objectives, governance arrangements and prescribed methods and standards in formal business policies. These may be communicated to company employees in written form or electronically via the company's intranet. They are also increasingly made publicly available, in whole or in part, on listed companies' external websites.

Content of procedural documentation

The number, style and format of policy and procedural documents will vary widely from company to company according to business complexity, regulatory and operating environment and management style. The following list sets out in summary form some typical elements of policy and procedural documentation:

> *Mission or vision statement* describing the company's identity and key objectives, such as customer satisfaction, market share, product development or territorial expansion, often accompanied by a statement of the company's values and its approach to social and environmental responsibility.

> *Governance arrangements*, including the schedule of matters reserved for the collective decision of the board (see above); the delegation of financial and non-financial authority to committees and individual directors and officers; and the terms of reference of committees established by the board.

> *Business planning cycle*, including planning assumptions and the company's criteria for investing in new business developments.

> *External accountability and communications*, including the protection and dissemination of price-sensitive information; compliance with listing requirements and the Model Code; media, investor and public relations; and the safeguarding of corporate identity and brands.

> *Internal control and risk management arrangements*, including the allocation of responsibility for identifying, managing and monitoring financial and non-financial risks to the achievement of the company's objectives.

> *Financial planning and reporting*, including accounting policies and procedures; treasury, taxation, and pensions policy; and procurement arrangements.

> *Safeguarding of assets*, including insurance; physical security of plant and buildings; disaster recovery and business continuity; information security and confidentiality; and data protection.

> *Health, safety and environment*, including the safeguarding of employees and the public from physical hazards; occupational health; accident reporting; and environmental protection policies.
> *Employment policies*, including remuneration arrangements; human resources policies; equal opportunities; and employee communications.
> *Standards and values*, including any employee code of conduct.

Chapter summary

> In the UK's unitary board system, all directors – both executive directors and NEDs – participate equally in the collective management and supervisory functions of the board.

> Accordingly, the board as a whole is actively responsible to shareholders for setting the company's strategic aims, ensuring that the necessary financial and human resources are in place, reviewing performance and monitoring progress towards objectives, setting the company's values and standards and ensuring that the company's strategic objectives and obligations to shareholders and other stakeholders are understood and met.

> In order to discharge its obligations to shareholders, the board must first define its own 'job description' and priorities by preparing a schedule of the key business decisions it intends to reserve to its collective decision – the schedule of matters reserved to the board is of the highest importance to the board's ability to control and direct the activities of the company, and demands both careful analysis and regular review.

> The board must define the conditions on which its collective decision-making powers are to be delegated to others, taking into account its ultimate responsibility for the exercise of the powers granted to it by the shareholders.

> The board must also ensure that the company's strategic aims and objectives are understood throughout the organisation and are translated into clear, binding guidance for the conduct of the company's business.

6

Composition of the board

❛ There should be a clear division of responsibilities at the head of the company between the running of the board and the executive responsibility for the running of the company's business. No one individual should have unfettered powers of decision.

Combined Code (2003) Main Principle A.2 ❜

❛ The board should include a balance of executive and non-executive directors (and in particular independent non-executive directors) such that no individual or small group of individuals can dominate the board's decision-taking.

Combined Code (2003) Main Principle A.3 ❜

This chapter considers the composition of the board, taking into account:

> ❭ the duties of individual directors, the risks and potential liabilities arising from these duties and the role of insurance and due diligence in mitigating them;
> ❭ the role and effectiveness of non-executive directors (NEDs) in ensuring an appropriate balance of influence on the board;
> ❭ the definition of 'independence' and the specific roles allocated by the Combined Code to independent NEDs; and
> ❭ the division of authority at the top of the company, including the role of the chairman, the chief executive officer (CEO) and the senior independent director.

Introduction

As described in *Chapter 5*, the board is collectively responsible to the shareholders for the management of the company's business (encompassing entrepreneurial leadership, strategic direction, the assessment and management of risk and the decisions about the required level of resources), as well as for the review of management performance.

Although there is no distinction in law between directors, the UK's system of corporate governance recognises that in practice the boards of listed companies are composed of directors of two distinct types:

> executive directors, including the CEO, who are full-time employees of the company, with direct involvement in and delegated responsibility for the executive management of a defined area of the business; and

> NEDs, who are not employees of company, have no involvement in its management and may spend no more than 15–30 days a year on its business.

All directors, irrespective of type, are equally responsible for both management and supervision. Thus, the CEO and other executive directors participate in the board's collective responsibility for supervising management conduct and performance, despite their own direct involvement and responsibility as managers. Conversely, NEDs are responsible, as members of the collective board, both for contributing to the development of strategy and for scrutinising the conduct of the executive directors.

Successive codes of corporate governance have adopted provisions designed to ensure that the influence of executive management over board decisions is tempered by the contributions of objective and independent NEDs, and in certain cases – notably executive remuneration – to exclude executive directors from decision-making entirely. As a result, there is increasing emphasis on the composition of the board and the balance of power and influence over its decision-making, accompanied by an increasing differentiation between the roles and qualifications of different members of the board.

Directors as individuals

Directors' duties

As discussed in *Chapter 1*, all directors – whether executive or non-executive – owe to the company and its shareholders fiduciary duties of loyalty and good faith requiring them to:

> behave loyally towards the company and obey its constitution;
> use their powers under the company's constitution for their proper purposes;
> act in good faith in the company's best interests;
> maintain independence of judgment and avoid conflicts, actual and potential, between duties to the company and personal interests; and
> act fairly as between shareholders.

All directors are expected to apply reasonable care and skill in the exercise of their functions, subject to an objective test applicable to directors generally and to a more demanding subjective test applicable to each director personally. Although executive directors and NEDs are bound by the same duties, the application of the subjective test means in practice that a higher standard of skill, care and diligence is expected of executive directors, reflecting their closer involvement in the company's day-to-day affairs.

The proposed statutory statement of directors' general duties set out in the Company Law Reform Bill seeks to codify these fiduciary duties and to impose on each director a new statutory duty to act in the way which he or she considers, in good faith, will be most likely to promote the success of the company for the benefit of its members as a whole. The duties are cumulative, in that directors will be required to comply with every duty that applies to a given case and must also continue to comply with all other applicable laws.

Directors' legal liabilities

All directors, whether executive or non-executive, are potentially exposed to claims for damages in respect of the following:

> *Breach of fiduciary duties*: directors may be held personally liable for breach of fiduciary duties and may be sued by the company for recovery of benefits wrongly obtained from such breaches.
> *Breach of duties of care and skill*: claims for damages may be brought, usually by the company, against directors who are considered to have breached their duties of care and skill.

In both cases, it is generally assumed that the company as a whole, rather than shareholders individually, will initiate any legal proceedings against directors who are considered to be in breach of their duties. As explained in *Chapter 1*, routes do exist to enable aggrieved shareholders, acting on their own account or on behalf of the company, to pursue legal actions against directors, but these are often difficult, complex and expensive and are therefore rarely used in practice.

The Company Law Reform Bill proposes to replace the existing common law right of a shareholder to bring a derivative action on the company's behalf and to introduce a new statutory derivative procedure. If successful, this measure is expected to make it easier for shareholders to sue directors or others (for example, those who have knowingly received money or property transferred by a director in breach of trust) for a broader range of conduct than would be possible at present.

In addition to actions for breach of directors' general duties, the Companies Act 1985 (CA 1985) identifies more than 200 offences for which directors may be punished on conviction, including failure to keep proper accounting records and making loans on uncommercial terms to an associated company. The directors and officers of a company may also face claims arising from areas such as employment law, health and safety, takeovers and mergers, misrepresentation, liability under the Environmental Protection Act 1990 and the Financial Services and Markets Act 2000 (FSMA 2000).

Further, the Company Directors Disqualification Act 1986 (CDDA 1986) and insolvency legislation provide for the disqualification and personal liability of directors who have permitted a company to continue to trade when they were, or should have been, aware that it had gone (or would soon go) into insolvent liquidation and thus negligently failed to act to minimise potential losses to creditors. Directors may also be convicted of the more serious criminal offence of fraudulent trading if it can be shown that they allowed the company to continue trading when insolvent, with the intent of defrauding creditors or for some other fraudulent purpose.

Indemnification of directors

It is well-established in company law that companies can properly indemnify their directors against actions, by the company or by third parties, where the directors are not in breach of their duties to the company. Recognising that, as a matter of principle, no such indemnity should offer complete mitigation of the personal risks faced by directors, CA 1985 stipulated that:

> ❯ a company could not validly exempt any director, officer or auditor from, or indemnify them against, any liability for negligence, default, breach of duty or breach of trust in relation to the company; and
> ❯ any advance commitment by the company to indemnify a director against his or her legal costs would be invalid unless it was made conditional on a successful defence by the director.

The Higgs Report, *Role and effectiveness of non-executive directors*, published in January 2003, observed that the potential risks and uncertainties associated with being a director appeared to be increasing, not least as a result of the growing scope and likelihood of litigation. In the light of concerns that potential candidates might be deterred from coming forward, particularly for non-executive appointments, the Government consulted in late 2003 on possible changes to the law on directors' liabilities. The outcome, in the form of the Companies (Audit, Investigations and Community Enterprise) Act 2004, has made it easier for companies to indemnify directors against liability.

Companies are still not permitted to exempt directors from, or indemnify them against, liabilities to the company itself. The Act does, however, introduce two important relaxations of the current prohibition:

> ❯ It permits (but does not require) companies to indemnify directors in respect of proceedings brought by third parties and applications for relief from liability (covering both legal costs and the financial costs of any adverse judgment except criminal penalties, penalties imposed by regulatory bodies such as the Financial Services Authority and the legal costs of unsuccessful criminal defences or applications for relief).
> ❯ It permits (but does not require) companies to pay directors' costs of defence proceedings as they are incurred, even if the action is brought by the company itself or is a derivative action.

Guidance on directors' and officers' insurance has been prepared by the ICSA in collaboration with the City of London Law Society, the Association of British Insurers (ABI) and the British Insurance Brokers Association, and is reproduced in *Appendix 5*.

Reputational risk and due diligence

In addition to their potential exposure to financial liabilities and other legal sanctions, all directors encounter reputational risks arising from their association with the company. These risks are likely to be particularly acute for new directors, whether executive or non-executive, who are recruited from outside the company on the basis of their past achievements. Such individuals will have established reputations for their business ability, sound judgment and personal probity and will want to preserve their reputational assets, both as matter of personal pride and as the basis on which to advance their careers.

The Higgs Report urged that, prior to appointment, potential new NEDs should carry out due diligence on the board and the company to satisfy themselves that they have the knowledge, skills, experience and time to make a positive contribution to the board.

Due diligence is equally relevant to new executive directors and NEDs, given that their reputations and future career prospects are equally likely to be impaired if the company runs into financial difficulties or engages in illegal or unethical behaviour. Guidance on the due diligence process to be undertaken by prospective directors before joining a company is provided in the ICSA's Guidance Note, *Due Diligence for Directors*, the full text of which is given in *Appendix 6*.

Board balance

Requirement for non-executive directors

Although it is now generally accepted that the boards of listed companies should have significant non-executive membership, this is a comparatively recent phenomenon. In the early 1990s, the Cadbury Committee found that some company boards had no NEDs at all and that, in companies where non-executives had been appointed, they were often outnumbered by executive directors. In many cases, NEDs had prior links with the company or its major shareholders or external advisers, impairing their independence.

The initial focus of corporate governance was therefore to reinforce the presence of NEDs as a numerical counterweight to the company's executive management. More recently, in the light of concerns about the effectiveness of NEDs aroused by Enron and other corporate scandals, attention has focused on the quality of the contribution made by NEDs, both as individuals and – more controversially – as a distinct group with a recognised senior member.

Numerical balance of the board

The desirability of appointing NEDs to the boards of listed companies was first formally advanced in the Cadbury Code, which recommended that NEDs should bring independent judgment to bear on issues of strategy, performance, resources (including key appointments) and standards of conduct. Although the Cadbury Code emphasised the need for a strong and independent element on the board, it gave no firm guidance on the proportion of the board that should be made up of NEDs, stating only that they should be 'of sufficient calibre and number for their views to carry significant weight in the board's decisions'.

More specific guidance on the numerical balance of the board was provided in the 1998 Combined Code, which recommended that, in order to ensure that no individual or small group of individuals could dominate the board's decision-taking, a least one-third of the board should be made up of NEDs, of whom the majority should be independent. This was superseded in the 2003 Combined Code by the recommendation that:

> ❭ except for smaller companies (defined for this purpose as listed companies below the FTSE 350) at least half the board, excluding the chairman, should be made up of independent NEDs; while
> ❭ the boards of smaller companies should contain at least two independent NEDs.

Effectiveness of non-executive directors

The emphasis in codes of corporate governance on the numerical balance of the board was challenged in 2001 by the collapse of Enron, a company whose board – like those of most US companies – consisted almost exclusively of outside directors. The failure of the board to detect and challenge questionable financial practices contributed to the eventual downfall of the company and demonstrated that numerical predominance is not sufficient by itself to ensure the effectiveness of NEDs.

In his report to HM Treasury on institutional investment in the UK, published in March 2001, Paul Myners characterised NEDs as the 'missing link' in the chain of accountability between the board and the company's shareholders, pointing out that the dominant position of executive directors meant that institutional shareholders rarely had the opportunity to communicate their concerns to non-executives: 'the only time shareholders actually meet non-executives is when something terrible has happened, which is too late'.

Further concerns about the effectiveness of NEDs were identified in the Higgs Report, published in January 2003. This concluded that the contribution of NEDs to effective governance was limited in practice by factors including:

> ❭ NEDs' lack of knowledge about the business of the company, compounded by the ability of executive management to withhold or manipulate information;
> ❭ the inability or unwillingness of some NEDs to devote sufficient time to the company's affairs, particularly because of the competing demands of other directorships; and
> ❭ reluctance on the part of some NEDs to question and challenge management, whether because of the dominant position of the CEO or because cross-directorships created a mutual interest in not 'rocking the boat'.

To address these concerns, the Higgs Report emphasised the need for at least a proportion of NEDs to be wholly independent (see below) and for improved practices in relation to the appointment, induction and training of NEDs (see *Chapter 8*). Key elements in the role of NEDs, as identified in the Higgs Report, are set out on page 70.

ROLE OF NON-EXECUTIVE DIRECTOR

- *Strategy:* Non-executive directors should constructively challenge and contribute to the development of strategy.
- *Performance:* Non-executive directors should scrutinise the performance of management in meeting agreed goals and objectives and monitor the reporting of performance.
- *Risk:* Non-executive directors should satisfy themselves that financial information is accurate and that financial controls and systems of risk management are robust and defensible.
- *People:* Non-executive directors are responsible for determining appropriate levels of remuneration of executive directors and have a prime role in appointing, and where necessary removing, senior management and in succession planning.

Source: Higgs (January 2003) *Role and effectiveness of non-executive directors*, Chapter 6

The recommendations of the Higgs Report are reflected in the 2003 Combined Code, Supporting Principle A.1 of which states that:

'As part of their role as members of a unitary board, non-executive directors should constructively challenge and help develop proposals on strategy. Non-executive directors should scrutinise the performance of management in meeting agreed goals and objectives and monitor the reporting of performance. They should satisfy themselves on the integrity of financial information and that financial controls and systems of risk management are robust and defensible. They are responsible for determining appropriate levels of remuneration of executive directors and have a prime role in appointing, and where necessary removing, executive directors, and in succession planning.'

The Combined Code also emphasises the need for NEDs to be proactive in the exercise of their responsibilities, stating that:

> where they have concerns which cannot be resolved about the running of the company or a proposed action, they should ensure that their concerns are recorded in the board minutes; and

> on resignation, an NED should provide a written statement to the chairman, for circulation to the board, if he or she has any such concerns.

Concept of independence

Definition of independence

The collective responsibility of the board for the leadership and direction of the company's activities and for supervising management conduct and performance imposes on all directors, whether executive or non-executive, a duty to act objectively in the interests of company as a whole. This point was reinforced in the Higgs Report, which drew attention to the need for all directors, without exception, to be 'independent of mind and willing and able to challenge, question and speak up'.

It is now generally accepted, however, that for the purposes of corporate governance at least a proportion of NEDs should meet a defined technical standard of independence, in particular to ensure that they are free of potential conflicts of interest over issues such as remuneration, appointment and audit.

The standard of strict technical independence considered necessary for at least a proportion of NEDs has evolved over time. Both the Cadbury Code and the 1998 version of the Combined Code stated that:

> *'the majority of non-executive directors should be independent of management and free from any business or other relationship which could materially interfere with the exercise of their independent judgement'*

leaving it to the discretion of the board to determine which of its members met this test.

The Higgs Report expressed concern that, in the absence of definitive guidance, both boards and shareholders were uncertain as to what the test of independence should entail. As a result, institutional investors and their representatives had developed their own, mutually inconsistent, definitions for use in determining their voting intentions. According to the Higgs Report, by 2002 there were over a dozen such definitions in the UK, all with different criteria. It therefore recommended that a new, definitive test of independence should be adopted, emphasising that this should address not only those relationships or circumstances that would impair an NED's objectivity, but also those that could appear to an outside observer to do so.

Accordingly, Provision A.3.1of the 2003 Combined Code states that the board of a listed company should:

> ❯ identify in the annual report each NED it considers to be independent;
> ❯ for this purpose, determine whether the director is independent in character and judgment and whether there are relationships or circumstances which are likely to affect, or could appear to affect, the director's judgment; and
> ❯ state its reasons if it determines that a particular director is independent notwithstanding the existence of relationships or circumstances which may appear relevant to its determination, including if the director:
>   - has been an employee of the company or group within the last five years;
>   - has, or has had within the last three years, a material business relationship with the company either directly, or as a partner, shareholder, director or senior employee of a body that has such a relationship with the company;
>   - has received or receives additional remuneration from the company apart from a director's fee, participates in the company's share option or a performance-related pay scheme, or is a member of the company's pension scheme;
>   - has close family ties with any of the company's advisers, directors or senior employees;

- holds cross-directorships or has significant links with other directors through involvement in other companies or bodies;
- represents a significant shareholder; or
- has served on the board for more than nine years from the date of their first election.

Implications for board composition

In determining the appropriate composition of the board, the 2003 Combined Code recommends that:

> except for smaller companies (defined for this purpose as listed companies below the FTSE 350) at least half the board, excluding the chairman, should be made up of NEDs who meet the above definition of independence; while
> the boards of smaller companies should contain at least two independent NEDs.

This numerical requirement does not in itself constitute a prohibition on the appointment as NEDs of individuals who do not comply with the formal definition of independence, for example because of a recent or ongoing connection with the company. Indeed, it is widely recognised that such individuals, who may include former executive directors, representatives of major shareholders and senior external advisers to the company, may contribute skills and expertise of great value in the board's decision-making. It must be acknowledged, however, that such individuals may be, or may appear to be, less willing to question the views of executive management.

The presence of non-independent NEDs will also have important practical consequences for the overall size and numerical balance of the board. In addition to any non-independent NEDs, there must be sufficient NEDs who do meet the standard of independence to enable the company to comply with the recommendation that at least half the board, excluding the chairman, should be independent and to enable members to be appointed to the key sub-committees of the board, given that:

> a majority of members of the nomination committee should be independent NEDs (see *Chapter 8*);
> the remuneration committee should consist of at least three, or in the case of smaller companies two, independent NEDs (see *Chapter 9*); and
> the audit committee should consist of at least three, or in the case of smaller companies two, independent NEDs (see *Chapter 11*).

Compliance with independence requirements

Despite some initial concerns about the practicability of the independence standards, the evidence is that most listed companies have been able to comply without undue difficulty with the recommendations of the 2003 Combined Code. According to the report *Board Effectiveness and Shareholder Engagement 2005* published by the proxy voting agency Research, Recommendations and Electronic Voting (RREV), the average percentage of independent members on boards in 2005 was 54 per cent in FTSE 100 companies and 49 per cent in FTSE 250 companies (compared with 50 per cent and 44 per cent respectively in 2004).

Concerns have also been expressed by some companies about the possibility that institutional investors may not accept as independent any NED who has served on the board for more than nine years. In its review of the implementation of the 2003 Combined Code, the Financial Reporting Council (FRC) found little evidence for this, pointing out that around 10 per cent of all NEDs in FTSE 350 companies had been in position for 10 years or more. It made clear that none of the factors listed in the definition of independence will automatically prevent an NED from being considered independent in character and judgment, provided that the company is able to provide a satisfactory explanation in circumstances where any of the factors apply.

The RREV report *Board Effectiveness and Shareholder Engagement 2005* provides useful clarification of the type of explanation likely to be accepted by institutional investors. This explains that NEDs whose tenure has exceeded nine years may still be considered independent where:

> the explanation given by the company focuses specifically on the director's independence of character and judgment, rather than on his or her expertise or experience;
> there is evidence that the board performance evaluation process has addressed and confirmed the independence of the director in question;
> where the director is a member of a board committee such as audit or remuneration, that committee has acted in a properly independent manner; and
> there are no other factors which could potentially compromise the director's independence, such as cross-directorships or a material business or financial relationship with the company.

Division of authority

Allocation of responsibilities at head of company

A key aim of corporate governance has been to prevent an excessive concentration of power and authority at the top of the company. The approach taken to this problem in successive codes of corporate governance has evolved in distinct stages, comprising:

> formal separation between the offices of chairman and CEO, with a strengthening presumption that both posts should not be held by the same individual;
> more detailed qualitative definition of the role of the chairman, with emphasis on the position of the chairman relative to the executive directors and NEDs;
> growing acceptance of the need for a senior independent director to lead the independent contingent on the board and provide a channel of communication for shareholders who have been unable to resolve concerns in discussion with either the chairman or CEO.

Chairman/CEO split

Table A, Regulation 91 provides that the directors may appoint one of their number to be chairman of the company, but gives no further guidance on which of the directors is eligible to be so appointed. There is thus no legal or constitutional prohibition on both offices being held by the same person: indeed, when the Cadbury Committee was established in 1991, it was still commonplace for the offices of chairman and CEO to be combined on the boards of UK listed companies.

The Cadbury Committee's study concluded, however, that the two offices entail different, and arguably irreconcilable, roles and responsibilities. According to this analysis, the chairman is responsible for the functioning of the board and for facilitating the discharge of its collective responsibility to shareholders, but is not directly involved in the day-to-day management of the business. By contrast, the CEO is responsible for the leadership of the management team and is accountable to the board as a whole for implementing its collective decisions.

Based on this analysis, the Cadbury Committee concluded that the chairman's role should, as a matter of principle, be separated from that of the CEO. However, the ensuing Cadbury Code stopped short of requiring a formal separation in listed companies, conceding that some companies might wish to continue to combine the roles of chairman and CEO. Where this was done, it recommended that there should be a strong and independent element on the board as a safeguard against an excessive concentration of power in the hands of one individual.

The 1998 Combined Code reinforced this presumption against the appointment of a combined chairman and CEO. It recommended that any decision to combine the two posts should be publicly justified and that, whether or not the posts were held by different people, the board should contain a strong and independent non-executive element.

Research carried out in 2002 on behalf of the Higgs Review of the role and effectiveness of NEDs found that the principle of separation between the positions of chairman and CEO was generally accepted, with around 90 per cent of listed companies splitting the roles. The Review concluded that the benefits of separation, in terms of the dispersal of authority and power and differentiation between leadership of the board and the running of the business, were so well established that there should now be a categorical presumption that the roles of chairman and chief executive should be separated.

Accordingly, the 2003 Combined Code provides that the functions of chairman and CEO should not be exercised by the same individual. Further, the division of responsibilities between the chairman and CEO should be clearly established, set out in writing and agreed by the full board.

Role of chairman

In addition to its conclusions on the separation of the roles of chairman and chief executive, the Higgs Report identified a need for definitive guidance on the distinctive responsibilities of the chairman within the unitary board structure. Following the recommendations of the Report, the 2003 Combined Code, Supporting Principle A.2 states that:

> *'The chairman is responsible for leadership of the board, ensuring its effectiveness on all aspects of its role and setting its agenda. The chairman is also responsible for ensuring that the directors receive accurate, timely and clear information. The chairman should ensure effective communication with shareholders. The chairman should also facilitate the effective contribution of non-executive directors in particular and ensure constructive relations between executive and non-executive directors.'*

Specific guidance for chairmen as offered in Annex D of the Higgs Report is set out on page 76.

Independence of chairman

Given the nature of the chairman's responsibilities, he or she must establish and maintain relationships of trust with all directors – executive and non-executive. For this reason, the 2003 Combined Code discourages the once common practice of appointing a former chief executive to the chairmanship of the company and recommends that, on first appointment, the chairman should meet the test of independence applied to NEDs (see above).

Once appointed, however, the chairman's role will differ significantly from that of either the NEDs or the executive directors. The chairman will have closer day-to-day involvement with the executive team than do the NEDs, and this involvement will inevitably have the effect of reducing his or her independence. For this reason, the 2003 Combined Code provides that, even where the chairman met the test of independence on first appointment, he or she must be excluded from any subsequent considerations involving the numerical balance of the board and cannot be counted as a member of the independent contingent.

It follows that, as a general principle, the chairman should not sit on those key committees which the Combined Code recommends should consist solely of independent NEDs. There is evidence, however, that many companies are electing not to comply with this limitation in the context of the remuneration committee. The FRC's review of the implementation of the 2003 Combined Code found that the chairman sits on the remuneration committee in nearly 30 per cent of FTSE 350 companies and that, in companies where the chairman is not a remuneration committee member, he or she is often invited to attend its meetings.

Recognising that presence of the chairman as a member of the remuneration committee could help to ensure that performance incentives and other elements of the remuneration policy are properly aligned with the company's strategic objectives, the FRC has proposed amendments to the Combined Code to allow the chairman to sit as a full member of the remuneration committee provided that he or she met the

GUIDANCE FOR CHAIRMAN

The chairman is pivotal in creating the conditions for overall board and individual director effectiveness, both inside and outside the boardroom. Specifically, it is the responsibility of the chairman to:

- run the board and set its agenda. The agenda should take full account of the issues and the concerns of all board members. Agendas should be forward-looking and concentrate on strategic matters rather than formulaic approvals of proposals which can be the subject of appropriate delegated powers to management;
- ensure that the members of the board receive accurate, timely and clear information, in particular about the company's performance, to enable the board to take sound decisions, monitor effectively and provide advice to promote the success of the company;
- ensure effective communication with shareholders and ensure that the members of the board develop an understanding of the views of major investors;
- manage the board to ensure that sufficient time is allowed for discussion of complex or contentious issues, where appropriate arranging for informal meetings beforehand to enable thorough preparation for the board discussion. It is particularly important that non-executive directors have sufficient time to consider critical issues and are not faced with unrealistic deadlines for decision-making;
- take the lead in providing a properly constructed induction programme for new directors that is comprehensive, formal and tailored, facilitated by the company secretary;
- take the lead in identifying and meeting the development needs of individual directors, with the company secretary having a key role in facilitating provision. It is the responsibility of the chairman to address the development needs of the board as a whole with a view to enhancing the overall effectiveness as a team;
- ensure that the performance of individuals and of the board as a whole and its committees is evaluated at least once a year; and
- encourage active engagement by all the members of the board.

The effective chairman:

- upholds the highest standards of integrity and probity;
- sets the agenda, style and tone of board discussions to promote effective decision-making and constructive debate;
- promotes effective relationships and open communication, both inside and outside the boardroom, between non-executive directors and the executive team;
- builds an effective and complementary board, initiating change and planning succession in board appointments, subject to board and shareholders' approval;
- promotes the highest standards of corporate governance and seeks compliance with the provisions of the Code wherever possible;
- ensures a clear structure for and the effective running of board committees;
- ensures effective implementation of board decisions;
- establishes a close relationship of trust with the chief executive, providing support and advice while respecting executive responsibility; and
- provides coherent leadership of the company, including representing the company and understanding the views of shareholders.

Source: Higgs (January 2003) *Role and effectiveness of non-executive directors*, Annex D

test of independence at the time of first appointment to the chairmanship. Depending on the outcome of consultation, the amendment will have effect for financial years beginning on or after 1 November 2006. It should be noted, however, that:

> the chairman's membership of the remuneration committee will be *in addition to* the current recommended minimum membership of three independent NEDs (two for smaller companies);
> the chairman of the company should not chair the remuneration committee; and
> the chairman's status with regard to independence will be otherwise unchanged, in that a chairman who met the test of independence on first appointment will still not count as a member of the independent contingent on the board.

Nomination and appointment of chairman

In view of the particular sensitivities surrounding the post of chairman, the Higgs Report concluded that special arrangements were required for the nomination and appointment of the chairman. It therefore recommended that the following principles should be observed when a board is appointing a new chairman:

> The nomination and appointment process should be led, not by the incumbent chairman, but by the senior independent director (see below) or by the deputy chairman (provided that the latter is independent).
> Any existing director who is putting himself or herself forward as a candidate for the chairmanship should be excluded from involvement in the appointment process.
> The nomination committee or another group comprising a majority of independent NEDs should lead the process and make a recommendation to the board as a whole.
> A systematic approach should be taken to identify the skills and expertise required for the role of chairman and a job specification should be prepared.
> A shortlist of potential candidates should be considered, preferably with the benefit of external advice, rather than possible individuals being considered in isolation.

Further information on the selection and appointment and the role of the nomination committee is set out in *Chapter 8*.

Senior independent director

The concept of the senior independent director originated in the Cadbury Code and applied to companies in which the posts of chairman and CEO were still held by the same individual. This was taken further in the 1998 Combined Code, which recommended that, even where the posts of chairman and CEO were separated, the non-executive element on the board should have a recognised senior member other than the chairman. A particular role envisaged for the senior NED was to provide a channel of communication for shareholders who had concerns about the company's performance or proposed developments, but who had been unable to resolve these in discussion with the chairman or CEO.

By 2002, the Higgs Report found that many listed companies were still unconvinced of the case for a senior NED, not least because of concerns that the role might be unnecessary, and even potentially divisive. Despite these concerns, the 2003 Combined Code recommended that:

> ❭ the board should appoint one of the independent NEDs to be the senior independent director (Provision A.3.3);
> ❭ the senior independent director should be available to shareholders if they have concerns which contact through the normal channels of chairman, chief executive or finance director has failed to resolve or for which such contact is inappropriate (Provision A.3.3);
> ❭ the senior independent director should lead meetings of the NEDs which it is inappropriate for the chairman to attend (Provision A.1.3);
> ❭ the senior independent director, together with the chairman, the deputy chairman (where there is one), the chief executive, and the chairmen and members of the nomination, audit and remuneration committees, should be identified in the annual report (Provision A.1.2); and
> ❭ for the purpose of appraising the chairman's performance the NEDs, led by the senior independent director, should meet without the chairman present at least annually, and additionally as necessary (Provision A.1.3).

According to the RREV report *Board Effectiveness and Shareholder Engagement 2005*, the case for the appointment of a senior independent director is now gaining ground. By 2005, some 85 per cent of FTSE 350 companies reported that they had appointed a senior independent director. Further, senior independent directors appear to be taking on a distinct corporate governance role encompassing the following:

> ❭ *Relations with shareholders*: companies typically report that their senior independent director is available to shareholders if they have concerns which contact through the normal channels of chairman, chief executive or finance director has failed to resolve or for which such contact is inappropriate. In support of this role, many companies state that their senior independent director attends sufficient meetings of major shareholders and financial analysts to develop an understanding of their objectives and concerns.
> ❭ *Appraisal and appointment of the chairman*: in many companies, the senior independent director meets other directors at least annually to evaluate and appraise the performance of the chairman and also chairs the nomination committee when it considers succession to the role of the chairman.

The role of the senior independent director as described in the guidance on board governance adopted by Barclays plc in December 2004 is set out below.

BARCLAYS PLC BOARD GOVERNANCE – SENIOR INDEPENDENT DIRECTOR

Role profile

The role of the Senior Independent Director is to:

- Be available to shareholders if they have concerns relating to matters which contact through the normal channels of Chairman, Chief Executive or Finance Director has failed to resolve, or for which such contact is inappropriate.
- Maintain contact as required with major shareholders to understand their issues and concerns, including attending meetings where necessary with shareholders to listen to their views in order to help develop a balanced understanding of the issues and concerns of major shareholders.
- Meet with the Non-Executive Directors without the Chairman present at least annually and lead the Board in the ongoing monitoring and annual evaluation of the Group Chairman, including communicating results of the evaluation to the Chairman.

Charter of expectations

Role requirements

- Time commitment – The Senior Independent Director will be expected to commit at least 3 to 4 days per year but be able to commit significantly more time to the role in exceptional circumstances.
- Experience – Significant experience of serving on a Board of a major international organisation.

Key competencies and behaviours

- Trust/respect – Must be able to command the trust and respect of his fellow Directors and be seen as an individual to whom Directors and Institutional Shareholders can raise concerns which contact through normal channels has failed to resolve or for which such contact is inappropriate.
- Political awareness – Must have experience in managing politically sensitive situations in a large and complex organisation.
- Judgement – must have ability to demonstrate excellent judgement under pressure.

Source: Barclays plc (December 2004) Board Governance

Chapter summary

> Recent corporate failures have increased the perceived risks associated with being a director, leading to renewed emphasis on the need for companies and individuals to satisfy themselves that prospective new directors have the knowledge, skills, experience and time to make a positive contribution to the board.

> Although there is no distinction in law between directors, there is an increasing focus for corporate governance purposes on the composition and balance of the board, involving a growing differentiation between the roles and contributions of executive and NEDs.

> In addition, recent corporate failures have led to close scrutiny of the role and effectiveness of NEDs, leading to a more stringent definition of independence.

> There is a strengthening presumption that the posts of chairman and CEO should not be held by the same individual and that the boards of listed companies should appoint one of their independent NEDs to be the senior independent director.

7

Board effectiveness

> The board should be supplied in a timely manner with information in a form and of a quality appropriate to enable it to discharge its duties. All directors should receive induction on joining the board and should regularly update and refresh their skills and knowledge.
>
> Combined Code (2003) Main Principle A.5

> The board should undertake a formal and rigorous annual evaluation of its own performance and that of its committees and individual directors.
>
> Combined Code (2003) Main Principle A.6

This chapter explores:

> ❭ company and individual responsibilities for the induction of new directors and the professional development of directors in service;
> ❭ the operation of the board, including the roles of the chairman and the company secretary in ensuring the effectiveness of its decision-making processes; and
> ❭ the expectation that boards and individual directors should undertake regular, formal evaluation of their own performance and the evolution of techniques and processes for that purpose.

Introduction

The ability of the board to lead and control the company in the interests of shareholders is critically dependent on the quality of its decision-making. This in turn is determined by the skills and capacities of individual directors, by the existence of an open and constructive boardroom culture and by the availability to the board of accurate, timely and meaningful information.

While these factors have long been recognised, the traditional assumption has been that the board collectively, and directors individually, are merely the recipients and consumers of information and that responsibility for ensuring that the board is well informed lies primarily with the company's management.

Recent corporate failures demonstrate that this assumption is no longer tenable. The increased technological complexity and geographical dispersal of business activity mean that serious problems may materialise very quickly and that boards cannot rely passively on information provided by management (who may have their own reasons for preferring not to draw the board's attention to potential problems). Given the potential legal and reputational risks involved, directors cannot afford to adopt a passive attitude to information, but must instead be ready to define their information requirements and to ask searching and, if necessary, repeated questions.

Current developments in corporate governance in the UK are designed to increase board effectiveness through an increased emphasis on the need for directors, individually and collectively, to take responsibility for their own professional development and ability to contribute to the work of the board. In addition, there is a growing recognition of the board's obligation regularly and objectively to re-evaluate the mix of skills and experience it needs and to change its membership in an orderly manner over time.

Directors' induction and professional development

Induction of new directors

Newly appointed directors need to familiarise themselves quickly with the company's activities so that the skills and experience for which they have been appointed can be used for the benefit of the company and its shareholders. The need for a proper induction process for this purpose has long been recognised: the Cadbury Report made clear in 1992 that newly appointed board members are entitled to expect proper induction into the company's affairs.

Despite this recognition, research carried out in 2002 for the Higgs Review found that half of all newly appointed chairmen, and nearly one-fifth of newly appointed non-executive directors (NEDs), received no induction at all for their roles, while less than one-quarter of NEDs received formal briefing or induction after appointment. In many cases, new NEDs were left to take the initiative in seeking an induction programme and to ask the right questions in order to receive the information they needed.

Commenting that this position was not acceptable, the Higgs Review concluded that companies must set aside adequate resources and ensure that sufficient time is available for a thorough induction for new directors. It recommended that the chairman should take the lead in providing a properly constructed induction programme, which should be facilitated by the company secretary.

The Higgs Review suggested that induction programmes should consist of a combination of written briefing material, together with presentations and activities such as meetings and site visits, and should be designed to develop the new director's understanding in the following main areas:

> the company's business and the markets in which it operates, including its products and services, principal assets, liabilities and significant contracts, major competitors, significant risks and risk management strategy, key performance indicators and regulatory constraints;

> the culture of the company and the board, including the company's constitution; board procedures and matters reserved for the board; the behaviours needed for effective board performance; and, for foreign directors, the working of the UK unitary board;
> the company's people, including fellow directors, the senior management team and employees, through visits to company locations, attending company events and other informal contacts; and
> the company's external relationships with, for example, its auditors, major customers, major suppliers and principal shareholders.

The ICSA has developed a checklist of written material that should be considered for inclusion in an induction pack to be provided to all new directors. The full text of the ICSA Guidance Note, *Induction of Directors*, can be found at *Appendix 7*.

Professional development of existing directors

The Higgs Review found that few directors received structured training or development: two-thirds of NEDs and chairmen received no formal training beyond the experience acquired through their involvement in the company's business and participation in board discussions. Questioning whether this experience alone was sufficient to ensure the effectiveness of the board, Higgs called on companies to provide the resources needed to develop and update the knowledge and skills of their directors. To this end, it recommended that the chairman should address the development needs of the board as a whole, and should also take the lead in identifying the development needs of individual directors, with the company secretary playing a key role in facilitating provision.

Professional development for existing directors should ideally draw on practical lessons drawn from real events and situations, rather than relying on formal lectures and presentations. Training should be tailored closely to company and individual requirements:

> Company-specific elements are likely to include updating and expanding the knowledge of directors in strategic areas, including technological developments, new and potential markets and changes in the company's legal and regulatory environment.
> Individual development needs may include personal behaviours and competencies, such as influencing and negotiating skills, conflict resolution, chairing skills and board dynamics.

NEDs may have specific needs for technical education and development to enable them to evaluate the strategic proposals brought forward by the executive management team and to fulfil their roles as members of the audit, remuneration or nomination committees. For these purposes, development may be needed in areas such as, for example: risk management; the company's treasury policies, including its use of new and complex financial instruments; recruitment and evaluation methodologies; and developments in the design of performance incentives.

The Higgs Review acknowledged, however, that there may be significant cultural and practical barriers to the effective professional development of directors. Long-standing directors may assume – not necessarily correctly – that they already have all the skills and knowledge needed to carry out their role and may therefore be reluctant to recognise their own development needs. Where development needs are recognised, however, training programmes appropriate to the needs of boards and individual directors may not be readily available.

Following the publication of the Higgs Report, a task force of business leaders, under the chairmanship of Laura D'Andrea Tyson, Dean of London Business School, was commissioned by the DTI to consider the recruitment and development of NEDs. The Tyson Report, published in June 2003, looked more broadly at the availability of development opportunities for directors. The report concluded that although training programmes for directors were available from a range of providers, including the Institute of Directors (IoD), the Confederation of British Industry (CBI), and business schools and consultancies, these were in general not well matched to the needs of companies and individual directors.

The DTI paper, *Building Better Boards*, issued in December 2004, reviewed progress since the publication of the Higgs and Tyson Reports and identified improvements in the availability and take-up of structured training programmes for directors. Examples highlighted in the paper included:

> the IoD's Company Direction programme for current and aspiring directors, which deals with skill areas such as: directors' duties, liabilities and legal responsibilities; finance; setting strategic direction; human resource strategy; marketing; leading and directing change; decision-making; and performance management;

> the IoD Chartered Director Qualification Scheme, participation of which is now increasing rapidly, from a total of 280 chartered directors in November 2004 to 600 examination candidates in 2004 alone; and

> programmes developed by companies themselves to develop the skills of potential directors: an example cited in *Building Better Boards* is 3i's Independent Directors Programme for candidates for non-executive appointments on the boards of businesses backed by 3i.

In addition to wider availability of structured training for directors, the DTI found a growing number of mentoring and networking initiatives, such as the FTSE-100 Cross-Company Mentoring Programme, which are intended to help potential directors to develop their skills and enhance their credibility as candidates for board appointments through one-to-one encouragement and guidance.

Whatever type of training and development is provided for directors, it will have greater impact if it is planned and implemented within a coherent framework comprising:

> *an analysis of training needs* to identify which directors need what kind of training and to determine whether individual training needs can be met most effectively through in-house briefings, open courses or specially tailored programmes;

> *a realistic training and development plan* for each director, recognising the need for flexibility and ensuring that the format and pitch are appropriate;

> *evaluation of training* to identify particular aspects of training which worked more or less well for each participant; and

> *a formal budget and programme* to ensure that funds are allocated to director training and development in the same way as for staff development.

Operation of the board

However well qualified for their roles, individual directors can only make an effective contribution to the leadership of the company in the context of a well-organised and supportive board culture. Key considerations include:

> the size of the board and the frequency and duration of its meetings;

> the clarity of the board's role and the quality and timeliness of the information provided by management to support the board's decision-making;

> the conduct of board meetings and the extent to which full and open discussion is promoted; and

> the contributions of the chairman and the company secretary.

Size of the board

Research carried out in 2002 for the Higgs Review found that the average size of the board of a UK listed company was seven, typically comprising three executive directors, three NEDs and a chairman. A FTSE 100 board was generally bigger, with an average of 12 members, of whom six were NEDs, five were executive directors and one was the chairman. Nearly half FTSE 100 boards had 12 or more members.

While the 2003 Combined Code cautions that the board should not be so large as to be unwieldy, boards need to be large enough to provide diversity and challenge and to ensure that key committees are appropriately resourced, bearing in mind the Combined Code recommendations that:

> the audit and remuneration committees of smaller companies should consist of at least two independent NEDs, increasing to three for larger companies; and

> all nomination committees should have a majority of independent NEDs.

In combination with guidance from the ICSA that, to avoid potential conflict, there should be no overlap of membership between the remuneration and nomination committees, this would seem to imply a minimum requirement, even for smaller companies, of four NEDs.

Frequency of board meetings

The 2003 Combined Code gives no specific recommendation on the frequency of board meetings, stating only that the board should meet sufficiently regularly to discharge its duties effectively. The frequency of meetings of the full board will therefore depend on the internal and external circumstances of the business and on any specific issues with which the company needs to deal at a given time. The typical pattern for listed company boards appears to be around eight meetings a year, often supplemented by strategy 'away days', with additional meetings as necessary at times of rapid change.

The 2003 Combined Code emphasises the need for directors to attend meetings and devote the time needed for proper debate. To enable shareholders to monitor the extent of directors' participation in the board's activities, Provision A.1.2 recommends that the annual report disclose the number of meetings of the board and its committees and individual attendance by directors.

In its report *Board Effectiveness and Shareholder Engagement 2005*, the proxy voting agency Research, Recommendations and Electronic Voting (RREV), confirmed that the majority of listed companies now provide tabulated disclosure on directors' attendance at board and committee meetings, although they rarely give explanations for any non-attendance.

Duration of board meetings

The length of board meetings should be sufficient to enable directors to give appropriate attention to the issues at hand, while still representing a sensible investment of the time of individual directors. While excessively long meetings devoted to routine business are clearly a waste of time, care is equally needed to ensure that important issues are not being missed or that discussions on potentially contentious matters are not being unduly curtailed.

Underlining this point, the DTI paper, *Building Better Boards*, cites the results of a survey of 100 independent NEDs carried out by the consultancy firm Convivium in 2004, which found that 70 per cent of respondents considered that their boards were functioning at less than their potential effectiveness because insufficient time was allowed for decision-making by the board.

Planning board meetings

Annual calendar

It was suggested in *Chapter 5* that the schedule of matters reserved for collective decision by directors effectively constitutes the board's 'job description' and will to a large extent determine the business of a cyclical nature which is to be transacted by the board at its meetings. Such business will clearly vary from company to company, but is likely to include:

> ❯ approval of the annual report and accounts and other financial statements, proposed dividends, the calling of the AGM and the despatch of notices and other documentation to shareholders;
> ❯ consideration of periodic reports from board committees, the chief executive officer (CEO) and executive management and business units; and
> ❯ consideration of the company's business plan, annual operating and capital expenditure budgets and review of the effectiveness of its internal control and risk management arrangements.

To assist in the planning of meetings and to help maximise the attendance of individual directors, it is generally desirable for the chairman, assisted by the company secretary, to draw up an annual calendar of meetings, with an outline of the cyclical business to be considered at each meeting, and to present this for advance agreement by the full board.

Quality and timeliness of information

As a matter of principle, all directors should receive the same information at the same time and should be given sufficient time in which to consider such information.

In most companies, management is primarily responsible for providing the board with information. The company secretary will typically circulate to directors, a week to 10 days before each board meeting:

> an agenda listing the items to be covered during the meeting, with cross-references to the relevant board papers;

> the minutes of the previous meeting, together with the minutes or action notes of board committees (including any executive committee) which have taken place since the last board meeting; and

> papers relating to agenda items, including regular financial and other business reports and specific proposals for board approval: where appropriate, these should specify the wording of any formal resolution which the board is being asked to approve.

In addition, advance copies of the company's annual report and accounts and any other significant external publications would usually be sent to all directors as soon as available, even if not intended for discussion at a scheduled board meeting.

In practice, the preparation of the agenda for board meetings and the collation and circulation of papers are generally the responsibility of the company secretary, subject to the approval of the chairman. As in the case of the schedule of matters reserved for the collective decision of directors, however, it is essential that the board should 'own' its agenda and be actively involved in and responsible for defining and controlling its own role and information requirements.

Research carried out by the consultancy firm Convivium in 2004 and quoted in the DTI paper, *Building Better Boards*, suggests that, although the quality, relevance and timeliness of information provided to directors has improved since the adoption of the 2003 Combined Code, there is still some way to go: of the independent NEDs surveyed, 50 per cent (compared with 70 per cent in 2000) considered that information provided was inadequate in quality and was received too late, while 75 per cent (compared with 85 per cent in 2000) felt that the content of papers, and subsequent discussion at meetings, was insufficiently issues-led.

Conduct of board meetings

Role of chairman

The chairman has a pivotal role in creating the conditions in which the board collectively and directors individually can perform effectively. In addition to the strategic role outlined in *Chapter 6*, the chairman is accountable to the board for the management of its business and must therefore ensure that:

> the board's agenda takes full account of the issues and concerns of all directors, and focuses on strategic issues;

> sufficient time is available for the consideration of complex or contentious issues;

> all directors have the necessary time and information to consider critical issues and are not faced with unrealistic deadlines for decision-making; and

> where appropriate, informal discussions are held before the meetings of the full board to facilitate thorough preparation for the board discussion.

The complex nature of the chairman's responsibilities in relation to the board is illustrated by the role description set out in the guidance on board governance adopted by Barclays plc in December 2004, reproduced below.

Role of company secretary

The company secretary should be accountable to the board as a whole, through the chairman, for the proper administration of the meetings of the board and its

---

BARCLAYS PLC BOARD GOVERNANCE – CHAIRMAN'S ROLE REQUIREMENTS

- **Time commitment** – The Chairman is expected to commit to expend whatever time is necessary to fulfil his duties. It is expected this will be equivalent to approximately 60% of a full time position.

- **Experience** – Experience on the Board of a major international organisation. Good understanding of the role of a Chairman and able to operate effectively in such a role at the highest level.

- **Knowledge** – The Chairman must have a good understanding and experience of UK boardroom and corporate governance issues.

KEY COMPETENCIES AND BEHAVIOURS

In addition to the required competencies and behaviours of a Non-Executive Director, the Chairman must demonstrate the following:

Provision of effective leadership to the Board

- In conjunction with the Corporate Governance and Nominations Committee, ensures high quality Board composition with an appropriate balance of skills and experience.

- Pro-actively manages annual calendar of business to ensure most appropriate use of Board's time.

committees. To carry out this responsibility, the company secretary should be entitled to be present or represented at all such meetings and should be responsible for preparing, or arranging for the preparation of, the minutes of the meetings. In addition to ensuring that the board's deliberations and decisions reached are correctly recorded in the minutes, the company secretary has a key responsibility for ensuring that actions placed by the board are communicated to the appropriate responsible officers and carried out on a timely basis.

The company secretary should also support the chairman in assessing the information required by the board and in facilitating the induction of new directors and the professional development of existing directors. The recommendation in Provision A.1.4 of the Combined Code, that any question of the removal of the company secretary should be a matter for the board as a whole, underlines the need for the company secretary to be independent in order to provide impartial information and guidance to all directors on issues relating to board procedures, legal requirements and corporate governance.

The distinctive role of the company secretary in relation to corporate governance and wider issues of accountability and corporate social responsibility has been set out by the ICSA in a specimen job description for the corporate governance role of the company secretary, reproduced on pages 90 and 91.

- Engages and supports individual members to enhance Board activities and discussions.
- Ensures that the Board operates effectively as a team.
- Ensures that membership of the Board is a stimulating and enjoyable experience for Board members.

Effective Chairmanship of meetings

- Empowers all Board members to challenge issues openly whilst preventing unnecessary or acrimonious conflict.
- Encourages and manages vigorous debate whilst achieving closure on issues.
- Ensures time is allocated appropriately, ensuring business of meeting is completed whilst allowing appropriate discussion of individual items.

Be a respected Ambassador for the Group

- Be comfortable dealing with political and regulatory interests.
- Able to command respect of key opinion formers.
- Has the skills to Chair an Annual General Meeting and deal with challenging and diverse shareholder questions.

Source: Barclays plc (December 2004) Board Governance

ICSA GUIDANCE NOTE: SPECIMEN JOB DESCRIPTION FOR THE CORPORATE GOVERNANCE ROLE OF THE COMPANY SECRETARY

- Ensuring the smooth running of the board's and board committees' activities by helping the chairman to set agendas, preparing papers and presenting papers to the board and board committees, advising on board procedures and ensuring the board follows them.
- Keeping under close review all legislative, regulatory and corporate governance developments that might affect the company's operations, and ensuring that the board is fully briefed on these and that it has regard to them when taking decisions.
- Ensuring that the concept of stakeholders (particularly employees – see section 309 Companies Act 1985) is in the board's mind when important business decisions are being taken. Keeping in touch with the debate on corporate social responsibility and stakeholders, and monitoring all developments in this area and advising the board in relation to its policy and practices with regard to corporate social responsibility and its reporting on that matter.

- To act as a confidential sounding board to the chairman, non-executive directors and executive directors on points that may concern them, and to take a lead role in managing difficult inter-personal issues on the board, e.g. the exit of the directors from the business.
- To act as a primary point of contact and source of advice and guidance for, particularly, non executive directors as regards the company and its activities in order to support the decision making process.
- To act as an additional enquiring voice in relation to board decisions which particularly affect the company, drawing on his experience and knowledge of the practical aspects of management including law, tax and business finance. To act as the 'conscience of the company'.
- To ensure, where applicable, that the standards and/or disclosures required by the Combined Code annexed to the UK Listing Rules are observed and, where required, reflected in the annual report of the directors – the secretary usually takes

Board meeting management and procedures

The board should establish written procedures for the formal conduct of its business and should ensure that a copy is given to each director. These should include:

> the role, functions and powers of the chairman, and arrangements for the nomination of a person to preside over board meetings if the chairman is not present;

> the quorum of the board and board committees and the consequences of lack of an adequate quorum;

> arrangements for the disclosure and recording of individual directors' interests in items proposed for discussion;

> the general order of business for board meetings, including the recording of apologies for absence; confirmation and approval of the minutes of the last

the lead role in drafting the annual report, including the remuneration disclosures and agreeing these with the board and board committee.

- Compliance with the continuing obligations of the Listing Rules eg ensuring publications and dissemination of report and accounts and interim reports within the periods laid down in the Listing Rules; dissemination of regulatory news announcements such as trading statements to the market; ensuring that proper notification is made of directors' dealings and the acquisition of interests in the company's incentive arrangements.
- Managing relations with investors, particularly institutional investors, with regard to corporate governance issues and the board's practices in relation to corporate governance.
- To induct new directors into the business and their roles and responsibilities.
- As regards offences under the Financial Services and Markets Act (eg s395), ensuring that the board is fully aware of its

responsibility to ensure that it does not mislead the market by putting out or allowing the release of misleading information about its financial performance or trading condition, or by omitting to state information which it should state, or by engaging in a course of conduct which could amount to misleading the market.

- Ensuring compliance with all statutory filings, eg Forms 288, 88(2), annual returns, filing of resolutions adopted at annual general meetings/new Articles of Association and any other filings required to be made with Companies House.
- Making arrangements for and managing the whole process of the annual general meeting and establishing, with the board's agreement, the items to be considered at the AGM, including resolutions dealing with governance type matters, e.g. the vote on the remuneration report and votes on special incentive schemes involving directors. Information about proxy votes etc.

Source: ICSA

meeting; any matters arising or deferred from previous minutes; receipt and consideration of reports from the CEO and board committees; and consideration of matters requiring the express approval of the board;

❯ the procedure for consideration of business without notice; and

❯ the rules of debate and procedures for voting on formal resolutions of the board.

Further guidance on the conduct of board meetings is given in the ICSA *Code of Good Boardroom Practice*, the full text of which is set out in *Appendix 8.*

While it is clearly essential that the business of the board should be conducted and recorded with an appropriate degree of formality, it is equally important for the effectiveness of the board that open and constructive dialogue should be facilitated in an environment of trust and mutual respect.

The central challenge for effective governance is to ensure that the full range of opinions represented by the directors individually are brought out, discussed and resolved into a single position which can command the collective support of the board. To enable this to be achieved, all directors, including new or inexperienced directors, must be able to express divergent views.

Once a clear policy position has been reached, it is the duty of the board to ensure that it is clearly stated: vagueness in this area will merely lead to uncertainty and hence to waste of the company's resources. Further, there must be agreement from the outset that any position arising from a fair and open process represents the collective position of the board: individual directors who continue to disagree must uphold any collective position which has been reached correctly and must not seek to undermine it.

Board performance evaluation

Need for board performance evaluation

As described above, the 2003 Combined Code places heightened emphasis on the induction and professional development of directors and the effectiveness of the board as a whole. In addition, it introduces for the first time a formal expectation that the boards of UK listed companies will undertake regular evaluation of their own performance and, where necessary, act on the results by changing their membership.

It is now commonplace for organisations of all kinds to review the performance of their key contributors periodically, whether individual employees, work teams, business units or senior managers. Moreover, well-publicised increases in executive remuneration have reinforced shareholder and wider public expectations that rewards will be linked to measurable performance. Research carried out for the Higgs Review in 2002 indicated, however, that more than one-third of boards did not evaluate their collective performance, while over three-quarters of NEDs and over one half of chairmen had never had a formal review of their personal performance.

The Higgs Review concluded that listed company boards could benefit significantly from formal performance evaluation, encompassing both individual and collective board performance, including committees. Review of individual performance could assist directors in identifying and addressing their own development needs. Additionally, it would enable the chairman to identify problems and take appropriate action, if necessary by seeking the resignation of underperforming directors and proposing new appointments to the board. At the same time, appraisal of the collective performance of the board would facilitate the chairman's management and development of the board by helping to identify and address its strengths and weaknesses.

In line with the conclusions of the Higgs Review, the 2003 Combined Code recommends that there should be a formal and rigorous annual evaluation of the performance of the board and its committees and of individual directors, and that:

> ❯ the aim of the individual evaluation process should be to show whether each director continues to contribute effectively and to demonstrate commitment to

the role (including commitment of time for board and committee meetings and any other duties);

> the chairman should lead the evaluation process and should act on its results by recognising the strengths and addressing the weaknesses of the board and, where appropriate, proposing that new members be appointed to the board or seeking the resignation of directors; and

> the chairman's own performance should be evaluated by the NEDs, led by the senior independent director, and should take into account the views of the executive directors.

Compliance with Combined Code recommendations

In 2005, listed companies were required to report for the first time on their compliance with the new Code provisions in respect of board performance evaluation, with a majority of companies confirming that they had carried out such evaluations. Research carried out on behalf of the Financial Reporting Council (FRC) by the corporate governance consultancy Edis-Bates Associates suggests, however, that relatively few companies are currently complying in full with the recommended scope of the evaluation and that the degree of rigour and formality varies widely. Specifically:

> 90 per cent of all evaluations included a review of the performance of the board as a whole;

> only two-thirds of individual directors received performance assessments (with a slightly higher figure for chairmen); and

> the performance of the audit and remuneration committees was assessed in about 70 per cent of companies, but the nomination committee was reviewed by just 58 per cent of companies.

Although specialist board evaluation services are available from the ICSA, the IoD and a wide range of consultancy firms, the great majority of evaluations carried out to date appear to have been conducted entirely in-house, with no external involvement.

Of those conducted with some degree of external support, only about half appear to have used an external facilitator. Given the novelty and sensitivity of board performance evaluation, the preference for an internally driven process is understandable at this early stage. However, institutional investors will increasingly look for evidence that rigorous, in-depth and objective evaluation processes are being carried out. This is likely to increase the pressure on boards to involve external facilitators, perhaps by alternating internal and external reviews over a two- or three-year cycle.

Evaluation methodologies

The DTI paper, *Building Better Boards*, suggests that any board evaluation process, whether conducted in-house or externally facilitated, can usefully involve six key stages:

I collecting the views of individual directors on the basis of an agreed questionnaire addressing specific topics but also giving them the opportunity to raise points of their own;

2003 COMBINED CODE: GUIDANCE ON PERFORMANCE EVALUATION

- How well has the board performed against any performance objectives that have been set?
- What has been the board's contribution to the testing and development of strategy?
- What has been the board's contribution to ensuring robust and effective risk management?
- Is the composition of the board and its committees appropriate, with the right mix of knowledge and skills to maximise performance in the light of future strategy? Are inside and outside the board relationships working effectively?
- How has the board responded to any problems or crises that have emerged and could or should these have been foreseen?
- Are the matters specifically reserved for the board the right ones?
- How well does the board communicate with the management team, company employees and others? How effectively does it use mechanisms such as the AGM and the annual report?
- Is the board as a whole up to date with latest developments in the regulatory environment and the market?
- How effective are the board's committees? [Specific questions on the performance of each committee should be included such as, for example, their role, their composition and their interaction with the board.]

2 one-to-one interviews with the chairman to discuss individual performance, including the performance of colleagues;

3 the preparation of a report to the board based on responses to the questionnaire, identifying strengths and weaknesses and making recommendations for action;

4 discussion of the report by the nomination committee or NEDs collectively as well as by the board as a whole;

5 production of an action plan recording areas for improvement for consideration and approval by the full board; and

6 regular monitoring by the board of progress against plan.

The Combined Code recognises that each company will need to develop its own approach to board performance evaluation, taking into account the nature of its business, the concerns of its shareholders and other stakeholders, and the current composition of its board. However, guidance appended to the main Code sets out a list of questions for consideration by the board, which might form the basis of any questionnaire used at stage 1 of the process outlined by the DTI. The suggested questions are reproduced above.

Whatever evaluation methodology is adopted, it is important that the evaluation process should not focus exclusively on the performance and contribution of individual directors but should consider carefully how well the board works as a team. The consultancy firm RSM Robson Rhodes suggests that relevant questions which the board should ask itself are:

> Is constructive challenge welcomed, or is it seen as dissent?
> Does it feel like a unitary board, or is there evidence of different factions?

The processes that help underpin the board's effectiveness should also be evaluated eg:

- Is appropriate, timely information of the right length and quality provided to the board and is management responsive to requests for clarification or amplification? Does the board provide helpful feedback to management on its requirements?
- Are sufficient board and committee meetings of appropriate length held to enable proper consideration of issues? Is time used effectively?
- Are board procedures conducive to effective performance and flexible enough to deal with all eventualities?

- In addition, there are some specific issues relating to the chairman which should be included as part of an evaluation of the board's performance e.g.:
  - Is the chairman demonstrating effective leadership of the board?
  - Are relationships and communications with shareholders well managed?
  - Are relationships and communications within the board constructive?
  - Are the processes for setting the agenda working? Do they enable board members to raise issues and concerns?
  - Is the company secretary being used appropriately and to maximum value?

> Are there dominant players who may – perhaps accidentally – be restricting the contribution of others?

Chapter summary

> Recent corporate failures have led investors, regulators and the general public to question the effectiveness of company boards, focusing on the quality of collective decision-making and the competence, skills and capacities of individual directors.

> The response of corporate governance has been to emphasise a need for better induction of new directors and for more focused attention to be paid to the professional development of directors already in service, who may assume – not necessarily correctly – that they have all the skills and knowledge needed to carry out their role.

> There is also increased recognition of the need for a well-organised, open and supportive board culture, including the timely availability of high-quality information, to enable individual directors to make an effective contribution to the leadership of the company.

> At the same time, there is emphasis on the responsibilities of directors themselves to undertake regular, formal and objective evaluation of their own performance, and on the obligation of the board as a whole to re-evaluate the mix of skills and experience it needs and to change its membership in an orderly manner over time.

8

Appointment of directors

> There should be a formal, rigorous and transparent procedure for the appointment of new directors to the board.
>
> Combined Code (2003) Main Principle A.4

> All directors should be submitted for re-election at regular intervals, subject to continued satisfactory performance. The board should ensure planned and progressive refreshing of the board.
>
> Combined Code (2003) Main Principle A.7

This chapter examines:

> ❯ the ability of the shareholders in general meeting to influence the appointment, reappointment and removal of directors;
> ❯ the role and responsibilities of the nomination committee, as reflected in successive codes of corporate governance; and
> ❯ strategic and qualitative issues relating to the appointment of directors, including succession planning, terms of office and board diversity.

Introduction

According to the report of the Cadbury Committee (1992):

'The formal relationship between the shareholders and the board of directors is that the shareholders elect the directors, the directors report on their stewardship to the shareholders and the shareholders appoint the auditors to provide an external check on the directors' financial statements. Thus, the shareholders as owners of the company elect the directors to run the business on their behalf and hold them accountable for its progress. The issue for corporate governance is how to strengthen the accountability of boards of directors to shareholders.'

In principle, then, the directors as the managers of the company are the agents of its owners and can be appointed, reappointed or dismissed by them at any time. In practice, direct shareholder involvement in appointing and dismissing directors is limited. As discussed below, institutional shareholders sometimes succeed, albeit with difficulty, in removing underperforming directors from the boards of investee companies, and more rarely in persuading shareholders in general meeting to appoint their own nominees to the board. In almost all cases, however, the board determines the selection of candidates and recommends the reappointment of current directors, with shareholder involvement being limited to formal ratification of the board's decision at the next AGM.

The ability of boards largely to determine their own membership gives rise to several concerns for corporate governance, in particular that:

> the chairman and/or the chief executive officer (CEO) may seek to influence the selection and appointment of new directors, thus impairing the independence and objectivity of the process;
> boards may be self-perpetuating, limiting their recruitment searches to individuals of similar outlook and experience to themselves and thus protecting themselves from unwelcome challenge; and
> where the same individuals hold several directorships, influence may be concentrated unhealthily and independence and diversity of outlook diminished.

To address these concerns and to ensure that the interests of shareholders are properly observed, successive codes of corporate governance have focused on increasing the transparency of the nomination and appointment process. More recently, events such as the failure of Enron have underlined the importance of strategic and qualitative issues, including independence and diversity of view, in ensuring the effectiveness of the board as a whole.

Shareholders' powers

Removal of a director

Under the Companies Act 1985 (CA 1985), shareholders who are dissatisfied with the performance of a director have the right to remove him or her from office by ordinary resolution in general meeting. Shareholders may requisition an appropriate resolution at a scheduled general meeting of shareholders, or requisition a general meeting for the specific purpose of considering the proposed removal, provided that they represent at least 5 per cent of the company's voting share capital. Where a general meeting or a shareholder resolution has been properly requisitioned, the board cannot refuse to comply, but is free to recommend that shareholders vote against any resolution for the removal of a director. Arrangements for the requisitioning of general meetings and shareholder resolutions are discussed in more detail in *Chapter 14*.

In practice, the use by shareholders of their legal powers to remove directors is comparatively rare, largely because institutional investors who are unhappy with the performance of a particular director are generally able to make their views known privately to the board. However, there have been two recent examples in FTSE 250 companies of the attempted use by institutional investors of legal powers to dismiss directors:

> *Wyevale Garden Centres plc:* the hedge fund, Laxey Partners, which controls 28 per cent of the voting share capital in Wyevale, has requisitioned two EGMs of the company's shareholders at which it has proposed resolutions to remove three of the existing directors (including the non-executive chairman) and to appoint its own nominee as a director. These resolutions were approved by the second EGM, held in December 2005. However, the board resisted pressure to appoint the shareholders' nominee as chairman of the company and has subsequently announced the appointment of a new chairman following a full search and nomination process.

> *SkyePharma plc:* in January 2006, three financial institutions, together control-ling 13.15 per cent of the voting share capital in the drug development company SkyePharma, requisitioned an EGM with the aim of removing the company's existing chairman and appointing its own nominee as his replacement. Follow-ing the voluntary resignation of the chairman, the board of the company made clear that it would not permit shareholders to impose a replacement against its will, and has since announced the appointment of a new chairman. Although the shareholders' resolutions to remove the remaining directors were defeated at an EGM in March 2006, the company has subsequently announced that it has agreed with the institutions' arrangements for the selection and appointment of two new independent non-executive directors (NEDs).

As the Wyevale example demonstrates, shareholders may succeed in using their legal powers to remove directors and to appoint their own nominees. However, the appoint-ment of particular directors to the post of chairman and other positions is a matter for the board, and shareholders have no authority to require the board to make specific appointments.

Election and re-election

Other than the provisions, described above, for the removal of a director, company law makes little formal provision for shareholder involvement. There are no formal statutory requirements for election or re-election of directors by the shareholders in general meeting, although the standard form of Articles set out in Table A to CA 1985 provides that, at each AGM:

> any director who has been appointed by the board since the company's last AGM should step down and submit himself or herself for re-election; and

> one-third of the directors who are subject to retirement by rotation should step down and submit themselves for re-election by the shareholders.

Retirement by rotation

In 1998 the Hampel Committee on Corporate Governance found that the requirement for newly appointed directors to be re-elected at the next AGM had been incorporated into the Listing Rules and was generally observed. However, not all companies complied with the principle of retirement by rotation. Even where Table A Articles had been adopted, some companies specifically exempted certain directors – usually the chairman and/or the CEO – from this requirement, thus enabling them to occupy entrenched positions until they chose (or were forced) to resign.

At the recommendation of the Hampel Committee, the 1998 Combined Code provided that:

> all directors, without exception, should submit themselves for re-election at the AGM at least every three years; and
> NEDs should be appointed for a specific term, subject to re-election, and their reappointment at the end of the period should not be automatic.

Hampel recommended in addition that all names submitted for election or re-election as directors should be accompanied by biographical details indicating their relevant qualifications and experience. This was reinforced in the 2003 Combined Code, which emphasised that the re-election of directors retiring by rotation should not be automatic, but subject to continued satisfactory performance. Further, the Higgs Report recommended that, in order to ensure that shareholders have sufficient information on which to base their approval of appointments, the board should explain why they believe a proposed director should be appointed and how the individual concerned meets the requirements of their prospective role as a director.

The requirement for directors to retire by rotation and submit themselves for re-election very rarely results in the removal of a director. However, it does enable shareholders to communicate concerns over the performance of the company or of the individual director, or to express disagreement with an aspect of company policy with which the director is closely associated. In its publication *Voting Review 2005*, the proxy voting agency Research, Recommendations and Electronic Voting (RREV) analysed the outcomes of shareholder voting at AGMs held between January and July 2005, during which period over 1,600 directors submitted themselves for election or re-election. Dissenting votes (including both votes against and abstentions) in excess of 20 per cent of the total votes cast were registered in 18 cases.

RREV's report also gave the following examples of circumstances in which it would consider recommending to its clients that they vote against a proposed re-election:

> an NED who does not meet the standard of independence set out in the 2003 Combined Code but who serves as a member of either the audit or the remuneration committee (see *Chapter 6*);
> a non-independent NED to a board where there are insufficient independent NEDs to meet the Combined Code recommendations on the balance of the board (see *Chapter 6*);
> a chairman who is a member of the audit committee (see *Chapter 11*);
> a chairman who is being proposed for election for the first time following appointment and who, on appointment, does not meet the independence standard set out in the Combined Code (see *Chapter 6*);
> a joint chairman/CEO or an executive chairman where the roles of chairman and CEO have not been separated and the division clearly explained to shareholders (see *Chapter 6*);

> an executive director who is a member of either the audit committee (see *Chapter 11*) or the remuneration committee (see *Chapter 9*);
> a chairman or NED with poor attendance at board and/or committee meetings; and
> a director with an excessive number of external directorships (see below).

Nomination committee

Although it is generally recognised that the appointment of directors is a matter for the full board, codes of corporate governance have not until recently provided definitive guidance on the process to be followed for the selection and appointment of new directors. Thus, the Cadbury Code identified the establishment of nomination committees as best practice, but did not formally recommend that all listed companies should establish such committees. Similarly, the 1998 Combined Code endorsed the use of nomination committees, but continued to accept that in some circumstances, particularly for smaller boards, it might be appropriate for the full board to be involved in the selection process.

Research carried out on behalf of the Higgs Review in 2002 found that although almost all FTSE 100 companies had nomination committees, these were the least developed of all committees of the board in terms of defined role and responsibilities and often had no clear understanding of the extent of their role in the appointment process. Nomination committees often met irregularly, and in many companies were convened only after a board-level vacancy had arisen. Similarly, some nomination committees lacked consistent membership: in some cases, directors who were not members of the nomination committee were present at its discussions, effectively making the committee indistinguishable from the board as a whole.

Reflecting the findings of the Higgs Review, the 2003 Combined Code makes clear that all listed companies should have a nomination committee. Further, it clarifies the required membership of such committees and provides more explicit guidance than was previously available on the committee's role and responsibilities.

Membership of nomination committee

The Combined Code recommends that a majority of the members of the nomination committee should be NEDs who meet the definition of independence discussed in *Chapter 6*. The committee may be chaired by either the chairman or an independent NED, although the Combined Code specifies that the company chairman should not chair the nomination committee when it is dealing with the appointment of a successor to the chairmanship.

In its Guidance Note, *Terms of Reference – Nomination Committee*, reproduced in full in *Appendix 9*, the ICSA makes further detailed recommendations designed to minimise the risk of conflicts of interest in the selection and appointment of directors. In particular, it recommends that:

> the chairman and members of the nomination committee should be rotated on a regular basis; and

> as far as possible, overlaps between the membership of the nomination committee and other committees of the board should be avoided.

Frequency of meetings

The 2003 Combined Code envisaged that the nomination committee should play a key strategic role in the ongoing development of the board, in particular by supporting a continuous process of succession planning and by keeping under review the leadership needs of the organisation. Reflecting this, the ICSA's Guidance Note recommends that the committee should not wait until a board vacancy occurs, but should meet at least once a year, close to the end of financial year, to consider whether or not directors retiring by rotation or reaching a predetermined age limit should be put forward for reappointment at the next AGM. It further recommends that, to maximise attendance, meetings of the nomination committee should take place on the same day as meetings of the full board.

Role and responsibilities of nomination committee

Provision A.4.1 of the Combined Code states that the nomination committee should lead the process for board appointments by evaluating the balance of skills, knowledge and experience of the existing directors and preparing a description of the role and capabilities required for a particular appointment. The nomination committee should also take the lead on succession planning for the board. To this end, it should ensure that plans are in place for orderly succession to appointments within the company, to both the board and to other senior management positions, and satisfy itself that the company has a programme of recruitment and retirement for board members, and adequate management development and succession planning arrangements.

Where a vacancy arises in the office of chairman, the appointment of a new chairman is a matter for the full board. In these circumstances, the nomination committee should prepare a job specification, including an assessment of the time commitment expected, recognising that the chairman will not normally be full time but will need to be available in the event of crises.

Where other board-level vacancies arise, the nomination committee is responsible for making recommendations to the board on proposed new appointments and for determining the terms of directors' appointments, including the duration of non-executive appointments, the required degree of independence and the time commitment required from each director. Relevant considerations detailed in the 2003 Combined Code include the following:

> *External directorships*: no individual should be appointed to a second chairmanship of a FTSE 100 company; a full-time executive director should not take on more than one non-executive directorship in a FTSE 100 company and should not become chairman of such a company; and NEDs should disclose other significant commitments before appointment and inform the board of subsequent changes.

> *Duration of appointments*: the initial terms of appointment of the chairman and NEDs should be for not less than three years (subject to satisfactory performance); most NEDs should be expected to serve a second term of three years, but if it is proposed that an NED should serve for more than two three-year terms, the reasons must be explained to shareholders.
> *Time commitment and other expectations*: the nomination committee should specify the expected time commitment required from NEDs and should evaluate the performance of each NED at least annually, including an assessment of whether the individual is committing enough time to fulfil his or her duties.

The role requirements of directors of Barclays plc, as described in the document *Board Governance: Role Requirements and Charter of Expectations*, adopted by the company in December 2004, is set out below.

Reporting to shareholders

Following the recommendations of the Higgs Review, the 2003 Combined Code requires that the nomination committee should make a statement about its activities in a separate section of the annual report. This should, as a minimum:

BARCLAYS PLC BOARD GOVERNANCE – ROLE PROFILES AND CHARTER OF EXPECTATIONS

Directors' role requirements

Chairman
- Time commitment – The Chairman is expected to commit to expend whatever time is necessary to fulfil his duties. It is expected this will be equivalent to approximately 60% of a full time position.
- Experience – Experience on the Board of a major international organisation. Good understanding of the role of a Chairman and able to operate effectively in such a role at the highest level.
- Knowledge – The Chairman must have a good understanding and experience of UK boardroom and corporate governance issues.

Deputy Chairman
- Time commitment – The Deputy Chairman will be expected to commit a minimum of one day per week to the role.

- Experience – Significant experience of serving on the Board of a major international organisation. Good understanding of the role of a Chairman and able to conduct such a role effectively at the highest level.
- Knowledge – The Deputy Chairman must have a good understanding and experience of UK boardroom and corporate governance issues.

Senior Independent Director
- Time commitment – The Senior Independent Director will be expected to commit at least 3 to 4 days per year but be able to commit significantly more time to the role in exceptional circumstances.
- Experience – Significant experience of serving on a Board of a major international organisation.

> identify the chairman and members of the committee;

> give the number of committee meetings held during the year and the attendance of individual members; and

> describe the process used for the selection and appointment of directors, with an explanation, if external advice or open advertising has not been used in making the appointment of a new chairman or NED.

The terms of reference of the nomination committee must be made publicly available, for example through publication on the company's website, and must explain clearly the role of the nomination committee and the nature and extent of the authority delegated to it by the board.

Board diversity

Higgs Report

As discussed in *Chapter 6*, the 2003 Combined Code introduced a new and more stringent standard whereby the independence of NEDs was to be assessed. Concerns were expressed by some companies that this more demanding standard, together with

Non-executive director

- Time Commitment – A Non-Executive Director will be expected to commit a minimum of 20–25 days per annum to the role.
- Attendance – Attends all Board and Board Committee meetings unless exceptional circumstances prevail.
- Independence – Maintenance of own independence as measured by the Combined Code and/or by fellow Directors.
- Conflict of Interest – Takes all reasonable actions to avoid potential conflicts of interest and discloses any that may arise.
- Shareholding – 2,000 ordinary shares held within two months of appointment to meet Directors share qualification requirement. Directors must comply with the Group Share Dealing Code.

Executive director

- Group Executive Committee member.
- Time commitment – Executive Directors are expected to attend all Board meetings each year and be available to attend meetings of Board Committees when required to do so by the Chairman of that Committee. Executive Directors will be well prepared for meetings of the Board.
- Group view – Be able to take a 'Group' shareholder value viewpoint notwithstanding personal responsibility for a cluster or function.
- Knowledge – Be knowledgeable of own areas of responsibility as well as understanding the strategic priorities facing the Group.

Source: Barclays plc (December 2004)
Board Governance

the enhanced responsibilities envisaged for the non-executive role, might make it more difficult for companies to recruit NEDs.

The Higgs Report pointed out, however, that the population of NEDs was drawn from a very narrow base (dubbed by Higgs 'the usual suspects'). Research carried out for the Review in 2002 showed that non-executives were typically white males nearing retirement age with previous experience as directors of public limited companies. In particular:

> only 4 per cent of executive director posts and 6 per cent of NED posts were held by women, while fewer than 1 per cent of listed company boards were chaired by women; and

> only 7 per cent of NEDs were non-British and only 6 per cent were from black and minority ethnic groups.

The Higgs Review warned that difficulties in recruiting new directors would be exacerbated if companies continued to restrict their selection and recruitment processes to the existing narrow pool of candidates. Consideration of candidates from a wider range of backgrounds was therefore needed, both to ensure that the best available people were recruited to the boards of listed companies and to demonstrate the reality of companies' stated commitments to the principle of equal opportunity. As the Review pointed out, the motivational value of such commitments would be severely undermined if it became apparent to employees that the board did not comply with its own policies in this respect.

Options identified by Higgs for broadening the recruitment base included:

> the appointment of individuals from wider and more diverse backgrounds to the boards of subsidiary companies as a possible stepping-stone to the full board of a listed company;

> encouragement of senior managers just below board level to take an NED position on a non-competitor board;

> consideration of private companies and the non-commercial sector, including major charitable or public sector bodies, as potential sources of NEDs with strong commercial and market understanding as well as breadth and diversity of experience; and

> where companies operate in international markets, the appointment of at least one international NED with relevant skills and experience, providing training as necessary.

In support of these objectives, nomination committees should insist that any executive search or recruitment consultants employed by the company should look beyond the usual suspects to find candidates who would make good board members.

Tyson Report

These themes were developed in more detail in the Tyson Report on the recruitment and development of NEDs, published in June 2003, which called for more rigorous and transparent processes for the selection of NEDs, better induction, training and evaluation of directors, and increased research and measurement of board diversity.

Specific recommendations were that companies should broaden their searches for new NEDs to include:

> the so-called 'marzipan layer' (the layer of corporate management just below board level);
> professional services firms;
> unlisted companies and private equity firms;
> the non-commercial sector; and
> the commercial and non-commercial sectors in other countries.

Progress on board diversity

There are signs that companies are beginning to recruit new directors from a broader range of backgrounds. According to research carried out for the FRC, nearly 80 per cent of FTSE 100 companies had at least one female director by 2005, while over half of all FTSE 100 directors report international experience.

The ethnic diversity of boards appears to be little changed, however. A study by the Cranfield School of Management for the DTI found that approximately 80 per cent of FTSE 100 companies still have no non-white directors. Of the 27 directors from minority ethnic backgrounds in 2004, only six were resident in the UK, and there were no directors from the UK black population.

The DTI paper, *Building Better Boards* (January 2004), drew attention to a range of initiatives intended to remove barriers to increased diversity, including the acquisition of basic skills by aspiring directors through schemes such as the Institute of Directors' Chartered Director Programme (see www.iod.com for further information) and participation in mentoring and networking schemes such as the FTSE 100 Cross-Company Mentoring Programme.

In addition, the Institute of Chartered Accountants in England and Wales (ICAEW) maintains an online register of suitably qualified chartered accountants as potential candidates for appointment as NEDs. The register seeks to promote greater diversity in UK boardrooms by focusing on women and chartered accountants working overseas, and is targeted at senior managers who have the requisite experience and expertise to serve on boards, but who have not previously been brought to the attention of those involved in recruiting for non-executive vacancies. The ICAEW register is available at www.icaew.co.uk/idregister.

Chapter summary

> The need for transparent processes for the nomination and appointment of directors is well established as a principle of corporate governance in the UK.

> However, Enron and other corporate failures have underlined the importance of longer-term strategic and qualitative issues in the selection and appointment of directors, leading to wider recognition that these should be regarded as a

continuous process, to be carried out objectively and with close attention to the independence and effectiveness of the board as a whole.

> As part of this process, there is now greater emphasis on the evolving role and responsibilities of the nomination committee, especially in relation to appointment of the chairman and the evaluation of the performance of individual directors and the board as a whole.

> In addition, there is growing pressure on boards and nomination committees to look beyond the usual suspects in making appointments, in particular by seeking well-qualified candidates from the public and not-for-profit sectors and other potential sources beyond the limited sphere of listed companies.

9

Directors' remuneration

> Levels of remuneration should be sufficient to attract, retain and motivate direc-
> tors of the quality required to run the company successfully, but a company
> should avoid paying more than is necessary for this purpose. A significant pro-
> portion of executive directors' remuneration should be structured so as to link
> rewards to corporate and individual performance.
>
> Combined Code (2003) Main Principle B.1

> There should be a formal and transparent procedure for developing policy on
> executive remuneration and for fixing the remuneration packages of individual
> directors. No director should be involved in deciding his or her own remuner-
> ation.
>
> Combined Code (2003) Main Principle B.2

This chapter examines the issues for corporate governance arising from the remuneration of directors, focusing on four key areas:

> ❭ the governance of remuneration, including the role, composition and indepen-
> dence of the remuneration committee;
> ❭ the level and structure of executive remuneration, including the use of perfor-
> mance-related incentives;
> ❭ the disclosure of remuneration policy and individual directors' remuneration
> and the circumstances in which shareholder approval must be obtained; and
> ❭ directors' service contracts, particularly in respect of notice periods and the
> provisions for termination or compensation payments.

In each area, the chapter looks at core regulatory requirements, as set out in legislation
and/or the Combined Code, and at institutional investor guidelines, in particular
the *Principles and Guidelines on Remuneration* issued by the Association of British
Insurers (ABI) reproduced in *Appendix 10*.

Introduction

Of all the issues dealt with by codes of corporate governance, executive remuneration is at once the most visible and most contentious. The combination of mandatory disclosure and newsworthiness guarantees that executive pay awards will be highly publicised and dissected in detail in the media.

The issues involved become particularly stark at times of economic uncertainty, when the pay and other benefits received by directors are seen against the background of falling share prices, profits warnings, employee redundancies and funding crises in many occupational pension schemes. Adverse investor and public reactions to apparently unjustified levels of executive pay can inflict serious reputational damage, on both the company and the individual directors concerned.

The high public profile of executive remuneration reflects one of the fundamental concerns for the governance of widely held companies: that the separation between ownership and day-to-day control may provide opportunities for self-interested managers to enrich themselves at the expense of the owners by appropriating or misusing the company's assets.

The potential for conflict of interest between shareholders and directors over matters of pay, performance and job security has long been recognised in principle. It was not until the early 1990s, however, that executive remuneration began to be addressed as a specific issue for corporate governance. The Cadbury Code recommended that executive pay should be determined by the board as a whole on the basis of recommendations from a remuneration committee made up wholly or mainly of non-executive directors (NEDs). However, it gave no guidance on the level or composition of executive remuneration.

The first detailed investigation into executive pay in the UK was carried out by the Greenbury Study Group on Directors' Remuneration. This was set up in 1995 by the Confederation of British Industry (CBI) in response to public controversy over seemingly undeserved increases in the level of directors' remuneration, particularly in recently privatised utilities. The Greenbury Study Group's work still represents the most comprehensive and detailed analysis of the remuneration issue carried out in the UK to date, while its Code of Best Practice on directors' remuneration has been widely influential on subsequent governance developments, in the UK and beyond.

The Greenbury Code and its successors have achieved some successes. The vast majority of listed companies now have remuneration committees consisting exclusively of independent NEDs, while most executive directors' service contracts now contain notice periods of 12 months or less.

Despite these reforms, there is continuing unease, on the part of institutional investors, private shareholders and the general public, about executive remuneration. Frequently expressed concerns are that in many cases:

> the level of remuneration is excessive, both in absolute terms and relative to average salaries;

> the link between incentive pay and the performance of individual directors has not been adequately demonstrated;

> shareholders are now invited to approve remuneration policy, but still have no powers to vote against individual packages; and

> 'rewards for failure' are paid, in the form of over-generous compensation payments to departing executives.

There is currently little prospect of further regulatory or legislative change to address these concerns. However, institutional shareholders have shown that they are willing to confront companies on remuneration issues, through the publication of explicit guidelines, through behind-the-scenes debate with boards and remuneration committees and, where necessary, through their voting practices at AGMs.

Governance of executive remuneration

Remuneration committee

Role

The Greenbury Code recommended that remuneration committees should have delegated authority to determine, on behalf of the board and shareholders, company policy on executive remuneration and the specific remuneration of each executive director. This broad authority is reflected in Provision B2.2 of the Combined Code, which stipulates that:

> 'The remuneration committee should have delegated responsibility for setting remuneration for all executive directors and the chairman, including pension rights and any compensation payments. The committee should also recommend and monitor the level and structure of remuneration for senior management...'

Guidance on the role and duties of the remuneration committee compiled by the ICSA is appended to the 2003 Combined Code on Corporate Governance: this is reproduced at pages 110 and 111.

Membership

In keeping with the principle that no director should be involved in deciding his or her own remuneration, the Greenbury Code and its successors have stipulated that remuneration committees should consist exclusively of NEDs with no personal financial interests other than as shareholders, no cross-directorships and no day-to-day involvement in running the business. Under the definition of non-executive independence set out in the 2003 Combined Code, all members of the remuneration committee must be independent in character and judgment and free from relationships or circumstances which are likely to affect, or could appear to affect, his or her judgment. Relationships or circumstances which might be considered to impair the independence of an NED are summarised in *Chapter 6*.

In combination, the definition of non-executive independence and the requirement that the remuneration committee should consist exclusively of independent NEDs has given rise to a presumption that the chairman of the company cannot be regarded as independent and is therefore ineligible to serve on the remuneration committee.

2003 COMBINED CODE: SUMMARY OF THE PRINCIPAL DUTIES OF THE REMUNERATION COMMITTEE

The Code provides that the remuneration committee should consist exclusively of independent NEDs and should comprise at least three or, in the case of smaller companies,[1] two such directors.

Duties

The committee should:

- determine and agree with the board the framework or broad policy for the remuneration of the chief executive, the chairman of the company and such other members of the executive management as it is designated to consider.[2] At a minimum, the committee should have delegated responsibility for setting remuneration for all executive directors, the chairman and, to maintain and assure their independence, the company secretary. The remuneration of NEDs shall be a matter for the chairman and

executive members of the board. No director or manager should be involved in any decisions as to their own remuneration;

- determine targets for any performance-related pay schemes operated by the company;
- determine the policy for and scope of pension arrangements for each executive director;
- ensure that contractual terms on termination, and any payments made, are fair to the individual and the company, that failure is not rewarded and that the duty to mitigate loss is fully recognised;[3]
- within the terms of the agreed policy, determine the total individual remuneration package of each executive director including, where appropriate, bonuses, incentive payments and share options;
- in determining such packages and arrangements, give due regard to the

Following its review of the implementation of the 2003 Combined Code, the Financial Reporting Council (FRC) announced in January 2006 that it had concluded in the light of comments from companies and investors that this was an unnecessarily restrictive approach. Subject to consultation, it is therefore proposed to amend Provision B.2.1 of the Combined Code to allow the chairman to sit on the remuneration committee where he or she was considered independent at the time of appointment. If adopted, the revised provision will apply to financial years beginning on or after 1 November 2006.

Additional safeguards of the independence of the remuneration committee are outlined in the ICSA Guidance Note, *Terms of Reference – Remuneration Committee* (see *Appendix 11*). This recommends that, in order to minimise the risk of any conflict of interest that might be seen to give rise to an unacceptable influence on the remuneration committee or its members:

> the chairman and members of the remuneration committee should be rotated on a regular basis;

> no member of the remuneration committee should also be a member of the nomination committee; and

contents of the Code as well as the UK Listing Authority's Listing Rules and associated guidance;

- be aware of and advise on any major changes in employee benefit structures throughout the company or group;
- agree the policy for authorising claims for expenses from the chief executive and chairman;
- ensure that provisions regarding disclosure of remuneration, including pensions, as set out in the Directors' Remuneration Report Regulations 2002 and the Code, are fulfilled;
- be exclusively responsible for establishing the selection criteria, selecting, appointing and setting the terms of reference for any remuneration consultants who advise the committee;
- report the frequency of, and attendance by members at, remuneration committee meetings in the annual reports; and

- make available the committee's terms of reference. These should set out the committee's delegated responsibilities and be reviewed and, where necessary, updated annually.

Notes

1. A smaller company is one that is below the FTSE 350 throughout the year immediately prior to the reporting year.
2. Some companies require the remuneration committee to consider the packages of all executives at or above a specified level such as those reporting to a main board director whilst others require the committee to deal with all packages above a certain figure.
3. Remuneration committees should consider reviewing and agreeing a standard form of contract for their executive directors, and ensuring that new appointees are offered and accept terms within the previously agreed level.

❯ (except for small companies which do not have sufficient NEDs) no member of the remuneration committee should also be a member of both the audit and nomination committee.

Remuneration of non-executive directors

In order to preserve the independence of the remuneration committee, successive Codes have stated that the remuneration of NEDs should not be determined by the remuneration committee. Thus, Provision B.2.3 of the Combined Code recommends that the full board (or, where required by the company's Articles of Association, the shareholders) should determine the remuneration of NEDs within the limits set in the Articles.

The remuneration of an NED is typically in the form of a fixed annual fee, with an additional sum for chairing a committee. Consistent with the Combined Code definition of independence, NEDs should not participate in bonus, share option or pension arrangements operated by the company, nor should they receive payments from the company for consultancy or other services or otherwise enter into relationships with the company that might impair their ability to make independent judgments.

The ABI *Principles and Guidelines on Remuneration* reinforce and extend this principle, making clear that, in the view of institutional investors, similar restrictions should apply to the remuneration of chairmen:

> '*The chairman and NEDs should be appropriately remunerated either in cash or in shares bought or allocated at market price. The granting of incentives linked to the share price or performance is not appropriate as this could impair the ability of chairmen and independent directors to provide impartial oversight and advice. Where, in exceptional circumstances, specific reasons arise for wishing to grant share incentives to a chairman, these should be fully discussed and approved by shareholders in advance.*'

Role of internal and external advisers

Successive codes have acknowledged that it will be appropriate for remuneration committees to consult the chairman or chief executive about their proposals relating to the remuneration of executive directors and to have access to professional advice from within and beyond the company.

It is increasingly recognised, however, that internal and external advisers may be in a position to influence remuneration committee deliberations to a point at which independence may be impaired. In addition to the self-evident risk that directors and senior managers within the company may seek to persuade the remuneration committee to increase rewards, there is growing concern about the involvement of external remuneration consultants. Some specific concerns are as follows:

> ❯ The objectivity of remuneration consultants' advice may be reduced by conflicts of interest, for example where firms are also employed as 'headhunters' or are engaged by prospective directors to help them to negotiate their terms of contract.
>
> ❯ Remuneration consultants may contribute to an upward spiral in remuneration levels by failing to challenge the assumption that companies need to match or exceed the remuneration paid by other similar companies, irrespective of individual circumstances.
>
> ❯ The highly concentrated nature of the remuneration consultancy market in remuneration advice (with fewer than six firms advising nearly 90 per cent of FTSE 100 companies in 2004/2005) may be hindering innovation, particularly in the design of schemes which link executive pay more closely to performance.
>
> ❯ The involvement of remuneration consultants in the design of incentive schemes may lead to an increased level of technical complexity, making it more difficult for shareholders to evaluate the linkage between performance and potential rewards.

Reflecting these concerns, the Directors' Remuneration Report Regulations 2002 (see 'Disclosure and shareholder approval' below) require quoted companies to disclose in their annual remuneration reports the names of: remuneration committee members;

any directors, other than remuneration committee members, who have provided material advice to the committee during the year; and any other person, inside or outside the company, who has advised the committee during the year, with details of any other services provided by that person to the company and whether the person was appointed by the remuneration committee itself.

Research carried out by Deloitte and Touche, *Report on the impact of the Directors' Remuneration Report Regulations – A report for the Department of Trade and Industry* (November 2005; available at www.dti.gov.uk) has found that in financial years ending on or after 31 December 2002 – the first full year of reporting under the Directors' Remuneration Report Regulations 2002 – virtually all FTSE 350 companies complied with the requirements to name remuneration committee members and identify external advisers. However:

> ⟩ nearly 10 per cent of FTSE 100 companies and almost 20 per cent of FTSE 250 companies failed to identify internal advisers to the remuneration committee;
> ⟩ more than 10 per cent of FTSE 100 companies and over 20 per cent of FTSE 250 companies failed to disclose the nature of other services provided to the company by advisers to the remuneration committee; and
> ⟩ based on companies' disclosures, it was not possible to determine whether remuneration committees had selected and appointed their own advisers, or were simply using the services of individuals already employed within the company or engaged to advise on other matters.

Level and structure of executive remuneration

Principles

Basic principles for the development of remuneration policy and the determination of individual directors' packages were identified in the Greenbury Code. This recommended that executive remuneration packages should be sufficient to attract, retain and motivate directors of the quality required by the company, but emphasised that the total rewards available to directors should not be excessive and that companies should avoid paying more than necessary. Remuneration committees should be aware of remuneration levels elsewhere, taking into account their own company's performance relative to that of comparable companies. However, they should be sensitive to the wider scene, including pay and employment conditions elsewhere in the company.

These basic principles are amplified and developed in the ABI *Principles and Guidelines on Remuneration*, which set out the criteria against which institutional investors will evaluate companies' remuneration policies and proposals in order to determine whether they are prepared to endorse them. Emphasising that the key determinant for investors in assessing remuneration is the performance of the company and its directors in the creation of shareholder value, the *Principles and Guidelines* state that:

EXECUTIVE SHARE OPTIONS

Share options have traditionally been the most common form of long-term incentive arrangement for executive directors. Under an executive share option scheme:

- participants are granted the right to 'exercise' by purchasing shares in the company at a predetermined option price at a specified future period;
- options cannot normally be exercised before the third anniversary of the date of grant and lapse if not exercised by the tenth anniversary of the date of grant;
- if the company's share price has risen between the date of grant and the exercise period, the director can make a gain equal to the difference between the option price set at grant and the price for which the shares can be sold after exercise;
- if the share price has fallen or remained the same, there is no benefit to the director and the options are said to be 'underwater'.

Problems with share options

Although share options are intended to align the interests of directors with those of shareholders by linking part of the directors' future rewards to the company's share price, it was found that the grant of share options could in some circumstances encourage behaviour which was not necessarily in shareholders' interests, such as:

- the link to share price could create an incentive for directors to overstate the company's profits to meet or exceed market expectations in the hope of boosting the share price;
- the granting of share options in large blocks could encourage directors to focus on share price performance in a narrow window of time, at the expense of long-term development;
- the potential for large personal profits could motivate directors to sell their shares immediately after exercise, frustrating the intention that share options should align directors' and shareholders' interests;
- in rising market conditions, an increase in the company's share price might not necessarily reflect the efforts of the directors, so share options could reward indifferent performance; and
- in falling market conditions, share options were occasionally re-priced to ensure that they remained exercisable, thus insulating directors from the financial risks faced by shareholders.

Current practices

The design of executive share options has evolved in response to these criticisms such that:

- it is now usual practice to grant options in relatively small annual tranches rather than in large blocks in order to ensure that directors are incentivised to improve performance over a sustained period;
- options can no longer be exercised simply on the basis of increased share price at the time of exercise, but become exercisable only if other predetermined performance criteria have been met over a longer period; and
- the practice of re-pricing share options is strongly discouraged.

> remuneration committees should take into consideration the requirements of the market, bearing in mind competitive forces applicable to the sector in which their company operates and the particular challenges facing their company;
> overall remuneration, and the associated employment costs to the company, must be weighed against the company's ability to recruit, retain and incentivise individuals;
> external comparisons should be used with caution, in view of the risk of an upward ratchet of remuneration levels with no corresponding improvement in performance; and
> an appropriate balance should be maintained between fixed and variable remuneration and between the short- and longer-term components of variable remuneration.

Fixed components of executive remuneration

The fixed components of executive remuneration are typically basic annual salary, benefits in kind, such as car and medical insurance, and pension contributions made by the company on behalf of individual directors under defined benefit or defined contribution pension schemes.

Basic annual salary

The ABI *Principles and Guidelines* recommend that:

> the fixed component of annual salary should be set at a modest level relative to the variable component, in order to link remuneration more closely to performance;
> remuneration committees should consider setting salary levels below the median level for their company's comparator group, thus providing more scope for increasing the amount of variable performance-based pay and participation in longer-term incentive arrangements; and
> where companies seek to pay basic salaries above the median, they should be prepared to justify this to their shareholders.

Benefits in kind

Remuneration committees should scrutinise all benefits, including benefits in kind and other financial arrangements, to ensure that they are justified, appropriately valued and suitably disclosed.

Pension contributions

Recognising that pension entitlements accruing to directors can represent a significant, and potentially costly, item of remuneration, the ABI *Principles and Guidelines* stipulate that:

> the full economic costs of pension contributions and pension enhancements must be fully evaluated and disclosed to shareholders;

LONG-TERM INCENTIVE PLANS (LTIPS)

In response to concerns about the effectiveness of traditional executive share option schemes (see page 114), various forms of LTIP have been devised. The intention of LTIPs is to link rewards more closely to the achievement of demanding performance conditions and to encourage executive directors to build up and retain meaningful holdings of shares in their company.

There is no single form of LTIP, each company designing its own according to its circumstances and the views of its shareholders. Some typical variations include:

- *Restricted shares*: legal ownership of a given number of shares is vested in the executive director, but the shares themselves are placed in trust, typically for three years. The release of the shares from trust at the end of the retention period is linked to the achievement of specific performance conditions, with the proportion of shares released varying according to how the company has performed. The shares may also be forfeit if performance targets are not met or if the director leaves the company.
- *Matching shares*: executive directors purchase shares in the company, at the current market price and with their own money, and retain them for an agreed period (typically three years). At the end of the retention period, the company provides matching shares, the number of which will vary according to the performance of the company during the retention period.
- *Deferred bonus plans*: executive directors are required by the company to use a proportion of any performance-related annual bonus to purchase shares in the company at the current market price. The shares are held in trust for an agreed period (typically three years), at the end of which the company provides an equivalent number of matching shares.

Current developments

The design of LTIPs is continuing to evolve in response to guidance from institutional investors. Recent recommendations set out in the ABI's *Principles and Guidelines* are that:

- Where directors are required to use a proportion of annual bonus to purchase shares in the company, institutional investors increasingly expect further performance criteria to be met before any matching shares can vest at the end of the retention period.
- Where shares conditionally awarded to a director do not vest at the end of the retention period, the director should not receive any scrip or cash amounts representing rolled-up dividends on the shares.
- Conversely, where shares do vest, the director should also receive equivalent value to that which has accrued to shareholders by way of dividends during the retention period.

> where potential liabilities are unfunded, remuneration committees must be able to demonstrate to shareholders that the approach adopted involves the least overall cost to the company;
> given impending changes to pensions taxation, remuneration committees should consider the role of additional pension accrual and, in particular, whether other forms of remuneration might more clearly align with the creation of shareholder value; and
> companies should not assume financial responsibility for compensating individual directors for changes in their personal tax liabilities.

Variable components of executive remuneration

The variable components of executive remuneration are typically annual bonus payments (normally paid in cash) and longer-term arrangements such as executive share option schemes (see page 114) and long-term incentive plans (LTIPs – see page 116).

The Greenbury Code established as a basic principle that performance-related remuneration should be designed to align the interests of directors and shareholders and should give directors incentives to perform at the highest levels. Performance conditions should be relevant, stretching and designed to enhance the business. To minimise the risk of directors receiving undeserved windfalls, remuneration committees should consider the need for an upper limit to be placed on potential gains, and should also consider ways in which directors could be encouraged to retain meaningful long-term shareholdings in the company.

The ABI *Principles and Guidelines* build on these broad principles, stipulating that performance-based remuneration arrangements must be demonstrably aligned with business strategy and objectives and regularly reviewed. To this end, remuneration committees must guard against the possibility of unjustified windfall gains when designing and implementing incentives and must ensure that performance measurement is robust before any variable remuneration is paid. Performance-related remuneration arrangements should align participants' risks, as well as their rewards, as closely as possible with those faced by shareholders: to facilitate this, companies should consider introducing a requirement for directors to retain a proportion of any shares to which they become entitled under a share-based incentive scheme until a predetermined shareholding level has been met.

Bonus payments

Specific recommendations of the ABI's *Principles and Guidelines* are that:

> directors must not be automatically entitled to annual bonuses;
> bonuses should be cut or eliminated when company or individual performance is poor; and
> transaction bonuses which reward directors simply for completing transactions, such as mergers and acquisitions, irrespective of the future financial consequences, are not acceptable.

Long-term performance-related remuneration

The Greenbury Code specified that awards to directors under longer-term performance arrangements should be subject to challenging performance conditions, and should preferably measure the company's performance against that of a group of comparator companies. To ensure that performance conditions are sufficiently challenging over a sustained period, it recommended that remuneration committees should consider the use of LTIPs as alternatives to traditional share option schemes.

In the light of the Greenbury recommendations, many companies introduced LTIPs of varying design and complexity. These typically involve a requirement for shares to be retained for a minimum period – usually three years – and make the potential gains receivable by executive directors conditional on the achievement of performance conditions.

Despite these developments, there are continuing concerns that executive remuneration and 'perks' are excessive and that performance-related awards are still insufficiently related to the long-term interests of shareholders. These concerns are reflected in the ABI's *Principles and Guidelines*, which state that:

> ❯ The vesting of awards under share-incentive schemes should be conditional on the achievement of demanding and stretching financial performance criteria over the incentivisation period, which should not be less than three years.
> ❯ The performance criteria governing the vesting of awards or exercise of options should demonstrate the achievement of a level of corporate performance which is demanding in the context of company's prospects and operating environment and should be measured relative to an appropriate benchmark, such as Total Shareholder Return (TSR – for definition see below) relative to a relevant index or peer group.
> ❯ Shareholder approval should be obtained for any changes which make it easier to achieve performance targets.
> ❯ Performance targets must not be subject to automatic waiver in the event of a change of control of the company or on the early termination of a director's employment.

TOTAL SHAREHOLDER RETURN (TSR)

Institutional investors have identified Total Shareholder Return (TSR) relative to a relevant index or peer group as a generally acceptable performance measure for use in executive share option schemes and LTIPs. TSR also forms the basis of the comparative performance chart required under the Directors' Remuneration Report Regulations 2002.

TSR measures the percentage increase in the value of a given holding of the company's shares over a specified period, based on the change in the market share price and assuming that all dividends received on the holding are reinvested in the company's shares. For this reason, TSR is considered to provide an evaluation of the total benefits received by shareholders over time which is more balanced

> Shares or options should not be granted at a discount: equally, setting of a premium exercise price should not be used as a substitute for the adoption of demanding performance conditions.
> The re-pricing, or surrender and re-grant, of awards or 'underwater' share options is strongly discouraged.

Disclosure and shareholder approval

Principle of full disclosure

Although the Cadbury Code stated in 1993 that there should be full and complete disclosure of directors' total emoluments, it did not demand a detailed breakdown of the remuneration package of each director. It was not until 1995, when the recommendations of the Greenbury Study Group were incorporated into the Listing Rules, that companies were required for the first time to provide a detailed breakdown of the actual remuneration and other benefits received by each director individually. Greenbury also introduced a broader concept of accountability for remuneration matters, recommending that:

> remuneration committees should account directly to shareholders through a separate remuneration report in the company's annual report and accounts; and
> remuneration committee chairmen should attend AGMs to answer shareholders' questions on remuneration matters and should be responsible for keeping institutional shareholders informed on remuneration issues.

Directors' Remuneration Report Regulations 2002

Requirements

Despite the increased volume of information made available by companies in response to the Greenbury recommendations, shareholders continued to express concerns

than alternative performance criteria (for example a requirement that the company's earnings per share should outperform the Retail Price Index by a given percentage, usually 2–3 per cent over three or more years).

Where TSR is used, a director's right to exercise share options may be conditional on the achievement of further performance conditions:

for example, exercise may be subject to the company's TSR equalling, or outperforming, the median TSR of a comparator group consisting of companies of similar size and business activity. Additionally, in some companies, the number of shares over which the director is permitted to exercise options may increase on a sliding scale related to the extent to the company's TSR has outperformed the TSR of the comparator group.

about the increasing levels of executive remuneration and, specifically, the continuing opacity of the relationship between company performance and directors' bonuses and other incentive payments.

The Government responded to these concerns by issuing the Directors' Remuneration Report Regulations 2002. These apply to quoted company reports for all financial years ending on or after 31 December 2002 and require the inclusion in the annual report and accounts of a detailed remuneration report. As discussed further below, the Regulations also require quoted companies to put their remuneration reports to a vote of shareholders at their AGMs.

SUMMARY OF THE DIRECTORS' REMUNERATION REPORT REGULATIONS 2002

The Regulations require a quoted company[1] to include in its annual report and accounts[2] a directors' remuneration report setting out the information summarised below.[3]

Information subject to review by the company's external auditors

Remuneration of individual directors by name:

- total emoluments, including salary and fees; bonuses; expenses; estimated non-cash benefits; and compensation for loss of office and any other termination payments;
- share options awarded, exercised or lapsing during the year, including performance criteria and details of any options whose terms and conditions have been varied during the year;
- benefits received or potentially receivable from the director's participation in a long-term incentive scheme, including the period within which performance conditions must be met;
- pension entitlements under defined benefit or money purchase schemes, including excess retirement benefits paid

to or receivable by directors and past directors.

Information not subject to review by the company's external auditors

The remuneration committee:

- the names of the remuneration committee members;
- any directors, other than remuneration committee members, who provided material advice to the committee during the year;
- any other person (such as a remuneration consultant) who advised the committee during the year, with details of any other services provided by that person to the company.

Statement of policy on directors' remuneration:

- the company's remuneration policy for future years;
- the performance criteria in respect of long-term incentive schemes and share options;
- explaining why the performance

Impact

In its report for the DTI on the impact of the Regulations, Deloitte found that in financial years ending on or after 31 December 2002, most companies in the FTSE 350 complied with the majority of the new disclosure requirements. Further, there was evidence that, in some areas at least, the new requirements have prompted remuneration committees and boards to re-examine their underlying policies and processes in the expectation of questions from shareholders. While it is not suggested that these are the direct result of the disclosure requirements, some observable changes of practice have taken place since the introduction of the Regulations:

conditions were chosen, use of comparator groups and other external factors, and how actual performance will be measured against the criteria;

- the division between basic and performance-related elements of pay and their relative importance;
- the company's policy on contract duration, notice periods and termination payments.

Comparative performance graph:

- a line graph comparing, for the year under review and the preceding four years, the TSR on a holding of the company's listed shares to the TSR on a hypothetical holding of shares in a broad equity market index; and
- the name of the index selected for the purposes of the graph and the company's reasons for selecting that index.

Service contracts of directors and former directors:

- the date of the individual's service contract, the unexpired term and notice period;

- any provision for compensation payable on early termination of the contract;
- any other information needed to enable shareholders to estimate the company's liability in the event of early termination of the contract;
- an explanation of any significant award paid during the year on early termination of a director's service contract.

Notes
1. For the purposes of the Regulations, a 'quoted company' includes a UK listed company, a company listed in any state of the EEA (the EU plus Iceland, Norway and Liechtenstein) and a company listed on the New York Stock Exchange or Nasdaq.
2. Where the company publishes a short-form annual review/summary financial statement in addition to its full annual report and accounts, the short-form document must contain the information on aggregate directors' emoluments required under the Companies Act 1985. The comparative performance graph described above and information on the company's remuneration policy should also be disclosed.
3. This summary is provided for ease of reference only: the drafting of the regulations is complex and should be studied in full before attempting to draft the directors' remuneration report.

> Share option schemes and LTIPs increasingly specify that performance con-
  ditions must be met before share options can be exercised, whether at the
  exercise date or in the event of a change of control.
> Greater use is being made of sliding scales for the vesting of awards, whereby
  only a proportion of any award can vest for a target level of performance, with
  full vesting requiring the achievement of more stretching performance.
> Few share option schemes now make any provision for the re-pricing of options
  or re-testing of performance conditions.

Reflecting these findings, Deloitte reported that most institutional investors believe
that the introduction of the Regulations, in combination with the remuneration
guidelines issued by the ABI and other investor bodies, has contributed to improved
communication and closer consultation between companies and their major shareholders.

According to Deloitte's findings, the majority of investors do not favour further
regulation, or indeed the provision by companies of more detailed or more volumin-
ous information. They do, however, identify a need for more effective communication
on some key aspects of remuneration policy, in particular:

> the rationale for the selection of performance conditions for share option
  schemes and LTIPs;
> the methods used to assess whether performance conditions have been met;
> the relationship between remuneration and performance, particularly in rela-
  tion to annual bonus plans (which are not covered by the Regulations);
> cases where remuneration committees exercise their discretion, for example to
  award bonuses which appear to be outside companies' declared remuneration
  policies; and
> the details of possible future termination payments.

Investor expectations on disclosure

As noted above, the improvements in remuneration practice which have taken place
since the introduction of the Directors' Remuneration Report Regulations 2002
have been attributed in part to the influence of the ABI *Principles and Guidelines on
Remuneration*. The revised version issued in December 2005 gives a clear signal to
companies that full disclosure (and, where appropriate, prior consultation and
justification) will be the best way of avoiding public confrontation with institutional
investors, particularly in respect of share option schemes and other performance-
incentive arrangements.

While the *Principles and Guidelines* are broadly consistent with the requirements
set out in the Regulations, they seek more detailed disclosures in those areas, such as
dilution and potential costs and liabilities, where remuneration practices have a
potential direct impact on shareholder interests. Specific instances in which the
Principles and Guidelines seek detailed disclosure beyond that required under the
Regulations include:

> ❭ the expected value at the outset of any options granted under a share incentive scheme, taking account of the present value of all possible outcomes at the time of vesting or exercise of the options and reflecting the probability of achieving each of a range of possible outcomes;
> ❭ the potential value at the time of vesting or exercise of an option or share award, assuming full vesting;
> ❭ the costs to shareholders of the potential liabilities associated with all elements of remuneration, including pension arrangements, share options and other share-based payments awarded under incentive schemes; and
> ❭ the potential dilutive effects of the issue of new shares to satisfy the exercise of options granted under executive and employee share option schemes, including available dilution capacity, scheme and individual participation limits and the number of shares held by Employee Share Ownership Trusts (ESOTs).

Shareholder approval

In addition to requiring the inclusion in annual reports of a detailed directors' remuneration report, the Directors' Remuneration Report Regulations 2002 require, for the first time, that quoted companies put the remuneration report to a vote of shareholders at each AGM. The vote has 'advisory' status only and the Regulations state explicitly that the contractual entitlements of individual directors are not subject to shareholder approval of the remuneration report.

The first mandatory shareholder votes on the remuneration report coincided with a period of considerable financial uncertainty, characterised by falling share prices, diminished company profits and reduced or passed dividends. In addition, a number of prominent companies had recently terminated executive directors' contracts for poor performance and had been obliged by the Regulations to disclose embarrassingly generous compensation arrangements.

At AGMs held between March 2003 and March 2004, significant shareholder votes were registered against remuneration reports in some high-profile companies. In the case of GlaxoSmithKline, for example, over 50 per cent of shareholders either voted against or abstained on the remuneration report as a means of registering their dissatisfaction with the lavish compensation and pension arrangements provided for the chief executive officer (CEO). Other major companies, including Tesco, WPP, Barclays, Reckitt Benckiser and Cadbury Schweppes, experienced severely reduced majorities.

In its report to the DTI on the impact of the Regulations, Deloitte suggested that there have subsequently been fewer occasions on which significant shareholder votes have been lodged against remuneration reports, a trend which it attributes to increased prior consultation on remuneration matters between companies and institutional investors. While this may be true overall, the 2005 AGM season provided continuing evidence that shareholders are prepared to publicly confront companies whose remuneration practices they consider to be inappropriate: examples of defeats or large dissenting votes, with the reasons for shareholders' objections, include:

> *MFI Furniture Group* (lost vote): provision for exercise of options on change of control; discretionary bonuses awarded where targets had not been met; vesting of awards for average performance;
> *United Business Media* (lost vote): proposed payment of *ex gratia* bonus to departing chief executive in recognition of successful handover to successor;
> *Xstrata* (reduced majority): special bonus awards to chief executive and chief financial officer;
> *J Sainsbury* (reduced majority): 'golden goodbye' to departing chairman.

Directors' service contracts

Rewards for failure?

With the exception of long-term incentive arrangements, the most contentious issue currently arising in the area of directors' remuneration relates to potential payments to directors in the event of early termination of their service contracts for reasons of unsatisfactory performance.

Where a director leaves a company involuntarily, following inadequate personal performance or policy disagreements with the other directors, his or her service contract will normally require the company to provide a severance package. Such packages may include some or all of a lump-sum termination payment, continuation of salary and other benefits, either for a defined period or until a new job is obtained, and pension enhancements. The period for which the company will be required to continue to pay the director's salary and other benefits will depend on the terms of the director's service contract. If the contract has a fixed term, the company may be required to pay throughout the unexpired term of the contract; alternatively, if the contract has a rolling notice period, the company may have to continue to pay for the entire duration of the notice period.

Regulatory responses

The risk that termination provisions could result in excessive and unjustified severance payments was recognised in the Greenbury Code, which achieved a measure of success in limiting the duration of notice periods, typically to one year or less.

Greenbury was less successful, however, in its attempts to moderate the level of potential termination payments. Following a number of high-profile cases – most recently the unsuccessful attempt by J Sainsbury to avoid paying a £2.3 million bonus to its departing chairman – there is now a widespread shareholder and public perception that underperforming directors are 'rewarded for failure', while shareholders suffer reduced investment values and employees potentially lose their jobs.

Reflecting these concerns, a DTI consultative document, *Rewards For Failure: Directors' Remuneration – Contracts, Performance and Severance* (June 2003), sought views on how best to improve shareholder scrutiny and accountability in relation to compensation and severance payments made to directors. The Government announced in March 2004 its conclusion that legislation or amendment of the Combined Code to address directors' service contracts and termination arrangements would be inappropriate. It is therefore probable that, for the foreseeable future, the main source of pressure on companies to control termination payments will continue to come from institutional investors.

Institutional investor guidelines

Although guidelines on directors' contracts and severance have now been issued by a number of different bodies, including the CBI and individual institutional investors, the most authoritative guidance issued to date is the *Joint Statement of Best Practice on Executive Contracts and Severance* published by the ABI and the National Association of Pension Funds (NAPF).

The *Joint Statement* makes clear that, while executive directors are entitled to some protection against the risk of removal from office, investors consider that executive remuneration is already at a level that allows for this risk. Remuneration committees should therefore seek to minimise their companies' potential liability to make severance payments, and to this end should consider the inclusion in directors' service contracts of provisions such as:

> ❯ *phased payments*, whereby the company would continue to pay a departing executive on a normal monthly basis for the outstanding term of his or her contract or until the director finds fresh employment, thus avoiding the need to pay a large lump sum which cannot be recovered;

> ❯ *liquidated damages*, whereby the amount to be paid in the event of severance is agreed in advance with the director, thus providing certainty for the company (but also precluding the opportunity for the company to reduce the amount to take account of underperformance); and

> ❯ *reliance on mitigation*, whereby the departing executive is legally obliged to mitigate his or her own loss, for example by seeking other employment and thus reducing the need for compensation from the company.

Chapter summary

> ❯ Companies face continuing questions from shareholders about the independence of remuneration committees and the range of influences on their decision-making.

> ❯ Boards, individual directors and their advisers need to be sensitive to shareholder and wider public concerns about the level and structure of executive remuneration, taking into account company performance, and employment conditions elsewhere in the company and in the wider economy.

> ❯ Boards and remuneration committee members must assume that they will be required to defend their policies and practices at the company's AGM. Before

finalising their proposals, they should therefore satisfy themselves that they can answer in good faith questions about whether levels of executive remuneration are justifiable.

> Boards and remuneration committees must be able to demonstrate that in designing directors' service contracts, all possible measures have been taken to ensure that the company will not be obliged to pay 'rewards for failure'.

10

Reporting to shareholders

The board should present a balanced and understandable assessment of the company's position and prospects.

Combined Code (2003) Main Principle C.1

This chapter considers:

> the limitations of current statutory and regulatory requirements for reporting by listed companies to their shareholders;
> the growing recognition, within the UK and more widely, of the need for improved disclosure of balanced, forward-looking information on company performance and prospects; and
> current prospects for statutory reform of reporting requirements in the UK.

Introduction

The majority of shareholders do not have regular access to the directors in person and must therefore rely on the information contained in the annual report and accounts as a means of assessing the stewardship of the directors and the state of the company. From the point of view of corporate governance, therefore, the annual report and accounts and other externally published reports are fundamental to ensuring that the directors are properly accountable to the generality of shareholders. The annual report and accounts thus have important procedural links to the annual general meeting (AGM), where they provide the context by which shareholders can assess and vote on the proposals recommended by the directors for their approval. Further discussion of the procedural links between the annual report and accounts and the AGM can be found in *Chapter 14.*

The company's external reporting is also an important element in its relationship with other stakeholders, such as employees, customers, suppliers and local communities, whose decisions on whether to do business with the company or otherwise to support its activities may be influenced by its published information. In addition, the annual report and accounts may be widely circulated and commented on, and may therefore have a significant impact on the company's reputation among a wide range of external audiences, including politicians, the media, pressure groups and the general public.

Despite the importance of the annual report and accounts, there are significant concerns about whether information produced in compliance with current statutory provisions can provide the balanced and understandable assessment of the company's position and prospects required by the revised Combined Code. Some of these concerns have been reinforced by Enron and other corporate scandals and relate to the integrity and reliability of financial reporting. Other concerns address the adequacy of traditional financially based reporting and its ability to provide shareholders and other users with insights into the risks and opportunities facing the company, the quality of its management and the effectiveness of its key relationships.

Current reporting requirements and their limitations

Statutory requirements

Financial reporting

The minimum content of the annual report and accounts, as currently determined by the Companies Act 1985 (CA 1985), is heavily weighted towards financial disclosure. The annual report and accounts must contain accounting statements comprising:

> a profit and loss account setting out the financial performance of the company over the previous financial year and incorporating a statement of recognised gains and losses;

> a balance sheet describing the company's financial position at the end of that year; and

> notes setting out the assumptions and estimates necessary to support and explain the information in the accounting statements. The notes must also

---

ENFORCEMENT OF REPORTING STANDARDS

The company's directors have ultimate responsibility for ensuring that the accounting statements are properly prepared, free from deliberate fraud or unintended error and presented to shareholders in an accessible and understandable form. Without diluting the responsibilities of the directors, the ASB, the Financial Reporting Review Panel (FRRP) and the FSA also exercise influence over reporting techniques and standards.

The ASB and the FFRP are subsidiary bodies of the Financial Reporting Council.

The ASB is responsible for making accounting standards and, where necessary, for amending existing accounting standards in response to the use by companies of accounting techniques which might appear to violate the principles of prudence and conservatism. It also has responsibilities in respect of non-financial reporting, including the development of guidance on the preparation of OFRs (see below). The FRRP is responsible for monitoring the compliance of public and large private companies with the reporting requirements of CA 1985 and applicable accounting

provide other specified information, including details of related undertakings and, unless a specific exemption has been granted, information on the aggregate emoluments of directors.

In preparing the accounting statements, the directors must adopt suitable accounting policies and apply them consistently from one financial year to the next. They must also observe the principles of prudence and conservatism, particularly in the recognition of income and the valuation of assets and liabilities. Where applicable, they must treat the company as a going concern – that is, as if it will continue in business and operations on its present scale for the foreseeable future.

Non-financial reporting

By contrast, the narrative content of the annual report as defined in current statutory provisions is selective and, in some respects, oddly assorted. Under CA 1985, the annual report and accounts of a public company must include a directors' report setting out:

> the principal activities of the company and any subsidiaries during the year, and any changes in these activities;

> the names of directors who held office during the year and details of their interests in the company's shares, including share options held or exercised during the year;

> particulars of any purchases of its own shares made by the company during the year;

> any political or charitable contribution made by the company in excess of £200; and

> where applicable, additional disclosures stipulated by statutory instrument, for example on directors' remuneration (see *Chapter 9*) and payments to the company's external auditors in respect of non-audit work (see *Chapter 11*).

standards, including International Financial Reporting Standards (IFRSs).

Until recently, the FRRP had a largely reactive role in responding to matters drawn to its attention. However, the Co-ordinating Group on Audit and Accounting Issues (CGAA), established by the Government following the collapse of Enron, identified a need for more active regulatory review of companies' published reports. In accordance with the CGAA's recommendations, the Companies (Audit, Investigations and Community Enterprise)

Act 2004 gave the FRRP new powers to review reports and to require companies, directors and auditors to provide documents, information and explanations. It was also authorised to review periodic accounts and reports produced in accordance with accounting requirements imposed by the Listing Rules, and to take action jointly with the FSA in respect of discovered infringements. In February 2006, the FRRP published the results of its first review of listed companies' interim reports.

The directors' report of a medium-sized or large company must also provide information including:

> a fair review of the business of the company and its subsidiaries during the year, the position at the end of the year and any likely future developments;
> the amount of any dividend recommended by the directors;
> important post-balance sheet events;
> details of research and development carried out by the company; and
> where the company is a public company or a subsidiary of a public company, its policy on the payment of trade creditors.

Where the average number of employees exceeds 250 during the year, the directors' report must also explain the company's policy on the employment of disabled people and set out a statement of employee involvement, including employee consultation procedures and arrangements for encouraging participation by employees in the company's performance, for example through an employee share scheme.

Requirements of the Listing Rules

Annual report and accounts

The Listing Rules specify that a listed company must include in its annual report and accounts additional information designed to assist a proper understanding of the company's position and performance. The additional disclosures required for this purpose include:

> an explanation of any significant differences (that is, more than 10 per cent) between the company's actual results for the period under review and any published estimate or forecast;
> details of matters affecting the relative interests of shareholders in the company's securities, including any shareholdings in excess of 3 per cent of the company's issued share capital; and
> details of directors' interests (whether beneficial or non-beneficial) in the shares of the company and in significant contracts or other transactions involving the company.

The directors of a UK listed company must also include in the annual report and accounts an explicit statement, reviewed in advance with the company's external auditors, that the business is a going concern, with supporting assumptions and qualifications as necessary. This requirement has significant implications for the personal responsibilities and liabilities of the directors: if the company subsequently suffers a financial collapse, each director may be liable to any investor who has suffered a loss having relied on the going concern statement.

Periodic reporting by listed companies

Under the Listing Rules, the directors of a listed company must publish two periodic financial statements in addition to the annual report and accounts. These are:

> An *interim report* setting out the company's financial results in the first six months of its financial year, with the amount of any interim dividend to be paid to shareholders where applicable. The interim report (which need not be audited) must be published via one of the Regulatory Information Services designated by the Financial Services Authority (FSA) within 90 days of the end of the half-year period to which it relates.
> A *preliminary results announcement* setting out the company's full-year results, including the profit and loss account, cash flow statement and balance sheet, in a format consistent with that adopted in the full annual report and accounts, together with details of any dividend or distribution recommended by the directors. The preliminary results announcement must be agreed in advance with the company's external auditors and must include any additional information necessary to enable shareholders and others to assess the significance of the reported position. The preliminary results announcement must be published via one of the Regulatory Information Services within 120 days of the year-end.

Limitations of financially based reporting

Historically, the statutory and regulatory focus on the disclosure of financial information has reflected an assumption that shareholders' interests in listed companies are limited to issues of short-term profitability. As a result, companies' published reports have traditionally been quantitative and backward-looking, providing users with little insight into future plans, opportunities, risks and strategies. In most cases, only limited information has been provided on qualitative and intangible factors, such as companies' business relationships, the skills and knowledge of their employees, reputation and the effectiveness of risk management.

They may also fail shareholders in a number of other ways. For example, accounting statements themselves may fail to present a balanced and understandable picture of the company's financial position and performance, whether through deliberate misrepresentation, through the use of 'creative' or 'aggressive' accounting techniques or simply through over-complexity or the use of technical jargon, making it difficult for shareholders to understand the company's real position.

The case for improved narrative reporting

The need for more accessible and objective narrative reporting on a wide range of financial and non-financial matters has been increasing recognised, particularly since the early 1990s. Key developments have included:

> the introduction of the 'comply or explain' regime described in *Chapter 2*, whereby the directors of UK listed companies are required by the Listing Rules to disclose in their annual reports whether or not they have complied with corporate governance recommendations;
> the issue by the Accounting Standards Board (ASB) in 1993 (subsequently revised in 2003) of a voluntary reporting framework, the Operating and Financial Review (OFR), which emphasised the need for qualitative disclosure of the

directors' assessment of the key dependencies of the business, including relationships with customers, suppliers and employees, and for analysis of the factors and influences likely to affect future performance;

❭ provision for a shortened version of the annual report and accounts, known as the Summary Financial Statement (SFS) (see below), to be sent to shareholders and other recipients who do not elect to receive a copy of the full annual report and accounts; and

❭ increasing investor demand for disclosure on companies' social, ethical and environmental policies and practices, as discussed in *Chapter 4*.

Recommendations of the Company Law Review

The Company Law Review (CLR) concluded that, despite intended improvements, the piecemeal development of reporting requirements failed to hold directors to account for their key stewardship responsibilities and resulted in an unsatisfactory mixture of public interest and functional reporting. Accordingly, it recommended in its final report, published in 2001, that the publication of an annual OFR should be made a statutory requirement for major public and private companies.

To enable users of such companies' annual reports to make an informed assessment of their operations, financial position and future business strategies and prospects, the directors would be required to include in the OFR a statement of the company's business in the financial year under review; a fair review of performance during the year

SUMMARY FINANCIAL STATEMENT

Under the Companies (Summary Financial Statement) Regulations 1995, directors of listed companies are permitted to send a short-form version of the annual report and accounts, known as the Summary Financial Statement (SFS), to shareholders and other recipients who do not specifically elect to receive a copy of the full document.

The minimum content of the SFS is specified in the Regulations and includes summaries of the profit and loss account and balance sheet derived from the company's full accounting statements, together with a summary of the directors' report from that document. In practice, most companies taking advantage of the Regulations to produce a short-form

document voluntarily include in it narrative sections similar to those included in the full annual report and accounts. In this case, the short-form document is often known as the annual review.

The SFS option has been widely adopted by listed companies with large shareholder registers, including utilities and former building societies. It can provide significant benefits for the company and its shareholders:

• The simplified format enables private shareholders in particular, who may lack the time or expertise to grapple with the full accounting statements, to monitor the progress of their investment.

and of the company's position at the end of the year; and a fair projection of the prospects for the business and events which might substantially affect the business. In addition, the directors would be required to consider whether the OFR should include information about: the company's management structure; receipts from, and returns to, shareholders during the financial year; the company's policies on employment, the environment and social and community issues; the company's performance in carrying out these policies during the year; and any other matters affecting the company's reputation.

EU Modernisation Directive

The need for more balanced and informative narrative reporting was also recognised in the EU Accounts Modernisation Directive adopted by the European Council in June 2003. With effect from 2005, most companies in Member States are required by the Directive to include in their annual reports a fair review of the development and performance of the business and its position, including a description of the principal risks and uncertainties that it faces. The review must provide a balanced and comprehensive analysis of the development and performance of the business. To the extent necessary for a proper understanding of the development, performance and position of the business, the review must also include key financial and non-financial performance indicators, including indicators relevant to environmental and employee matters.

- The shorter length of the document provides savings for the company in terms of lower production and mailing costs.

However, great care must be taken to ensure that the SFS communicates properly and effectively with recipients without talking down or trivialising their concerns. The following points must also be observed:

- the SFS must be approved and signed by a director on behalf of the board;
- it must state in a prominent position that it does not contain sufficient information to allow as full an understanding of the results and state of affairs as would be provided by the full annual report and accounts;
- even where a shareholder has not previously objected to the receipt of an SFS, he or she is entitled at any time to receive a copy of the current annual report and accounts free of charge, and to elect to receive a copy of the full document in all future financial years; and
- even where an SFS is sent to the majority of the company's shareholders, the full annual report and accounts must be laid before the shareholders in general meeting.

See: Companies (Summary Financial Statements) Regulations 1995

Prospects for change

Companies Act 1985 (Operating and Financial Review and Directors' Report etc) Regulations 2005

In the White Paper *Modernising Company Law*, published in July 2002, the DTI confirmed that the Government had accepted the CLR's recommendation for a statutory OFR. Following extensive consultations, the Companies Act 1985 (Operating and Financial Review and Directors' Report etc) Regulations 2005 were introduced with effect for financial years beginning on or after 1 April 2005.

The Regulations were intended to serve the dual purpose of fulfilling the Government's commitment to a mandatory OFR and implementing those provisions of the

KEY DIFFERENCES BETWEEN STATUTORY OFR AND BUSINESS REVIEW		
	OFR	**Business Review**
Applicable to	All UK quoted companies	All UK and EU companies (except small companies)
Effective for	Financial years beginning 1 April 2005	Financial years beginning 1 April 2005

Main requirement	Balanced and comprehensive review of:
	 • performance and development during year;
	 • position at end of year;
	 • main trends and factors:
	   – affecting development and performance;
	   – likely to affect future development and performance.
		Balanced and comprehensive review of performance and development during year

Must include	• Business objectives and strategies • Resources • Principal risks and uncertainties • Capital structure and treasury	• Principal risks and uncertainties
Include to extent necessary	• Financial and non-financial KPIs • Environment • Employees • Social and community • Receipts from and returns to shareholders • Persons with whom company has key relationships	• Financial and non-financial KPIs (including where appropriate environmental and employee matters)

Accounts Modernisation Directive which require an enhanced Business Review in the directors' report. In order to minimise overlap between the requirements of the Directive (which apply to all medium and large companies) and the OFR (which would apply to fewer companies but would set out more detailed reporting requirements), the drafting of some key aspects of the Regulations followed the wording of the Directive rather than that recommended by the CLR and used in the subsequent White Paper.

Acting under its statutory powers, the ASB issued a formal Reporting Standard for the OFR (RS1) in May 2005. In November 2005, however, the Chancellor of the Exchequer unexpectedly announced that the Government had decided to repeal the mandatory requirement on quoted companies to prepare an OFR as set out in the Regulations, ostensibly to avoid imposing on UK companies reporting requirements over and above those contained in the Accounts Modernisation Directive.

Regulations to repeal the requirement for the OFR came into effect in January 2006, although the requirement for an enhanced Business Review remains in force. The key differences between the mandatory OFR and the requirements of the Accounts Modernisation Directive are outlined above, while a summary of the guidance issued by the Department for the Environment, Food and Rural Affairs (DEFRA) on environmental Key Performance Indicators (KPIs) which companies should use in preparing their Business Reviews, is set out below.

DEFRA GUIDELINES ON ENVIRONMENTAL KPIS FOR USE IN BUSINESS REVIEWS

Emissions to air

- *Greenhouse gases*: gases which increase the Earth's surface temperature, such as methane and nitrous oxide.
- *Acid rain, eutrophication and smog precursors*: emissions into the air, which are dispersed over great distances via rain, snow or smog.
- *Dust and particles*: matter that can be inhaled, such as particles emitted from vehicles.
- *Ozone-depleting substances*: substances that are harmful to the Earth's atmosphere, such as hydrochloroflurocarbon used in air-conditioning systems, but are often only emitted into the environment by accident.
- *Volatile organic compounds*: a group of chemicals that evaporate when exposed to air. They are commonly used as cleaning agents and degreasers, but are also a byproduct of fossil fuel combustion.
- *Metal emissions to air*: these can be emitted through burning coal or oil.

Emissions to water

- *Nutrients and organic pollutants*: waste such as human sewage, oil and contaminants discharged into bodies of water.

continued

DEFRA GUIDELINES ON ENVIRONMENTAL KPIS FOR USE IN BUSINESS REVIEWS *continued*

- *Metal emissions to water*: discharges of metal waste which can poison the aquatic environment.

Emissions to land

- *Pesticides and fertilisers*: distributed predominantly on farmland to increase production and limit damaging effects to crops.
- *Metal emissions to land*: can be found in sewage sludge, which is used as a fertiliser, but is extremely toxic to certain types of agriculture.
- *Acids and organic pollutants*: any process which uses oil-based fuels can leave a discharge as well as spillages.
- *Waste (landfill, incinerated and recycled)*: waste incineration is a significant source of renewable energy. However, it produces vast amounts of carbon dioxide.
- *Radioactive waste*: a by-product of nuclear fuel and production of electricity.

Resource use

Most of these resources are considered non-renewable and their continued extraction will lead to their depletion. The extraction itself can also have detrimental effects on the environment.

- *Water use and abstraction*: due to climate change, depleting water resources are a concern – companies should use water more efficiently and reduce waste, such as sewage and chemical companies.
- *Natural gas*: ethane which can be refined and turned into liquid gas.
- *Oil*: fossil fuel.
- *Metals*: the most commonly used are gold, silver and aluminium.
- *Coal*: fossil fuel, used as an energy source.
- *Minerals*: diamonds, salt and graphite.
- *Aggregates*: crushed stone, sand and gravel.
- *Forestry*: the harvesting of wood products, although considered a renewable resource, can lead to depletion if overexploited.
- *Agriculture*: including meat and fish.

KPIs should be measurable and, therefore, quantitative in nature, but, in addition, a general narrative should accompany them explaining their purpose and impact. To compile the report on KPIs companies are advised to:

- classify the sector of the company;
- assess direct KPIs;
- assess indirect KPIs; and
- measure and report on KPIs.

The full guidelines can be downloaded at www.defra.gov.uk/environment/business/index.htm

Statutory OFR – current position

The decision to repeal the requirement for a mandatory OFR was less well received than the Government might have expected, not least because many of the companies affected by the requirement were already engaged in the preparation of reports in accordance with the Regulations. More fundamentally, as institutional investors and lobby groups such as Friends of the Earth have pointed out, the introduction of the mandatory OFR implemented the recommendations of the CLR and followed lengthy consultations over several years, in the course of which companies, investors and other key stakeholders generally supported the need for broader-based reporting.

In the light of these concerns, the DTI has invited comments on whether, and if so how, amendments should be proposed to the Company Law Reform Bill to ensure effective and proportionate narrative reporting by quoted companies, including on social, community, employee and environmental matters. In addition, the Government has indicated that it will also consider whether new Regulations to amend business reporting requirements should be introduced as an interim measure before the Bill comes into force. The consultation on narrative reporting closed on 24 March 2006, and at the time of writing the Government was considering the responses received.

OFR as a voluntary reporting framework

Alhough the position of the OFR as a statutory reporting requirement remains uncertain, it is likely that the format and associated guidance will be widely adopted as a voluntary reporting framework. To this end, the ASB has 'converted' its RS1 Reporting Standard into a statement of best practice, subject to minimal changes to take account of the repeal of the OFR requirement. The key principles of the OFR are set out in the ASB's Statement, the full text of which can be found at www.frc.org.uk.

PRINCIPLES OF THE OPERATING AND FINANCIAL REVIEW

The OFR should set out an analysis of the business through the eyes of the directors

The OFR should reflect the directors' view of the business. Accordingly, the entity should disclose appropriate elements of information used in managing the entity, including its subsidiary undertakings. Where appropriate, the review may give greater emphasis to those matters which are significant to the entity and its subsidiary undertakings taken as a whole. Such matters may include issues specific to business segments where relevant to the understanding of the business as a whole. Directors should develop the presentation of their OFR in a way that complements the format of their annual report as a whole.

The OFR should focus on matters that are relevant to the interests of members

Members' needs are paramount when directors consider what information should be contained in the OFR. Information in the OFR will also be of interest to users other than

continued

PRINCIPLES OF THE OPERATING AND FINANCIAL REVIEW
continued

members, for example other investors, potential investors, creditors, customers, suppliers, employees and society more widely. The directors should consider the extent to which they should report on issues relevant to those other users where, because of those issues' influence on the performance of the business and its value, they are also of significance to members. The OFR should not, however, be seen as a replacement for other forms of reporting addressed to a wider stakeholder group.

The OFR should have a forward-looking orientation, identifying those trends and factors relevant to members' assessment of the current and future performance of the business and the progress towards the achievement of long-term business objectives

The particular factors discussed should be those that have affected development, performance and position during the financial year and those which are likely to affect the entity's future development, performance and position.

Given the nature of some forward-looking information, in particular elements that cannot be objectively verified but have been made in good faith, directors may want to include a statement in the OFR to treat such elements with caution, explaining the uncertainties underpinning such information.

The OFR should comment on the impact on future performance of significant events after the balance sheet date.

The OFR should also discuss predictive comments, both positive and negative, made in previous reviews and whether or not these have been borne out by events.

The OFR should complement as well as supplement the financial statements, in order to enhance the overall corporate disclosure

In complementing the financial statements, the OFR should provide useful financial and non-financial information about the business and its performance that is not reported in financial statements but which the directors judge might be relevant to members' evaluation of past results and assessment of future prospects.

In supplementing the financial statements, the OFR should where relevant:

- provide additional explanations of amounts recorded in the financial statements;
- explain the conditions and events that shaped the information contained in the financial statements.

Where amounts from the financial statements have been adjusted for inclusion in the OFR, that fact should be recorded and a reconciliation provided.

The OFR should be comprehensive and understandable

Directors should consider whether the omission of information might reasonably be expected to influence significantly the assessment made by members.

PRINCIPLES OF THE OPERATING AND FINANCIAL REVIEW
continued

The recommendation for the OFR to be comprehensive does not mean that the OFR should cover all possible matters: the objective is quality, not quantity of content. It is neither possible nor desirable for a Reporting Statement to list all the elements that might need to be included, since these will vary depending on the nature and circumstances of the particular business and how the business is run.

Directors should consider the evidence underpinning the information to be included in the OFR. Where relevant, directors should explain the source of the information and the degree to which the information is objectively supportable, to allow members to assess the reliability of the information presented for themselves.

Directors should consider the key issues to include in the OFR that will provide members with focused and relevant information. The inclusion of too much information may obscure judgements and will not promote understanding. Where additional information is discussed elsewhere in the annual report, or in other reports, cross-referencing to those sources will assist members.

The OFR should be written in a clear and readily understandable style.

The OFR should be balanced and neutral, dealing even-handedly with both good and bad aspects

The directors should ensure that the OFR retains balance and that members are not misled as a result of the omission of any information on unfavourable aspects.

The OFR should be comparable over time

Disclosure should be sufficient for the members to be able to compare the information presented with similar information about the entity for previous financial years. Comparability enables identification of the main trends and factors and their analysis over successive financial years. Directors may wish to consider the extent to which the OFR is comparable with reviews prepared by other entities in the same industry or sector.

Source: ASB (January 2006) *Reporting Statement: Operating and Financial Review*

Other relevant guidance on the preparation and content of the OFR was commissioned by the DTI in preparation for the introduction of the regulations, but will be equally applicable to the adoption of the OFR format as a voluntary reporting framework. The Operating and Financial Review Working Group led by Rosemary Radcliffe published its report *Practical Guidance for Directors* in May 2004. The full text can be found at www.dti.gov.uk/cld/financialreview.htm and relevant extracts are set out below.

PREPARING THE OPERATING AND FINANCIAL REVIEW

Criteria for assessing the OFR preparation process

1. The process should be **planned** in the same way as any other major board-led project, with responsibilities for key tasks assigned within a clear timetable. In the light of the objective of the OFR, there should be an emphasis on **transparency**, with the process being recorded (written down and/or mapped in some way), and communicated to, and hence understood by, all those involved with the preparation of the OFR. There will also be merit in discussing with the firm's auditors how best to plan and record the process.

2. The process should provide for **appropriate consultation, within the business** (management and employees), **with members**, and with **other key groups** whose decisions can affect performance.

3. The process should ensure that all **relevant existing information and comparators** are taken into account. This may involve looking **within the business** (examination of prior years' OFRs, other published reports and information etc) and **externally** (examination of models of best practice, industry guidance, reports produced by other companies in the same sector etc).

4. The process should be **comprehensive** (i.e. it should be applied across the whole business unless there are sound, documented reasons for not doing so).

5. The process should be **consistent** (i.e. it should be applied the same way both across the business and from year to year, unless there are sound, documented reasons for not doing so).

6. The process should be **subject to review**, both internally and by the external auditors. (Review by external auditors is a requirement of the draft Regulations.) This might, for example, include a review after each cycle, with a major review perhaps every three to five years, linked to the strategic planning cycle. As with

Applicable guidance was also provided by the Task Force on Human Capital Management chaired by Denise Kingsmill in its report *Accounting for People*, published in October 2003. The full text of the report can be found at www.accounting forpeople.gov.uk. and key recommendations for company reporting are set out at page 142.

appropriate consultation, such reviews could with benefit involve not only the company and its members but also the other key groups whose decisions can affect company performance. Meeting the OFR's objective implies an inclusive process that takes into account all relevant views.

Key questions for the board

Q1 Does the board already have, or does it have ready access to, all the relevant knowledge and skills to make its judgements as to what should or should not be included in the OFR? If not, how will this be addressed?

Q2 An early task for the board will be to approve the process and satisfy itself that the process is being properly applied before it can exercise its judgements. How will the board work in discharging these key responsibilities?

Q3 What information should be considered at the outset for possible inclusion in the OFR?

Q4 What other sources might be important and should be considered for inclusion?

Q5 What key information do the corporate management information systems provide now on these topics?

Q6 What, in the light of all this, are the information gaps? What should the plans be for filling these gaps? How will the information be put together?

Q7 How should the information put before the board be validated, and by whom?

Q8 How, once the information has been put together, does the board decide whether it should be included or not? What processes of challenge, both internal and external, should be used? What sign-off procedures should be in place?

Q9 How should the information that is to be included be presented in the OFR? And how should the information in the OFR be linked to other information published by the company?

Q10 What feedback arrangements and review procedures should be in place between one OFR cycle and another?

Source: DTI (May 2004) *The Operating and Financial Review: Practical Guidance for Directors*

ACCOUNTING FOR PEOPLE IN THE OFR

Recommendation 1

We recommend that reports on Human Capital Management (HCM) should:

- have a strategic focus:
  - communicating clearly, fairly and unambiguously the Board's current understanding of the links between the HCM policies and practices, its business strategy and its performance; and
  - including information on:
    - the size and composition of the workforce;
    - retention and motivation of employees;
    - the skills and competencies necessary for business success, and training to achieve these;
    - remuneration and fair employment practices;
    - leadership and succession planning.
- be balanced and objective, following a process that is susceptible to review by auditors;
- provide information in a form that enables comparison over time and uses commonly accepted definitions where available and appropriate.

Recommendation 2

We recommend that directors of companies producing OFRs, and all public and other bodies that produce OFRs or reports with similar aims, should include within them information on HCM within the organisation, or explain why it is not material.

Source: Task Force On Human Capital Management (October 2003) *Accounting for People*

Chapter summary

❭ A balanced and understandable assessment of the company's position and prospects is fundamental to ensuring that the directors are properly accountable and that shareholders can assess the stewardship of the directors and the financial health of the company.

❭ There is a broad consensus on the need for improved reporting by companies on non-financial issues, including their social, ethical and environmental policies and performance, as a means of providing shareholders and other users with a more balanced assessment of the company's performance and prospects.

Audit committee and auditors

This chapter considers:

> the UK's statutory and regulatory response to concerns about accounting and audit integrity raised by Enron and other major corporate failures;
> the specific responsibilities of the audit committee for safeguarding the independence and objectivity of the audit process;
> other responsibilities of the audit committee, particularly in respect of financial reporting, internal control and risk management, and accountability to shareholders; and
> the membership and resourcing of the audit committee.

Introduction

The company's directors are responsible for preparing accounting statements which give a true and fair view of the position and state of affairs of the company, selecting and applying suitable accounting policies for this purpose. In the case of a listed company, the Combined Code requires the directors to include in the annual report and accounts an explicit statement of their responsibilities. This should include:

> making prudent and reasonable judgments and estimates;
> following applicable accounting standards, subject to the disclosure and explanation of any material departures;
> preparing accounts on a going concern basis where appropriate;
> maintaining proper accounting records; and
> safeguarding the company's assets and taking reasonable steps to prevent and detect fraud or other irregularities by implementing an effective system of internal control.

In all but very limited circumstances, the annual report and accounts of a public company must also include a report to shareholders from the company's external auditors. The aim of the auditors' report is to give an expert and independent opinion about whether the accounting statements give a true and fair view of the company's financial position and performance during the year and comply with the relevant laws. It does not, however, diminish the directors' responsibilities for the preparation of the accounting statements; nor does it constitute an absolute guarantee that the accounting statements prepared by the directors are free from all fraud or error. This allocation of responsibilities was summarised as following by the Cadbury Committee on the Financial Aspects of Corporate Governance (1992):

> '...the specifically financial aspects of corporate governance (the Committee's remit) are the way in which boards set financial policy and oversee its implementation, including the use of financial controls, and the process whereby they report on the activities and progress of the company to the shareholders... The role of the auditors is to provide the shareholders with an external and objective check on the directors' financial statements...'

The resulting Cadbury Code of Best Practice created a general expectation that every listed company in the UK would have an audit committee of non-executive directors (NEDs), which would safeguard shareholders' interests by overseeing the financial reporting and audit process. By providing an effective counterbalance to executive management, it was assumed, audit committees would uphold the independence of the audit process and would thus help to ensure that audits were carried out properly and that the accounting statements gave a true and fair view of the organisation's financial position and performance.

The collapse of Enron in 2001, amid allegations of serious financial malpractice by senior executives and collusion by external auditors, raised serious questions about the effectiveness of audit committees and the adequacy of the regulatory arrangements and professional and ethical standards applicable to the accounting and auditing professions. In response, governments and financial regulators in the US and internationally initiated the wide-ranging programmes of legal and regulatory reform outlined in *Chapter 3*.

In the UK, the Government established a Co-ordinating Group on Auditing and Accounting Issues (CGAA) to review existing regulatory arrangements for statutory audit and financial reporting. The resulting programme of reform of the UK's regulatory regime for the accounting and auditing profession is outlined below. In addition, the DTI invited a working group led by Sir Robert Smith to review the provisions of the 1998 Combined Code dealing with the role and effectiveness of audit committees. Its detailed recommendations were incorporated into the revised Combined Code published in July 2003, and their substance is described below.

Regulation of the audit profession

Organisational arrangements

The Companies (Audit, Investigations and Community Enterprise) Act 2004 has reinforced the existing statutory framework for the regulation of auditors, in particular by delegating statutory powers to the Financial Reporting Council (FRC) and its associated organisations, and by providing public funding for their activities. The FRC's organisational framework and the roles and responsibilbities of its associate bodies are summarised below.

REGULATION OF THE UK ACCOUNTING AND AUDITING PROFESSION

Under the provisions of the Companies (Audit, Investigations and Community Enterprise) Act 2004, the FRC is established as the independent regulator of the accountancy profession, with responsibility for promoting transparent and full reporting of relevant and reliable financial, governance and other information and effective and independent audit. Specific areas of activity include: the setting, enforcement and monitoring of accounting and audit standards; oversight of the major professional accountancy bodies; and statutory oversight and regulation of auditors.

The FRC's statutory functions are exercised principally by its operating bodies, the roles and responsibilities of which are as follows:

- The *Accounting Standards Board* (ASB) has responsibility for issuing and amending accounting standards in response to evolving business practice and for liaison with the International Accounting Standards Board (IASB) on the adoption of international accounting standards.
- The *Auditing Practices Board* (APB) is responsible: for establishing auditing standards with which external auditors are required to comply; for setting ethical standards to ensure the independence, objectivity and integrity of external auditors and other assurance providers; and for the implementation of international auditing standards.
- *The Financial Reporting Review Panel* (FRRP) is responsible for reviewing companies' published reports for compliance with reporting requirements (see Chapter 10).
- A new body, the *Professional Oversight Board for Accountancy* (POBA) is responsible for independent oversight of the accountancy and auditing profession and, through its Audit Inspection Unit (AIU), for monitoring the audit quality of economically significant entities.
- A new *Accountancy Investigation and Discipline Board* (AIDB) is responsible for the investigation of significant public interest disciplinary cases involving the accountancy profession and for imposing appropriate sanctions.

A further new body, the *Board for Actuarial Standards*, came into operation in April 2006.

Further information on the activities of the FRC and its operating bodies can be found on its website at www.frc.org.uk.

Auditor objectivity and independence: the APB's approach

Integrity, independence and objectivity (ES1)

In its Ethical Standard 1 (ES1: Integrity, independence and objectivity) published in December 2004, the Auditing Practices Board (APB) identified the following principal types of threats to auditors' objectivity and independence:

> *Self-interest threat*: a self-interest threat arises when auditors have financial or other interests which might cause them to be reluctant to take actions that would be adverse to the interests of the audit firm or any individual in a position to influence the conduct or outcome of the audit (for example, where they have an investment in the client, are seeking to provide additional services to the client or need to recover long-outstanding fees from the client).

> *Self-review threat*: a self-review threat arises when the results of a non-audit service performed by the auditors or by others within the audit firm are reflected in the amounts included or disclosed in the financial statements (for example, where the audit firm has been involved in maintaining the accounting records or undertaking valuations that are incorporated in the financial statements). In the course of the audit, the auditors may need to re-evaluate the work performed in the non-audit service. Since, by virtue of providing the non-audit service, the audit firm is associated with aspects of the preparation of the financial statements, it may be (or may be perceived to be) unable to take an impartial view of relevant aspects of those financial statements.

> *Management threat*: a management threat arises when the audit firm undertakes work that involves making judgments and taking decisions which are the responsibility of management (for example where it has been involved in the design, selection and implementation of financial information technology systems). In such work, the audit firm may become closely aligned with the views and interests of management, and the auditors' objectivity and independence may be impaired, or may be perceived to be impaired.

> *Advocacy threat*: an advocacy threat arises when the audit firm undertakes work that involves acting as an advocate for an audit client and supporting a position taken by management in an adversarial context (for example, by acting as a legal advocate for the client in litigation). In order to act in an advocacy role, the audit firm has to adopt a position closely aligned to that of management. This creates both actual and perceived threats to the auditors' objectivity and independence.

> *Familiarity (or trust) threat*: a familiarity (or trust) threat arises when the auditors are pre-disposed to accept or are insufficiently questioning of the client's point of view (for example, where they develop close personal relationships with client personnel through long association with the client).

> *Intimidation threat*: an intimidation threat arises where the auditors' conduct is influenced by fear or threats (for example, where they encounter an aggressive or dominating individual).

Specific circumstances which may give rise to these threats are identified in other Ethical Standards issued by the APB, which set out requirements and guidance on safeguards whereby such threats may be eliminated or reduced to acceptable levels. These are described briefly below.

Financial, business, employment and personal relationships (ES2)

Ethical Statement 2 seeks to ensure that the conduct and outcome of audits are not vulnerable to undue influence because of financial, business, employment or personal relationships between the audit firm, its partners and its employees, on the one hand, and the audit client, its affiliates and its directors, managers and staff, on the other. It requires audit forms to establish appropriate policies, procedures and safeguards and identifies circumstances (for example where an audit partner joins an audit client as a director or senior manager) in which the firm may need to resign as auditor.

Long association with the audit engagement (ES3)

Ethical Standard 3 addresses concerns that auditor independence may be compromised by a developing personal relationship with the client company.

In relation to the auditing of a listed company, ES3 requires audit firms to ensure that no individual is permitted to act as audit engagement partner or independent partner for more than five years, and states that a further five years should elapse before the individual is again permitted to hold a position of responsibility in relation to the same audit client. In addition, firms are required to ensure that key audit partners and senior audit staff are not involved in the audit of the same listed company for more than seven years and that a further two years should elapse before they are again involved in its audit.

Fees, remuneration and evaluation policies, litigation, gifts and hospitality (ES4)

Ethical Standard 4 seeks to ensure that the objectivity of the audit process is not jeopardised by the financial dependence of the audit firm on the business provided by a particular client. Key provisions include a requirement on audit firms to resign (or not stand for reappointment) in circumstances where the total fees from audit and non-audit work for a listed company client exceed 10 per cent of their annual fee income.

Non-audit services (ES5)

Ethical Standard 5 addresses concerns about the risks to auditor independence represented by the provision to audit clients of non-audit services such as tax advice, corporate finance, information technology and management consultancy, particularly where the income from non-audit work for an audit client equals or exceeds the statutory audit fee. Although these concerns have long been recognised within and beyond the UK, events at Enron and WorldCom (where Arthur Andersen's consultancy income in the company's final year of trading was $12.4 million, compared with the statutory audit fee of $4.4 million) underlined a need for tighter controls.

Against this background, Ethical Standard 5 requires audit firms to evaluate the threats to the independence and objectivity of the audit arising from the provision of non-audit services to an audit client, to assess the effectiveness of the available safeguards and, where appropriate, to decline to provide non-audit services. In addition, it applies this general approach to a range of specific circumstances which represent a potentially unacceptable level of risk to auditor independence, including the provision of: internal audit services; IT consultancy; valuation and actuarial valuation services; tax advice; litigation support and other legal services; recruitment and remuneration consultancy; corporate finance and transaction-related services; and accountancy advice.

Further information on the activities of the APB, including its Ethical Standards, can be found on the FRC's website at www.frc.org.uk/apb

Market issues affecting audit independence, objectivity and quality

Competition and choice in the audit market

As noted above, provisions introduced by the APB require audit firms to ensure that their partners and staff are not involved for excessive periods of time in the audit of particular clients. Although auditors are in principle subject to annual reappointment by the shareholders, there is no equivalent requirement on listed companies to replace their external auditors at prescribed maximum intervals, and formal re-tendering of audit appointments is in practice very rare. In its report *Competition and Choice in the UK Audit Market* (April 2006) for the DTI and the FRC, the economic research consultancy Oxera found that, amongst FTSE 100 companies, there had been only 33 competitive tendering exercises involving 28 companies in the 15 years to December 2004.

Companies may be reluctant to undertake formal re-tendering of audit appointments for a variety of reasons, including the cost of the tendering exercise and concerns about the disruption and enhanced risks arising from a change of auditor. A further barrier to change identified in the Oxera report was the lack of effective choice of audit firm, particularly for larger listed companies, because of the increasing concentration of the global audit market, as a result of which 97 per cent of FTSE 350 companies are currently audited by one of the 'Big Four' accountancy firms.

In response to the Oxera report, the FRC has stated that it intends to issue a discussion paper in May 2006 as a basis for consultation with stakeholders on the public interest issues arising from the existing competitive environment for audit services and on possible measures to reduce actual and perceived barriers to entry to the audit market, particularly for listed companies.

Auditor liability

One possible barrier to entry into the listed company audit market may be the current legal position whereby auditors are exposed to unlimited liability for their mistakes. As a result, it is suggested, capable mid-tier audit firms may be deterred from taking on listed company audit work by the prospect of extending their potential liabilities beyond the point at which they would be able to secure insurance.

The Company Law Review (CLR) considered the question of auditors' liability and concluded that auditors should be allowed to negotiate limits on their liability in their contracts with audit clients, subject to shareholder approval. Following the publication by the DTI of the consultative document *Director and Auditor Liability* (December 2003), the following proposals have been included in the Company Law Reform Bill:

> *Auditors' limitation of liability*: it is proposed that auditors should be able to agree contractually with clients, subject to annual shareholder approval, to limit their liability in respect of any negligence, default, breach of duty or breach of trust occurring in the course of the audit to an amount that is fair and reasonable, having regard to the auditors' responsibilities, obligations and professional standards expected of them.

> *A new criminal offence in relation to the audit*: it is proposed to create a new criminal offence for an auditor knowingly or recklessly to include in an audit report anything that is materially misleading, false or deceptive and to omit any statement required to be included in the report (for example that proper accounting records or returns have not been kept).

Both of these proposals are contentious and, at the time of writing, it is unclear whether, and in what form, they will survive the process of Parliamentary debate and amendment.

Audit committee and audit independence

Terms of reference in respect of independence and objectivity

The 2003 Combined Code allocates to the audit committees of listed companies specific responsibilities for safeguarding the independence and objectivity of the audit process. Provision C.3.2 recommends that the audit committee should have written terms of reference, which should include its responsibility for:

> making recommendations to the board, for it to put to the shareholders for their approval in general meeting, in relation to the appointment, reappointment and removal of the external auditor and approving the remuneration and terms of engagement of the external auditor;

> reviewing and monitoring the external auditor's independence and objectivity and the effectiveness of the audit process, taking into consideration relevant UK professional and regulatory requirements;

> developing and implementing policy on the engagement of the external auditor to supply non-audit services, taking into account relevant ethical guidance regarding the provision of non-audit services by the external audit firm; and

> monitoring and reviewing the effectiveness of the company's internal audit function.

More detailed guidance on the terms of reference of the audit committee in the light of the 2003 Combined Code is set out in the ICSA Guidance Note, *Terms of Reference – Audit Committee*, the full text of which can be found at *Appendix 13*.

The responsibilities of the audit committee in relation to auditor independence and objectivity are amplified in the Smith Guidance appended to the Combined Code, which recommends that the audit committee should:

> seek reassurance that the audit firm, and individual partners and staff involved in the audit, have no family, financial, employment, investment or business relationship with the company;

> seek from the audit firm, on an annual basis, information about the firm's policies and processes for maintaining independence;

> monitor the audit firm's compliance with relevant requirements, including those relating to the rotation of audit partners and staff; and

> agree with the board and monitor the company's policy for the employment of former employees of the external auditor, paying particular attention to employees of the audit firm who were part of the audit team and moved directly to the company.

The Smith Guidance on audit committees is reproduced in full at *Appendix 14.*

Appointment and reappointment of external auditors

In principle, external auditors are appointed by the shareholders in general meeting and report directly to them through their statement in the annual report and accounts. In practice, however, the views of executive management have typically shaped the recommendation on the appointment or reappointment of the external auditors, giving shareholders little opportunity or encouragement to participate in the appointment process. As the CGAA pointed out in its 2003 report to the Government, the effect has been to relegate shareholders to the role of spectators in the appointment and reappointment of the external auditors.

The independence of external auditors is clearly at risk if they are dependent for future work on the views of the executive management whose financial statements it is their job to audit. The pitfalls inherent in this situation were highlighted by the Enron affair, where the external auditors failed to challenge (or even colluded in) questionable accounting practices rather than jeopardise their ongoing relationship with management.

For these reasons, the 2003 Combined Code states that the audit committee, rather than executive management, should have formal responsibility for recommending to shareholders, via the board, the appointment, reappointment and removal of external auditors. In the event that the board does not accept the audit committee's recommendation, this should be drawn to the shareholders' attention through an explicit statement in the annual report and accounts, with an account of the audit committee's recommendation and an explanation of the board's reasons for taking a different position.

If, on the basis of its assessment of the incumbent firm's performance, the audit committee proposes to the board that the firm should be replaced as the company's external auditors, it should oversee the selection process and make appropriate recommendations, through the board, for consideration by the shareholders in general meeting.

In its recent report *Competition and Choice in the UK Audit Market*, the economic research consultancy Oxera found that, although listed companies, auditors and investors believe that audit committees now have a key role in the auditor selection process, executive directors (particularly finance directors) still have significant influence on the choice of auditor, including final selection and fee negotiation.

Auditor remuneration

In addition to its responsibilities in relation to the appointment and reappointment of the external auditors, the audit committee its required by the Combined Code to approve the auditors' terms of engagement and remuneration and, in doing so, to satisfy itself that the level of fee payable represents value for money and is sufficient to enable an effective audit to be conducted.

The Smith Guidance focuses on the threat to auditor independence represented by the provision to the audit client of non-audit services, and recommends in this context that the audit committee should:

> specify in advance the types of non-audit work from which, in its view, the external auditors should be totally excluded;

> identify the types of non-audit work which it may be permissible for the external auditors to carry out, distinguishing between categories of work for which the auditors can be engaged without referral to the audit committee and those for which case-by-case approval by the audit committee is necessary;

> ensure that, where non-audit work is carried out by the external auditors, adequate safeguards are in place to ensure that the provision of non-audit services does not threaten the objectivity and independence of the external audit;

> consider the fees paid by the company for the provision of non-audit services by the external auditor, on a case-by-case basis and in aggregate, relative to the statutory audit fee; and

> explain to shareholders, in its statement in the annual report and accounts, how its policy on the provision of non-audit services by the external auditor provides adequate protection of auditor independence.

In addition to their requirements of the Combined Code, companies other than small or medium-sized companies will be required by the Companies (Disclosure of Auditor Remuneration) Regulations 2005 to disclose in their accounts for financial years beginning on or after 1 October 2005 the remuneration payable to the auditors for carrying out the statutory audit, together with any additional remuneration payable in respect of non-audit services. The Regulations require separate disclosure in respect of the statutory audit fee and of each type of non-audit service, including: taxation advice; IT consultancy; internal audit services; valuation and actuarial services; litigation support; recruitment and remuneration consultancy; and corporate finance and transaction-related services.

Oversight of the audit cycle

The Combined Code also allocates to the audit committee broad responsibilities for oversight of the activities of the external auditors, including the planning and execution of the annual audit cycle, and for monitoring the external auditors' effectiveness and any risks to their independence arising from their relationships with the company's management.

While the audit committee must be careful not to duplicate the role of the external auditors, it therefore should seek to satisfy itself, before the beginning of the annual audit cycle, that the intended scope of the audit is adequate, and that the audit firm has in place appropriate quality control procedures and has taken proper steps to respond to changes in regulatory or other requirements. To this end, the audit committee should be involved in the planning of the annual audit. It should review and agree the engagement letter issued by the external auditor at the start of each audit and should establish that the auditors' work plan and resources, including the seniority, expertise and experience of the audit team, are consistent with the terms of the audit engagement. If the audit committee is not satisfied with the proposed scope of the audit, it should request that additional work be undertaken.

On completion of the audit, the audit committee should review with the external auditors, in the absence of executive management where appropriate, the findings of their work as reflected in the management letter or equivalent. The review should address the key accounting and auditing judgments encountered in the course of the audit and should consider, on the basis of the external auditors' opinion and the audit committee's own knowledge, whether the information provided by the company's management has been accurate and complete. In addition, the audit committee should review the level of errors and misstatements revealed during the audit and establish, in discussion with management and the external auditors, whether adjustments recommended by the external auditors have been made and, if not, the reasons why not.

At the end of each annual audit cycle, the audit committee should review the quality and effectiveness of the audit process. It should assess whether the external auditors have performed the audit as planned and establish the reasons for any changes, obtaining feedback as necessary about the conduct of the audit from key members of the company's management, including the finance director and the head of internal audit.

In the course of its annual assessment, the audit committee should also consider the relationships between the company and the audit firm, including the provision of non-audit services, taking into account the views of the external auditor, the company's management and the internal audit function. Based on its assessment, the audit committee should determine whether any potential risks to the external auditors' judgment or independence arise from its relationships with management.

Internal audit

In a departure from earlier codes of corporate governance, which recommended only that companies without an internal audit function should 'from time to time' review the need for one, the 2003 Combined Code states explicitly that, where there is no internal audit function, the audit committee should consider annually whether there is a need for one and should make a recommendation to the board. The Code also proposes that the reasons for the absence of an internal audit function should be explained to shareholders in the audit committee section of the annual report and accounts.

The Combined Code also envisages that the audit committee should play a key role in ensuring that the internal audit function is independent and has the necessary resources, standing and authority within the company to enable it to discharge its functions. To this end, the Smith Guidance recommends that the audit committee should:

> ensure that the internal auditor has direct access to the board chairman and to the audit committee and is accountable to the audit committee;
> review and assess the annual internal audit work plan;
> receive a report on the results of the internal auditors' work on a periodic basis;
> review and monitor management's responsiveness to the internal auditor's findings and recommendations;
> meet with the head of internal audit at least once a year without the presence of management; and
> monitor and assess the role and effectiveness of the internal audit function in the overall context of the company's risk management system.

Other responsibilities of the audit committee

Terms of reference

In addition to the specific responsibilities, outlined above, in relation to audit independence and objectivity, Provision C.3.2 of the Combined Code assigns to the audit committee responsibility for:

> monitoring the integrity of the financial statements of the company and any formal announcements relating to the company's financial performance, and reviewing significant financial reporting judgments contained in them;
> reviewing the company's internal financial controls and, unless expressly addressed by a separate board risk committee composed of independent directors or by the board itself, reviewing the company's internal control and risk management systems; and
> reporting to the board, identifying any matters in respect of which it considers that action or improvement is needed and making recommendations as to the steps to be taken.

The company should make the audit committee's terms of reference publicly available by publishing these on its website and by making copies available on request.

The Smith Guidance recommends in addition that the audit committee should review its terms of reference and assess its own performance and effectiveness annually, bringing forward any necessary changes for approval by the board. In its report for the FRC on board performance evaluation, published in October 2005, the consultancy firm Edis-Bates Associates found that, in those listed companies which undertook performance evaluations of their key committees in 2005, the audit committee was assessed in more than 70 per cent of cases, making it the committee most frequently assessed.

Financial reporting

Although management, rather than the audit committee, is responsible for the preparation of financial disclosures and for compliance with applicable accounting standards and other relevant rules, the Combined Code gives the audit committee a key role in monitoring the integrity of the company's financial statements. The audit committee must therefore satisfy itself that the executive directors are carrying out their responsibilities, while taking care not to duplicate the role of the executive directors by becoming too closely involved in matters of detail or making decisions on behalf of the company.

The Smith Guidance recommends that the audit committee should review all significant statements proposed for publication before they are submitted to the full board for approval. The audit committee's review should encompass the annual report and accounts, the interim report and preliminary results announcement, and any other intended release of price-sensitive information. Scrutiny by the audit committee should not be confined to the accounting statements, however, but should extend to all relevant narrative information, including the company's statement of compliance with the Combined Code. For further discussion on the narrative content of the annual report and accounts, see *Chapter 10*.

In carrying out its review, the audit committee should:

> evaluate the judgments and reporting decisions made by the executive directors, including changes in critical accounting policies, decisions requiring a major element of judgment, and the clarity and completeness of the proposed disclosures;

> receive explanations from management of the methods used to account for any significant or unusual transaction, taking account of the external auditor's views; and

> take into account any factors that might predispose management to present an incomplete or misleading picture of the company's financial position and performance, including a perceived need to counter adverse market sentiment or to report the achievement of performance targets on which bonus payments depend.

The audit committee has clear responsibility for challenging inadequate accounting and auditing practices and for ensuring that weaknesses in these processes are not permitted to result in poor or misleading financial disclosures. While the Smith Guidance acknowledges the need for an open working relationship and a high level of mutual respect between the audit committee and the other directors of the company, particularly the chairman, the chief executive officer (CEO) and the finance director, it stresses that the audit committee must be prepared, where necessary, to take a robust stand on issues of principle.

Internal control and risk management

As discussed in *Chapter 12*, the board has collective responsibility for ensuring the effectiveness of the company's system of internal control. The 2003 Combined Code envisages that the audit committee should have primary responsibility on behalf of the board for the review of the company's system of internal financial control and, where so determined by the board, for reviewing the effectiveness of the company's operational and compliance controls and risk management.

The precise scope of the audit committee's responsibility for reviewing the effectiveness of internal control and risk management is therefore likely to vary widely from company to company. In each case, however, operational management will be responsible for developing, operating and monitoring the system of internal control and for providing assurance that it has done so. The role of the audit committee, by contrast, will be to receive reports from those managers who are responsible for identifying and managing risks on the nature and effectiveness of the systems in place.

In addition, the audit committee will generally consider the results of reviews and investigations carried out by other assurance providers. Where the company's financial controls are under consideration, the audit committee may seek confirmation from the internal audit function and/or the company's external auditors on the adequacy and effectiveness of the controls. Where controls relate to non-financial matters, such as legal and regulatory compliance, health and safety and environmental protection, the audit committee may receive reports from the internal auditor or from other internal assurance providers, including the company secretary, with policy responsibilities for these areas of the company's activities.

Whistleblowing

As part of its wider responsibilities in relation to internal control and risk management, the audit committee is required by the 2003 Combined Code to review the company's arrangements to enable employee whistleblowers to report concerns about possible improprieties in matters of financial reporting or related issues. In particular, the audit committee should ensure that arrangements are in place for the proportionate and independent investigation of such reports and for taking any necessary follow-up action.

These recommendations reflect the failure of Enron, prior to its collapse, to take seriously the warnings of a senior employee who attempted to draw attention to the potential risks to the company's business of the unorthodox financial arrangements which contributed to its ultimate demise. Similar provisions are contained in the Sarbanes-Oxley Act and in other international responses to the Enron scandal. It is important to note, however, that improprieties and malpractice with potentially significant effects on the company's well-being are not limited to financial and accounting matters. Corporate failures in other areas, such as those relating to product quality, the safety of employees and the general public, and the protection of the environment, may also inflict serious and long-lasting damage on the company's reputation and standing. Care is needed to ensure that the scope of the whistleblowing procedure is wide enough to ensure that all matters of concern are surfaced and investigated. Further details on employee whistleblowing procedures can be found in *Chapter 12*.

In its guidance for audit committees on whistleblowing arrangements, published in October 2005, the Institute of Chartered Accountants in England and Wales (ICAEW) emphasises that audit committees are not responsible for making or operating whistleblowing arrangements, although it may be appropriate to allow whistleblowers to contact the audit committee chairman direct as an effective method of demonstrating the board's commitment to the success of the process and its independence. The ICAEW suggests that the audit committee's review of whistleblowing arrangements should comprise two types of activity, described as direct and indirect:

> ❭ the direct element of the review could include questions to senior management, directors and relevant employees about the arrangements and issues that have come to light; while
> ❭ the indirect element can be described as the committee becoming aware, through its other functions, of matters which indicate that the arrangements may not be effective.

Guidance for audit committees on whistleblowing arrangements and other aspects of their remit can be downloaded from the ICAEW's website at www.icaew.co.uk

Reporting to shareholders

In a significant departure from the provisions of earlier codes of corporate governance, the 2003 Combined Code recommended that audit committee should report to shareholders on the discharge of its responsibilities in a separate section of the annual report and accounts. More specific suggestions on the content of the audit committee's report are given in the Smith Guidance (see *Appendix 15*), which recommends that the report should, as a minimum, provide:

> ❭ a summary of the role of the audit committee;
> ❭ the names and qualifications of all members of the audit committee during the period under review;
> ❭ the number of audit committee meetings held during the period;
> ❭ how the audit committee has discharged its responsibilities in the period under review, including an explanation of how auditor independence and objectivity are safeguarded in circumstances where non-audit services are provided by the company's external auditors.

The Smith Guidance also recommends that the chairman of the audit committee should be present at the AGM to answer questions, through the chairman of the board, on the report on the audit committee's activities and matters within the scope of audit committee's responsibilities.

Membership and resources of the audit committee

Composition

Prior to 2003, UK codes of corporate governance recommended that audit commit-tees should consist of NEDs, but specified only that a majority of them should be independent. In the light of recommendations in the Smith Guidance, this provision is strengthened in the 2003 Combined Code, which states that the board of every listed company should establish an audit committee of at least three (or, in the case of smaller companies, two) NEDs, all of whom should be independent. On the definition of independence, see *Chapter 6*.

In addition, the Smith Guidance recommends that, in order to preserve the col-lective independence of the audit committee, appointments to the audit committee should be for periods of no more than three years, extendable by no more than two additional three-year periods, and should terminate if a director ceases to be independent. Further, the Smith Guidance recommends that the chairman of the company should not be eligible for appointment as an audit committee member.

In its 2005 *Corporate Governance Review*, the consultancy firm Grant Thornton found that 86 per cent of FTSE 100 companies had established audit committees consisting solely of independent NEDs, compared with just under 84 per cent in 2004. This trend towards compliance was broadly confirmed by the proxy voting agency Research, Recommendations and Electronic Voting (RREV), whose publication *Board Effectiveness and Shareholder Engagement 2005* noted that the proportion of chairmen sitting on audit committees had fallen in FTSE 100 companies, from 14 per cent in 2004 to 4 per cent in 2005.

Qualifications of audit committee members

Unlike earlier codes of corporate governance, which offered no guidance on the quali-fications of audit committee members, the 2003 Combined Code states explicitly that the board should satisfy itself that at least one member of the audit committee has 'recent and relevant' financial experience. A similar provision is set out in the revised EU Eighth Company Law Directive, which contains a requirement for audit com-mittees to include an individual with 'competence in accounting or auditing'.

The Combined Code recommendation is amplified in the Smith Guidance, which states that the audit committee member whom the board considers to have recent and relevant financial experience should have a professional qualification from one of the professional accountancy bodies. The Guidance further explains that the depth of financial know-how needed by other members of the audit committee will vary according to the nature of the company's business, but that experience of corporate financial matters will normally be required. Where the company's activities involve specialised financial activities, it will be particularly important for audit committee members to have appropriate financial expertise.

Despite this new emphasis on the qualifications required for audit committee membership, there is a general recognition that specialist financial expertise alone will not ensure that audit committees are able to operate effectively. The Smith Guidance drew attention to the importance of personal qualities, in particular the need for audit committee members to be 'tough, knowledgeable and independent-minded' and to be willing to ask challenging questions of executive colleagues, senior managers and internal and external auditors. In this regard, the Guidance suggested that an intelligent and independent audit committee member without significant financial experience might contribute to the work of the committee by cutting through technicalities to ask relevant and straightforward questions.

In its report, published in January 2006, on the implementation of the 2003 Combined Code, the FRC observed that some companies appeared to have experienced difficulties in finding suitably qualified candidates willing to serve as the audit committee member with 'recent and relevant financial experience', perhaps because potential candidates were reluctant to be held accountable in case this increased their potential exposure to liability. This position was confirmed by Grant Thornton in its 2005 *Corporate Governance Review*, which found that 55 per cent of companies did not identify an audit committee member with recent and relevant financial experience. While some companies stated instead that the audit committee as a whole had the necessary experience, nearly 30 per cent of companies made no comment on the audit committee's financial expertise.

Training

The 2003 Combined Code emphasises the need for all directors, whether executive or non-executive, to receive training on first appointment and throughout their period of office. The Smith Guidance builds on this recommendation, identifying a need for the company to provide an induction programme for new audit committee members. This should cover the role of the audit committee, including its terms of reference and expected time commitment for members, and should also provide an overview of the company's main businesses and key financial dynamics and risks. Ongoing training should also be provided to enable audit committee members to improve their understanding of the principles of financial reporting, related company law and key developments

Access to information and other resources

The Smith Guidance emphasises the need for the audit committee to be provided with sufficient resources to undertake its duties. The resources available to the audit committee should include access to the services of the company secretary and his or her staff, who should assist the chairman in:

> planning the audit committee's meeting agendas;
> preparing minutes;
> collecting and distributing information required by the audit committee;
> drafting the report on the audit committee's activities for inclusion in the annual report; and
> providing administrative, professional and other necessary practical support.

In addition, the board should make funds available to the audit committee to enable it to take independent legal, accounting or other advice when the audit committee reasonably considers it necessary to do so.

Most importantly, the Smith Guidance underlines the audit committee's need for access to information from the company's directors, managers and employees, and also from the external auditors. To this end, it recommends that the board should make clear to all directors and staff that they must cooperate with the audit committee and provide it with any information it requires.

Chapter summary

> The collapse of Enron and other major US corporations amid allegations of serious financial malpractice by senior executives and collusion by external auditors has raised serious questions about the extent to which audit committees can ensure the reliability of reporting and auditing processes.

> Reviews undertaken by governments and financial regulators in the US, the UK and elsewhere have established a consensus on the need to strengthen the framework of corporate governance generally and, more particularly, to clarify and enhance the role of the audit committee.

> In the UK, the Combined Code envisages that the role and responsibilities of the audit committee will become more onerous in future, with significant implications for the composition and resources of the audit committee and the skills, personal qualities and remuneration of its members.

> Among its other responsibilities, the audit committee has primary responsibility for recommending to shareholders the appointment, reappointment and removal of the external auditors and for safeguarding the independence and objectivity of both internal and external auditors.

12

Internal control and risk management

This chapter describes:

- ❯ the evolving approach to internal control and risk management in successive codes of corporate governance;
- ❯ the elements of an embedded system of internal control and risk management;
- ❯ the allocation of responsibility for internal control and risk management between the board, management and employees; and
- ❯ reporting to shareholders.

Introduction

The effective management of risk is central to the discharge of directors' responsibilities for the safeguarding of shareholder investments and company assets. In general terms, a risk can be defined as the combination of the probability of an event and of its consequences (ISO/IEC Guide 73). Potential risks to shareholder investments and company assets can be categorised in a number of different ways, including:

- ❯ *operational risk*: exposure to uncertainty arising from day-to-day business activities;
- ❯ *hazard risk*: exposure to loss arising from harm to employees, the public or the environment or from damage to property;
- ❯ *strategic risk*: exposure to uncertainty arising from long-term policy decisions;
- ❯ *market risk*: exposure to uncertainty due to changes in, for example, interest rates or share prices; and
- ❯ *reputational risk*: exposure to loss due to impaired customer, investor or public perceptions, particularly in circumstances where the company is considered to have acted unlawfully or unethically.

Bearing in mind that entrepreneurial risk-taking in pursuit of profit is a normal part of business life, possible responses to risk can be divided into four broad categories:

1 *Terminate*: where a risk presents an unacceptable threat to the viability of the business or the achievement of its objectives and cannot cost-effectively be contained to an acceptable level, the company may respond by terminating the activity from which the risk arises.

2 *Tolerate*: where the magnitude of a risk is not so great as to threaten the viability of the business or the achievement of its objectives, but the practical scope for containing the risk is limited or involves costs disproportionate to the potential benefit gained, the company may simply decide to tolerate the risk.

3 *Transfer*: where a risk involves financially quantifiable consequences (for example theft, fire or flood damage, personal injury or product liability) it may be possible for the company to transfer the risk to a third party, for example through commercial insurance or by out-sourcing or contracting the activity from which the risk arises.

4 *Treat*: in the majority of cases for which other responses are inappropriate, the company is likely to seek to identify and manage risks to acceptable levels through its system of internal controls.

Internal procedures are essential elements of any company's system of internal control. However, there is increasing recognition that, although prescriptive rules may be effective in some situations and in the short term, reliance on prescription alone may result in failure to identify and manage more subtle and less quantifiable forms of risk, particularly those which may impact on the company's reputation. This recognition is reflected in the evolving approach to internal control taken in successive codes of corporate governance, from the relatively narrow focus on financial risks in the Cadbury Code, to the more holistic approach taken in the 2003 Combined Code and the associated Turnbull Guidance.

Internal control in codes of corporate governance

Combined Code recommendations

In its report, published in 1992, the Cadbury Committee on the Financial Aspects of Corporate Governance acknowledged that directors' responsibilities in relation to internal control should not be limited to the management of financial risks, but should encompass a systematic approach to risks of all kinds. After consultation, however, a narrower focus was accepted, with the result that the final Cadbury Code and the subsequent guidance produced by the Rutteman Working Group recommended that the board should have responsibility for the company's system of internal *financial* control.

Returning to the broad view originally taken by Cadbury, the Hampel Committee on Corporate Governance recommended that boards should take responsibility for all aspects of internal control, including financial, operational and compliance controls and risk management. Accordingly, the 1998 Combined Code stated that:

❯ the board should maintain a sound system of internal control to safeguard shareholders' investment and the company's assets (Principle D.2);

❯ the directors should, at least annually, conduct a review of the effectiveness of the group's system of internal control and should report to shareholders that they have done so (Provision D.2.1); and

❯ companies which did not have an internal audit function should from time to time review the need for one (Provision D.2.2).

Turnbull Guidance

Internal Control: Guidance for Directors on the Combined Code (1999)

Following the publication of the 1998 Combined Code, the Institute of Chartered Accountants in England and Wales (ICAEW) undertook to provide guidance on the recommendations relating to internal control, and established a working party led by Nigel Turnbull for this purpose.

In its report, *Internal Control: Guidance for Directors on the Combined Code*, published by the ICAEW in September 1999, the Turnbull Working Party acknowledged that profits are in part the reward for successful risk-taking. The purpose of a system of internal control is therefore to minimise the company's exposure to unnecessary risks, rather than to eliminate risk altogether. While even a sound system of internal control cannot exclude the possibility that a company will incur losses, it should facilitate effective and efficient operation, enabling the company to manage significant known risks to the achievement of its business objectives and to respond quickly to new risks as they emerge.

The Turnbull Guidance emphasised that, to be effective, the company's internal control and risk management arrangements must:

❯ be embedded in the company's day-to-day business processes, including its investment appraisal methodology, decision-making structures, performance assessment and reward system and internal communication arrangements;

❯ be led by the directors through their demonstrable personal commitment to effective risk management and their own behaviour in terms of ethical conduct and decision-making; and

❯ extend beyond quantifiable financial and physical risks to include risks arising from technological, legal, health and safety, environmental, reputational and business probity issues.

The Flint review

In July 2004, the Financial Reporting Council (FRC) announced that it had appointed a team led by Douglas Flint, the Group Finance Director of HSBC Holdings plc, to carry out a review of the continued appropriateness of the Turnbull Guidance.

The timing of the review reflected the recommendation of the Turnbull working party that the guidance should be revisited after five years to address any problems encountered in operation and to take account of new issues. However, its scope has needed to be considerably broader than envisaged in 1999: in addition to company and investor experience with the implementation of the guidance, it has had to take account of significant developments, both internationally and within the UK. These include:

> the requirements of the US Sarbanes-Oxley Act of 2002 (SOX), in particular that directors should make public their assessment of the effectiveness of their companies' internal financial controls and that external auditors should issue an attestation report on directors' assessments;

> the publication in July 2003 of the revised Combined Code incorporating the Smith Guidance on the role and responsibilities of audit committees in assessing internal control;

> intended changes to the Fourth and Seventh Company Law (Accounting) Directives to establish directors' collective responsibility for financial statements, enforce disclosure of all off-balance sheet arrangements and require listed companies to provide corporate governance statements in their annual reports; and

> the inclusion in the Company Law Reform Bill of a proposed statutory statement of directors' duties, as recommended by the Company Law Review (CLR).

Revised guidance on internal control (October 2005)

In consultation with listed companies, institutional investors, major accountancy firms and other professional bodies, the review group found that, in the overwhelming view of respondents, the Turnbull Guidance has been highly successful, has been intelligently and appropriately applied by companies and has contributed to better understanding and management of risk. There was strong support both for the broad coverage of the guidance and for its non-prescriptive, principles-based approach, which required boards to think broadly about the risks faced by their companies and enabled them to apply the guidance in a way that suited their circumstances.

On this basis, the review group recommended that the guidance should continue to cover all internal controls and that there should be no changes which might have the effect of restricting a company's ability to apply the guidance in a manner suitable to its own particular circumstances. In addition, the review group explicitly rejected suggestions that the disclosure provisions contained in section 404 of SOX – which require directors to make a statement on the effectiveness of internal financial controls, and external auditors to attest to the accuracy of such statements – should be emulated in guidance to UK listed companies.

Concluding that no material changes to the original Turnbull Guidance were required, the review group proposed a small number of amendments including:

> the addition of a new preface designed to encourage boards to review their application of the guidance on a continuing basis and to communicate effectively to shareholders on their management of risk;

> reordering of the introduction to the guidance to reinforce the message that it is intended to reflect sound business practice as well as to help companies comply with the internal control requirements of the Combined Code;

> for consistency with the statutory statement of directors' duties proposed in the Company Law Reform Bill, the insertion of a requirement for directors to

exercise reasonable care, skill and diligence when forming a view on the effectiveness of their company's system of internal control (rather than forming a view 'after due and careful enquiry'); and

> the addition of a new requirement on boards to include in their annual reports to shareholders a statement confirming that necessary action has been or is being taken to remedy any significant failings or weaknesses identified from their review of the effectiveness of the system of internal control and any other information which the board considers necessary to help shareholders to understand the main features of the company's risk management processes and system of internal control.

Revised guidance incorporating the review group's recommendations was published by the FRC in October 2005 for application in listed companies' annual reports to shareholders for financial years beginning on or after 1 January 2006. The revised guidance is reproduced in full in *Appendix 16.*

Elements of internal control

In order to leave companies free to adopt the risk management approaches that best take account of their particular circumstances, the Turnbull Guidance does not require companies to adhere to any prescribed risk management framework. It does recognise, however, that some companies may find it helpful to refer to externally developed frameworks, such as the the Institute of Risk Management's Risk Management Standard, the Enterprise Risk Management Framework developed by the US Committee of Sponsoring Organizations of the Treadway Commission (COSO), or the Australia/New Zealand Risk Management Standard AS/NZS 4360:2004.

While these frameworks vary in the nomenclature they apply to the risk management and internal control process, certain activities are generic in nature. In any company, therefore, an embedded risk management system is likely to consist of a range of continuous and interacting activities covering:

> the establishment and maintenance of an appropriate control environment, encompassing the company's policies, values and standards supported by its arrangements for reporting and communications;

> the setting of strategic objectives and their translation into detailed business plans, targets and budgets;

> the identification and analysis of the significant risks to the achievement of objectives;

> the determination, for each risk, of the appropriate response – that is, whether to terminate, tolerate, treat or transfer the particular risk;

> the design and operation of internal controls to manage significant risks which cannot be transferred or terminated;

> monitoring the effectiveness of individual control mechanisms and the overall system of internal controls; and

> the modification of strategic objectives, plans and targets in the light of feedback from the company's system of internal control and changes in the external operating environment.

Roles and responsibilities

Role of the board

Establishing and maintaining the control environment

As discussed in *Chapter 5*, the board is responsible for determining its own role, for deciding which matters should be reserved for its collective decision and which can properly be delegated to others, and for defining the company's strategic objectives, policies, values and standards and communicating them clearly to employees, shareholders and other key stakeholders. As part of this process, the board must set out its policy on risk and allocate clear responsibilities and accountabilities for all aspects of risk management and internal control.

The effectiveness of the board's policy on risk activities will depend to a large extent on the company's organisational culture, values, competencies and reward structures, as reflected in the behaviour of directors, managers and staff. The board should therefore ensure that:

> consistent messages and priorities are set out in policy documents such as the company's mission statement or corporate vision, its employee code of conduct and its business procedures;

> the same messages and priorities are supported through staff training, performance management approaches and reward systems;

> procedures are established for the timely reporting of adverse events and failures or deficiencies in internal controls; and

> no 'blame culture' which might encourage the concealment of control deficiencies is allowed to exist at any level within the company.

The need to ensure that employees are able to report control failures, including suspected illegal or unethical practices, without fear of reprisal, was underlined by the Enron scandal, some of the consequences of which might have been averted had the company taken appropriate steps to investigate the concerns raised by an internal whistleblower. In the light of that experience, the Sarbanes-Oxley Act now requires quoted companies in the US to make arrangements for the receipt and investigation of whistleblower reports on financial, accounting and auditing matters.

As explained in *Chapter 11*, the 2003 Combined Code similarly recomends that the audit committee should be responsible for ensuring that employees can raise concerns about possible improprieties in financial reporting or related matters and that any such reports are properly investigated and acted upon. However, the board as a whole should satisfy itself that the scope of any whistleblowing procedure is wide enough to enable employees to report concerns about non-financial matters which might, if not investigated, impact adversely on the company's reputation. The statutory position in the UK in respect of whistleblower protection is set out below, together with a summary of some key points to be considered when establishing a whistleblowing policy.

WHISTLEBLOWING: THE STATUTORY POSITION IN THE UK

In the UK, workers who report known or suspected wrongdoings in their organisations are protected from victimisation or discrimination by the Public Interest Disclosure Act 1998 (PIDA 1998). The Act protects people who raise concerns about past, present and future malpractices in relation to: criminal acts; failure to comply with legal duties (such as negligence or breach of contract); miscarriages of justice; danger to health and safety; damage to the environment; and deliberate cover-up of any of these.

PIDA 1998 provides protection for all disclosures made in good faith, even if it is subsequently shown that the whistleblower had misunderstood or misinterpreted the circumstances. However, anyone who deliberately makes false or malicious allegations about an individual or corporate body cannot avail themselves of PIDA 1998 protection and will be subject to their employer's normal disciplinary procedures.

PIDA 1998 encourages workers to raise their concerns with their employers in the first instance, but it also allows external disclosure, for instance to a regulatory body, the police or the media, as long as there are good reasons for doing so. The Act details four such good reasons:

- the concern was raised internally or with a prescribed regulator, but has not been properly addressed; or
- the concern was not raised internally or with a prescribed regulator because the whistleblower reasonably believed that he or she would be victimised; or
- the concern was not raised internally or with a prescribed regulator because the whistleblower reasonably believed that a cover-up was likely and there was no prescribed regulator; or
- the concern was exceptionally serious.

Under the Act, employers are not allowed to treat legitimate whistleblowers as troublemakers or ignore their concerns. Confidentiality clauses and gagging clauses in contracts of employment and severance agreements are ineffective in so far as they conflict with the provisions of the Act.

Legitimate whistleblowers are protected from detriments in their employment, including dismissal, reassignment of duties and refusal to grant a salary increase. Where someone has been victimised in breach of the Act (regardless of whether or not he or she has been dismissed) that person can bring a claim for compensation in an employment tribunal. Awards for victimisation are uncapped (so that, for example, employees who lose their jobs in breach of the Act will be fully compensated for all their losses). Dismissed employees may also obtain interim relief, before their case has been decided.

GOOD PRACTICE POINT ◉ ▶

Establishing a whistleblowing procedure

A whistleblowing procedure can help to ensure that cases of unlawful or unethical conduct are brought to the attention of management before they can damage a company's reputation.

To be effective, however, a whistleblowing procedure must have the confidence of the employees who are its intended users. A copy of the procedure should be distributed to every employee and should:

- set out clearly all aspects of the procedure, including the identity of the person or persons to whom concerns should be addressed;
- emphasise that the company takes malpractice and misconduct seriously, is committed to investigating all allegations and will protect employees who report concerns in good faith from reprisals even if, on investigation, their concerns prove to be honest mistakes;
- give examples of the types of misconduct for which employees should use the procedures and the

level of evidence needed, stressing that positive proof is not needed but that the reporter should be able to show good reasons;
- explain the process by which concerns will be investigated and the outcome reported to directors; and
- make clear that false and malicious allegations will result in disciplinary action against the person making them.

In some circumstances, employees with genuine concerns may be reluctant to use the company's internal whistleblowing procedure, perhaps because of fears that the procedure will be insufficient to protect them from intimidation by immediate colleagues or superiors. To ensure that all such concerns are reported, the company should offer an external reporting route as an alternative to its internal arrangements. Information and advice on external reporting processes can be provided by the registered charity Public Concern at Work (www.pcaw.co.uk).

Setting strategic objectives

The board is accountable to shareholders for defining the strategic objectives which are key to the company's long-term success, taking into account its main markets and the legal, social, political and cultural constraints on its activities. Where appropriate, the board should modify the company's strategic objectives in the light of new or increased risks identified through the operation of the internal control system and to take account of changes in the external operating environment.

Critically, the board is also responsible for determining the company's risk appetite – that is, how much risk the company is prepared to accept on behalf of its shareholders in the pursuit of value creation. Depending on assessment, the board may conclude at the outset that certain risks are unacceptable and may therefore decide to avoid them, either by discontinuing the activity from which the risk arises or by determining that the company will not enter into new high-risk activities.

Monitoring the system of internal control

In most companies, the board will need to delegate to line management responsibility for detailed risk identification and evaluation and the design of specific internal controls. However, it will still be accountable to shareholders for the operation of the company's system of internal control and must therefore establish and maintain effective oversight of management activities. To this end, boards will typically receive:

> regular reports from line managers on the outcome of the risk identification and analysis carried out within each business unit and the internal controls implemented as a result; and

> assurance that appropriate controls are in place from appropriate internal functions (see pages 170–171).

The board's responsibility for regular oversight of the company's system of internal control can be discharged by the full board, by the audit committee or by a committee of the board with specific responsibility for risk and control of these. Paragraph 25 of the revised Turnbull Guidance points out, however, that where designated board committees carry out activities on behalf of the board, the results of their work must be reported to and considered by the full board. Further, the board as a whole retains responsibility for disclosures on internal control in the annual report and accounts (see pages 172–173).

Responsibilities of line management

Identifying and analysing significant risks to objectives

As noted above, line managers will generally have delegated responsibility for identifying and analysing the significant risks arising in the business unit for which they are responsible. Although these activities can be carried out by external consultants, the process is more effectively conducted in-house by the managers and staff with immediate knowledge of the risks affecting their area of responsibility. Such direct involvement will also facilitate embedding, in that it gives those responsible for operation a degree of ownership of the resulting control processes.

There are numerous techniques and methodologies available for identifying and evaluating risk, including SWOT (Strengths, Weaknesses, Opportunities, Threats) and BPEST (Business, Political, Economic, Social, Technological) analyses and Hazard & Operability (HAZOP) studies. These can be used as the basis of questionnaires, or can provide a framework for discussion in workshops or team meetings. However, the exact choice of methodology is less important than ensuring that the risk identification and evaluation process is consistent, well-communicated and participative. Regardless of the methodology chosen, the process should seek to:

> identify all possible risks to the achievement of the business unit's operating targets and budgets; and

> assess the materiality of each risk, taking into account the probability of the risk actually occurring and the potential impact of an occurrence of the risk, including its possible financial, operational and reputational consequences.

The risks identified within each business unit can be ranked in order of materiality in a risk log or risk register. This can then be used to prioritise internal control and risk management activities and can also form the basis of regular reporting to the board on key risks.

Some typical elements of a risk register are outlined below.

GOOD PRACTICE POINT

Typical content of a business unit risk register

Once a business unit has identified and analysed the principal risks to the achievement of its operating targets and budgets, the outcome will need to be recorded systematically so that control activities can be prioritised on the most significant risks. A risk log or risk register is often used for this purpose and can usefully capture in tabular form the following types of information:

- the likelihood of the risk occurring (perhaps on a scale of 1 to 10, where 1 is 'unlikely' and 10 is 'very likely');
- the likely impact of an occurrence of the risk (again, this can be assessed on a scale of 1 to 10, where 1 represents 'very little impact' and 10 represents 'potentially very serious, or even catastrophic, impact');

- a brief description of the action to be taken to prevent an occurrence of the risk or to mitigate its impact;
- the name of the person or business unit with responsibility for managing the risk;
- the date by which the action is to be carried out;
- where appropriate, a statement of the objective of the relevant action and an assessment of whether further action is likely to be necessary to achieve the objective; and
- arrangements for review and for taking further action as necessary.

Designing and operating internal controls

Based on the outcome of the risk identification and analysis process, line managers are responsible for designing and implementing internal control measures as necessary to ensure that all risks which are considered material are managed to acceptable levels. Internal controls can take many different forms, including delegations of authority, requirements for approvals and authorisations, segregation of duties, reporting procedures, accounting and other reconciliations, data protection, operating procedures, safety and environmental protection rules and physical security measures. The principal generic categories of internal control are summarised at page 170.

Reviewing the operation of internal controls

Line managers are also responsible for keeping under review the operation of the internal controls they have implemented, for rectifying any weaknesses in existing control measures and for reporting promptly to the board on any new or emerging risks facing their business unit. To this end, they must develop self-assessment measures which enable them to monitor the key business and financial activities within their respective areas of operation and highlight significant variances from

CATEGORIES OF INTERNAL CONTROL

Internal controls can take many forms but can be broadly categorised as follows:

- *Directive controls*: controls which give instructions designed to ensure that a particular outcome is achieved or an undesirable event is avoided. Examples of directive controls include a requirement that protective clothing be worn during the performance of dangerous duties, or that staff be trained with required skills before being allowed to work unsupervised.
- *Preventive controls*: controls designed to limit the possibility of an undesirable outcome being realised. Examples of preventive controls include segregation of duties (for example to ensure that the same person cannot order goods and services and authorise payment of the relevant invoice), or limitation of action to authorised persons (for example to ensure that only suitably trained and authorised personnel are permitted to handle media enquiries).
- *Detective controls*: controls designed to identify the occurrence of undesirable outcomes so that action can be taken to limit the loss or damage incurred. Examples of detective controls include stock or asset checks (which detect whether stocks or assets have been removed without authorisation), reconciliation (which can detect unauthorised transactions), and post-implementation reviews designed to ensure that lessons learnt from particular events are recorded for application in future.
- *Corrective controls*: controls designed to correct undesirable outcomes once they have occurred, for example by facilitating some recovery against loss or damage. Examples of corrective controls include contractual terms which allow recovery of overpayment.

plan or other unexpected events at sufficient frequency to allow appropriate action to be taken. The ongoing nature of line managers' responsibilities for internal control is emphasised in research carried out by MORI in conjunction with the Turnbull Review: this found that in over 40 per cent of listed companies, senior management and their support teams kept internal control under continuous review, while in a further 20 per cent of companies, reviews took place at least monthly or quarterly.

Internal assurance providers

Ongoing review by line management is an essential part of an embedded system of internal control and risk management, but may not be sufficiently objective to provide adequate assurance of the effectiveness of the system. Independent assurance will therefore need to be provided by in-house specialists including the following:

> *The internal audit function*: the role of the internal audit function in respect of internal control and risk management will vary from one company to another depending on the nature of the business, the legal and regulatory environment in which the company operates and the availability of other specialist resources in-house. Internal audit will certainly be responsible for providing assurance to

the board on the adequacy of the internal controls relevant to significant financial and accounting risks, and in some circumstances may also take the lead in auditing all risk management processes across the company and in co-ordinating all risk reporting to the board.

> *Specialist risk managers*: many companies now have designated risk 'champions' or professional risk managers whose role includes advising the board on the company's overall policy and strategy for risk management, building a culture of risk awareness within the company and reporting to the board on the adequacy of the company's internal control and risk management arrangements as a whole.

> *Other functional specialists*: assurance may also be provided to the board on specific aspects of the company's internal control and risk arrangements by functional specialists in areas such as legal and regulatory compliance, health and safety and environmental policy.

In each case, the role of internal audit and other assurance providers should be to challenge the outcome of management's self-assessment and to report to the board on the effectiveness of the company's system of internal control and risk management. Key areas for review will be the completeness of the strategic objectives covered by the system, the adequacy of the process adopted by management for the identification, assessment and management of the significant business risks, and the transparency of reporting on control failures and weaknesses.

Accounting to shareholders

Reviewing the effectiveness of internal control

Provision C.2.1 of the 2003 Combined Code states that:

> 'The board should, at least annually, conduct a review of the effectiveness of the group's system of internal controls and should report to shareholders that they have done so. The review should cover all material controls, including financial, operational and compliance controls and risk management systems.'

As the revised Turnbull Guidance makes clear, however, boards cannot limit their involvement in the internal control and risk management process to a single annual review, but should instead ensure that they (or designated board committees on behalf of full boards) regularly receive and review reports on internal control. In practice, it appears that in a majority of listed companies the full board is actively involved in the oversight of internal control and risk management. Research carried out by MORI in conjunction with the review of the Turnbull Guidance found that almost 60 per cent of listed company boards included risk and internal control matters as a specific item on the agenda at all or most board meetings, while only 11 per cent of boards limiting their consideration of these matters to a formal annual review.

The revised Turnbull Guidance (paragraph 29) recommends that, when reviewing reports received from management during the year, the board should:

> ❯ consider what are the significant risks and assess how they have been identified, evaluated and managed;
> ❯ assess the effectiveness of the related system of internal control in managing the significant risks, having regard, in particular, to any significant failings or weaknesses that have been reported;
> ❯ consider whether necessary actions are being taken promptly to remedy any significant failings or weaknesses; and
> ❯ consider whether the findings indicate a need for more extensive monitoring of the system of internal control.

Whenever necessary during the year, the board should commission from appropriate internal assurance providers, such as the internal audit function, more detailed reports on any areas of concern highlighted by management, including any new or emerging risks or other issues which might also affect other areas of business or otherwise appear to represent an unacceptable degree of risk.

In its annual assessment of the system of internal control, the board should revisit the issues raised in reports considered during the year and should also ensure that it receives from line managers and internal assurance providers any additional information needed to enable it to review all significant aspects of internal control. The revised Turnbull Guidance (paragraph 31) recommends that the board should address the following matters in the course of its annual review:

> ❯ the changes since the last annual assessment in the nature and extent of significant risks, and the company's ability to respond to changes in its business and the external environment;
> ❯ the scope and quality of management's ongoing monitoring of risks and of the system of internal control, and, where applicable, the work of its internal audit function and other providers of assurance;
> ❯ the extent and frequency of the communication of the results of the monitoring to the board (or board committee(s)) which enables it to build up a cumulative assessment of the state of control in the company and the effectiveness with which risk is being managed;
> ❯ the incidence of significant control failings or weaknesses that have been identified at any time during the period and the extent to which they have resulted in unforeseen outcomes or contingencies that have had, could have had, or may in the future have, a material impact on the company's financial performance or condition; and
> ❯ the effectiveness of the company's public reporting processes.

Reporting to shareholders on internal control

The board's annual assessment of the company's system of internal control forms the basis of its statement to shareholders in the annual report and accounts. Paragraph 35 of the revised Turnbull Guidance specifies that this statement must acknowledge the board's responsibility for the company's system of internal control and for reviewing its effectiveness, but should also point out that the system is designed to manage rather than eliminate the risk of failure to achieve business objectives and can only provide reasonable and not absolute assurance against material misstatement or loss.

The statement should confirm that the board has ensured the existence of an ongoing system for identifying, evaluating and managing the significant risks faced by the company, that this system has been in place for the year under review and up to the date of approval of the annual report and accounts, and that it is regularly reviewed by the board in accordance with the Turnbull Guidance. It should summarise the process applied by the board in reviewing the effectiveness of the system and dealing with any significant problems revealed by its review. If the board is unable to make any of the required disclosures, it must identify the areas concerned and explain what it is doing to rectify the situation.

The FRC's review of the Turnbull Guidance has confirmed that the board should not be required to give an opinion on the effectiveness of the company's system of internal control or to identify specific risk areas. However, paragraph 33 of the revised Guidance emphasises the need for the annual report and accounts to include sufficient meaningful, high-level information to assist shareholders' understanding of the main featurees of the company's risk management processes and system of internal control, and to avoid giving a misleading impression.

Chapter summary

> Directors have a primary responsibility for the stewardship of investors' assets and the protection of their investment through the company's system of internal control and risk management.

> It is now firmly established that the requirement for effective internal control extends beyond financial controls to include controls relating to all significant risks to the achievement of objectives, including legal, health and safety, environmental, reputational and ethical risks.

> Alongside this recognition, there is strong emphasis on the need for internal control to be embedded in the company's day-to-day business processes, including its investment appraisal methodology, decision-making structures, performance assessment and reward system, and internal communication arrangements.

Relations with institutional investors

> There should be a dialogue with shareholders based on the mutual understanding of objectives. The board as a whole has responsibility for ensuring that a satisfactory dialogue with shareholders takes place.
>
> Combined Code (2003) Main Principle D.1

> Institutional shareholders should enter into a dialogue with companies based on the mutual understanding of objectives.
>
> Combined Code (2003) Main Principle E.1

> When evaluating companies' governance arrangements, particularly those relating to board structure and composition, institutional shareholders should give due weight to all relevant factors drawn to their attention.
>
> Combined Code (2003) Main Principle E.2

> Institutional shareholders have a responsibility to make considered use of their votes.
>
> Combined Code (2003) Main Principle E.3

This chapter explores the relationship between listed companies and their major shareholders, focusing on:

> ❯ the increasing pressure on financial institutions to engage proactively with investee companies in the fulfilment of their fiduciary duties to underlying savers and investors;
> ❯ the implications of institutional engagement for listed companies' wider duties in respect of equal treatment of all shareholders and the protection of price-sensitive information; and
> ❯ the responsibilities of companies and boards for fostering positive relationships with institutional shareholders.

In each of these areas, the chapter considers current and prospective requirements on companies and institutions, as set out in legislation, regulation and the Combined Code.

Introduction

Under UK law, shareholders in public companies delegate substantially all their powers as owners to the company's directors and thus relinquish the right to be directly involved in the direction and management of the business. As the share-holders' agents, the directors are required to:

> control and direct the business in the interests of the shareholders as a whole;
> act fairly as between shareholders;
> ensure that meaningful and reliable information about the position and prospects of the company is available to all shareholders; and
> contribute to the maintenance of an orderly and transparent market in the company's shares.

As explained in *Chapter 1*, shareholders retain two forms of power over the actions of the directors, namely:

> *Voice*: the shareholders in general meeting have the right to exercise the voting powers attaching to their shares to approve or reject significant decisions of the company, including the appointment and reappointment of directors, proposed dividend payments and other substantial transactions.
> *Exit*: shareholders can choose to maintain, increase or dispose of their share-holdings in the company according to their opinion of the performance of the business and the quality of its directors.

Until comparatively recently, it has been assumed that the decision to exercise their powers of voice and exit is a private matter for shareholders, who need only consult their own self-interest. Corollary to this assumption is a long-standing belief that share-holders may be 'rationally apathetic', especially towards the use of their power of voice.

The concept of 'rational apathy' derives from the observation by Berle and Means in the 1930s that, where ownership of shares in publicly quoted companies is widely dispersed amongst a large number of shareholders, individual shareholders may conclude that it is not worthwhile to engage in dialogue with company management in order to seek improved performance.

According to this model, the small size of most individual shareholdings means that the benefit to the individual shareholder arising from improved performance would be outweighed by the costs involved in seeking change, particularly in a large company where it may be difficult to achieve concerted action by shareholders. Even where successful action is possible, potential instigators are likely to be deterred by the prospect that shareholders who have not participated in the action will 'free ride' on their efforts. In these circumstances, the existence of a liquid market in the company's shares may mean that it is easier and cheaper for dissatisfied shareholders to exit (whether by selling their shares or by accepting a takeover offer) than to seek to use their power of voice to effect a change of policy or management.

In recent years, the balance of share ownership has shifted decisively away from private individuals towards financial institutions, dominated by pension funds, insur-ance companies and other collective investment vehicles. The following table briefly describes the principal bodies by which UK institutional investors are represented.

INSTITUTIONAL INVESTOR BODIES IN THE UK

Institutional investors in the UK are represented by a number of bodies, each of which has its own constituency and makes recommendations to its members on engagement with investee companies on matters of policy and governance. The principal representative bodies are as follows:

- The *Association of British Insurers* (ABI) is the trade association for the UK insurance industry, the members of which account for approximately 20 per cent of shares listed on the London Stock Exchange. The ABI recommends responsible voting within the framework of a considered corporate governance policy. In 2001, it issued guidelines setting out the disclosures on social, environmental and ethical matters that institutional investors should expect to be included in the annual reports of listed companies. The ABI's website can be found at www.abi.org.uk.
- The *National Association of Pension Funds* (NAPF) represents 75 per cent of occupational pension funds in the UK, accounting for some 25 per cent of shares listed on the London Stock Exchange. On its own account and jointly with the ABI and other investor bodies, the NAPF issues influential guidelines on corporate governance issues, particularly in relation to executive remuneration. The NAPF's website can be found at www.napf.co.uk.
- The *Institutional Shareholders' Committee* (ISC) is an umbrella group comprising the ABI, the NAPF, the Association of Investment Trust Companies, and the Investment Management Association. The ISC *Statement of Principles on the Responsibilities of Institutional Shareholders and Agents*, originally published in 2002, was revised in September 2005 and is reproduced in *Appendix 17*. The ISC's website can be found at www.investmentuk.org.uk.
- The *Investment Management Association* (IMA) is the trade body for the UK asset management industry. Its guidance document, *Relations with Investee Companies – Guidance on Good Practice*, is set out at pages 183–184. The IMA's website can be found at www.investmentuk.org.uk.

There are in addition a number of organisations which evaluate the corporate governance practices of companies and make recommendations to institutional investors on the use of their voting powers. The principal voting agencies are as follows:

- *Manifest* is an independent corporate governance and proxy voting service. Its website can be found at www.manifest.co.uk.
- *Research, Recommendations and Electronic Voting* (RREV) is a joint venture between the NAPF and the US-based proxy voting and research organisation Institutional Shareholder Services. Its website can be found at www.rrev.co.uk.
- *Pensions Investment Research Consultants Ltd* (PIRC) produces advice and voting recommendations for its clients, mainly local authority and other public sector pension funds. The PIRC is in some respects the most radical of the voting agencies and is active in the public policy debate on issues of corporate governance and socially responsible investment. Its website can be found at www.pirc.co.uk.

The concentration of ownership in the hands of financial institutions challenges the assumption that 'rational apathy' is a legitimate position for institutional share-holders, for a combination of reasons:

> *Commercial*: by the end of 2003, HM Treasury estimated that almost half of all UK listed equities, valued at nearly £660 billion, were owned by UK financial institutions: in these circumstances, it may be difficult for an institution simply to sell large numbers of shares in an underperforming company without depressing its share price and effectively disturbing the wider market.

> *Strategic*: many institutions operate according to 'index tracking' strategies, whereby they seek to match their investment portfolios to the components of a share index such as the FTSE 100 with the aim of ensuring that long-term returns from the investment portfolios are no lower than those from the selected index as a whole. The adoption of an index tracking strategy effectively commits the institution concerned to retaining a substantial long-term holding in each of the listed companies in the selected index and thus limits its ability to dispose of shares in underperforming companies.

> *Fiduciary*: it is increasingly accepted that, as providers of collective investment vehicles which aggregate and invest funds on behalf of individual savers and investors, financial institutions owe fiduciary duties to the underlying investors which require them to develop constructive relationships with the companies in which they invest and to use their powers as shareholders, including voting rights, where there is a reasonable prospect that this will result in improved governance and enhanced performance in the interests of beneficiaries.

For these reasons, listed companies and their major institutional investors are increas-ingly encouraged to enter into constructive dialogue. From the company's perspective, this may raise difficult questions relating to, for example, the wider obligation to act fairly as between shareholders, the consistency and predictability of institutions' expectations, and the quality and effectiveness of institutional engagement.

Responsibilities of institutional shareholders

The case for institutional engagement

Concerns about the level and effectiveness of institutional investor engagement with investee companies have typically focused on the extent to which institutional investors exercise their voting rights in the interests of the underlying beneficiaries.

In its final report (June 2000), the Company Law Review (CLR) identified a need for greater transparency in the way in which institutional investors exercise their powers, recommending that institutional investors who manage funds on behalf of others should be required to disclose publicly how they have voted their shares. *Chapter 14* describes efforts to facilitate voting, in particular through the introduction of electronic proxy appointment and instruction.

A more broad-based critique of institutional investor engagement was provided by Paul Myners in his report to HM Treasury, published in March 2001, on institutional investment in the UK. This concluded that:

> fund managers responsible for managing institutional investments, especially those in pension funds, were generally unwilling to engage proactively in dialogue with investee companies;
> even where there were strong grounds for concern about strategy, personnel or other potential causes of corporate underperformance, fund managers were reluctant to tackle corporate underperformance or to intervene to prevent troubled companies from developing serious problems; and
> as a result, value was being lost to institutional investors (and ultimately to pension fund beneficiaries and other individual savers and investors) through the reluctance of fund managers to engage actively with companies.

The Myners Report proposed the adoption by pension funds of a voluntary set of investment decision-making principles, compliance with which would be monitored via a 'comply or explain' regime based on that used for the Combined Code. In respect of shareholder activism, the principles would require all pension fund trustees to incorporate into the mandates agreed with fund managers provisions similar to those set out in the US Department of Labor Interpretative Bulletin on the Employment Retirement Income Security Act (ERISA) 1974. The Bulletin defines the fiduciary duties of fund managers, including the obligation to intervene in companies, through active monitoring and voting where appropriate, if there is a reasonable expectation that doing so might raise the value of the investment in the interests of their clients.

Formal requirements on institutions

Myners Investment Principle 6: Activism

Following consultation, the Myners Principles for Institutional Investment Decision-making were adopted in October 2001. Myners Principle 6 (Activism) states that:

> pension fund investment mandates and trust deeds should incorporate the principles of the US Department of Labor Interpretative Bulletin on activism;
> fund managers should have an explicit strategy, setting out the circumstances in which they will intervene in a company, the approach they will use in doing so, and how they measure the effectiveness of this strategy; and
> the trustees of defined benefit pension schemes should take responsibility for ensuring that their fund managers have an appropriate strategy for intervention in investee companies.

In addition to these voluntary measures, the Myners Report recommended that the Government should ultimately incorporate into UK law the principles set out in the Department of Labor Interpretative Bulletin. While this recommendation was initially accepted, the Government agreed, following consultation, that the principles set out in the Interpretative Bulletin should be pursued voluntarily through the *Statement of Principles on the Responsibilities of Institutional Shareholders and Agents* developed by the Institutional Shareholders' Committee (ISC) comprising the Association of British Insurers (ABI), the Association of Investment Trust Companies (AITC), the

National Association of Pension Funds (NAPF) and the Investment Management Association (IMA).

ISC Statement of Principles on the Responsibilities of Institutional Shareholders and Agents

The ISC *Statement of Principles*, as updated in September 2005, is reproduced in *Appendix 17*. Amongst its other provisions, the *Statement* recommends that each institutional shareholder should have a clear statement of its policy on activism setting out:

> ❭ how investee companies will be monitored, including the institution's approach to active dialogue with the investee company's board and senior management;
> ❭ the institution's policy for requiring investee companies to comply with the core standards of the Combined Code;
> ❭ the policy for meetings with an investee company's board and senior management;
> ❭ how situations where the institution and/or its agent has a conflict of interest will be minimised or dealt with;
> ❭ the institution's strategy on intervention;
> ❭ an indication of the type of circumstances when the institution may take further action and details of the type of action that may be taken; and
> ❭ the institution's policy on voting.

2003 Combined Code

The 2003 Combined Code stressed the obligations of institutional shareholders towards underlying beneficiaries, recommending at Principle E.2 that institutions should:

> ❭ account to their clients for the use of their voting powers by making available, on request, information on the proportion of resolutions on which votes were cast and non-discretionary proxies lodged; and
> ❭ attend the AGMs of investee companies where appropriate and practicable.

Importantly, however, the Combined Code also emphasised the responsibilities of institutional shareholders towards investee companies, in particular to ensure that dialogue is constructive and is based on a mutual understanding of objectives. Particular concerns of investee companies addressed in the Code are as follows:

> ❭ *Consistency between institutions' corporate governance policies*: there is long-standing concern on the part of companies that the corporate governance policies adopted by individual institutions and voting agencies may involve expectations and standards which are inconsistent both with each other and with the provisions of the Combined Code itself. As an example, the Higgs Review discovered in 2002 that more than a dozen different definitions, all with different criteria, were being used by financial institutions to evaluate the independence of non-executive directors (NEDs). To counter this inconsistency of approach, Supporting Principle E.1 of the Combined Code recommended that all institutional shareholders should adopt the ISC *Statement of Principles on*

the Responsibilities of Institutional Shareholders and Agents, in particular by publishing clear statements of their policies.

> '*Box-ticking*': in the experience of companies, some institutions have tended to adopt an inflexible stance where companies have not complied in full with the recommendations of the Combined Code, despite the 'comply or explain' approach to corporate governance adopted in the Listing Rules. The 2003 Combined Code therefore recommended at Principle E.2 that institutional shareholders should:

– give due weight to all relevant factors drawn to their attention when evaluating companies' governance arrangements, particularly those relating to board structure and composition: in particular, they should consider carefully explanations given for departure from this Code and make reasoned judgments in each case, avoiding a 'box-ticking' approach to assessing a company's corporate governance; and

– give an explanation to the company, in writing where appropriate, and be prepared to enter a dialogue if they do not accept the company's position.

Evidence for increased engagement

Voting by institutions

There is some evidence of increased shareholder voting activity: according to data collected by the voting agency Manifest, the average voting level for FTSE 100 companies in the year to August 2005 was 59 per cent, compared to 54 per cent in 2003.

It is difficult, however, to establish the extent to which this represents a real increase in participation in voting by UK financial institutions. With a few notable exceptions (amongst them Prudential, Friends Provident and Co-operative Insurance Society), institutions have to date continued to be reluctant to publish their voting records. In line with the recommendations of the CLR, which identified a need for greater transparency in the way in which institutional investors exercise their powers, the Company Law Reform Bill introduced in Parliament in November 2005 seeks to give the Government reserve powers to require institutions to disclose their voting records if voluntary disclosure fails to deliver progress.

Implementation of Myners Principle 6

The implementation of the Myners Principles for Institutional Investment Decision-making is being monitored by HM Treasury, whose initial report, published in December 2004, found that pension schemes are taking action voluntarily on many of the areas covered by the Principles. However, progress with the promotion of shareholder engagement appears to be lagging: according to the report, only 25 per cent of schemes had reviewed their policies in relation to shareholder activism, while only 15 per cent had taken a formal decision to adopt a positive engagement policy.

Specific findings were that:

> pension fund trustees typically rely on the engagement policies of their investment managers, rather than developing their own approaches;

> trustees are not generally active in pushing fund managers to undertake share-holder engagement;

> the development of engagement activity continues to be impeded by perceived conflicts of interest facing both fund managers and trustees; and

> the quality of engagement, the extent to which engagement is integrated into the investment decision-making and asset management processes, the quantity and quality of resources committed by institutions to engagement and the level of qualitative reporting provided by fund managers to their clients have not increased at the rate envisaged by the Myners Report.

In response to these findings, the Government has indicated that it intends to strengthen Myners Principle 6 in order to make clear the responsibility of trustees for ensuring that appropriate shareholder engagement is undertaken. Intended detailed changes will require trustees to:

> comply with the ISC *Statement of Principles on the Responsibilities of Institutional Shareholders and Agents* (replacing the current reference to the US Labor Department Interpretative Bulletin);

> ensure that fund managers' mandates incorporate the ISC principles;

> ensure that fund managers have an explicit strategy, elucidating the circumstances in which they will intervene in a company, the approach they will use in doing so and how they will measure the effectiveness of this strategy; and

> monitor and evaluate the performance of fund managers against the ISC principles.

ISC review of implementation of Statement of Principles

A more upbeat assessment of the development of institutional engagement is given in the ISC's report, published in September 2005, on the implementation of its *Statement of Principles on the Responsibilities of Institutional Shareholders and Agents*. This suggests that there has been a significant change in the approach of institutional share-holders and their agents. Positive trends identified by the ISC include:

> increased engagement by fund managers in meetings with investee companies' independent directors to discuss issues and concerns, and more frequent communications with company management over and above routine meetings;

> express undertakings by a majority of fund managers to vote all their UK shares; and

> improved resourcing of engagement, including the employment by the majority of fund managers of specialist staff dedicated to engagement on corporate governance or social responsibility issues.

The ISC concluded on this basis that major revisions to the *Statement of Principles* were not needed. It recognised, however, that greater progress needs to be made by institutions, in particular to ensure that the corporate governance aspect of engagement is integrated with the investment process and to improve the interface between pension funds and fund managers, with greater emphasis on the quality of the fund managers' relationships with investee companies and the effectiveness of interventions undertaken.

Financial Reporting Council review of Combined Code 2003

During its broader review of progress made by companies and investors in implementing the 2003 Combined Code, the Financial Reporting Council (FRC) has also addressed the issue of investor engagement. Its report, published in January 2006, confirmed that dialogue between boards and their main shareholders is generally more constructive than previously. However, some concerns remain in specific areas identified in the Combined Code:

> *Consistency between institutions' corporate governance policies*: the FRC found that there is still a perception that some investment institutions and rating agencies apply criteria different to those set out in the Combined Code when assessing a company's corporate governance practices. In this context, the FRC welcomed the decision by Hermes, the fund manager responsible for the BT Pension Scheme, to discontinue its separate corporate governance guidelines in favour of the principles and provisions set out in the Combined Code, and encouraged other institutions to follow this example.

> The FRC also noted concerns that fund managers and corporate governance specialists within the same institution do not necessarily take a consistent position or place the same importance on governance issues. It drew attention to guidance on this issue produced by the IMA in October 2004, which recommended that institutions identify a lead contact for each of their investee companies, and urged institutions to adopt this as good practice.

> The IMA's guidance, *Relations with Investee Companies – Guidance on Good Practice*, is set out on pages 183–184.

> *Box-ticking*: the FRC's review found that most institutions strongly support the principle of 'comply or explain' and are generally willing to consider on their merits companies' explanations for governance practices which differ from those set out in the Combined Code. However, there is continuing concern that some institutions and rating agencies regard the Combined Code as a rigid set of rules, with the result that some companies adopt structures and practices which are compliant but sub-optimal rather than take the risk of explaining their circumstances.

> Pointing out that corporate governance is intended to support, not constrain, the board's ability to provide entrepreneurial leadership, the FRC underlined the need for companies to provide considered and meaningful explanations of their governance practices and for institutions to demonstrate that they are willing in principle to accept such explanations.

Responsibilities of the company and the board

Acting fairly as between shareholders

The company's directors, as the managers of its business, are responsible for controlling and directing the business in the interests of the shareholders as a whole. There is no legal expectation that shareholders' views will be consulted in detail, except where

Investment Management Association *Relations with Investee Companies – Guidance on Good Practice* **(October 2004)**

Introduction

This paper sets out a number of examples of good practice in communicating with the boards of investee companies, which the IMA Board commends to Members. It follows discussions earlier in 2004 with the Confederation of British Industry (CBI) at which a number of concerns were expressed.

The suggestions in this paper should not be read either as a mandatory or an exhaustive list.

They are intended to be examples drawn from experience which may help to facilitate good communications with the companies in which fund managers invest.

Facilitating understanding of the investment process

In certain instances, it may be necessary for managers to facilitate companies' understanding of the investment process. Examples are set out below:

- fund managers do not act as principals but are fiduciaries acting on behalf of their clients, the beneficial owners. In many cases, decisions about voting and other issues are delegated by the client to the fund manager, although some clients will give specific instructions, for example, to follow the recommendations of a particular voting service. As they act for different beneficial owners, fund managers may vote a particular block of shares different ways according to their clients' instructions.
- different fund managers may have different views, in which case they will vote their shares different ways.
- most company meetings with fund managers will be on issues about company strategy/performance and not on longer-term stewardship and

therefore are attended in the main by portfolio managers and research analysts. Fund managers often, however, employ governance experts, with voting and other agencies to assist, and in some cases these individuals may have different lines of communication with companies, for example, via the Company Secretary rather than the head of investor relations. Fund managers seek to ensure that different messages do not pass along these different channels of communication. If companies feel they do, then they should raise their concerns at an appropriately senior level (see below).

- most corporate governance issues are not price sensitive and communication between portfolio managers and corporate governance specialists does not raise conflicts of interest. However, in the few instances when information is price sensitive and conflicts do arise, Chinese walls operate between the corporate governance specialists and those that actively trade shares.

Providing clarity

The fact that different individuals handle different aspects of engagement can cause confusion in that companies may be unclear as to whom enquiries should be directed and how issues relating to engagement should be escalated as and when they arise.

Managers can help this by:

- making available to companies – perhaps by publishing on their website – a list of contacts within their forms, together with the issues each will cover;
- including in this, one individual as the nominated central contact point for companies, who is able to direct enquiries to the appropriate person to deal with, including those relating to voting matters; and *continued*

Investment Management Association *Relations with Investee Companies – Guidance on Good Practice* (October 2004) *continued*

- nominating a senior member of staff (perhaps the Chief executive or the Chief Investment Officer) as the person to whom a company Chairman or other senior individual can turn in the event on an issue having arisen which cannot be resolved otherwise.

Raising issues in a timely manner

If issues are raised in a timely manner then the parties involved may be able to resolve them easily. To facilitate this, IMA intends to discuss with the Institute of Chartered Secretaries and Administrators the development of a timetable as to when issues should be raised.

Communicating voting decisions

A particular concern of companies is that fund managers may sometimes vote against management without explaining why or vote against management when previous communications indicated that they were likely to support it. This is exacerbated by the fact that, as voting is concentrated in the Spring, the timeframes for discussion are inevitably limited.

The Institutional Shareholders' Committee's Statement of Principles on the Responsibilities of Institutional Shareholders and Agents states in Section 4: 'institutional shareholders and agents ... will not automatically support the board; if they have been unable to reach a satisfactory outcome through active dialogue then they will register an abstention or vote against the resolution. In both instances it is good practice to inform the company in advance of their intention and the reasons why.' In addition, the Combined code states that institutional shareholders have a responsibility to make considered use of their votes and to apply the principles set out by the Institutional Shareholders' Committee.

Specifically, therefore, fund managers could help meet these concerns by:

- agreeing to a dialogue with companies on their rationale for voting, particularly if that vote is negative (most already do this);
- alerting companies in advance to any negative vote; and
- where a vote is particularly contentious, making the appropriate level of seniority available to the Chairman of the company.

Media relations

There is a widespread perception that damage may be caused to relations between companies and fund managers by public disagreement and unattributed press comments. While the circumstances by which such comments come to appear are sometimes contentious – unattributed comments in the media may not always reflect the actual words used by an individual fund manager – there is no doubt about the potential harm that can be done.

Fund managers may therefore wish to consider a written policy on media relations and a list of individuals that are authorised to speak to the media, including procedures for those not authorised to seek temporary permission to do so.

the consent of the shareholders in general meeting is needed for specific proposals of the board.

Principles enshrined in company law and the Listing Rules seek to protect the interests of all investors by achieving an orderly market in the shares of listed companies and ensuring that all market participants, whether actual or potential, have simultaneous access to information on companies' performance and prospects. The principles are reflected in the continuing obligations of listed companies, under Chapter 9 of the Listing Rules, to ensure that:

> all companies make timely disclosure of information relevant to investment decisions, including information which might affect the price of their listed securities; and
> all shareholders are given equal access to the same relevant information.

Against this background, the proposition in successive codes of corporate governance that the board should maintain direct contact with a limited number of major shareholders has significant legal, regulatory and procedural implications for companies. This was recognised in the Cadbury Report, which acknowledged that institutions would inevitably have greater access to boards than would individual shareholders: given that boards could not put all shareholders on equal footing, they must be careful to ensure that any significant statements are made publicly and so are available to all shareholders.

Protection of price-sensitive information

The Listing Rules identify certain matters that a listed company must always announce to the market because they may lead to substantial movement in the price of the company's listed securities. These include:

> acquisitions and disposals above certain size criteria set out in the Listing Rules;
> interim and preliminary results and forthcoming and recommended dividends;
> board appointments and departures, and details of share dealings by directors or substantial shareholders;
> profit warnings; and
> rights issues and other offers of securities.

In addition to the matters specifically identified in the Listing Rules, listed companies have a general obligation of disclosure to give sufficient and timely information to the market as a whole on any major new developments, including any changes in their financial condition or in the actual or expected performance of their businesses, which are not already public knowledge and which, if known, may lead to a substantial movement (whether up or down) in the prices of their listed securities. In fulfilment of this obligation, an announcement must be made without delay by the listed company concerned, via one of the Regulatory Information Services (RISs) designated by the UKLA.

There are two main areas of uncertainty for the company in deciding whether an announcement is needed:

> *When is information already public knowledge?* Certain information, such as a change in UK interest rates, may be potentially price-sensitive information but will already be in the public domain. In these circumstances, the company

would not normally be required to make an announcement unless the change could have an unusual or disproportionate effect on its business. The FSA has pointed out that, just because it is possible for information to be obtained by the public, it does not necessarily make it 'public knowledge': in particular, if a fee is required to obtain information, or if its availability is not generally known, the information is not 'public knowledge' and the company must make an announcement.

> *What kinds of information are price-sensitive?* There is no definitive formula for determining what might constitute price-sensitive information: this will vary widely from company to company, depending on a company's size, developments in its recent past and activity in its sector. Major new developments, changes in the company's financial condition or business performance or changes in the expectation of future performance could all trigger a significant movement – up or down – in the company's share price. There are therefore many events which may need to be announced. These could include, for example: the launch of a new product or service; the failure of a particular product or service to meet expectations; the winning or placing of a large contract; the initiation of a major internal restructuring; or the discovery of a major technical defect or health hazard associated with a particular product or process.

In order to determine whether a particular item of information is potentially price sensitive, the company must be able to assess the likely impact of the information on the key factors which affect its share price, such as its reported earnings per share, pre-tax profits or borrowings. If the company believes that information may be price sensitive, it must make an announcement to the market without delay.

Management of investor relations

Given the constraints described above, any dialogue between a listed company and its institutional shareholders must be carefully planned, with clear objectives and procedures.

The directors have overall responsibility both for the control and dissemination of price-sensitive information and for maintaining a constructive dialogue with institutional shareholders. In practice, day-to-day activities in these areas are usually delegated to designated investor relations staff. In addition, listed companies are generally advised by their brokers on external financing and investment matters, and may also use the services of specialist financial communications consultants. It is therefore essential for listed companies to establish consistent procedures for the management of their investor relations. Key items should include the following:

> *A clear allocation of responsibilities*: in order to control the dissemination of price-sensitive information and reduce the chance of unauthorised or inadvertent disclosure, the company should identify those employees who have responsibility for communicating with shareholders, analysts and the press, and should

ensure that all employees so designated are kept aware of the company's policy and relevant legal and regulatory requirements. It should be made clear to all employees that, unless they have been given specific responsibility, they are prohibited from communicating information to anyone outside the company. In addition, the company should notify external parties, including institutional shareholders, analysts and the press, of the identity of those employees who are responsible for communicating with them and of the company's policies on the treatment of price-sensitive information.

> *Consistent treatment of price-sensitive information*: the company should establish a consistent procedure for determining what information is sufficiently significant for it to be price sensitive and for releasing that information to the market. For this purpose, the company, with the assistance of its advisers, should identify and keep under review the types of information that are likely to be price sensitive given the company's particular circumstances, and incorporating these in their communications policy.

> *Protection of price-sensitive information prior to announcement*: the company must make arrangements to keep price-sensitive information confidential until the moment of announcement: in particular, it must not allow such information to 'seep' into the public domain. All employees, whether they have regular or occasional access to price-sensitive information, must be made aware of the need at all times to observe the confidentiality of unpublished information given to them.

> *Content of announcements*: under the Listing Rules, a listed company must exercise a reasonable standard of care to ensure that its announcements are accurate and not misleading, present a balanced picture of its performance and prospects, and that price-sensitive information is given due prominence.

> *Making recipients of information 'insider'*: in some circumstances, the company may wish to disclose price-sensitive information in confidence to, for example, institutional shareholders or other parties with whom they are negotiating. Where this takes place, however, the recipients of the information will become 'insiders' and will be unable to deal in the company's shares until after the information has been announced to the market. For this reason, potential recipients will not necessarily wish to become 'insiders' and the company must therefore have an established procedure for obtaining the consent of potential recipients before any price-sensitive information is disclosed to them.

Detailed advice on the obligations of listed companies to protect price-sensitive information can be found on the FSA's website at www.fsa.gov.uk.

Involvement of the board

In many listed companies, contact with institutional shareholders has traditionally been regarded as the primary responsibility of the chief executive officer (CEO) and the finance director, with the support of the chairman and the other executive directors. This was confirmed in research carried out on behalf of the Higgs Review, which found that NEDs were rarely involved in discussions with major shareholders: under normal circumstances, there was therefore little communication, and direct contact was likely to be made only when there was a serious problem. In consequence, there were few opportunities to develop mutual understanding of the roles of NEDs and institutional shareholders. As a result, NEDs often perceived institutions as distant and disengaged, while institutions experienced difficulty in making contact with NEDs in order to discuss issues in a timely manner.

The 2003 Combined Code recognised that most shareholder contact is with the chief executive and finance director, but emphasised that the board as a whole should keep in touch with shareholder opinion. To this end, Combined Code Provision D.1.1 recommends that:

> *the chairman* should discuss governance and strategy with major shareholders and should ensure that the views of shareholders are communicated to the board as a whole;

> *NEDs* should be offered the opportunity to attend meetings with major shareholders, and should expect to attend such meetings if requested to do so by major shareholders;

> *the senior independent director* should attend sufficient meetings with a range of major shareholders to develop a balanced understanding of their issues and concerns.

In addition, Provision D.1.2 requires the board to disclose in the annual report and accounts the steps taken to ensure that the board, and in particular the NEDs, are able to develop an understanding of the views of major shareholders about the company.

Implementation of the Combined Code provisions by listed companies

In its review of the implementation of the 2003 Combined Code, the FRC found that, in the overwhelming view of respondents, the overall standard of corporate governance in listed companies has improved since the introduction of the revised Code in 2003. Similarly, investors consider that the overall quality of disclosure in annual reports has improved (although there is still scope for corporate governance statements to be more informative, particularly on how the principles of the Combined Code have been applied, with company-specific explanations when the company chooses not to follow the provisions of the Code).

Both companies and institutions reported that the revised Combined Code has contributed to an overall improvement in the level and quality of the dialogue between boards and institutional investors: relations are generally more constructive than previously, with company chairmen in particular taking a more proactive approach in meeting institutional investors. In the light of these findings, the FRC has not proposed any changes to the current provisions of the Combined Code which deal with the responsibilities of companies for maintaining constructive dialogue with institutions.

Chapter summary

> There is growing recognition of the obligation on institutions, as fiduciaries acting on behalf of underlying savers and investors, to exercise their voting powers actively and responsibly, when necessary by voting against board resolutions where companies have declined to address the legitimate concerns of shareholders.

> In addition, there is increasing emphasis on the need for closer relationships between company boards and institutional shareholders, both to enable directors to gain a proper understanding of the issues and concerns of major shareholders and to provide institutions with a channel of communication with the board on issues of concern.

> The expectation in codes of corporate governance that boards of listed companies should establish and maintain an active dialogue with major shareholders has significant legal, regulatory and procedural implications, given the presumption in law that all shareholders should be treated equally.

> Boards must therefore take care to ensure that any information disclosed to institutions and market intermediaries is also made available to shareholders as a whole.

> Dialogue between listed companies and their institutional shareholders must be carefully planned, with clear objectives and procedures and consistent treatment of price-sensitive information.

14

Constructive use of the AGM

> The board should use the AGM to communicate with investors and to encourage their participation.
>
> Combined Code (2003) Main Principle D.2

This chapter considers the part played by the AGM in the governance relationship between the company's owners and its directors. It focuses on:

> ❭ the requirement to convene an AGM and to provide advance notice to those entitled to attend and vote, including the use of electronic communications for this purpose;
> ❭ the use of formal resolutions to put forward the business of the AGM, including the rights of shareholders to propose their own resolutions;
> ❭ arrangements for voting on resolutions, in person and by proxy; and
> ❭ best practice for the open and constructive conduct of business at the AGM.

In each area, the chapter examines current statutory and regulatory requirements and considers the intended legal changes set out in the Company Law Reform Bill, including measures to improve the timeliness of the AGM and to extend participation rights to investors whose shares are held indirectly.

While this chapter focuses on the AGM, other types of shareholder meeting, particularly extraordinary general meetings (EGMs) and court meetings, are convened with increasing frequency in connection with corporate transactions. The legal and other technical arrangements for meetings of these types are outside the scope of this book, but the need for open, constructive and courteous debate is the same for all meetings between shareholders and directors.

Introduction

Under current legislation all companies – whether public or private – are required to hold a general meeting at least once a year, at which the annual accounts are laid before the members. Private companies are permitted to dispense with this requirement, but only if an explicit resolution to this effect has been passed by all members.

It was recognised by the Company Law Review (CLR) that the obligation to hold an AGM is burdensome for all companies and that, for a small private company with few shareholders, a formal AGM may be irrelevant to the conduct of the company's business. In the light of this finding, the Company Law Reform Bill seeks to abolish the current requirement for private companies to hold AGMs (although those private companies that wish to continue to hold AGMs will be able to do so voluntarily).

The CLR also considered whether public companies should be permitted to opt out of the requirement to hold an AGM, subject to the unanimous agreement of their members. Following extensive consultation, the Government concluded that such a provision would have little practical application, in that it is very unlikely that a public company would be able to demonstrate that not a single shareholder wished to hold an AGM. The current statutory requirement for all public companies to hold AGMs will therefore continue.

In listed companies, the pattern of attendance and voting in person at the AGM is generally unrepresentative of the true balance of share ownership. As discussed elsewhere in this book, the great majority of shares, and hence voting rights, in listed companies are typically held by a relatively small number of financial institutions, whose relationship with the company's management is conducted as a continuing dialogue outside the forum of general meetings. Although institutions are actively encouraged to vote on resolutions proposed at the AGM, they generally do so by proxy and their active participation in AGMs is comparatively rare.

Because AGM attendance is typically dominated by private shareholders who do not exercise significant voting power, directors have sometimes been reluctant to devote significant time and effort to the meeting. However, there is strong evidence that private shareholders value the AGM as an opportunity – often the only one available to them – to meet the company's directors face to face and to voice their opinions about the company's affairs. Moreover, as Sir Adrian Cadbury points out in his book *Corporate Governance and Chairmanship: A Personal View* (2002):

> '...Chairmen who pride themselves on the speed with which their AGMs are con-cluded are losing sight of the advantages to be won from encouraging shareholders to ask questions. Such questions give chairmen a feel for the issues which are on the minds of shareholders and in answering them they have the chance to put forward the company's point of view, persuasively and in a public forum.'

Convening the meeting

Frequency and timing of AGM

Current requirements

Public companies are required to hold an AGM in each calendar year. Under current legislation, the AGM must be held in time to allow the annual report and accounts to be laid before the shareholders not more than seven months after the end of the financial year to which they relate, with each AGM taking place no more than 15 months after the previous year's meeting.

As a general rule, it is for the directors of the company to call general meetings. However, under existing and prospective legislation, shareholders holding 10 per cent or more of the company's voting share capital are able to require the directors to call a general meeting. Until lately, this provision has been little used, but in recent years institutional investors have been increasingly willing to requisition general meetings as a means of challenging, and sometimes removing, directors: notable examples are British Land (targeted by the hedge fund Laxey Partners) and SkyePharma (targeted by a group of institutions comprising North Atlantic Value, Morley Fund Management and Insight Investment).

The requirement for the annual report and accounts to be laid at the AGM has given rise to the standard practice of despatching the AGM notice, the related proxy voting materials and the annual report and accounts (or the annual review and summary financial statement where relevant) to shareholders as a single package.

For listed companies, the date of issue of the annual report and accounts and the AGM notice, and hence the date of the AGM itself, are generally determined by reference to the timing of the company's preliminary results announcement. This linkage arises from the requirements of the Listing Rules, which stipulate that:

> ❯ a listed company must issue a preliminary statement of its annual results, including, as a minimum, a balance sheet, profit and loss account and cash flow statement) within 120 days of its financial year-end;
> ❯ the presentation of audited financial information in the annual report and accounts should be consistent with that in the preliminary results announcement; and
> ❯ to minimise the risk of inconsistency, the annual report and accounts should be published as soon as practicable following approval by the directors.

In combination, these requirements dictate that, under normal circumstances, the preliminary results announcement and the annual report and accounts should be approved by the directors and signed off by the company's external auditors immediately prior to the results announcement, and the annual report and accounts should be published as quickly as possible thereafter. In practice, several weeks can elapse between the results announcement and publication, particularly in companies with large shareholder registers where long print runs and complex mailing operations are needed.

Proposed legislative changes

The CLR was critical of some aspects of current year-end reporting requirements, which in its view fail to ensure timely and equitable shareholder access to company information. Reflecting these concerns, the Company Law Reform Bill contains measures designed to speed up the reporting process, in particular through enhanced use of electronic communications, in order to ensure that all shareholders have timely opportunities to hold directors to account for company performance. To this end, the Bill proposes the following:

> ❯ To ensure that the generality of shareholders have access to any new and potentially price-sensitive information about the company's position and performance

set out in the preliminary statement of annual results, quoted companies should post their preliminary results announcements on their websites immediately after release to the market, with email notifications to those shareholders who have requested them.

> Similarly, quoted companies should publish their AGM notices and full annual report and accounts on their websites as soon as reasonably practicable, again with email notifications to those shareholders who have requested them (although hard copies of the AGM notice and the annual report and accounts, or annual review/summary financial statement where applicable, will still have to be sent to those shareholders who wish to receive the documents in printed form).

> Public companies should in future to hold their AGMs (also described in the Bill as the 'accounts meeting') within six months of each financial year-end.

A further recommendation of the CLR was that the annual report and accounts of quoted companies should be published in advance of the AGM notice, such that the annual reports and accounts would be posted on the company's website no later than 120 days after the year-end. Publication would be followed by a 15-day 'holding period' during which shareholders could consider the contents of the annual report and accounts and, if they so wished, requisition AGM resolutions. On expiry of the holding period, the AGM notice would be finalised and circulated to shareholders with the annual report and accounts.

This recommendation was initially accepted by the Government and appeared in early draft legislation, but has not been incorporated in the Company Law Reform Bill. Instead, as explained in this chapter, shareholders in public companies will be able to require the company to circulate resolutions and any accompanying statement at the company's expense (rather than their own) if the materials are provided to the company before the end of the financial year.

Notice requirements

Under current and proposed legislation, the directors of a public company must ensure that written notice of the AGM is sent to those entitled to receive it at least 21 clear days before the date of the meeting (or longer if required by the company's Articles). For listed companies, the Combined Code recommends that the AGM notice and related documents are sent to shareholders at least 20 *working* days before the meeting.

A general meeting may be called on shorter notice if the requisite majority of members agree. For public companies, the majority required to agree a short notice period is (and will remain) 95 per cent of the voting rights.

Entitlement to receive notice

Current requirements

The right to receive notice of the AGM is currently limited to those shareholders who are entitled to attend, speak and vote at the meeting. This entitlement is restricted at present to registered shareholders, with the result that underlying beneficial owners –

whether institutional or private investors – who hold their shares through a corporate sponsored nominee, ISA or other intermediary have no direct governance rights in relation to their shares. Such indirect investors are thus effectively disenfranchised unless the intermediary, as the registered shareholder, undertakes to pass on company information and to accept investors' instructions as to how their shares should be voted.

Proposed legislative changes

In the course of its review, the CLR considered the rights of persons other than registered shareholders and made a number of recommendations designed to make it easier for underlying investors to exercise their governance rights. In the light of these recommendations, the Company Law Reform Bill seeks to enable companies to amend their Articles to allow registered holders to nominate someone else (such as an underlying beneficial owner) to exercise some or all of their shareholder rights, including the right to receive notice of the AGM and to attend, speak and vote at the meeting. The proposed changes will apply to all companies, but will have most relevance to public and quoted companies. The Government has indicated that, if sufficient companies do not change their Articles, it will consider making regulations to give registered shareholders automatic rights of nomination. Related proposals to enhance the rights of proxies are described at page 198.

Contents of AGM notice

The AGM notice must give the date, time and location of the meeting and specify the business to be conducted in sufficient detail to enable recipients to decide whether to attend the meeting. The notice must identify any special resolutions (see page 195) and give details of shareholders' rights in respect of the meeting, including the right to appoint a proxy (see page 198).

Business of AGM

The formal business to be transacted at the AGM is set out in the notice in the form of resolutions for discussion and approval. The Combined Code recommends that each substantially separate matter for discussion and approval should be the subject of a separate resolution and vote. This is intended to prevent the practice of combining in a single resolution two or more issues, one popular and one contentious, in the hope that the contentious issue will be carried 'under cover' of the more popular proposal.

Currently, the great majority of the resolutions proposed at AGMs originate with the company's directors although, as discussed below, statutory changes are proposed to make it easier for shareholders to propose their own resolutions.

Resolutions proposed by directors

Ordinary resolutions

Unless another type of resolution is specified by law or the company's Articles, the business of the AGM will take the form of ordinary resolutions. The routine business of the AGM – including receipt of the company's annual report and accounts, receipt of the directors' remuneration report, approval of any dividend recommended by the directors, appointment and reappointment of directors, and appointment and remuneration of the company's external auditors – can be passed by ordinary resolution. Where voting is by show of hands (see page 199), an ordinary resolution can be passed by a simple majority of the votes cast by shareholders present at the meeting.

Special resolutions

Proposals for significant changes to the company's constitution – such as amendments to the Memorandum and Articles, change of name, disapplication of members' pre-emption rights and reductions in share capital – must be approved by the members in general meeting, either at the AGM or at an EGM convened for the purpose. In either case, the proposal must be set out in the form of a special resolution: where voting is by show of hands, a three-fourths majority of those present at the meeting and voting in person or by proxy is required to pass a special resolution.

Directors must ensure that special resolutions are identified as such in the notice of meeting, that the required period of notice is given and that all resolutions, whether ordinary or special, are passed by appropriate majorities.

Other forms of resolution

Two further forms of resolution are currently recognised by company law, but are expected to be abolished by the Company Law Reform Bill:

> *Extraordinary resolutions* must be passed by a three-fourths majority, but are required only for certain matters connected with winding up or where a class meeting is asked to agree to a modification of class rights. The Company Law Reform Bill envisages that the matters currently covered by extraordinary resolutions will in future by the subject of special resolutions.

> *Elective resolutions* are available only to private companies and, if passed unanimously, enable such companies to 'opt out' of certain statutory requirements (including the obligation to hold an AGM). The simplified arrangements for private companies envisaged by the Company Law Reform Bill are intended to make 'opt out' unnecessary, and no provision will be made for elective resolutions.

Resolutions proposed by shareholders

Current arrangements

Currently, shareholders have the right to require the company to circulate, at the expense of the shareholders making the request, a resolution proposed by the shareholders or a statement of not more than 1,000 words relating to the resolution or to any other business of the AGM. The request for circulation must be given by either:

> no fewer than 100 shareholders holding shares with an average paid-up value of not less than £100; or

> shareholders holding 5 per cent or more of the voting rights at the relevant meeting.

RESPONDING TO SHAREHOLDER RESOLUTIONS

Under current and proposed legislation, a company may be relieved of its obligation to circulate a shareholder resolution where the court is satisfied that its purpose is to secure publicity for defamatory material. Otherwise, there are no formal restrictions on the subject matter of shareholder resolutions, provided that they are requisitioned on time and with the appropriate level of shareholder support.

Although in the past some companies have declined, or attempted to decline, to circulate shareholder resolutions on the grounds that they were imprecise or otherwise invalid, impeding legislative changes are clearly intended to make it easier for shareholders to propose their own resolutions and to have them circulated at the company's, rather than their own, expense. There is therefore an obvious danger that the use of technicalities to avoid discussion on shareholder resolutions will be viewed externally as censorship, with adverse effects on the reputation of the company and its directors.

For a resolution, a written requisition accompanied by the signatures of all the shareholders making the request must be lodged with the company not less than six weeks before the meeting. For a statement, the written requisition and accompanying signatures must be lodged at least one week before the meeting.

A company may be relieved of its obligation to circulate a shareholder resolution where the court is satisfied that its purpose is to secure publicity for defamatory material. Otherwise, there are no formal restrictions on the subject matter of shareholder resolutions, provided that they are requisitioned on time and with the appropriate level of shareholder support.

Shareholder resolutions are regularly used by pressure groups to draw attention to aspects of company conduct in respect of human rights and the environment. In recent years, prominent companies such as BP, Shell, Balfour Beatty and Rio Tinto have been the targets of shareholder resolutions of this kind.

Proposed legislative changes

As part of its examination of shareholder participation in governance, the CLR concluded that it should be made easier for shareholders to requisition their own resolutions.

In the light of the CLR's recommendations, the Company Law Reform Bill proposes to permit requests to be made in electronic form and remove the requirement for the shareholders concerned to cover the company's costs in circulating a resolution or statement, provided that the material and accompanying signatures are received before the company's financial year-end.

The Bill leaves unchanged the current numerical requirements in respect of shareholder support and specifies in addition that the shares relied on to support a

The directors and company secretary should therefore:

- ensure that the dates of forthcoming AGMs are published well in advance in company documents and websites so that the appropriate deadlines are clear to prospective requisitionists;
- decide in principle whether requisitions will be accepted from indirect investors or only from registered shareholders, communicate this decision to the company's share registrars and apply it consistently to all requisitions;
- agree arrangements with the share registrars for timely validation of all requisitions received; and
- decide in principle whether the company will waive its existing right to demand that successful requisitionists should pay for the circulation of their resolution and accompanying statement, given proposed legislative changes to require companies to absorb the costs of circulation.

requisition must carry specific rights to vote on the subject matter of the resolution, rather than just a general right to vote at the meeting.

Voting

Right to vote

As a general rule, ownership of an ordinary share in a listed company confers the right to vote on any question put before the shareholders in general meeting.

Voting rights are defined in the company's Articles and will typically provide that shareholders attending in person are entitled to speak at the meeting, to demand or join in a demand for a poll and to participate in any vote, whether by show of hands or by poll. Corporate representatives appointed by institutional investors and other corporate shareholders are also entitled to speak, demand or join in a demand for a poll and to participate in any vote (although only one representative from each corporate shareholder is permitted to vote). Proxies attending the meeting on behalf of a shareholder may vote in the event that a poll is called, and may also join in a demand for a poll; however, proxies are not entitled to vote on a show of hands, nor are they entitled to speak unless permitted to do so by the chairman of the meeting.

Much of company law in its current form assumes that, in normal circumstances, decisions at general meetings will be taken by those physically present at the meeting. In these circumstances, voting will usually be by show of hands on the basis of one vote per shareholder. Unless a poll is called, no account will be taken of the relative sizes of shareholdings or of the wishes of shareholders who are not present but who have appointed proxies to whom they have given instructions as to how their votes are to be used.

The difficulty with this approach is that voting by show of hands does not reflect the real distribution of ownership and voting power within the company. As explained in the introduction to this chapter, institutional investors will typically hold the great majority of shares and voting rights, but will usually vote in advance and by proxy, rather than attending the meeting. Where decisions are taken by show of hands at general meetings, participation is therefore typically limited to small numbers of private investors.

Voting by proxy

Appointing a proxy

Under the Companies Act 1985 (CA 1985), any shareholder who is entitled to attend and vote at a general meeting is also entitled to appoint another person to attend and vote on his or her behalf in the event that a poll is called. Shareholders must be advised in the notice of meeting of their right to appoint a proxy.

In listed companies, shareholders who do not intend to go to the meeting are typically invited to appoint the chairman of the meeting as their proxy: however, shareholders have the right to nominate anyone of their choosing (who need not be a shareholder). Having appointed a proxy or proxies, the shareholders may indicate how their votes are to be used in the event that a poll is called on one or more of the resolutions; alternatively, the proxy may be given discretion to vote as he or she sees fit, having heard the discussion at the meeting.

Traditionally, companies have sent pre-printed proxy forms to shareholders with the AGM notice and associated documents. More recently, however, the principal firms of share registrars have offered facilities to enable shareholders to appoint a proxy and lodge their voting instructions electronically using a secure website or to give the necessary instructions by telephone.

Whether paper-based or electronic, proxy appointments and voting instructions must be received by the company (or, where appropriate, its share registrar) no later than 48 hours before the meeting. Where shareholders have given instructions as to how their votes should be cast in the event of a poll, the total instructions to vote for, vote against or abstain on each resolution will be counted in advance of the meeting.

Rights of proxies

As noted above, proxies are not currently entitled to speak at a general meeting or to vote by show of hands. Alongside the proposed enhancements to the rights of beneficial holders described above, the Company Law Reform Bill sets out provisions to extend the rights of proxies to enable indirect investors who have been appointed as proxies by an intermediary to exercise the same participation rights as registered shareholders. Under these provisions, proxies will be able to speak at general meetings and to vote, both by show of hands and on a poll.

Voting at meetings

The conduct of voting at the AGM is the responsibility of the chairman, to whom relevant authorities are generally given in the company's Articles. These include authority to rule on any question of the validity of votes cast at the meeting, to declare the result of any vote taken by show of hands and to demand that a poll be taken. Where voting is by show of hands, the chairman will normally have a casting vote in the event of an equality of votes.

Voting by show of hands

Where voting is by show of hands, the chairman of the meeting will normally ask for those present at the meeting to indicate whether they are for or against each resolution by raising the voting card handed to them on arrival at the meeting. With the help of the company secretary, he or she will then visually assess the votes for and against each resolution and declare the outcome immediately.

It is not usually necessary for a formal count to be made of a show of hands on an ordinary resolution, where a visual check alone should be sufficient to establish whether there is a simple majority for or against a resolution. However, it may be necessary to account a show of hands on a special resolution, which must be passed by a 75 per cent majority, or otherwise if a show of hands is very close. Where a count is needed on a show of hands, it is generally carried out by scrutineers provided by the company's share registrars.

Voting by poll

The chairman of the meeting has absolute authority to call for a poll if he or she thinks fit, and must do so if the outcome of a show of hands is unclear. Shareholders, corporate representatives and proxies present at the meeting may also call for a poll, which must be held if the demand is supported by not less than five shareholders entitled to vote.

Until recently, voting at AGMs has typically been by show of hands, with polls being taken by exception where the outcome of voting is unclear or where the question before the meeting is controversial. The growing demand for transparency, particularly in relation to the exercise of institutional voting powers, has prompted an increasing number of listed companies to change their Articles to enable polls to be conducted automatically on all resolutions put to shareholders in general meeting. During the 2005 calendar year, polls were held on all resolutions at the AGMs of nearly 40 per cent of FTSE 100 companies. There is no currently no provision in the Company Law Reform Bill for the introduction of compulsory polling under UK legislation. However, the draft EC Directive on shareholders' rights proposes that all votes cast in relation to a resolution should be taken into account.

Where a poll is required, the process will usually be carried out by the company's share registrars at the direction of the chairman or company secretary. There are two basic polling methodologies:

> *Manual*: pre-printed poll cards are either handed to shareholders, corporate representatives and proxies on arrival at the meeting or distributed by hand when a poll is called. The completed poll cards (including poll cards held by chairman and other directors as proxies for shareholders) are then collected by the share registrars' representatives and taken away for manual verification and counting.
> *Electronic*: share registrars are now able to provide each shareholder, corporate representative and proxy, on arrival at the meeting, with electronic voting handsets programmed according to the number of shares held using data derived from the company's shareholder register. When a poll is called, votes are cast using the handsets, providing almost immediate poll results and an electronic audit trail.

Disclosing proxy votes

The Combined Code recommends that the company should count and record all proxy votes lodged by post in advance of the meeting and that, where a resolution has been dealt with on a show of hands, the level of proxy votes lodged for and against should be announced. The numbers of proxy votes lodged can be disclosed at the AGM in various ways, including an oral announcement by the chairman, the screening of a slide showing the relevant numbers, or the production of a printed slip which can be given to interested shareholders at the end of the meeting. Irrespective of the method used at the meeting, the company should also publish on its website the details of the proxy votes lodged: guidance on disclosure is set out in the ICSA's *Guidance Note: Disclosing Proxy Votes*, reproduced in *Appendix 18*.

Proposals set out in the Company Law Reform Bill will give statutory force to existing best practice by requiring quoted companies to disclose on a website the results of all polls taken at a general meeting.

Independent assessment of poll procedure

In addition, the Company Law Reform Bill sets out intended new provisions to give members of a quoted company the right to demand independent assessment of any poll taken at a general meeting, for example on a controversial resolution or where there appears to be a problem relating to voting procedures. The demand must be supported by shareholders holding 5 per cent of the company's voting share capital rights or of 100 shareholders holding on average £100 of paid-up capital, and must be made within one week of the meeting at which the poll is taken.

Where an independent assessment is requested by shareholders, the assessor must be not be an employee of the company or otherwise involved in the voting process on behalf of the company; however, the company's external auditor is permitted to be appointed as the independent assessor. The independent assessor's report must as a minimum give an opinion as to whether the procedures adopted in connection with the poll or polls were adequate, the votes cast (including proxy votes) were fairly and accurately recorded and counted, the validity of members' appointments of proxies was fairly assessed, and the notice of meeting and invitation to appoint proxies complied with relevant statutory requirements. The company will be required to publish the independent assessor's report on a website.

Conduct of meeting

Formal requirements

As a minimum, the directors and the company secretary must ensure that the business of the AGM is conducted in compliance with statutory requirements and the provisions of the company's Articles so that the validity of the meeting and of the resolutions, once approved, is not open to challenge. However, compliance with formal requirements may be insufficient by itself to ensure that the AGM functions effectively as a forum for debate between the shareholders and directors.

Thus, the Combined Code emphasises the need to keep shareholders informed and enable them to comment on the work of the main board committees and issues of corporate governance generally. To this end, it recommends that the chairmen of the audit, remuneration and nomination committees should attend the AGM, where the opportunity should be given to shareholders to put questions to them.

In practice, many public and listed companies have expanded the business of the AGM beyond the basic statutory requirements, for example by opening the meeting with a presentation, often by the chairman, on the company's performance over the past year and by inviting questions from shareholders. While such developments are clearly in the spirit of the Combined Code recommendations, care must be taken to ensure that there is no inadvertent disclosure, in presentations or answers to shareholders' questions, of price-sensitive information which has not already been announced to the market. Further information on the obligations of listed companies to identify and manage price-sensitive information is given in *Chapter 13*.

Role of chairman

The role of the chairman, supported as necessary by the company secretary, is critical to the proper conduct of the AGM. Although it is possible in principle for another person – another director or, in the absence of any directors, one of the shareholders present – to chair the AGM, it is customary for the chairman of the board to chair the meeting.

This involves a potential conflict of interest: as a director of the company, the chairman has a vested interest in securing the shareholders' approval for the resolutions proposed by the board. Against this, as the chairman of the meeting, he or she is responsible to the shareholders present for ensuring that the AGM is conducted fairly and openly and that there is an opportunity for all shades of opinion, including those critical of the directors, to be expressed. It is important for the chairman to recognise that, although the voting rights of different shareholders vary with the size of their respective ownership interests in the company, all shareholders are equally entitled to

Organising the AGM

Holding the AGM is complex and expensive, involving time-consuming preparations which are generally the responsibility of the company secretary. Key tasks include the following:

Advance preparation:
- ensuring that the date of the AGM is included in the programme of board meetings and the financial calendar in the annual report and accounts and on the company's website;
- booking the venue for the AGM and ensuring that the venue is big enough and has adequate overflow facilities, with appropriate audio-visual links, in case of unexpectedly large shareholder attendance.

Between the posting of the AGM notice and the date of the meeting:
- monitoring the progress of proxy voting, with particular attention to proxy votes lodged against resolutions proposed by the directors;
- collating any manuscript comments written on returned proxy cards – these can be a valuable source of intelligence on the questions shareholders are likely to ask at the AGM;
- considering with the directors possible shareholder questions and how to deal with them;
- preparing the chairman's opening address and other presentations by directors;
- finalising venue arrangements, including shareholder registration, catering, marshalling and security;

- arranging facilities for shareholders with special needs, including sign language interpreters and wheelchair access.

In the 48 hours before the meeting:
- checking all venue arrangements;
- running through possible shareholders' questions with directors – if possible as part of a full dress rehearsal at the meeting venue;
- where any pool would be carried out manually, preparing poll cards and identification cards for shareholders and corporate representatives, proxies and non-voting observers and arranging with the share registrar for these to be handed to attendees on arrival at the meeting;
- arranging for the register of members, directors' service contracts and other documents for inspection to be available at the venue and other designated locations;
- arranging for the announcement, via a designated Regulatory Information Service, of any potentially price-sensitive information to be disclosed at the AGM, including the outcome of voting on resolutions where appropriate;
- arranging for publication of voting results on all resolutions, including abstentions, on the company's website or an appropriate alternative as soon as possible following the meeting.

attend and participate in the AGM. These rights extend to pressure groups with token holdings, and companies are not entitled to discriminate against them.

In this context, the directors of public companies should consider whether speaking rights should automatically be extended to proxies attending the AGM on behalf of shareholders who are not able to be present in person. A decision on the speaking rights of proxies should be taken in advance of the AGM and applied consistently at the meeting.

Order of business

At the advertised time for the start of the AGM, the company secretary should check that the necessary quorum is present: unless the company's Articles specify a different quorum, the meeting is quorate when two shareholders are present. The chairman will then typically propose that the AGM notice be taken as read, although the company secretary should be ready to read out the notice of AGM if the meeting so determines.

Once these formalities have been concluded, the chairman will normally explain the procedures to be adopted for the conduct of the meeting. In addition, he or she will often make an opening statement on the company's performance and prospects, handing over as appropriate to the chief executive officer (CEO) or any other director who is to make a presentation to shareholders or explain a particular aspect of the company's business. As a general rule, the chairman will then invite shareholders' questions and comments on each of the resolutions appearing in the AGM notice. The chairman may answer shareholders' questions in person, or may hand over to one or more of the other directors for reply.

The chairman must ensure that any ensuing debate between shareholders and directors is properly and fairly conducted and that an opportunity is provided for shareholders present to express their opinions. While all shareholders have a right to speak at the AGM, this does not necessarily imply that everyone who wishes to must be allowed to address the meeting: however, it does mean that the business of the meeting must not be rushed or unduly curtailed, perhaps to avoid discussion on matters which the directors regard as inconvenient.

After a reasonable period for debate on each resolution, the chairman should wind up the discussion, formally propose the resolution and invite the shareholders present to vote on it, as described at page pages 198–199.

Dealing with interruptions

The chairman's responsibility for ensuring the orderly and businesslike conduct of the AGM may involve a requirement to adjudicate, with the help of the company secretary, on points of order and a variety of other potential interruptions to the flow of business. The company secretary should therefore have ready procedural notes covering all reasonably foreseeable types of event and may also find it helpful to have a telephone link to assistants backstage.

In a small number of cases, protests and other forms of deliberate disruption to the AGM have led to the forcible removal of individual shareholders, or even to the adjournment or abandonment of the meeting. While it is of course essential for the chairman and company secretary to ensure the orderly conduct of business and the safety of everyone present, it is also important to distinguish between genuine disruption and persistent but proper questioning of the directors and to avoid an inappropriately heavy-handed response.

Chapter summary

› Although institutional shareholders control the great majority of voting shares in most large and public companies, the AGM provides the opportunity for private shareholders to hold the directors to account for company performance, to ask questions about the directors' stewardship of their assets and to express their own opinions.

› Constructive use of the AGM depends on careful advance planning to ensure that all shareholders receive high quality and timely information about the company and the business of the AGM, together with sensitive chairing of the meeting to facilitate open discussion and mutual respect in which all shades of shareholder opinion can be debated.

› Proposed legislative changes will speed up the year-end reporting timetable so as to ensure that all shareholders have timely opportunities to hold directors to account for company performance.

› Legislative changes are also proposed to enhance the rights of beneficial owners to participate in governance, extend the rights of proxies and increase the transparency of shareholder voting.

› To enable the AGM to function effectively as a forum for debate, shareholders present at the meeting should have the opportunity to ask questions about the company's business, the work of the board and its main committees and issues of corporate governance generally.

Source materials

Part 3 of the Handbook contains the text of the relevant reports, documents and Codes referred to in Parts 1 and 2.

Appendix 1	Combined Code of Corporate Governance (July 2003)	207
Appendix 2	Association of British Insurers: Disclosure Guidelines on Socially Responsible Investment (October 2001)	225
Appendix 3	ICSA Guidance Note: Matters Reserved for the Board (November 2003)	229
Appendix 4	ICSA Guidance Note: Terms of Reference – Executive Committees (September 2004)	232
Appendix 5	ICSA Guidance Note: Directors' and Officers' Insurance (April 2005)	237
Appendix 6	ICSA Guidance Note: Due Diligence for Directors (July 2003)	245
Appendix 7	ICSA Guidance Note: Induction of Directors (February 2003)	248
Appendix 8	ICSA Code of Good Boardroom Practice	252
Appendix 9	ICSA Guidance Note: Terms of Reference – Nomination Committee (October 2003)	254

Appendix 10   Association of British Insurers: Principles and
              Guidelines on Remuneration (December
              2005)   259

Appendix 11   ICSA Guidance Note: Terms of Reference
              – Remuneration Committee (October 2003)   273

Appendix 12   Association of British Insurers and National
              Association of Pension Funds: Joint Statement
              on Best Practice on Executive Contracts and
              Severance (December 2005)   278

Appendix 13   ICSA Guidance Note: Terms of Reference –
              Audit Committee (October 2003)   283

Appendix 14   Combined Code of Corporate Governance:
              Smith Guidance on Audit Committees
              (July 2003)   289

Appendix 15   Smith Report: Outline Report to
              Shareholders on the Activities of the Audit
              Committee   300

Appendix 16   Financial Reporting Council: Internal Control
              – Revised Guidance for Directors on the
              Combined Code (October 2005)   301

Appendix 17   Institutional Shareholders' Committee:
              The Responsibilities of Institutional
              Shareholders and Agents – Statement of
              Principles (September 2005)   310

Appendix 18   ICSA Guidance Note: Disclosing Proxy
              Votes (August 2004)   314

Appendix I

COMBINED CODE OF CORPORATE GOVERNANCE
(July 2003)

PREAMBLE

1. This Code supersedes and replaces the Combined Code issued by the Hampel Committee on Corporate Governance in June 1998. It derives from a review of the role and effectiveness of non-executive directors by Derek Higgs[1] and a review of audit committees[2] by a group led by Sir Robert Smith.

2. The Financial Services Authority has said that it will replace the 1998 Code that is annexed to the Listing Rules with the revised Code and will seek to make consequential Rule changes. There will be consultation on the necessary Rule changes but not further consultation on the Code provisions themselves.

3. It is intended that the new Code will apply for reporting years beginning on or after 1 November 2003.

4. The Code contains main and supporting principles and provisions. The existing Listing Rules require listed companies to make a disclosure statement in two parts in relation to the Code. In the first part of the statement, the company has to report on how it applies the principles in the Code. In future this will need to cover both main and supporting principles. The form and content of this part of the statement are not prescribed, the intention being that companies should have a free hand to explain their governance policies in the light of the principles, including any special circumstances applying to them which have led to a particular approach. In the second part of the statement the company has either to confirm that it complies with the Code's provisions or – where it does not – to provide an explanation. This 'comply or explain' approach has been in operation for over ten years and the flexibility it offers has been widely welcomed both by company boards and by investors. It is for shareholders and others to evaluate the company's statement

5. While it is expected that listed companies will comply with the Code's provisions most of the time, it is recognised that departure from the provisions of the Code may be justified in particular circumstances. Every company must review each provision carefully and give a considered explanation if it departs from the Code provisions. Smaller listed companies, in particular those new to listing, may judge that some of the provisions are disproportionate or less relevant in their case. Some of the provisions do not apply to companies below FTSE 350. Such companies may nonetheless consider that it would be appropriate to adopt the approach in the Code and they are encouraged

---

1 'Review of the role and effectiveness of non-executive directors', published January 2003.
2 'Audit Committees Combined Code Guidance', published January 2003.

to consider this. Investment companies typically have a different board structure, which may affect the relevance of particular provisions.

7. Whilst recognising that directors are appointed by shareholders who are the owners of companies, it is important that those concerned with the evaluation of governance should do so with common sense in order to promote partnership and trust, based on mutual understanding. They should pay due regard to companies' individual circumstances and bear in mind in particular the size and complexity of the company and the nature of the risks and challenges it faces. Whilst shareholders have every right to challenge companies' explanations if they are unconvincing, they should not be evaluated in a mechanistic way and departures from the Code should not be automatically treated as breaches. Institutional shareholders and their agents should be careful to respond to the statements from companies in a manner that supports the 'comply or explain' principle. As the principles in Section 2 make clear, institutional shareholders should carefully consider explanations given for departure from the Code and make reasoned judgements in each case. They should put their views to the company and be prepared to enter a dialogue if they do not accept the company's position. Institutional shareholders should be prepared to put such views in writing where appropriate.

8. Nothing in this Code should be taken to override the general requirements of law to treat shareholders equally in access to information.

9. This publication includes guidance on how to comply with particular parts of the Code: first, 'Internal Control: Guidance for Directors on the Combined Code',[3] produced by the Turnbull Committee, which relates to Code provisions on internal control (C.2 and part of C.3 in the Code); and, second, 'Audit Committees: Combined Code Guidance', produced by the Smith Group, which relates to the provisions on audit committees and auditors (C.3 of the Code). In both cases, the guidance suggests ways of applying the relevant Code principles and of complying with the relevant Code provisions.

10. In addition, this volume also includes suggestions for good practice from the Higgs report.

11. The revised Code does not include material in the previous Code on the disclosure of directors' remuneration. This is because 'The Directors' Remuneration Report Regulations 2002'[4] are now in force and supersede the earlier Code provisions. These require the directors of a company to prepare a remuneration report. It is important that this report is clear, transparent and understandable to shareholders.

---

3 'Internal Control: Guidance for Directors on the Combined Code', published by the Institute of Chartered Accountants in England and Wales in September 1999.
4 The Directors' Remuneration Report Regulations 2002 (SI 2002/1986).

CODE OF BEST PRACTICE
Section 1 Companies

A. DIRECTORS

A.1 The Board

MAIN PRINCIPLE

Every company should be headed by an effective board, which is collectively responsible for the success of the company.

Supporting Principles

The board's role is to provide entrepreneurial leadership of the company within a framework of prudent and effective controls which enables risk to be assessed and managed. The board should set the company's strategic aims, ensure that the necessary financial and human resources are in place for the company to meet its objectives and review management performance. The board should set the company's values and standards and ensure that its obligations to its shareholders and others are understood and met.

All directors must take decisions objectively in the interests of the company.

As part of their role as members of a unitary board, non-executive directors should constructively challenge and help develop proposals on strategy. Non-executive directors should scrutinise the performance of management in meeting agreed goals and objectives and monitor the reporting of performance. They should satisfy themselves on the integrity of financial information and that financial controls and systems of risk management are robust and defensible. They are responsible for determining appropriate levels of remuneration of executive directors and have a prime role in appointing, and where necessary removing, executive directors, and in succession planning.

Code Provisions

A.1.1   The board should meet sufficiently regularly to discharge its duties effectively. There should be a formal schedule of matters specifically reserved for its decision. The annual report should include a statement of how the board operates, including a high level statement of which types of decisions are to be taken by the board and which are to be delegated to management.

A.1.2   The annual report should identify the chairman, the deputy chairman (where there is one), the chief executive, the senior independent director and the chairmen and members of the nomination, audit and remuneration committees. It should also set out the number of meetings of the board and those committees and individual attendance by directors.

A.1.3   The chairman should hold meetings with the non-executive directors without the executives present. Led by the senior independent director, the non-executive directors should meet without the chairman present at least annually to appraise the chairman's performance (as described in A.6.1) and on such other occasions as are deemed appropriate.

A.1.4   Where directors have concerns which cannot be resolved about the running of the company or a proposed action, they should ensure that their concerns are recorded in the board minutes. On resignation, a non-executive director should provide a written statement to the chairman, for circulation to the board, if they have any such concerns.

A.1.5   The company should arrange appropriate insurance cover in respect of legal action against its directors.

A.2 Chairman and chief executive

MAIN PRINCIPLE

There should be a clear division of responsibilities at the head of the company between the running of the board and the executive responsibility for the running of the company's business. No one individual should have unfettered powers of decision.

Supporting Principle

The chairman is responsible for leadership of the board, ensuring its effectiveness on all aspects of its role and setting its agenda. The chairman is also responsible for ensuring that the directors receive accurate, timely and clear information. The chairman should ensure effective communication with shareholders. The chairman should also facilitate the effective contribution of non-executive directors in particular and ensure constructive relations between executive and non-executive directors.

Code Provisions

A.2.1   The roles of chairman and chief executive should not be exercised by the same individual. The division of responsibilities between the chairman and chief executive should be clearly established, set out in writing and agreed by the board.

A.2.2[5]   The chairman should on appointment meet the independence criteria set out in A.3.1 below. A chief executive should not go on to be chairman of the same company. If exceptionally a board decides that a chief executive should become chairman, the board should consult major shareholders in advance and should set out its reasons to shareholders at the time of the appointment and in the next annual report.

A.3 Board balance and independence

MAIN PRINCIPLE

The board should include a balance of executive and non-executive directors (and in particular independent non-executive directors) such that no individual or small group of individuals can dominate the board's decision taking.

---

5 Compliance or otherwise with this provision need only be reported for the year in which the appointment is made.

Supporting Principles

The board should not be so large as to be unwieldy. The board should be of sufficient size that the balance of skills and experience is appropriate for the requirements of the business and that changes to the board's composition can be managed without undue disruption.

To ensure that power and information are not concentrated in one or two individuals, there should be a strong presence on the board of both executive and non-executive directors.

The value of ensuring that committee membership is refreshed and that undue reliance is not placed on particular individuals should be taken into account in deciding chairmanship and membership of committees.

No one other than the committee chairman and members is entitled to be present at a meeting of the nomination, audit or remuneration committee, but others may attend at the invitation of the committee.

Code Provisions

A.3.1 The board should identify in the annual report each non-executive director it considers to be independent.[6] The board should determine whether the director is independent in character and judgement and whether there are relationships or circumstances which are likely to affect, or could appear to affect, the director's judgement. The board should state its reasons if it determines that a director is independent notwithstanding the existence of relationships or circumstances which may appear relevant to its determination, including if the director:
- has been an employee of the company or group within the last five years;
- has, or has had within the last three years, a material business relationship with the company either directly, or as a partner, shareholder, director or senior employee of a body that has such a relationship with the company;
- has received or receives additional remuneration from the company apart from a director's fee, participates in the company's share option or a performance-related pay scheme, or is a member of the company's pension scheme;
- has close family ties with any of the company's advisers, directors or senior employees;
- holds cross-directorships or has significant links with other directors through involvement in other companies or bodies;
- represents a significant shareholder; or
- has served on the board for more than nine years from the date of their first election.

A.3.2 Except for smaller companies,[7] at least half the board, excluding the chairman, should comprise non-executive directors determined by the board to be independent. A smaller company should have at least two independent non-executive directors.

A.3.3 The board should appoint one of the independent non-executive directors to be the senior independent director. The senior independent director should be available to shareholders if they have concerns which contact through the normal channels of chairman, chief executive or finance director has failed to resolve or for which such contact is inappropriate.

---

6 A.2.2 states that the chairman should, on appointment, meet the independence criteria set out in this provision, but thereafter the test of independence is not appropriate in relation to the chairman.
7 A smaller company is one that is below the FTSE 350 throughout the year immediately prior to the reporting year.

A.4 Appointments to the Board

MAIN PRINCIPLE

There should be a formal, rigorous and transparent procedure for the appointment of new directors to the board.

Supporting Principles

Appointments to the board should be made on merit and against objective criteria. Care should be taken to ensure that appointees have enough time available to devote to the job. This is particularly important in the case of chairmanships.

The board should satisfy itself that plans are in place for orderly succession for appointments to the board and to senior management, so as to maintain an appropriate balance of skills and experience within the company and on the board.

Code Provisions

A.4.1 There should be a nomination committee which should lead the process for board appointments and make recommendations to the board. A majority of members of the nomination committee should be independent non-executive directors. The chairman or an independent non-executive director should chair the committee, but the chairman should not chair the nomination committee when it is dealing with the appointment of a successor to the chairmanship. The nomination committee should make available[8] its terms of reference, explaining its role and the authority delegated to it by the board.

A.4.2 The nomination committee should evaluate the balance of skills, knowledge and experience on the board and, in the light of this evaluation, prepare a description of the role and capabilities required for a particular appointment.

A.4.3 For the appointment of a chairman, the nomination committee should prepare a job specification, including an assessment of the time commitment expected, recognising the need for availability in the event of crises. A chairman's other significant commitments should be disclosed to the board before appointment and included in the annual report. Changes to such commitments should be reported to the board as they arise, and included in the next annual report. No individual should be appointed to a second chairmanship of a FTSE 100 company.[9]

A.4.4 The terms and conditions of appointment of non-executive directors should be made available for inspection.[10] The letter of appointment should set out the expected time commitment. Non-executive directors should undertake that they will have sufficient time to meet what is expected of them. Their other significant commitments should be disclosed to the board before appointment, with a broad indication of the time involved and the board should be informed of subsequent changes.

---

8 The requirement to make the information available would be met by making it available on request and by including the information on the company's website.
9 Compliance or otherwise with this provision need only be reported for the year in which the appointment is made.
10 The terms and conditions of appointment of non-executive directors should be made available for inspection by any person at the company's registered office during normal business hours and at the AGM (for 15 minutes prior to the meeting and during the meeting).

A.4.5 The board should not agree to a full time executive director taking on more than one non-executive directorship in a FTSE 100 company nor the chairmanship of such a company.

A.4.6 A separate section of the annual report should describe the work of the nomination committee, including the process it has used in relation to board appointments. An explanation should be given if neither an external search consultancy nor open advertising has been used in the appointment of a chairman or a non-executive director.

A.5 Information and professional development

MAIN PRINCIPLE

The board should be supplied in a timely manner with information in a form and of a quality appropriate to enable it to discharge its duties. All directors should receive induction on joining the board and should regularly update and refresh their skills and knowledge.

Supporting Principles

The chairman is responsible for ensuring that the directors receive accurate, timely and clear information. Management has an obligation to provide such information but directors should seek clarification or amplification where necessary.

The chairman should ensure that the directors continually update their skills and the knowledge and familiarity with the company required to fulfil their role both on the board and on board committees. The company should provide the necessary resources for developing and updating its directors' knowledge and capabilities. Under the direction of the chairman, the company secretary's responsibilities include ensuring good information flows within the board and its committees and between senior management and non-executive directors, as well as facilitating induction and assisting with professional development as required.

The company secretary should be responsible for advising the board through the chairman on all governance matters.

Code Provisions

A.5.1 The chairman should ensure that new directors receive a full, formal and tailored induction on joining the board. As part of this, the company should offer to major shareholders the opportunity to meet a new non-executive director.

A.5.2 The board should ensure that directors, especially non-executive directors, have access to independent professional advice at the company's expense where they judge it necessary to discharge their responsibilities as directors. Committees should be provided with sufficient resources to undertake their duties.

A.5.3 All directors should have access to the advice and services of the company secretary, who is responsible to the board for ensuring that board procedures are complied with. Both the appointment and removal of the company secretary should be a matter for the board as a whole.

A.6 Performance evaluation

MAIN PRINCIPLE

The board should undertake a formal and rigorous annual evaluation of its own performance and that of its committees and individual directors.

Supporting Principle

Individual evaluation should aim to show whether each director continues to contribute effectively and to demonstrate commitment to the role (including commitment of time for board and committee meetings and any other duties). The chairman should act on the results of the performance evaluation by recognising the strengths and addressing the weaknesses of the board and, where appropriate, proposing new members be appointed to the board or seeking the resignation of directors.

Code Provision

A.6.1   The board should state in the annual report how performance evaluation of the board, its committees and its individual directors has been conducted. The non-executive directors, led by the senior independent director, should be responsible for performance evaluation of the chairman, taking into account the views of executive directors.

A.7 Re-election

MAIN PRINCIPLE

All directors should be submitted for re-election at regular intervals, subject to continued satisfactory performance. The board should ensure planned and progressive refreshing of the board.

Code Provisions

A.7.1   All directors should be subject to election by shareholders at the first annual general meeting after their appointment, and to re-election thereafter at intervals of no more than three years. The names of directors submitted for election or re-election should be accompanied by sufficient biographical details and any other relevant information to enable shareholders to take an informed decision on their election.

A.7.2   Non-executive directors should be appointed for specified terms subject to re-election and to Companies Acts provisions relating to the removal of a director. The board should set out to shareholders in the papers accompanying a resolution to elect a non-executive director why they believe an individual should be elected. The chairman should confirm to shareholders when proposing re-election that, following formal performance evaluation, the individual's performance continues to be effective and to demonstrate commitment to the role. Any term beyond six years (e.g. two three-year terms) for a non-executive director should be subject to particularly rigorous review, and should take into account the need for progressive refreshing of the board. Non-executive directors may serve longer than nine years (e.g. three three-year terms), subject to annual re-election. Serving more than nine years could be relevant to the determination of a non-executive director's independence (as set out in provision A.3.1).

B. REMUNERATION

B.1 The level and make-up of remuneration[11]

MAIN PRINCIPLES

Levels of remuneration should be sufficient to attract, retain and motivate directors of the quality required to run the company successfully, but a company should avoid paying more than is necessary for this purpose. A significant proportion of executive directors' remuneration should be structured so as to link rewards to corporate and individual performance.

Supporting Principle

The remuneration committee should judge where to position their company relative to other companies. But they should use such comparisons with caution, in view of the risk of an upward ratchet of remuneration levels with no corresponding improvement in performance.

They should also be sensitive to pay and employment conditions elsewhere in the group, especially when determining annual salary increases.

Code Provisions

Remuneration policy

B.1.1 The performance-related elements of remuneration should form a significant proportion of the total remuneration package of executive directors and should be designed to align their interests with those of shareholders and to give these directors keen incentives to perform at the highest levels. In designing schemes of performance-related remuneration, the remuneration committee should follow the provisions in Schedule A to this Code.

B.1.2 Executive share options should not be offered at a discount save as permitted by the relevant provisions of the Listing Rules.

B.1.3 Levels of remuneration for non-executive directors should reflect the time commitment and responsibilities of the role. Remuneration for non-executive directors should not include share options. If, exceptionally, options are granted, shareholder approval should be sought in advance and any shares acquired by exercise of the options should be held until at least one year after the non-executive director leaves the board. Holding of share options could be relevant to the determination of a non-executive director's independence (as set out in provision A.3.1).

B.1.4 Where a company releases an executive director to serve as a non-executive director elsewhere, the remuneration report[12] should include a statement as to whether or not the director will retain such earnings and, if so, what the remuneration is.

11 Views have been sought by the Department of Trade and Industry by 30 September 2003 on whether, and if so how, further measures are required to enable shareholders to ensure that compensation reflects performance when directors' contracts are terminated: See 'Rewards for Failure': Directors' Remuneration – Contracts, performance and severance, June 2003.
12 As required under the Directors' Remuneration Report Regulations.

Service Contracts and Compensation

B.1.5   The remuneration committee should carefully consider what compensation commitments (including pension contributions and all other elements) their directors' terms of appointment would entail in the event of early termination. The aim should be to avoid rewarding poor performance. They should take a robust line on reducing compensation to reflect departing directors' obligations to mitigate loss.

B.1.6   Notice or contract periods should be set at one year or less. If it is necessary to offer longer notice or contract periods to new directors recruited from outside, such periods should reduce to one year or less after the initial period.

B.2 Procedure

MAIN PRINCIPLE

There should be a formal and transparent procedure for developing policy on executive remuneration and for fixing the remuneration packages of individual directors. No director should be involved in deciding his or her own remuneration.

Supporting Principles

The remuneration committee should consult the chairman and/or chief executive about their proposals relating to the remuneration of other executive directors. The remuneration committee should also be responsible for appointing any consultants in respect of executive director remuneration. Where executive directors or senior management are involved in advising or supporting the remuneration committee, care should be taken to recognise and avoid conflicts of interest.

The chairman of the board should ensure that the company maintains contact as required with its principal shareholders about remuneration in the same way as for other matters.

Code Provisions

B.2.1   The board should establish a remuneration committee of at least three, or in the case of smaller companies[13] two, members, who should all be independent non-executive directors. The remuneration committee should make available[14] its terms of reference, explaining its role and the authority delegated to it by the board. Where remuneration consultants are appointed, a statement should be made available[15] of whether they have any other connection with the company.

B.2.2   The remuneration committee should have delegated responsibility for setting remuneration for all executive directors and the chairman, including pension rights and any compensation payments. The committee should also recommend and monitor the level and structure of remuneration for senior management. The definition of 'senior management' for this purpose should be determined by the board but should normally include the first layer of management below board level.

---

13 See footnote 8.
14 See footnote 9.
15 See footnote 9.

B.2.3   The board itself or, where required by the Articles of Association, the shareholders should determine the remuneration of the non-executive directors within the limits set in the Articles of Association. Where permitted by the Articles, the board may however delegate this responsibility to a committee, which might include the chief executive.

B.2.4   Shareholders should be invited specifically to approve all new long-term incentive schemes (as defined in the Listing Rules) and significant changes to existing schemes, save in the circumstances permitted by the Listing Rules.

C. ACCOUNTABILITY AND AUDIT

C.1 Financial reporting

MAIN PRINCIPLE

The board should present a balanced and understandable assessment of the company's position and prospects.

Supporting Principle

The board's responsibility to present a balanced and understandable assessment extends to interim and other price-sensitive public reports and reports to regulators as well as to information required to be presented by statutory requirements.

Code Provisions

C.1.1   The directors should explain in the annual report their responsibility for preparing the accounts and there should be a statement by the auditors about their reporting responsibilities.

C.1.2   The directors should report that the business is a going concern, with supporting assumptions or qualifications as necessary.

C.2 Internal control[16]

MAIN PRINCIPLE

The board should maintain a sound system of internal control to safeguard shareholders' investment and the company's assets.

Code Provision

C.2.1   The board should, at least annually, conduct a review of the effectiveness of the group's system of internal controls and should report to shareholders that they have done so. The review should cover all material controls, including financial, operational and compliance controls and risk management systems.

---

16 The Turnbull guidance suggests means of applying this part of the Code.

C.3 Audit Committee and Auditors[17]

MAIN PRINCIPLE

The board should establish formal and transparent arrangements for considering how they should apply the financial reporting and internal control principles and for maintaining an appropriate relationship with the company's auditors.

Code Provisions

C.3.1 The board should establish an audit committee of at least three, or in the case of smaller companies[18] two, members, who should all be independent non-executive directors. The board should satisfy itself that at least one member of the audit committee has recent and relevant financial experience.

C.3.2 The main role and responsibilities of the audit committee should be set out in written terms of reference and should include:
- to monitor the integrity of the financial statements of the company, and any formal announcements relating to the company's financial performance, reviewing significant financial reporting judgements contained in them;
- to review the company's internal financial controls and, unless expressly addressed by a separate board risk committee composed of independent directors, or by the board itself, to review the company's internal control and risk management systems;
- to monitor and review the effectiveness of the company's internal audit function;
- to make recommendations to the board, for it to put to the shareholders for their approval in general meeting, in relation to the appointment, re-appointment and removal of the external auditor and to approve the remuneration and terms of engagement of the external auditor;
- to review and monitor the external auditor's independence and objectivity and the effectiveness of the audit process, taking into consideration relevant UK professional and regulatory requirements;
- to develop and implement policy on the engagement of the external auditor to supply non-audit services, taking into account relevant ethical guidance regarding the provision of non-audit services by the external audit firm; and
- to report to the board, identifying any matters in respect of which it considers that action or improvement is needed and making recommendations as to the steps to be taken.

C.3.3 The terms of reference of the audit committee, including its role and the authority delegated to it by the board, should be made available.[19] A separate section of the annual report should describe the work of the committee in discharging those responsibilities.

C.3.4 The audit committee should review arrangements by which staff of the company may, in confidence, raise concerns about possible improprieties in matters of financial reporting or other matters. The audit committee's objective should be

17 The Smith guidance suggests means of applying this part of the Code.
18 See footnote 7.
19 See footnote 8.

to ensure that arrangements are in place for the proportionate and independent investigation of such matters and for appropriate follow-up action.

C.3.5 The audit committee should monitor and review the effectiveness of the internal audit activities. Where there is no internal audit function, the audit committee should consider annually whether there is a need for an internal audit function and make a recommendation to the board, and the reasons for the absence of such a function should be explained in the relevant section of the annual report.

C.3.6 The audit committee should have primary responsibility for making a recommendation on the appointment, reappointment and removal of the external auditors. If the board does not accept the audit committee's recommendation, it should include in the annual report, and in any papers recommending appointment or re-appointment, a statement from the audit committee explaining the recommendation and should set out reasons why the board has taken a different position.

C.3.7 The annual report should explain to shareholders how, if the auditor provides non-audit services, auditor objectivity and independence is safeguarded.

D. RELATIONS WITH SHAREHOLDERS

D.1 Dialogue with institutional shareholders

MAIN PRINCIPLE

There should be a dialogue with shareholders based on the mutual understanding of objectives. The board as a whole has responsibility for ensuring that a satisfactory dialogue with shareholders takes place.[20]

Supporting Principles

Whilst recognising that most shareholder contact is with the chief executive and finance director, the chairman (and the senior independent director and other directors as appropriate) should maintain sufficient contact with major shareholders to understand their issues and concerns. The board should keep in touch with shareholder opinion in whatever ways are most practical and efficient.

Code Provisions

D.1.1 The chairman should ensure that the views of shareholders are communicated to the board as a whole. The chairman should discuss governance and strategy with major shareholders. Non-executive directors should be offered the opportunity to attend meetings with major shareholders and should expect to attend them if requested by major shareholders. The senior independent director should attend sufficient meetings with a range of major shareholders to listen to their views in order to help develop a balanced understanding of the issues and concerns of major shareholders.

---

20 Nothing in these principles or provisions should be taken to override the general requirements of law to treat shareholders equally in access to information.

D.1.2 The board should state in the annual report the steps they have taken to ensure that the members of the board, and in particular the non-executive directors, develop an understanding of the views of major shareholders about their company, for example through direct face-to-face contact, analysts' or brokers' briefings and surveys of shareholder opinion.

D.2 Constructive use of the AGM

MAIN PRINCIPLE

The board should use the AGM to communicate with investors and to encourage their participation.

Code Provisions

D.2.1 The company should count all proxy votes and, except where a poll is called, should indicate the level of proxies lodged on each resolution, and the balance for and against the resolution and the number of abstentions, after it has been dealt with on a show of hands. The company should ensure that votes cast are properly received and recorded.

D.2.2 The company should propose a separate resolution at the AGM on each substantially separate issue and should in particular propose a resolution at the AGM relating to the report and accounts.

D.2.3 The chairman should arrange for the chairmen of the audit, remuneration and nomination committees to be available to answer questions at the AGM and for all directors to attend.

D.2.4 The company should arrange for the Notice of the AGM and related papers to be sent to shareholders at least 20 working days before the meeting.

Section 2 Institutional Shareholders

E. INSTITUTIONAL SHAREHOLDERS[21]

E.1 Dialogue with companies

MAIN PRINCIPLE

Institutional shareholders should enter into a dialogue with companies based on the mutual understanding of objectives.

---

21 Agents such as investment managers, or voting services, are frequently appointed by institutional shareholders to act on their behalf and these principles should accordingly be read as applying where appropriate to the agents of institutional shareholders.

Supporting Principles

Institutional shareholders should apply the principles set out in the Institutional Shareholders' Committee's 'The Responsibilities of Institutional Shareholders and Agents – Statement of Principles'[22], which should be reflected in fund manager contracts.

E.2 Evaluation of governance disclosures

MAIN PRINCIPLE

When evaluating companies' governance arrangements, particularly those relating to board structure and composition, institutional shareholders should give due weight to all relevant factors drawn to their attention.

Supporting Principle

Institutional shareholders should consider carefully explanations given for departure from this Code and make reasoned judgements in each case. They should give an explanation to the company, in writing where appropriate, and be prepared to enter a dialogue if they do not accept the company's position. They should avoid a box-ticking approach to assessing a company's corporate governance. They should bear in mind in particular the size and complexity of the company and the nature of the risks and challenges it faces.

E.3 Shareholder voting

MAIN PRINCIPLE

Institutional shareholders have a responsibility to make considered use of their votes.

Supporting Principles

Institutional shareholders should take steps to ensure their voting intentions are being translated into practice.

Institutional shareholders should, on request, make available to their clients information on the proportion of resolutions on which votes were cast and non-discretionary proxies lodged.

Major shareholders should attend AGMs where appropriate and practicable. Companies and registrars should facilitate this.

Schedule A: Provisions on the design of performance related remuneration

1. The remuneration committee should consider whether the directors should be eligible for annual bonuses. If so, performance conditions should be relevant, stretching and designed to enhance shareholder value. Upper limits should be set and disclosed. There may be a case for part payment in shares to be held for a significant period.

2. The remuneration committee should consider whether the directors should be eligible for benefits under long-term incentive schemes. Traditional share option schemes

---

22 Available at website: www.investmentuk.org.uk/press/2002/20021021-01.pdf.

should be weighed against other kinds of long-term incentive scheme. In normal circumstances, shares granted or other forms of deferred remuneration should not vest, and options should not be exercisable, in less than three years. Directors should be encouraged to hold their shares for a further period after vesting or exercise, subject to the need to finance any costs of acquisition and associated tax liabilities.

3. Any new long-term incentive schemes which are proposed should be approved by shareholders and should preferably replace any existing schemes or at least form part of a well considered overall plan, incorporating existing schemes. The total rewards potentially available should not be excessive.

4. Payouts or grants under all incentive schemes, including new grants under existing share option schemes, should be subject to challenging performance criteria reflecting the company's objectives. Consideration should be given to criteria which reflect the company's performance relative to a group of comparator companies in some key variables such as total shareholder return.

5. Grants under executive share option and other long-term incentive schemes should normally be phased rather than awarded in one large block.

6. In general, only basic salary should be pensionable.

7. The remuneration committee should consider the pension consequences and associated costs to the company of basic salary increases and any other changes in pensionable remuneration, especially for directors close to retirement.

Schedule B: Guidance on liability of non-executive directors: care, skill and diligence

1. Although non-executive directors and executive directors have as board members the same legal duties and objectives, the time devoted to the company's affairs is likely to be significantly less for a non-executive director than for an executive director and the detailed knowledge and experience of a company's affairs that could reasonably be expected of a non-executive director will generally be less than for an executive director. These matters may be relevant in assessing the knowledge, skill and experience which may reasonably be expected of a non-executive director and therefore the care, skill and diligence that a non-executive director may be expected to exercise.

2. In this context, the following elements of the Code may also be particularly relevant.

    (i)   In order to enable directors to fulfil their duties, the Code states that:
          ● The letter of appointment of the director should set out the expected time commitment (Code provision A.4.4); and
          ● The board should be supplied in a timely manner with information in a form and of a quality appropriate to enable it to discharge its duties. The chairman is responsible for ensuring that the directors are provided by management with accurate, timely and clear information. (Code principles A.5).

    (ii) Non-executive directors should themselves:
          ● Undertake appropriate induction and regularly update and refresh their skills, knowledge and familiarity with the company (Code principle A.5 and provision A.5.1)
          ● Seek appropriate clarification or amplification of information and, where necessary, take and follow appropriate professional advice. (Code principle A.5 and provision A.5.2)

- Where they have concerns about the running of the company or a proposed action, ensure that these are addressed by the board and, to the extent that they are not resolved, ensure that they are recorded in the board minutes (Code provision A.1.4).
- Give a statement to the board if they have such unresolved concerns on resignation (Code provision A.1.4)

3. It is up to each non-executive director to reach a view as to what is necessary in particular circumstances to comply with the duty of care, skill and diligence they owe as a director to the company. In considering whether or not a person is in breach of that duty, a court would take into account all relevant circumstances. These may include having regard to the above where relevant to the issue of liability of a non-executive director.

Schedule C: Disclosure of corporate governance arrangements

The Listing Rules require a statement to be included in the annual report relating to compliance with the Code, as described in the preamble. For ease of reference, the specific requirements in the Code for disclosure are set out below:

The annual report should record:
- a statement of how the board operates, including a high level statement of which types of decisions are to be taken by the board and which are to be delegated to management (A.1.1);
- the names of the chairman, the deputy chairman (where there is one), the chief executive, the senior independent director and the chairmen and members of the nomination, audit and remuneration committees (A.1.2);
- the number of meetings of the board and those committees and individual attendance by directors (A.1.2);
- the names of the non-executive directors whom the board determines to be independent, with reasons where necessary (A.3.1);
- the other significant commitments of the chairman and any changes to them during the year (A.4.3);
- how performance evaluation of the board, its committees and its directors has been conducted (A.6.1);
- the steps the board has taken to ensure that members of the board, and in particular the non-executive directors, develop an understanding of the views of major shareholders about their company (D.1.2).

The report should also include:
- a separate section describing the work of the nomination committee, including the process it has used in relation to board appointments and an explanation if neither external search consultancy nor open advertising has been used in the appointment of a chairman or a non-executive director (A.4.6);
- a description of the work of the remuneration committee as required under the Directors' Remuneration Reporting Regulations 2002, and including, where an executive director serves as a non-executive director elsewhere, whether or not the director will retain such earnings and, if so, what the remuneration is (B.1.4);
- an explanation from the directors of their responsibility for preparing the accounts and a statement by the auditors about their reporting responsibilities (C.1.1);

- a statement from the directors that the business is a going concern, with supporting assumptions or qualifications as necessary (C.1.2);
- a report that the board has conducted a review of the effectiveness of the group's system of internal controls (C.2.1);
- a separate section describing the work of the audit committee in discharging its responsibilities (C.3.3);
- where there is no internal audit function, the reasons for the absence of such a function (C.3.5);
- where the board does not accept the audit committee's recommendation on the appointment, reappointment or removal of an external auditor, a statement from the audit committee explaining the recommendation and the reasons why the board has taken a different position (C.3.6); and
- an explanation of how, if the auditor provides non-audit services, auditor objectivity and independence is safeguarded (C.3.7).

The following information should be made available (which may be met by making it available on request and placing the information available on the company's website):

- the terms of reference of the nomination, remuneration and audit committees, explaining their role and the authority delegated to them by the board (A.4.1, B.2.1 and C.3.3);
- the terms and conditions of appointment of non-executive directors (A.4.4) (see footnote 10 on page 9); and
- the terms of reference of any remuneration consultants, together with a statement of whether they have any other connection with the company (B.2.1).

The board should set out to shareholders in the papers accompanying a resolution to elect or re-elect:

- sufficient biographical details to enable shareholders to take an informed decision on their election or re-election (A.7.1).
- why they believe an individual should be elected to a non-executive role (A.7.2).
- on re-election of a non-executive director, confirmation from the chairman that, following formal performance evaluation, the individual's performance continues to be effective and to demonstrate commitment to the role, including commitment of time for board and committee meetings and any other duties (A.7.2).

The board should set out to shareholders in the papers recommending appointment or reappointment of an external auditor:

- if the board does not accept the audit committee's recommendation, a statement from the audit committee explaining the recommendation and from the board setting out reasons why they have taken a different position (C.3.6).

Appendix 2

ASSOCIATION OF BRITISH INSURERS: DISCLOSURE GUIDELINES ON SOCIALLY RESPONSIBLE INVESTMENT (October 2001)

1. Background and introduction

Public interest in corporate social responsibility has grown to the point where it seems helpful for institutional shareholders to set out basic disclosure principles, which will guide them in seeking to engage with companies in which they invest.

In drawing up guidelines for this purpose they are mindful of statements made at multilateral level through the Guidelines for Multinational Corporations published in 2000 by the Organisation for Economic Cooperation and Development, as well as by the European Union and UK Government. These, coupled with legal disclosure obligations on UK pension funds and local authority investments, point to clear responsibilities both for companies and for institutions that invest in them.

Institutional shareholders are also anxious to avoid unnecessary prescription or the imposition of costly burdens, which can unnecessarily restrict the ability of companies to generate returns. Indeed, by focusing on the need to identify and manage risks to the long and short-term value of the business from social, environmental and ethical matters, the guidelines highlight an opportunity to enhance value through appropriate response to these risks.

It is not the intention of these guidelines to set a limit on the amount of information companies should provide on their response to social, environmental and ethical matters. Some shareholders with specific ethical investment objectives may seek more specific information. Some companies may choose to make additional information available in order to enhance their appeal to investors.

The ABI hopes that in elaborating these guidelines it will provide a helpful basic benchmark for companies seeking to develop best practice in this area.

2. The Disclosure Guidelines

The guidelines take the form of disclosures, which institutions would expect to see included in the annual report of listed companies. Specifically they refer to disclosures relating to Board responsibilities and to policies, procedures and verification.

With regard to the board, the company should state in its annual report whether:

1.1 The Board takes regular account of the significance of social, environmental and ethical (SEE) matters to the business of the company.

1.2   The Board has identified and assessed the significant risks to the company's short and long term value arising from SEE matters, as well as the opportunities to enhance value that may arise from an appropriate response.

1.3   The Board has received adequate information to make this assessment and that account is taken of SEE matters in the training of directors.

1.4   The Board has ensured that the company has in place effective systems for managing significant risks, which, where relevant, incorporate performance management systems and appropriate remuneration incentives.

With regard to policies, procedures and verification, the annual report should:

2.1   Include information on SEE-related risks and opportunities that may significantly affect the company's short and long term value, and how they might impact on the business.

2.2   Describe the company's policies and procedures for managing risks to short and long term value arising from SEE matters. If the annual report and accounts states that the company has no such policies and procedures, the Board should provide reasons for their absence.

2.3   Include information about the extent to which the company has complied with its policies and procedures for managing risks arising from SEE matters.

2.4   Describe the procedures for verification of SEE disclosures. The verification procedure should be such as to achieve a reasonable level of credibility.

Towards best practice

Institutional shareholders consider that adherence to the principles outlined above will help companies to develop appropriate policies on corporate social responsibility.

The principles should also provide a constructive basis for engagement between companies and their shareholders. Over time this will allow both parties jointly to develop a clear joint understanding of best practice in the handling of social, environmental and ethical matters which will help preserve and enhance value. It is the intention of the ABI to continue regular contact with companies and stakeholders with a view to refining the concept of best practice.

Current understanding of best practice leads to the following conclusions and indications as to how the guidelines should operate:

1. The guidelines are intended to apply to all companies, including small and medium companies.

2. The cost of managing risks should be proportionate to their significance. Ideally, procedures should be integrated into existing management structures and systems.

3. Statements relating to the guidelines should be made in the annual report, and not separately as part of the summary accounts or on a web site dedicated to social responsibility. In view of the close philosophical linkage between these guidelines and Turnbull reporting, it would make sense to include a brief statement in the Internal Control section of the annual report, although this would not preclude a cross reference

to other parts of the report where more detailed disclosure of the type of risks involved and systems for managing those risks may also fit with other content.

4. With regard to the implementation, shareholders are anxious to leave leeway for companies to establish their own systems best suited to their business. However, they believe that, with regard to clause 1.1, best practice would require the full Board to consider the issues on a regular basis, although some on-going detailed work might be delegated to a committee. Disclosure should include a brief description of the process undertaken by the Board for identifying significant risks and indicate which risks are the most significant in terms of their impact on the business.

5. Examples of initiatives for reducing and managing risks (see 1.4 and 2.2) include regular contact with stakeholders and mechanisms to ensure that appropriate standards are maintained in the supply chain. Evidence of such initiatives would be viewed positively by shareholders.

6. Reporting on performance over time in complying with policies to reduce risk will help shareholders monitor improvement in compliance.

7. Independent external verification of SEE disclosures would be regarded by shareholders as a highly significant advantage. Credible verification may also be achieved by other means, including internal audit. It would assist shareholders in their assessment of SEE policies if the reason for choosing a particular method of verification were explained in the annual report.

Appendix 1: Questions on social, environmental and ethical matters

Disclosure could be addressed by response in the annual report to the following questions:

1. Has the company made any reference to social, environmental and ethical matters? If so, does the board take these regularly into account?

2. Has the company identified and assessed significant risks and opportunities affecting its long and short term value arising from its handling of SEE matters?

3. Does the company state that it has adequate information for identification and assessment?

4. Are systems in place to manage the SEE risks?

5. Are any remuneration incentives relating to the handling of SEE risks included in risk management systems?

6. Does Directors' training include SEE matters?

7. Does the company disclose significant short and long term risks and opportunities arising from SEE issues? If so, how many different risks/opportunities are identified?

8. Are policies for managing risks to the company's value described?

9. Are procedures for managing risk described? If not, are reasons for non-disclosure given?

10. Does the Company report on the extent of its compliance with its policies and procedures?

11. Are verification procedures described?

Appendix 2: Questions for investment trusts

1.   Is the voting policy of the trust publicly available?

2.   Does the voting policy make reference to SEE matters?

3.   Is the manager encouraged actively to engage with companies to promote better SEE practice?

© Association of British Insurers. Reproduced with permission.

Appendix 3

ICSA GUIDANCE NOTE: MATTERS RESERVED
FOR THE BOARD
(November 2003)

No matter how effective a board of directors may be it is not possible for the directors to have hands-on involvement in every area of the company's business. An effective board controls the business but delegates day to day responsibility to the executive management. That said there are a number of matters which are required, or that should in the interests of the company, only [to] be decided by the board of directors as a whole.

It is incumbent upon the board to make it clear what these Matters Reserved for the Board are.

ICSA has produced this Guidance Note to aid directors and company secretaries in drawing up such a schedule of Matters Reserved for the Board. The original version of this document was first published in the February 1993 edition of The Company Secretary and has been adopted as a precedent by a number of writers on corporate governance. It has been updated to incorporate more recent developments in best practice.

The relative importance of some matters included in this Guidance Note will vary according to the size and nature of the company's business. For example all companies will have a different view on the establishment of the financial limits for transactions which should be referred to the board. Equally, there may well be items not mentioned in the Guidance Note which some companies (eg those subject to additional forms of external regulation) would wish to include in their own schedule.

Multiple signatures

In drawing up a schedule of Matters Reserved for the Board, companies should clarify which transactions require multiple board signatures on the relevant documentation.

Delegation

Certain of the matters included in this Guidance Note should, under the recommendations of the Cadbury Committee and/or Combined Code, be the responsibility of the audit, nomination or remuneration committee.

However, full delegation is not permitted in these cases as the final decision on the matter is required to be taken by the whole board.

Urgent matters

In drawing up a schedule of Matters Reserved for the Board it is important to establish procedures for dealing with matters which often have to be dealt with urgently, often between board meetings. It is recommended that, where practical, the approval of all the directors should be obtained by means of a written resolution. In all cases however the procedures should balance the need for urgency with the overriding principle that each director should be given as much information as possible and have an opportunity to requisition an emergency meeting of the board to discuss the matter prior to the commitment of the company.

The following schedule has been produced to assist boards of directors and company secretaries in preparing a schedule of Matters Reserved for the Board in accordance with good Corporate Governance.

Items marked * are not considered suitable for delegation to a committee of the board, eg because of Companies Act requirements or because, under the recommendations of the Cadbury Report or Combined Code, they are the responsibility of an audit, nomination or remuneration committee, with the final decision required to be taken by the board as a whole.

Companies Act Requirements

1.*   Approval of interim and final financial statements.
2.*   Approval of the interim dividend and recommendation of the final dividend.
3.*   Approval of any significant changes in accounting policies or practices.
4.*   Appointment or removal of the company secretary.
5.*   Remuneration of the auditors [where, as is usual, shareholders have delegated this power to the board] and recommendations for the appointment or removal of auditors [possibly following recommendations of the audit committee].
6.   Resolutions and corresponding documentation to be put forward to shareholders at a General Meeting.

Stock Exchange/Financial Services Authority

7.*   Approval of all circulars and listing particulars [approval of routine documents such as periodic circulars re scrip dividend procedures or exercise of conversion rights could be delegated to a committee].
8.*   Approval of press releases concerning matters decided by the board.

Board membership and board committees

9.*   Board appointments and removals and any special terms and conditions attached to the appointment [subject to the recommendations of the remuneration committee].
10.* Terms of reference of chairman, chief executive and other executive directors.
11.* Terms of reference and membership of board committees.

Management

12.   Approval of the group's long term objectives and commercial strategy.
13.   Approval of the annual operating and capital expenditure budgets.
14.   Changes relating to the group's capital structure or its status as a plc.
15.   Appointments to boards of subsidiaries.
16.* Terms and conditions of directors and senior executives.
17.   Changes to the group's management and control structure.

Cadbury/Combined Code recommendations

18. Major capital projects.
19. Material, either by reason of size or strategically, contracts of the company [or any subsidiary] in the ordinary course of business, eg bank borrowings [above £xxx] and acquisition or disposal of fixed assets [above £xxx].
20. Contracts of the company [or any subsidiary] not in the ordinary course of business, eg loans and repayments [above £xxx]; foreign currency transactions [above £xxx]; major acquisitions or disposals [above £xxx].
21. Major investments [including the acquisition or disposal of interests of more than (5) percent in the voting shares of any company or the making of any takeover bid].
22. Risk management strategy.
23. Treasury policies [including foreign currency exposure].

Miscellaneous

24. Review of the company's overall corporate governance arrangements.
25. Major changes in the rules of the company pension scheme, or changes of trustees or [when this subject is subject to the approval of the company] changes in the fund management arrangements.
26. Major changes in employee share schemes and the allocation of executive share options.
27. Formulation of policy regarding charitable donations.
28. Political donations.
29. Approval of the company's principal professional advisers.
30. Prosecution, defence or settlement of litigation [involving above £xxx or being otherwise material to the interests of the company].
31. Internal control arrangements.
32. Health & Safety policy.
33. Environmental policy.
34. Directors' & Officers' liability insurance.
35. This schedule of matters reserved for board decisions.

Appendix 4

ICSA GUIDANCE NOTE: TERMS OF REFERENCE
– EXECUTIVE COMMITTEES
(September 2004)

The Combined Code on Corporate Governance recommends that boards should appoint certain committees to deal with particular matters. These are the audit, remuneration and nomination committees. Descriptions of the roles of these committees and suggested terms of reference are the subject of separate ICSA guidance notes.

There may be other committees, in addition to these, to cover areas such as risk, health and safety, corporate social responsibility, share plans and so on. Some of these may be formally constituted by the board, others may be management committees.

One of the key committees is the executive committee, or Excom. This will not usually be formally appointed by the board as it is the Chief Executive's forum for major operational decisions. However, because the business it conducts will be of importance to the group it should report back to the board. This may be by the circulation of the Excom minutes to all directors, or by a report from the Chief Executive (oral or written), or both.

The Excom will typically be made up of the executive directors and the most senior members of the management team – those individuals one level down from the board who report directly to the Chief Executive or possibly to the finance director.

It is useful for the company secretary to act as secretary to the Excom. This can avoid problems arising with governance issues. The Excom needs to be clear about its powers and delegated authorities and about what decisions require board approval. Written terms of reference and delegated authorities are therefore essential and should be agreed by the board as a matter of good practice.

The Combined Code requires that companies make the terms of reference of their audit, remuneration and nomination committees available on their websites. There is no such requirement for other committees, such as the Excom. However, companies may wish to consider making the Excom terms of reference available in the interests of transparency and good governance.

The Appendix contains examples of certain administrative tasks which may be included in the terms of reference of the Excom but which are also often carried out by a General Purposes or Finance Committee. Some of these, which are of a routine nature (for example the allotment of new shares to satisfy the awards of shares under employee share plans) may be carried out equally well by written resolution of the Committee as no discussion is required.

Example terms of reference for an Executive Committee

1. Purpose

The purpose of the Committee is to assist the Chief Executive in the performance of their duties, including:

- the development and implementation of strategy, operational plans, policies, procedures and budgets;
- the monitoring of operating and financial performance;
- the assessment and control of risk;
- the prioritisation and allocation of resources;
- monitoring competitive forces in each area of operation.

2. Membership

The Committee shall be made up of the Chief Executive, Deputy Chief Executive, Finance Director, all other executive (main board) directors, the heads of each business division, human resources, risk, IT, strategy, operations, group legal, and the company secretary.[1]

Others may be invited by the Chief Executive (or in their absence, the Deputy Chief Executive) to attend all or part of any meeting.

3. Chair

The Chief Executive shall act as Chair of the Committee. In their absence, the [Deputy Chief Executive][Finance Director] shall act as Chair.

4. Secretary

The company secretary or their nominee shall act as the secretary of the Committee.

5. Quorum

The quorum necessary for the transaction of business shall be [3] members of whom at least one must be either the Chief Executive or [Deputy Chief Executive]/[Finance Director]. A duly convened meeting of the Committee at which a quorum is present shall be competent to exercise all or any of the authorities, powers and discretions vested in or exercisable by the Committee.

6. Frequency of Meetings

The Committee shall meet [monthly on the first Monday of each month] [fortnightly on a Tuesday] [every Monday].

7. Notice of Meetings

Meetings of the Committee, other than those regularly scheduled as above, shall be summoned by the secretary of the Committee at the request of the Chief Executive.

---

1 To the extent that the individuals holding these positions are not executive directors.

Unless otherwise agreed, notice of each meeting confirming the venue, time and date together with an agenda of items to be discussed and supporting papers, shall be forwarded to each member of the Committee, any other person required to attend, no later than [2] working days before the date of the meeting.

8. Conduct of Meetings

Except as outlined above, meetings of the Committee shall be conducted in accordance with the provisions of the Company's Articles of Association governing the proceedings of Directors.

9. Minutes of Meetings

The secretary shall minute the proceedings and resolutions of all meetings of the Committee, including recording the names of those present and in attendance.

Minutes of Committee meetings shall be circulated promptly to all members of the Committee and, once agreed, to all members of the board.

10. Duties

Recommending objectives and strategy for the group in the development of its business, having regard to the interests of its shareholders, customers, employees and other stakeholders;

Agreeing policy guidelines for business divisions based on approved group strategy;

The successful execution of strategy;

The presentation of the group's budgets and five year plan to the board and, following their adoption, the achievement of the budgets and plans;

Developing and reviewing business division objectives and budgets to ensure that they fall within the agreed group targets;

Ensuring appropriate levels of authority are delegated to senior management throughout the group;

Reviewing the organisational structure of the group and making recommendations for change;

Ensuring the control, co-ordination and monitoring within the group of risk and internal controls;

Ensuring compliance with relevant legislation and regulations;

Safeguarding the integrity of management information and financial reporting systems;

Identifying and executing new business opportunities outside the current core activities, including geographic diversification;

Examining all trade investments, divestments and major capital expenditure proposals and the recommendation to the group board of those which, in a group context, are material either by nature or cost;

Approving all strategic or material alliances and partnership agreements;

Optimising the allocation and adequacy of the group's resources;

Ensuring the provision of adequate management development and succession and recommendation and implementation of appropriate remuneration structures within business divisions;

Developing and implementing group policies, including:

- Codes of ethics and business practice
- Share dealing code
- Risk management policies
- Treasury policies
- Health and safety policy
- Communications policy (including procedures for the release of price sensitive information)
- Investor relations policy
- Corporate social responsibility policy (including environmental, employee communications and employee disability)
- Charitable donations policy; and

Ensuring the active liaison, co-ordination and co-operation between business divisions.

11. Reporting Responsibilities

The Chief Executive shall report formally to the board, at each board meeting, on the proceedings of the Committee since the previous board meeting.

Appendix

General Purposes Committee

The following duties and powers are often delegated to a general purposes or finance committee, rather than the executive committee.

Duties

To approve the opening of new ordinary current or deposit account banking facilities, the persons to act as the authorised signatories and the authority limits of all bank accounts in the United Kingdom and overseas;

To approve arrangements with financial institutions for dealing in the following:

- money market instruments
- currency instruments
- interest rate instruments
- exchange traded futures and options contracts
- sale and repurchase agreements;

To approve guarantees and indemnities up to a maximum liability in each case of £xx million or its equivalent (at the time of approval or authorisation) in any other currency required in connection with the issue of bonds, guarantees, indemnities or letters of credit or other financial accommodation by any bank, surety group or financial institution on its behalf;

To approve guarantees and indemnities (whether in respect of any financial obligation or otherwise) including (but not limited to) any such guarantee or indemnity required to be given in respect of the obligations of any group subsidiary company of up to £xx million in each case or its equivalent (at the time of approval or authorisation) in any other currency;

To issue comfort letters, whether in respect of any financial obligation or otherwise;

To allot shares in the Company to satisfy awards of shares under its executive and employee share plans and to approve the market purchase [or transfer out of treasury] of shares for the same purpose. Allotments of shares to directors following the exercise of awards under the plans must also be agreed by the Chairman of the Board, or in their absence, the Chairman of the Remuneration Committee;

To review the monthly summary of treasury activities and issues.

Powers

The Committee may authorise:

any director or the company secretary to execute and deliver any agreement, document or instrument and to do any act or thing for or in connection with any of the above transactions, arrangements and other matters, including but not limited to, a power of attorney or other document under which the execution and delivery of any agreement, document or instrument constituting or evidencing any of the transactions, arrangements or other matters referred to above will be effected; and

officials of the Company to sign declarations, affidavits, warrants, bills of lading and other official documents, relating to patents, trade marks, customs, shipping, government returns, taxation documents, bad debts, liquidations and other similar matters as may from time to time be required to be completed in the normal course of business;

the appointment of individuals to act on behalf of the Company in relation to matters for which it has authority or responsibility and specifically delegate to the Company Secretary the authority to approve the exercise of options and allotment of shares under any of the company share plans; and

any other matters specifically delegated to the Committee by the Board.

Appendix 5

ICSA GUIDANCE NOTE: DIRECTORS' AND OFFICERS' INSURANCE
(April 2005)

In 2002, at the request of the Secretary of State, Derek Higgs undertook a review of the role and effectiveness of non-executive directors. One point identified as causing concern related to the perceived inadequacies and high costs of Directors and Officers Liability cover (D & O). Following publication of the Report,[1] and at the request of the Higgs team, ICSA convened a meeting of representatives of:

- City of London Law Society;

- ICSA;

- The Association of British Insurers;

- British Insurance Brokers Association; and

- The ICSA Company Secretaries Forum

to produce guidance on this topic.

It was agreed that, given the wide variety of organisations, the range of industries in which they operate and the differing everyday business risks, it would not be practical to draft a 'specimen policy'. This note is therefore:

- a check-list of just some of the major issues that prospective directors (whether executive or non-executive) should consider, both to help them understand D & O insurance and also to evaluate the cover provided by companies they are considering joining; and

- a useful aide memoire for existing directors and for organisations when considering their own requirements for such cover.

The Guidance is not intended to be a comprehensive summary of the topic and should not be considered a substitute for specific advice from a good broker or legal adviser.

It should be remembered that D & O insurance is only one of the methods by which risk is transferred from directors. They may also, for example, have an indemnity from the company, but this will undoubtedly be restricted, either by its specific terms or by law.

D & O insurance is not compulsory. Although Section 310 of the Companies Act (1985) permits companies to take out insurance on behalf of their directors and to pay the premiums, it is not mandatory. However the newly published Combined Code[2] includes a provision (A.1.5) that 'The company should arrange appropriate insurance cover in respect of legal action against its directors'.

---

1 *Review of the role and effectiveness of non-executive directors*, DTI January 2003.
2 *The Combined Code on Corporate Governance* issued by the Financial Reporting Council, July 2003.

D & O insurance is normally taken out in one of three formats:

- A policy which is taken out by the company (and most usually the policy schedule will be in the name of that company) and which provides cover for indemnifiable risks under one section and non-indemnifiable risks under another – commonly referred to as sections A and B;

- A policy which is taken out by the company (again most usually the policy schedule will be in the name of that company) and which provides cover only for non-indemnifiable risks. This type of policy is particularly popular for companies that wish to provide significant limits of indemnity for directors and officers when the company does not, cannot or will not indemnify. Particular care and attention must be paid to the wording of the operative clause in such policies (i.e. regarding when indemnity can be provided);

- A policy covering an individual named person, e.g. Mr David Smith, who may have one and/or a number of directorships, executive and/or non-executive positions which he wishes to insure under his 'own personal policy'.

From this it is clear that individuals may find themselves covered by more than one policy which can cause major difficulties between parties. It is therefore important that due cognisance is made of potential overlap and/or gaps in cover.

The headings in this note are for general guidance; many of the issues raised overlap between areas.

Who does it cover?

Unless written as an 'individual' policy, the company itself, parent and/or subsidiary companies may be covered to the extent that they in turn have to indemnify their directors and officers. Associated companies[3] may not be included at all.

The policy normally covers the directors, the company secretary(ies) and any other nominated officers of the insured company(ies).

Those seeking to join a company as a director or officer should seek written confirmation that they will be included in the company's D & O insurance and notified of any changes in cover that might affect them.

This may be particularly important when considering the sufficiency of the amount of cover provided – see section headed 'Amount of cover'.

From the individual's point of view it is also important to check that the policy covers 'past and present directors' to ensure that cover continues after 'retirement'[4] – at least in respect of situations occurring during their period of office. There are examples where those who ceased to be directors prior to the inception of the policy were not covered, even where the claim arose after the policy's inception, – see section headed 'Automatic conversion to run-off'.

---

3 Whilst different insurers may define 'associated companies' differently, the Financial Reporting Standard FRS9 defines it as 'An entity (other than a subsidiary) in which another entity (the investor) has a participating interest and over whose operating and financial policies the investor exercises significant influence'.

4 'Retirement' is used here in its broadest sense and covers a director leaving the company for whatever reason.

Outside directors

Standard policies will not automatically cover directors and officers sitting on unconnected boards, i.e. boards outside the insured group, where the director sits at the request of the group. In such cases, 'Outside Directors' cover will be required. This will often only be available on different, more restricted terms, than the basic D & O cover. Typical wording of such an inclusion may read:

> '*a past, present or future director of an outside entity who has become or became a director of the entity at the specific request of the company.*'

Care will be needed to ensure that the particular needs of the company and individual are correctly catered for, e.g. directors or officers seconded to, or given an additional role in, an associated or unrelated company should check that they will be covered either under the main or the associated/unrelated company's policies.

Acquisitions

As with many issues in D & O insurance different insurers deal with acquisitions in differing ways. Some will cover acquisitions automatically, but this could be on any one of a number of different bases. It is essential to check. A typical clause may read:

> '*The benefit of the insurance cover provided by this policy shall extend automatically to all newly acquired or created subsidiaries of the company, other than those which have or have had a listing of any of its securities on any exchange in the USA or Canada; such extension to apply solely in respect of WRONGFUL ACTS alleged to have been committed whilst the newly acquired or created company was a subsidiary of the company.*'

Note the exclusion of US and Canadian listed companies. If such an organisation is involved, the insurer would undoubtedly seek to clarify the risk involved and quote specific terms and conditions for such an inclusion.

Period of cover

Cover will normally start from the date of appointment, but there may be a requirement to notify the insurer of the appointment. Frequently, the only obligation is to update the list of directors and officers at annual renewal.

Directors should ask the company to confirm that the appropriate notifications have been or will be made. In any event, companies would be wise to play safe and notify the insurer/broker of changes – especially in circumstances such as the appointment of a new US based director which may fundamentally alter the risk.

Care should be taken to ensure that the insurer will be or has been notified of the appointment within any prevailing time limits.

Basis of cover

D & O policies are almost exclusively written on a 'claims made' basis. Cover will normally cease when the appointment comes to an end, but an individual's liability may continue for some time in respect of actions or inactions occurring during the period of appointment. To cover this a policy can be extended to include 'run-off' cover.

Directors should obtain clear guidance on the extent of 'run-off' cover that is provided under the policy and what, if any, action is required to ensure that they are/will be included under such provision. Although there are examples of run-off cover being provided for up to six years, there are also examples where it has been restricted to just six months. This can pose particular problems for 'retiring' directors and officers or where divisions or parts of businesses are disposed of, and the continuity of cover is broken.

Automatic conversion to run-off

Some policies have an 'automatic run-off' option. More often, this will come under the condition of 'Extended Discovery Period'. Either approach usually involves payment of an additional premium, which varies in amount. It can be as little as 25% or up to 100% of the most recent annual premium, depending on the duration of the run-off period and the insurer's willingness to extend the policy on this basis.

It is vital to remember that indemnity contracts do not have any automatic extensions or 'periods of grace'. If renewal is required, the insurer must be advised long before the expiry of the existing contract otherwise continuity[5] of cover will be broken and then backdating the start of the cover can become a serious issue.

What is a 'claim'?

A 'claim' is usually defined quite narrowly e.g. 'a demand made in writing'. Anything else, such as a threat of legal action, has to be notified as a 'Circumstance' (which may give rise to a claim). As a 'Circumstance', if accepted by the insurer, will lodge in the year it is registered regardless of when the eventual claim may materialise, insurers are generally reluctant to accept them.

Duty of disclosure

As with all insurances, the policy will incorporate a duty of disclosure whether or not specifically mentioned. A director will therefore be obliged to disclose to the insurer any claims or circumstances which may give rise to a claim.

Some policies contain clauses which can be quite helpful to the insured e.g. severability clauses whereby one insured's knowledge, or facts pertaining to one insured, are not ascribed to other insureds. In addition, insurers will sometimes agree not to void a policy for non-disclosure or misrepresentation if the insured can establish that such non-disclosure or misrepresentation was entirely innocent.

Extent of cover

Policy wording, and the extent of cover, can vary widely and care should be taken to understand what is (and – more importantly – what is not) covered, and any areas of risk that may remain. It is usual and/or highly desirable to include the following:

- Damages awarded against an insured person;

---

5 We understand that the word 'continuity' may have a specific meaning within the realms of D & O insurance however in this text the word is used in its everyday sense.

- Out-of-court settlements – care should be taken to ensure that these are also specifically included;

- Costs, including fees, professional costs and expenses resulting from the investigation and/ or defence or settlement of a claim will normally be covered. However, material or information may come to light during a claim which causes the insurer to cease paying the defence costs half way through. In such cases the insurer may also seek to recover costs already paid out;

- Libel and slander – may be included, but not always;

- Wrongful Acts which can be defined as any error, mis-statement, misleading statement, act, omission, neglect or breach of duty committed or attempted or any matter claimed against the individual solely by reason of their serving in a capacity as a director or officer of the company. Whilst the definition of Wrongful Acts can vary and be very widely construed it is of vital importance to recognise that the act must be something done in the capacity of director or officer.

The following are common restrictions and/or exclusions:

- Fines, penalties and punitive damages levied by regulators or criminal courts. (Note that the Financial Services Authority has recently suggested that it will, in any event, ban insurance cover for regulatory fines.);

- Criminal defence costs can apply in respect of criminal proceedings, but only to the point of conviction/release. No cover is given for appeal costs in the event of a conviction – the premise of innocent until proven guilty applies only to a limited extent;

- Loss of earnings or expenses incurred by the insured themselves, such as PR expenses to preserve reputations;

- Personal injury or property damage are also frequently excluded (this will typically be covered elsewhere – see below);

- Fraudulent, dishonest or illegal acts. Cover will not extend to deliberate dishonesty or the deliberate committing of fraudulent or illegal acts as to do so would be against the public interest;

- Legal jurisdiction. Some policies may restrict cover to certain geographical areas or exclude specific jurisdictions, e.g. the highly litigious USA. Directors and potential directors should consider carefully the possibility of a claim arising in any area excluded under the policy;

- Taxes are rarely covered. It should also be noted that premiums may not be tax deductible by the insuring company but, if structured properly, they may not be taxable as a benefit in kind to the director or officer. Directors and potential directors should obtain confirmation of the tax treatment in relation to the policy and their personal position. Premiums paid by an individual where cover is taken out personally will, on the other hand, usually be tax deductible;

- Existing conditions. Cover will normally exclude any loss or liability arising from an action or inaction occurring prior to the commencement of the cover. Careful attention should be paid to 'Conditions precedent' clauses which can be quite onerous;

- Liabilities covered elsewhere – e.g. liabilities normally covered under Employer's or Public Liability policies or Prospectus Liability policies. Those who may find themselves covered by more than one policy should make a point of clarifying the precise position. Some policies, for example, will cover executive directors in non-executive positions of other companies who may also have their own cover;

- Insured v insured. Some policies will not cover actions between parties covered by the same policy, often now described as the 'Equitable Life Claim scenario'. This might be an action taken by the company against a director or one director against another covered by the same policy. This can be particularly complicated when one policy covers a Group of companies including directors and officers of the parent and various subsidiary companies. Policies differ widely in the wording here but it is critical that directors and potential directors recognise whether the policy would cover them against claims from the company itself and/or another director covered by the same policy;

- Additional services. D & O policies are designed to cover liabilities arising from the insured services as a director or officer and will not extend to services, e.g. professional services, outside the scope of their role as directors or officers of the company. Similarly D & O cover will not normally extend to personal guarantees and undertakings given by directors and officers. Although they may be given in connection with the role, e.g. personal guarantees to lenders, they do not arise out of the role itself;

- Service Companies. Additional complications can arise where a director may provide his/her services through a service company. If a director intends to act through a service company, care should be taken to clarify the position.

'Basis of contract' clause

The proposal form for the policy may include a 'basis of contract' clause. This seemingly innocuous phrase can have far-reaching consequences – its legal effect is to give every statement in the proposal form the status of a warranty so that a trivial error can be used by the insurer to avoid the policy.

This has been upheld by UK courts despite criticism of the potentially severe consequences it can have for the insured – while the Statement of General Insurance Practice issued by the ABI recommends that personal lines insurance is not written on this basis, Directors & Officers Liability cover is treated as corporate insurance and may still include a 'basis of contract' clause. Companies should therefore seek to have this removed in renewal negotiations and a director who hopes to benefit from cover under a D & O policy should establish whether the policy contains this clause, given its potential to negate the cover provided by the policy.

Amount of cover

Policies are usually written with a specific monetary limit but how this limit is applied may vary:

- Per claim – the policy will normally have a limit per claim or incident and may have sub-limits for different heads of claim;

- Per year – cover will frequently have an overall limit per year, often including defence costs. This can be particularly problematic where a number of companies or individuals are covered by the same policy. If the overall limit is exhausted by one or two claims, the unfortunate subject of a third claim may find they have no cover at all. This situation is often exacerbated when policy cover for one area is extended without due consideration to the impact on the overall or other parts of the policy. Directors and potential directors should clarify the amount of cover provided.

Automatic re-instatement of sums insured

This extension, if available, can be particularly useful in guarding against the using up of cover. Clauses vary between insurers. Many take the position that they would seek a higher initial sum insured – for example, several hundreds of millions. In the UK, the tendency has been to err on the side of caution, which sees the vast majority of limits in the tens of millions.

More recently, many new companies coming into the market have found it difficult to obtain this type of extension. Insurers are becoming more concerned over the complications of providing a 'top up' of sums insured – but existing policies with this cover built in may still be able to renew with the extension. In the current market, the availability of cover has been restricted – but the hope is that it will become easier as the liability market settles down in the coming months.

Deductibles

Any deductible will be a matter of commercial negotiation, and can vary from nil to quite a high 'excess'. Different deductibles will apply to different sections of a policy and directors should be clear when or whether a deductible applies and, if so, in which circumstances this will be paid by the company and when it might be for their own account. If, for example, deductibles apply 'per event' it is essential to be clear on what constitutes a single event. For example, was 9/11 a single act of terrorism or a series of separate hijackings?

Conditions

All D & O policies will have fairly strict conditions attached. These may cover such things as:

- notification of appointments or other changes in the list of insured persons;
- notification of potential or actual claims;
- what actually constitutes a 'claim' in the terms of the policy;
- admission of liability;
- the actual conduct of any claims; and
- an obligation to make oneself available to defend a claim;

most of which are dealt with individually within this Guidance Note.

The general point, however, is that the exact wording in some of these clauses can be critical. For example, where there is an obligation to 'notify', the language might refer to circumstances which 'may' or 'are likely' to give rise to a claim. Clearly the two situations are significantly different. It can however be a double-edged sword; if the duty is to notify 'promptly' or within a specified time limit then there is a greater risk of breaching the 'may' condition than there is if the threshold is 'likely to'.

If there is simply an obligation to notify (without a time limit) then 'may' reduces the prospect of insurers alleging that a claim is not sufficiently probable. Further difficulties can then arise because, in the ordinary way, the matter giving rise to concern would have to be disclosed to the next insurer for the following period and the new insurer might insist on an exclusion in respect of that particular matter.

As with all insurance policies, it is a contract of 'utmost good faith'. Additionally there will be a requirement to mitigate losses wherever possible. It may, for example, be financially beneficial to settle a claim out of court rather than bear the costs of a protracted and complicated defence, especially if advice is that the defence is unlikely to succeed – even though this may be damaging to the reputation of the individual concerned.

Right of litigation

The insurer will almost invariably have the right to act on behalf of the insured although, unlike most insurance policies, with D & O insurance it is the duty of the company/director actually to defend a claim. This can be an extremely onerous experience for the individual.

Whilst the choice of legal adviser might be agreed between the insured and insurer there will be a tendency to appoint a legal firm who will have a good degree of insurance knowledge – which is all well and good in major centres like London, Birmingham etc. but might raise problems in more remote areas.

Summary

The (July 2003) Combined Code contains a specimen appointment letter for new non-executive directors and suggests that a copy of the D & O policy is provided. Clearly this is a pragmatic and reasonable practice. Potential directors should make every effort to understand the D & O policy, what it does and does not cover and the manner in which cover operates when joining, serving or leaving the company. It may also be prudent to understand the company's procedures for renewing or amending the cover to ensure that the cover cannot be diluted without the knowledge of those affected. If anything is unclear, clarification should be sought from the company secretary.

Given the complexity of the topic we make no apologies for repeating the earlier warning. The purpose of this Guidance Note is to alert, particularly new, directors to some of the issues involved with D & O insurance. It is not intended to be, nor in just a few pages can it be, a comprehensive guide. For those requiring more detailed information there are some authoritative books available on the subject. The risks and extent of cover available are however changing all the time and anyone contemplating taking out D & O insurance is advised to seek good professional advice.

It has been suggested that a short guide such as this is likely to raise more questions than it answers. If that is what happens then it may be that this Guide has served its purpose.

Appendix 6

ICSA GUIDANCE NOTE: DUE DILIGENCE FOR DIRECTORS
(July 2003)

A Guide to the due diligence process that prospective directors should undertake before joining a company.

Why undertake due diligence?

The review carried out by Derek Higgs and published in January 2003 as the Review of the role and effectiveness of non-executive directors, recommended that before accepting an appointment, the prospective non-executive director should undertake their own thorough examination of the company to satisfy themselves that it is an organisation in which they can have faith and in which they will be well suited to working.

The Institute of Chartered Secretaries and Administrators assisted in the compilation of a list of questions for this purpose and undertook to keep them up to date. The questions as seen below are more or less as per the original Higgs report and as repeated in the Financial Reporting Council's re-issue of the Combined Code in July 2003. The order has, however, been re-arranged slightly and sub-headings added.

The following questions are not intended to be exhaustive, but are intended to be a helpful basis for the pre-appointment due diligence process that all non-executive directors should undertake. By making the right enquiries, asking the right questions and taking care to understand the replies, a prospective director can reduce the risk of nasty surprises and dramatically increase the likelihood of success.

Questions to ask

The business

What is the company's current financial position and what has its financial track record been over the last three years?

What are the exact nature and extent of the company's business activities?

What is the company's competitive position and market share in its main business areas?

What are the key dependencies (e.g. regulatory approvals, key licences)?

Governance and investor relations

What record does the company have on corporate governance issues?

Does the company have sound and effective systems of internal controls?

Who are the current executive and non-executive directors, what is their background and record and how long have they served on the board?

What is the size and structure of the board and board committees and what are the relationships between the chairman and the board, the chief executive and the management team?

Who owns the company i.e. who are the company's main shareholders and how has the profile changed over recent years?

What is the company's attitude towards, and relationship with, its shareholders?

The role of the non-executive director

Is the company clear and specific about the qualities, knowledge, skills and experience that it needs to complement the existing board?

If the company is not performing particularly well is there potential to turn it round and do I have the time, desire and capability to make a positive impact?

Am I satisfied that the size, structure and make-up of the board will enable me to make an effective contribution?

Would accepting the non-executive directorship put me in a position of having a conflict of interest?

Do I have the necessary knowledge, skills, experience and time to make a positive contribution to the board of this company?

How closely do I match the job specification and how well will I fulfil the board's expectations?

Risk management

Is there anything about the nature and extent of the company's business activities that would cause me concern both in terms of risk and any personal ethical considerations?

Is any material litigation presently being undertaken or threatened, either by the company or against it?

Am I satisfied that the internal regulation of the company is sound and that I can operate effectively within its stated corporate governance framework?

What insurance cover is available to directors and what is the company's policy on indemnifying directors?

Sources of information

- Company report and accounts, and/or any listing prospectus, for the recent years.
- Analysts' reports.
- Press reports.
- Company web site.

- Any Corporate Social Responsibility or Environmental Report issued by the company.

- Rating agency reports.

- Voting services reports.

Published material is unlikely to reveal wrongdoing, however a lack of transparency may be a reason to proceed with caution.

Further information may be obtained from discussions with existing directors, senior management, employees, suppliers and customers although care should be taken to preserve confidentiality especially considering that, in itself, the fact that an approach has been made will undoubtedly be deemed to be price sensitive information.

Appendix 7

ICSA GUIDANCE NOTE: INDUCTION OF DIRECTORS
(February 2003)

Since the publication of the ICSA Best Practice Guide *The Appointment and Induction of Directors*, it has become apparent that some newly appointed directors have been completely overwhelmed with the sheer volume of documents and other papers provided by the well meaning company secretary to such an extent that some have been completely put off by it.

The objective of induction is to inform the director such that he or she can become as effective as possible in their new role as soon as possible. The provision of reams of paper in one go is, obviously, not conducive to this process. It is therefore recommended that, on appointment, a new director be provided with certain key, essential information together with a comprehensive list of other information that will be made available subsequently.

More recently we have seen the publication of the Higgs Report on the role and effectiveness of non-executive directors. That report includes various recommendations including, as Annex I, an induction checklist. ICSA worked closely with the Higgs Review team on the creation of that checklist and, in order to enable it to be kept brief and to the point, undertook to produce this Guidance Note providing more comprehensive details of the material that should be considered for inclusion in an induction pack provided to new directors on, or during the weeks immediately following their appointment.

The following list is divided into three parts. The first includes the essential material that should be provided immediately and the second, material that should be provided over the first few weeks following the appointment, as and when deemed most appropriate. The director should, however, be provided immediately with a comprehensive list of the material being made available in total, together with an undertaking to provide it earlier if required.

The third list covers items which the company secretary might consider making the director aware of.

Note that some information may have already been provided during the director's due diligence process prior to appointment, or along with the appointment letter. Whilst duplication should be avoided, care should be taken to provide any updates that may be necessary.

The topics contained within this note should be supplied to all newly appointed directors, both executive and non-executive, however the secretary will need to gauge the level of previous knowledge and adjust them accordingly, particularly in regard to the appointment of executive directors.

Essential information to be provided immediately

The following information is felt to be essential and needs to be given to the director prior to the first board meeting.

Methods of delivery vary. Some of the information needs to be sent to the director with his appointment letter; but some could be deferred until a meeting after the board papers have been issued, so that the company secretary can review the board pack with the director before the first meeting highlighting any relevant issues.

Directors' Duties

Brief outline of the role of a director and a summary of his/her responsibilities and ongoing obligations under legislation, regulation and best practice.

Copy of UKLA Model Code, and details of the company's procedure regarding directors' share dealings and the disclosure of price sensitive information.

The company's guidelines on:

- Matters reserved for the board;

- Delegated Authorities;

- The policy for obtaining independent professional advice for directors;

- Other standing orders, policies and procedures of which the director should be aware.

'Fire Drill' procedures (the procedures in place to deal with such as hostile takeover bids).

The Company's Business

Current strategic/business plan, market analysis and budgets for the year with revised forecast, and three/five year plan.

Latest annual report and accounts, and interims as appropriate.

Explanation of key performance indicators.

List of major domestic and overseas subsidiaries, associated companies and joint ventures, including any parent company(ies).

Summary details of major group insurance policies including D & O liability insurance.

Details of any major litigation, either current or potential, being undertaken by the company or against the company.

Treasury issues:

- Funding position and arrangements;

- Dividend policy.

The corporate brochure, mission statement and any other reports issued by the company such as an environmental report, with a summary of the main events (such as mergers, divestments, introductions of new products, diversification into new areas, restructuring etc.) over the last three years.

Board Issues

Up to date copy of the company's Memorandum and Articles of Association /Constitution, with a summary of the most important provisions.

Minutes of the last 3 to 6 board meetings.

Schedule of dates of future board meetings and board subcommittees if appropriate.

Description of board procedures covering details such as when papers are sent out, the normal location of meetings, how long they last and an indication of the routine business transacted.

Brief biographical and contact details of all directors of the company, the company secretary and other key executives. This should include any executive responsibilities of directors, their dates of appointment and any board committees upon which individual directors sit.

Details of board subcommittees together with terms of reference and, where the director will be joining a committee, copies of the minutes of meetings of that committee during the previous 12 months.

Additional material to be provided during the first few months

The following information is crucial to assist the director to develop his/her knowledge of the company, its operations and staff, but is not necessary for him/her to commence his/her involvement. It is suggested, however, that a detailed schedule of the information available is provided to him/her, and the information is supplied either on request or within three months of appointment. It would also be appropriate to involve senior members of staff in the induction programme, for example the Investor Relations Manager could give a presentation on the IR programme, so that the non-executive director begins to get a view of the depth of management available and the executive director is exposed to areas of the business he/she has less previous knowledge of.

Copies of the company's main product/service brochures.

Copies of recent press cuttings, reports and articles concerning the company.

Details of the company's advisers (lawyers, bankers, auditors, registrars etc.), both internal and external, with the name of the partner dealing with the company's affairs.

The company's risk management procedures and relevant disaster recovery plans.

An outline of the provisions of the Combined Code as appended to the UK Listing Rules together with details of the company's corporate governance guidelines and any Investor's corporate governance guidelines which the company seeks to follow.

Brief history of the company including when it was incorporated and any significant events during its history.

Notices of any general meetings held in the last 3 years, and accompanying circulars as appropriate.

Company organisation chart and management succession plans.

Copy of all management accounts prepared since the company's last audited accounts.

The company's investor relations policy and details of the major shareholders.

Details of the five largest customers with the level of business done over the last five years.

Details of the five largest suppliers to the company.

Policies as regards:

- Health & Safety;

- Environmental;

- Ethics and Whistleblowing;

- Charitable & Political donations.

Internal company telephone directory (including any overseas contact numbers and names).

Additional information which the company secretary might consider making the director aware of

The final section includes information which will differ for all companies depending on the sector and the company secretary will need to use his/her experience and knowledge to pass on information to allow the director to feel accustomed to the business as soon as possible.

Protocol, procedures and dress code for:

- Board meetings;

- General meetings;

- Formal dinners, staff social events, site visits etc. including the involvement of partners where appropriate.

Procedures for:

- Accounts sign off;

- Results announcements;

- Items requiring approval outside of board meetings.

Expenses policy and method of re-imbursement.

Appendix 8

ICSA CODE OF GOOD BOARDROOM PRACTICE

1. The board should establish written procedures for the conduct of its business which should include the matters covered in this Code. A copy of these written procedures should be given to each director. Compliance should be monitored, preferably by an audit committee of the board, and breaches of the procedures should be reported to the board.

2. The board should ensure that each director is given on appointment sufficient information to allow him or her to perform his or her duties. In particular, guidance for non-executive directors should cover the procedures:
    - for obtaining information concerning the company; and
    - for requisitioning a meeting of the board.

3. In the conduct of board business, two fundamental concepts should be observed:
    - each director should receive the same information at the same time; and
    - each director should be given sufficient time in which to consider such information.

4. The board should identify matters which require the prior approval of the board and lay down procedures to be followed when, exceptionally, a decision is required before its next meeting on any matter not required by law to be considered at board level.

5. As a basic principle, all material contracts, and especially those not in the ordinary course of business, should be referred to the board for decision prior to the commitment of the company.

6. The board should approve definition of the terms 'material' and 'not in the ordinary course of business' and these definitions should be brought to the attention of all relevant persons.

7. Where there is any doubt about the materiality or nature of a contract, it should normally be assumed that the contract should be brought before the board.

8. Decisions regarding the content of the agenda for individual meetings of the board and concerning the presentation of agenda items should be taken by the chairman in consultation with the company secretary.

9. The company secretary should be responsible to the chairman for the proper administration of the meetings of the company, the board and any committees of the board. To carry out this responsibility, the company secretary should be entitled to be present at, or represented at, all such meetings and should be responsible for preparing, or arranging for the preparation of, the minute of the proceedings of all such meetings.

10. The minutes of meetings should record the decisions taken and provide sufficient background to those decisions. All papers presented at meetings should be clearly identified in the minutes and retained for reference. Procedures for the approval and circulation of minutes should be established.

11. Where the articles of association allow the board to delegate any of its powers to a committee, the board should give its prior approval to:
    - the membership and quorum of any such committee;
    - its terms of reference; and
    - the extent of any powers delegated to it.

12. The minutes of all meetings of committees of the board (or a written summary thereof) should be circulated to the board prior to its next meeting and the opportunity should be given at that meeting for any member of the board to ask questions thereon.

13. Notwithstanding the absence of a formal agenda item, the chairman should permit any director or the company secretary to raise at any board meeting any matter concerning the company's compliance with this Code of Practice, with the company's Memorandum and Articles of association and with any other legal or regulatory requirement.

Notes

1. If it is practicable, the approval of all of the directors for matters reserved to the board should be obtained by means of a written resolution. In all cases, however, the procedures should balance the need for urgency with the overriding principle that each director should be given as much information as possible and have an opportunity to requisition an emergency meeting of the board to discuss the matter prior to the commitment of the company.

2. Different definitions of the term 'material' should be established for 'contracts not in the ordinary course of business'. Financial limits should be set where appropriate.

Appendix 9

ICSA GUIDANCE NOTE: TERMS OF REFERENCE – NOMINATION COMMITTEE
(October 2003)

Following the publication of the Higgs Review[1] the Financial Reporting Council has indicated its intention of introducing the revised Combined Code with effect from 1 July 2003. This Guidance Note advises on best practice in light of the Higgs recommendations and has been drafted referring to the provisions in the suggested code.

The Combined Code states as one of its principles that:

> *'There should be a formal, rigorous and transparent procedure for the appointment of new directors to the board.'*[2]

Previous guidance has permitted smaller listed companies to allow the Board to act as a Nomination Committee. This is no longer the case, and although the Higgs Review recognised that it may take time for time for smaller companies to comply, it states 'there should be no differentiation in the Code's provision for larger and smaller companies.'

The recommendation is that companies should go through a formal process of reviewing the balance and effectiveness of its Board, identifying the skills needed and those individuals who might best provide them. In particular the committee must assess the time commitments of the Board posts and ensure that the individual has sufficient available time to undertake them.

As with most aspects of Corporate Governance, however, the company must be seen to be doing so in a fair and thorough manner. It is, therefore, essential that a Nomination Committee be properly constituted with a clear remit and identified authority.

The Combined Code states that the majority of members of a Nomination Committee should be independent non-executive directors.[3] The Chairman of the Board may be a member but, as he or she is not deemed to be independent under the revised definition, the Committee should be chaired by another independent non-executive director. It is, however, recognised in some companies, that there may be a valid reason for the Chairman of the company to chair the Nomination Committee if only for a period of time. In this case we would draw attention to the 'comply or explain' principle behind the Combined Code and suggest that, in such a case the matter be discussed with major shareholders and a full explanation for the company's decision to be included in the company's Annual Report.

The Code gives no guidance on the overall size of the Committee, we have recommended a Committee of three but companies with larger Boards should consider increasing this to four or five.

---

1 *Review of the role and effectiveness of non-executive directors*, published January 2003.
2 Principles of Good Governance and Code of Best Practice (The Combined Code), A.4.
3 The definition of independence is given in Code Provision A.3.4.

Although not a provision in the Code, the Higgs Review states as good practice, in its Non-Code Recommendations, that the Company Secretary (or their nominee) should act as Secretary to the Committee. It is the Company Secretary's responsibility to ensure that the Board and its Committees are properly constituted and advised. There also needs to be a clear co-ordination between the main Board and the various Committees where the Company Secretary would normally act as a valued intermediary.

The frequency with which the Committee needs to meet will vary considerably from company to company and will no doubt change from time to time. It is, however, clear that it must meet at least once each year prior or close to the year-end if only to consider whether or not directors retiring by rotation or reaching a pre-determined age limit should be put forward for re-appointment at the next the Annual General Meeting (AGM).

The list of duties we have proposed are those contained in the Summary of The Principal Duties of the Nomination Committee which ICSA drew up for the Higgs Review, which we believe all Nomination Committees should consider. Some companies may wish to add to this list and some smaller companies may need to modify it in other ways.

The Chairman of the Committee should attend the AGM and be prepared to respond to any questions which may be raised by shareholders on matters within the Committee's area of responsibility.

The reporting requirements within the Annual Report suggested by Higgs, means that the following has to be disclosed by the Board each year:

- The Chairman and members of the Committee need to be identified;

- The terms of reference need to be explained, to an extent that the role and authority is clearly demonstrated;

- A statement, detailing the activities and process used for appointments to the Board, for both Executive and Non-Executive appointments, explaining the reasons why external advice (recruitment consultants) or open advertising were not used;

- The number of Committee meetings held and attendance levels by members; and

- The reasons why a director should be appointed by the shareholders at the forthcoming AGM.

These recommendations and explanations clearly indicate a need for a guiding document. Further, the provisions of the Combined Code also advocate terms of reference for a Nomination Committee. This has led the ICSA to produce this Guidance Note proposing model terms of reference for a Nomination Committee to support the Summary of Principal Duties of the Nomination Committee contained within the Higgs Review. The document draws on the experience of senior Company Secretaries and Best Practice as carried out in some of the country's leading companies.

Reference to 'The Committee' shall mean The Nomination Committee.

Reference to 'The Board' shall mean The Board of Directors.

The square brackets contain recommendations which are in line with Best Practice but which may need to be changed to suit the circumstances of the particular organisation.

1. Membership

1.1.   The Committee shall be appointed by The Board and shall comprise of a Chairman and at least [2] other members.

1.2.   A majority of members of The Committee shall be independent non-executive directors.

1.3.   The Board shall appoint The Committee Chairman who should not be the Chairman of The Board. In the absence of The Committee Chairman and/or an appointed deputy, the remaining members present shall elect one of their number to chair the meeting.

1.4.   If a regular member is unable to act due to absence, illness or any other cause, the Chairman of The Committee may appoint another director of the company to serve as an alternate member having due regard to maintaining the required balance of executive and independent non-executive members.

1.5.   Care should be taken to minimise the risk of any conflict of interest that might be seen to give rise to an unacceptable influence. (It is recommended that, where possible, the Chairman and members of the Committee should be rotated on a regular basis.) No member of the Committee shall also be a member of both the Audit and Remuneration Committee.[4]

2. Secretary

2.1   The Company Secretary or their nominee shall act as the Secretary of The Committee.

3. Quorum

3.1.   The quorum necessary for the transaction of business shall be [2] of whom at least [1] must be a non-executive director. A duly convened meeting of The Committee at which a quorum is present shall be competent to exercise all or any of the authorities, powers and discretions vested in or exercisable by The Committee.

4. Frequency of Meetings

4.1.   The Committee shall meet [not less than once a year][quarterly on the first Wednesday in each of January, April, July and October] and at such other times as the Chairman of The Committee shall require.[5]

5. Notice of Meetings

5.1.   Meetings of The Committee shall be summoned by the Secretary of The Committee at the request of the Chairman of The Committee.

---

4 It is recognised that small companies who do not have sufficient NEDs may not always be able to comply with this rule. Although not stated in the Code, ICSA consider it best practice that no member of the Nomination Committee be a Member of the Remuneration Committee, so that no conflict of interest can arise following a new appointment.
5 The frequency and timing of meetings will differ according to the needs of the company. Meetings should be organised so that attendance is maximised (eg by timetabling them to coincide with Board meetings).

5.2. Unless otherwise agreed, notice of each meeting confirming the venue, time and date together with an agenda of items to be discussed, shall be forwarded to each member of The Committee no fewer than [5] working days prior to the date of the meeting.

6. Minutes of Meetings

6.1. The Secretary shall minute the proceedings and resolutions of all Committee meetings, including the names of those present and in attendance.

6.2. Minutes of Committee meetings shall be circulated to all members of The Committee and to the Chairman of The Board and made available on request to other members of The Board.

7. Annual General Meeting

7.1. The Chairman of The Committee shall attend the Annual General Meeting prepared to respond to any shareholder questions on The Committee's activities.

8. Duties

8.1. The Committee shall:

8.1.1. regularly review the structure, size and composition of The Board and make recommendations to The Board with regard to any adjustments that are deemed necessary;

8.1.2. prepare a description of the role and capabilities required for a particular appointment;

8.1.3. be responsible for identifying and nominating for the approval of The Board candidates to fill board vacancies as and when they arise;

8.1.4. satisfy itself with regard to succession planning, that the processes and plans are in place with regard to both Board and senior appointments;

8.1.5. assess and articulate the time needed to fulfil the role of Chairman, senior independent director and non executive director, and undertake an annual performance evaluation to ensure that the all members of the board have devoted sufficient time to their duties.

8.1.6. ensure on appointment that a candidate has sufficient time to undertake the role and review his commitments, ensuring that if he is an executive of another company this will be his sole non-executive appointment; and in the event that a candidate for chairman is being considered take note that he can not be a Chairman of more than one FTSE100 company or equivalent;[6] and

8.1.7. Ensure that the Secretary on behalf of the Board has formally written to any appointees, detailing the role and time commitments and proposing an induction plan produced in conjunction with the Chairman.

---

6 Combined Code Provision A.4.8.

8.2.   It shall also make recommendations to The Board:

8.2.1.   with regard to the Chairman having assessed every three years whether the present incumbent shall continue in post, taking into account the needs of continuity versus freshness of approach;

8.2.2.   as regards the re-appointment of any non-executive director at the conclusion of his or her specified term of office; especially when they have concluded their second term;[7]

8.2.3.   for the continuation (or not) in service of any director who has reached the age of [70];

8.2.4.   concerning the re-election by shareholders of any director under the 'retirement by rotation' provisions in the company's articles of association;

8.2.5.   concerning any matters relating to the continuation in office as a director of any director at any time;

8.2.6.   concerning the appointment of any director to executive or other office other than to the positions of Chairman and Chief Executive, the recommendation for which would be considered at a meeting of:

8.2.6.1.   all the non-executive directors regarding the position of Chief Executive;

8.2.6.2.   all the directors regarding the position of Chairman;[8]

8.2.7.   detailing items that should be published in the company's Annual Report relating to the activities of The Committee; and

8.2.8.   with regard to the membership and chairmanship of the Audit Committee.[9]

9. Authority

9.1.   The Committee is authorised to seek any information it requires from any employee of the company in order to perform its duties.

9.2.   The Committee is authorised to obtain, at the company's expense, outside legal or other professional advice on any matters within its terms of reference.

---

7 Combined Code Provision A.7.3 recommends only two terms of three years, where a third term is proposed for a NED, the reasons must be explained in the Annual Report. After nine years the NED must submit to annual re-election and The Board must continue to give its reasons.
8 The appointment of a chairman should be led by the senior independent director, leading a committee which will exclude the present incumbent and any potential candidates for the position.
9 *Audit Committees, Combined Code Guidance, A Report and Proposed Guidance* by an FRC appointed group chaired by Sir Robert Smith, published January 2003, clause 3.3.

Appendix 10

ASSOCIATION OF BRITISH INSURERS: PRINCIPLES AND GUIDELINES ON REMUNERATION
(December 2005)

Introduction

The ABI Guidelines on remuneration are designed to provide a practical framework and reference point for both shareholders in reaching voting decisions and for companies in deciding upon their remuneration policy.

In conjunction with these Guidelines, institutional shareholders continue to expect companies to follow good practice under the Combined Code by establishing Remuneration Committees of independent non-executive directors. They will also expect companies to demonstrate best practice as regards disclosure as well as compliance with statutory regulation.

Shareholders believe that the key determinant for assessing remuneration is performance in the creation of shareholder value. The overall quantum of the remuneration package and the employment costs to companies must be weighed against the company's ability to recruit, retain and incentivise individuals.

Remuneration Reports should provide a full and clear explanation of the policy, establishing a clear link between reward and performance. Effective consultation by companies when formulating policy can help to avoid inappropriate outcomes. Companies should ensure that an appropriate policy is in place and followed, rather than to risk controversy when remuneration outcomes are disclosed in the Annual Report. Appropriate disclosures on remuneration for executives at below board level can be best achieved on a banded basis in order to illustrate the coherence of the company's remuneration policy.

During the transition to international accounting standards, shareholders expect Remuneration Committees to confirm that they are using a consistent approach to performance measurement and to explain how they are achieving this. In the context of impending changes to pensions taxation we expect companies will be addressing any appropriate structural changes to remuneration. The Remuneration Report should disclose the policy intentions in this area.

Remuneration – principles

1. Remuneration Committees should maintain a constructive and timely dialogue with their major institutional shareholders and the ABI on matters relating to remuneration such as contemplated changes to remuneration policy and practice, including issues relating to share-based incentive schemes. Any proposed departure from the stated remuneration policy should be subject to prior approval by shareholders.

2. Companies should ensure that Remuneration Committees are properly established and constituted to exercise independent judgment with appropriate powers of authority delegated from Company Boards.

3. Boards should demonstrate that performance based remuneration arrangements are clearly aligned with business strategy and objectives and are regularly reviewed. They should ensure that overall arrangements are prudent, well communicated, incentivise effectively and recognise shareholder expectations.

    It is particularly important that Remuneration Committees should bring independent thought and scrutiny to the development and review process together with an understanding of the drivers of the business which contribute to shareholder value.

4. Remuneration Committees must guard against the possibility of unjustified windfall gains when designing and implementing share-based incentives and other associated entitlements. They must also ensure that variable and share-based remuneration is not payable unless the performance measurement governing this is robust. They should satisfy themselves as to the accuracy of recorded performance measures that govern vesting of such remuneration. They should work with audit committees in evaluating performance criteria.

5. Remuneration Committees should have regard to pay and conditions throughout the company and demonstrate that appropriate analysis supports the level of remuneration. They should use external comparisons with caution, in view of the risk of an upward ratchet of remuneration levels with no corresponding improvement in performance and should avoid paying more than is necessary.

6. Remuneration Committees should pay particular attention to arrangements for senior executives who are not board members but have a significant influence over the company's ability to meet its strategic objectives.

7. All new share-based incentive schemes should be subject to approval by shareholders by means of a separate and binding resolution. Where the rules of share-based incentive schemes, or the basis on which the scheme was approved by shareholders, permit some degree of latitude as regards quantum of grant or performance criteria it is expected that any changes will be detailed in the Remuneration Report. Any substantive changes in practical operation of schemes resulting from policy changes or modifications of scheme rules as previously approved should be subject to prior shareholder approval.

8. Where there is any type of matching arrangement or performance-linked enhancement in respect of shares awarded under deferred bonus arrangements, there should be a separate shareholder vote. (see Paragraphs 6.6 and 13.4)

9. There should be transparency on all components of remuneration of present and past directors and where appropriate other senior executives. Shareholders' attention should be drawn to any special arrangements and significant changes since the previous Remuneration Report.

10. Remuneration paid and awards made should be within the scope of the policy outlined in the Remuneration Report approved by shareholders. Where, in exceptional circumstances for reasons of recruitment or retention, Remuneration Committees have made provision for remuneration beyond the scope of the previously outlined remuneration policy relevant details must be disclosed and the reasons for this explained to shareholders.

11. Shareholders consider it inappropriate for chairmen and independent directors to be in receipt of incentive awards geared to the share price or performance, as this could impair their ability to provide impartial oversight and advice.

12. Awards should be structured to promote as close as possible an alignment of participants with the risks and rewards faced by shareholders. It is undesirable for directors to seek out leveraged arrangements on the price of the company's securities.

Guidelines for the structure of remuneration

1. Remuneration Committees should look at overall remuneration, at whether there is an appropriate balance between fixed and variable remuneration and between short and long-term variable components of long-term remuneration, and, if not, how the remuneration package should be rebalanced in order to accommodate new elements.

2. When setting salary levels Remuneration Committees should take into consideration the requirements of the market, bearing in mind competitive forces applicable to the sector in which the company operates and to the particular challenges facing the company. Disclosure of policy in this regard is helpful to shareholders. Remuneration Committees should be able to satisfy shareholders that the company is not paying more than is necessary to attract and retain the directors needed to run the company successfully. It is also appropriate to evaluate other elements of the overall remuneration package, which are usually expressed by reference to base salary. Simple structures assist with motivation and enhance the prospects of successful communication with the employees involved and with shareholders.

3. A policy of setting salary levels below the comparator group median can provide more scope for increasing the amount of variable performance based pay and incentive scheme participation. Where a company seeks to pay salaries at above median, justification is required.

4. Annual bonuses, normally payable in cash, can provide a useful means of short-term incentivisation, but should be related to performance. Both individual and corporate performance targets are relevant and should be tailored to the requirements of the business and reviewed regularly to ensure they remain appropriate.

5. Shareholders understand that considerations of commercial confidentiality may prevent disclosure of specific short-term targets. However they expect to be informed about the main performance parameters, both corporate and personal, adopted in the financial year being reported on. When the bonus has been paid, shareholders expect to see analysis in the Remuneration Report of the extent to which the relevant targets were actually met. The maximum participation levels should be disclosed, and any increases in the maximum from one year to the next should be explicitly justified. As provided for under the Combined Code, annual bonuses should not be pensionable.

6. Remuneration Committees are responsible for ensuring that targets set out in bonus arrangements have been properly fulfilled. Where there is doubt they should work with the Audit Committee to ensure that the basis for their decision is correct.

7. Any material payments that may be viewed as being ex-gratia in nature should be fully explained, justified and subject to shareholder approval prior to payment. Shareholders

are not supportive of transaction bonuses which reward directors and other executives for effecting transactions irrespective of their future financial consequences.

8. Boards should review regularly the potential liabilities associated with all elements of remuneration including share incentive participation and pension arrangements and should make appropriate disclosures to shareholders.

9. Shareholders recognise that pension entitlements accruing to directors represent a significant, and potentially costly, item of remuneration which is not directly linked to the performance of the company.

    There should be informative disclosure identifying incremental value accruing to pension scheme participation and any other superannuation arrangements and related contingent commitments, arising from service during the year in question.

    Changes to transfer values should be fully explained. Where there are discretionary increases in pension entitlement, significant changes in actuarial and other relevant assumptions, or ex-gratia awards or contributions, these should be fully explained and justified.

    Companies should recognise the risks of changes to future mortality rates and investment returns and how to limit the potential liability created by pension commitments.

10. Companies are not responsible for compensating individuals for changes in personal tax liabilities such as those resulting from changes to pensions taxation. In the context of the changes coming into effect in 2006 companies may wish to consider whether there may be ways of delivering remuneration that are more cost-effective than a pension fund and more aligned with shareholder value creation.

    The extent to which actual and potential liabilities such as pension promises or early retirement benefits are funded should be disclosed, together with any aggregate outstanding unfunded liabilities.

11. Remuneration Committees should scrutinise all other benefits, including benefits in kind and other financial arrangements to ensure they are justified, appropriately valued and suitably disclosed.

12. Remuneration Committees should have regard to outstanding dilution in accordance with Guideline limits (see Section 20) and where appropriate available dilution capacity should be disclosed so that this can be compared with previous years.

13. Institutional shareholders encourage companies to require their senior executives to build up meaningful shareholdings in the companies for which they work. Consistent with this approach, consideration should be given to incorporating provisions in the rules of incentive schemes to require retention of a proportion of shares to which participants become entitled until such times as shareholding guidelines are met.

14. The chairman and non-executive directors should be appropriately remunerated either in cash or in shares bought or allocated at market price. The granting of incentives linked to the share price or performance is not appropriate as this could impair the ability of chairmen and independent directors to provide impartial oversight and advice.

    Where, in exceptional circumstances, specific reasons arise for wishing to grant share incentives to a chairman, these should be fully discussed and approved by shareholders in advance. Recipients would be expected to hold all shares awarded under such schemes for the duration of their term of office.

1. **Guidelines for share incentive schemes**

   1.1   Institutional shareholders generally support share incentive schemes that link remuneration to performance and align the interests of participating executive directors and senior executives with those of shareholders.

   1.2   The implementation of such schemes involves either the commitment of shareholder funds or the dilution of shareholders' equity. It is important, therefore, that they be objectively costed, well-designed and form a coherent part of the overall remuneration package.

   1.3   These Guidelines apply to all share-based schemes including any arrangements whereby the value of an option gain will be paid either in the form of cash or shares (cash or share-settled share appreciation rights respectively).

   1.4   Shareholders expect all share incentive schemes to follow the spirit of the Guidelines.

2. **General principles**

   2.1   Share incentive schemes should emphasise the importance of linking remuneration to performance, limits on dilution and individual participation, and a structure that effectively aligns the long-term interests of management with those of shareholders, having due regard to the cost of the schemes, which should be disclosed.

   2.2   Shareholders strongly encourage the adoption of phased grants and welcome the trend towards awards being applied on a sliding scale in relation to the achievement of demanding and stretching financial performance against a target group or other relevant benchmark.

   2.3   Dilution is a matter of particular concern to investors. These Guidelines re-affirm the basic principle that overall dilution under all schemes should not exceed 10% in any 10-year period with the further limitations of 5% in any 10-year period on discretionary schemes (see Section 20).

3. **Scope**

   3.1   These Guidelines apply to all share incentive schemes or arrangements sponsored by UK listed companies whether option-based or involving conditional awards of shares, and including arrangements whereby awards on vesting or exercise are made in cash, or the transfer of shares to the value of the imputed gain at vesting date. Other companies should have regard for them, whenever possible.

4. **Remuneration Committees**

   4.1   Remuneration Committees should:

   - regularly review share incentive schemes to ensure their continued effectiveness, compliance with current Guidelines and contribution to shareholder value

- provide a statement in the Remuneration Report as to whether a review of the current share incentive schemes has been undertaken both as regards their operation, including how discretion has been exercised, and whether grant levels, performance criteria and vesting schedules which have been previously approved by shareholders remain appropriate to the company's current circumstances and prospects

- obtain prior shareholder authorisation for any substantive or exceptional amendments to scheme rules and practice including changes to limits and changes which make it easier to achieve performance targets, and where significant exercise of discretion is proposed by the Remuneration Committee.

5. Disclosure

5.1   Companies must make full and relevant disclosure in their Remuneration Reports and in new proposals regarding share incentive schemes. Their rationale should be fully explained in order to enable shareholders to make informed decisions. In the absence of clear disclosure, shareholders may not be able to take the informed decision that will enable them to give their support.

5.2   Scheme and individual participation limits must be fully disclosed in share incentive schemes. Disclosure should, inter alia, cover performance conditions and related costs and dilution limits as set out in the relevant sections below. The reasons for selecting the performance conditions and target levels, together with the overall policy for granting conditional share or option awards, should be fully explained to shareholders.

6. Performance conditions

6.1   It is now widely recognised that the desired alignment of interests is best achieved through the vesting of awards under share incentive schemes being conditional on satisfaction of performance criteria. These should demonstrate the achievement of demanding and stretching financial performance over the incentivisation period.

6.2   Challenging performance conditions should govern the vesting of awards or the exercise of options under any form of long-term share-based incentive scheme. These should:

- relate to overall corporate performance

- demonstrate the achievement of a level of performance which is demanding in the context of the prospects for the company and the prevailing economic environment in which it operates

- be measured relative to an appropriate defined peer group or other relevant benchmark

- be disclosed and transparent.

The reasons for selecting the performance condition(s), together with the overall policy for granting conditional share or share option incentive awards, should be fully explained to shareholders.

6.3 Threshold vesting levels should not be significant by comparison to annual base salary. Furthermore, award structures with a marked 'cliff-edge' vesting profile are considered inappropriate, particularly where there may be clustering of performance outcomes around the average.

6.4 Where companies have a policy of making awards with high potential value shareholders expect the vesting of such awards to be linked to commensurately higher levels of performance i.e. the greater the level of potential reward to individual participants the more stretching and demanding the performance conditions should be. Full vesting should be dependent upon achievement of significantly greater value creation than that applicable to threshold vesting. Companies should explain clearly how this is achieved, especially when annual grants of options in excess of one times salary, or equivalent long term share incentive awards, are made.

6.5 Sliding scales that correlate the reward potential with a performance scale that incorporates the provisions of these Guidelines are a useful way of ensuring that performance conditions are genuinely stretching. They generally provide a better motivator for improving corporate performance than a 'single hurdle'.

6.6 When Share Schemes provide for awards of matching shares in respect of annual bonuses, such awards should be kept within reasonable limits and further performance conditions should be satisfied before the matching shares are permitted to vest (see Paragraph 13.4).

7. Performance criteria

7.1 All types of performance measures should be fully explained. It should be demonstrated that they are robust and demanding, and linked clearly to the achievement of enhanced shareholder value. Remuneration Committees should satisfy themselves that the vesting of awards accords with these objectives.

7.2 Remuneration Committees should take particular care to ensure that comparator groups used for performance purposes remain both relevant and representative. Where only a small number of companies are used for a comparator group, Remuneration Committees should satisfy themselves that the comparative performance will not result in arbitrary outcomes which are inconsistent with the Guidelines. Awards should not be made for less than median performance.

7.3 Total shareholder return (TSR) relative to a relevant index or peer group is one of a number of generally acceptable performance criteria. However, Remuneration Committees should satisfy themselves prior to vesting that the recorded TSR or other criterion is a genuine reflection of the company's underlying financial performance, and explain their reasoning.

7.4 Where TSR is used as a performance criterion and the chosen comparator group includes companies listed in overseas markets, it is essential that TSR be measured on a consistent basis. The standard approach should be for a common currency to be used. Where there are compelling grounds for the calculation to be based on local currency TSR of comparator group companies, then the reasons for choosing this approach should be fully explained.

7.5   Remuneration Committees should be careful to ensure that the definition of earnings per share (EPS) or any other financial measure that they may employ will fully reflect performance of the business on a consistent basis in respect of the measurement period.

7.6   Shareholders need to have sufficient data to judge the appropriate size of the award for any given performance level. They also expect a maximum level of grant to be disclosed.

7.7   Other than in exceptional circumstances, the setting of a premium exercise price is not of itself a substitute for the adoption of relative performance conditions in accordance with these Guidelines.

8.   Retesting

8.1   It is increasingly recognised that retesting of performance conditions for all share-based incentive schemes is unnecessary and unjustified as is clearly the case for Long Term Incentive Plans (LTIPs) and similar nil-priced option schemes. The stipulated performance conditions should never combine a fixed performance hurdle with measurement from a variable base date.

9.   Vesting of awards

9.1   Performance conditions should be measured over a period of three or more years. Strong encouragement is given to use of longer performance measurement periods of more than 3 years and deferred vesting schedules, in order to motivate the achievement of sustained improvements in financial performance.

9.2   Where LTIP awards are made over whole shares,[1] a better alignment of interest with shareholders will be achieved if, in respect of those shares that do vest, equivalent value to that which has accrued to shareholders by way of dividends during the period from date of grant also vests in the hands of LTIP recipients. To the extent that the shares conditionally awarded do not vest then nor should any scrip or cash amounts representing the rolled-up dividends.

Remuneration Committees should also be mindful to ensure that the size of grants made on this basis takes into account reasonable expectations as to the value of the dividend stream on the company's shares over the period to vesting. Where the facility for rolled-up dividends is introduced a smaller initial grant size is required in order to target a similar level of value in the conditional share award.

10. Performance on grant

10.1   Where competitive factors genuinely make awards of performance-linked grants impossible then shareholders will consider alternative proposals carefully and only in the most exceptional circumstances approve them. For example, Remuneration Committees may consider the application of challenging performance conditions

---

1   This term covers awards structured in the form of either 'restricted shares' or 'nil-cost options'.

to govern the grant instead of the vesting of options. However shareholders are likely only to consider such proposals in certain specific and exceptional circumstances, and in particular that the company has clearly demonstrated to the satisfaction of shareholders that it is operating in a global environment which genuinely requires it to pay attention to global remuneration practices. Shareholders will expect that at least the conditions (see Appendix A) have been met.

11. Change of control provisions

11.1 Scheme rules should state that there will be no automatic waiving of performance conditions either in the event of a change of control or where subsisting options and awards are 'rolled-over' in the event of a capital reconstruction, and/or the early termination of the participant's employment. Remuneration Committees should use best endeavours to provide meaningful disclosure that quantifies the aggregate payments arising on a change of control.

11.2 Shareholders expect that the underlying financial performance of a company that is subject to a change of control should be a key determinant of what share-based awards, if any, should vest for participants. Remuneration Committees should satisfy themselves that the performance criterion genuinely reflects a robust measure of underlying financial achievement over any shorter time period. They should explain their reasoning in the Remuneration Report or other relevant documentation sent to shareholders.

11.3 Where share incentive awards vest early as a consequence of a change of control, awards should vest on a time pro-rata basis i.e. taking into account the vesting period that has elapsed at the time of change of control.

12. Cost

12.1 The cost of share incentive schemes (and any amendments to existing schemes) should be disclosed at the time shareholder approval is sought in order that shareholders can assess the benefits of the proposal against the total costs and award justification. The following information should be disclosed:

- The total cost of all incentive arrangements.

- The potential value of awards (see Appendix B Note 1) due to individual scheme participants on full vesting. This should be expressed by reference to the face value of shares or shares under option at point of grant, and expressed as a multiple of base salary.

- The expected value (see Appendix B Note 2) of the award at the outset, bearing in mind the probability of achieving the stipulated performance criteria.

- The maximum dilution which may arise through the issue of shares to satisfy entitlements.

12.2 There should be prudent and appropriate arrangements governing acquisition of shares, and financing thereof, to meet contingent obligations under share-based incentive schemes.

12.3   The use of phased grants of share options and restricted shares, and utilisation of both new and purchased shares to satisfy the vesting of awards, requires a comprehensive approach to valuation. Assessment should focus on expected value, which should be disclosed, and it should take account of the performance vesting schedule which is adopted as well as the existence of any 'retesting' and 'replacement option' facilities such as have been prevalent under traditional schemes. Shareholders are helped in this task by disclosure of face value of any share award or option grant as well as of expected value.

13. Participation

13.1   Participation in share incentive schemes should be restricted to bona-fide employees and executive directors, and be subject to appropriate limits for individual participation which should be disclosed.

13.2   There should be no absolute right of participation in share incentive schemes. Grant policy should be disclosed and consistently applied and, within the limits approved by shareholders, reflect changing commercial and competitive conditions. In the event of declining share price levels it is particularly important to avoid unjustified increases in the actual number of shares or options awarded.

13.3   Participation in more than one share incentive scheme must form part of a well-considered remuneration policy, and should not be part of a multiple arrangement designed to raise the prospects of payout.

13.4   Institutional shareholders are not supportive of arrangements whereby shares or options may, in effect, be granted at a discount. This principle applies in circumstances where Remuneration Committees provide for awards of matching shares in respect of annual bonuses payable in the form of shares where these are then held for a qualifying period of, say, 3 years. In these cases, institutional shareholders will generally expect that satisfaction of further performance criteria will be required in order for the matching element to vest (see Paragraph 6.6).

14. Phasing of awards and grants

14.1   The regular phasing of share incentive awards and option grants, generally on an annual basis, is encouraged because:

- It reduces the risk of unanticipated outcomes that arise out of share price volatility and cyclical factors.

- It eliminates the perceived problem that a limit on subsisting options encourages early exercise.

- It allows the adoption of a single performance measurement period.

- It lessens the possible incidence of 'underwater' options, where the share price falls below the exercise price.

The phased vesting of awards in specific tranches following the minimum three-year performance measurement period is not an alternative to phased grants. However, it can help to enhance the linking of vesting of awards to sustained performance and maintain incentivisation.

15. Pricing of options and shares

15.1 The price at which shares are issued under a scheme should not be less than the mid-market price (or similar formula) immediately preceding grant of the shares under the scheme.

15.2 Options granted under executive (discretionary) schemes should not be granted at a discount to the prevailing mid-market price.

15.3 Repricing or surrender and regrant of awards or 'underwater' share options is not appropriate.

16. Timing of grant

6.1 The rules of a scheme should provide that share or option awards normally be granted only within a 42 day period following the publication of the company's results.

17. Life of schemes and incentive awards

17.1 No awards should be made beyond the life of the scheme approved on adoption by shareholders, which should not exceed 10 years.

17.2 Shares and options should not vest or be exercisable within three years from the date of grant. In addition, options should not be exercisable more than 10 years from the date of grant.

17.3 Options or other conditional share awards are normally granted in respect of the year in question and in expectation of service over the performance measurement period of not less than 3 years.

17.4 Where individuals choose to terminate their employment before the end of the service period, or in the event that employment is terminated for cause, any unvested options or conditional share-based award should normally lapse.

17.5 In circumstances where the individual is unable to complete the period of service, it is to be expected that some portion of the award will vest, at least to the extent of the service period that has been completed but subject to the achievement of the appropriate performance criteria.

17.6 Where, in the event of death or cessation of employment of the option holder or where a company is taken over (except where arrangements are made for a switch to options of the offeror company), outstanding options vest or have already vested, they must be exercised (or lapse) within 12 months.

17.7 Any shares or options that a company may grant in exchange for those released under the schemes of acquired companies should normally be taken into account for the purposes of dilution and individual participation limits determined in accordance with these Guidelines.

18. Retirement

18.1 The treatment of awards in the event of retirement of the holder should reflect the principle that awards are granted in respect of the year in question and in expectation of service over the performance period of at least 3 years. Where the treatment does not follow that provided for in Paragraph 17.5, awards made within 12 months of actual retirement date must in any event be subject to pro-rating in respect of the balance of the 12 month period following grant which falls after the actual date of retirement. In determining the size and other terms of a grant made within 3 years of the anticipated retirement date, Remuneration Committees should have regard to the executive's ability to contribute to the achievement of the performance conditions.

18.2 Any unvested options or other conditional share awards which are outstanding at a participant's retirement date should be subject to performance measurement over the original stipulated period. Where the rules of the scheme require early exercise on retirement, performance should be pro-rated over the shorter period. In any event options should vest no later than the end of the initial performance measurement period, and should be finally exercisable no later than 12 months following the date of vesting.

19. Subsidiary companies and joint venture companies

19.1 It is generally undesirable for options to be granted over the share capital in a joint venture company.

19.2 In normal circumstances grants over the shares in a subsidiary company should not be made. However shareholders may consider exceptions where the condition of exercise is subject to flotation or sale of the subsidiary company. In such circumstances, grants should be conditional so that vesting is dependent on a return on investment that exceeds the cost of capital and that the market value of the shares at date of grant is subject to external validation. Exceptions will apply in the case of an overseas subsidiary where required by local legislation, or in circumstances where at least 25% of the ordinary share capital of the subsidiary is listed and held outside the group.

20. Dilution limits

20.1 Where the terms of any incentive scheme provide that entitlements may be satisfied through the issue of new shares or utilisation of treasury shares, then the rules of that scheme must provide that, when aggregated with awards under all of the company's other schemes, commitments to issue new shares or re-issue treasury shares must not exceed 10% of the issued ordinary share capital (adjusted for scrip/bonus and rights issues) in any rolling 10 year period. Remuneration Committees should ensure that appropriate policies regarding flow-rates exist in order to spread the potential issue of new shares over the life of relevant schemes in order to ensure the limit is not breached.

20.2 Commitments to issue new shares or re-issue treasury shares under executive (discretionary) schemes should not exceed 5% of the issued ordinary share capital of the company (adjusted for scrip/bonus and rights issues) in any rolling 10 year period. This may be exceeded where vesting is dependent on the achievement of significantly more stretching performance criteria, with full vesting threshold at top quartile or above.

20.3 The implicit dilution commitment should always be provided for at point of grant even where, as in the case of share-settled share appreciation rights, it is recognised that only a proportion of shares may in practice be used.

20.4 For small companies, up to 10% of the ordinary share capital may be utilised for executive (discretionary) schemes, provided that the total market value of the capital utilised for the scheme at the time of grant does not exceed £500,000.

21. Employee Share Ownership Trusts – ESOTs

21.1 ESOTs should not hold more shares at any one time than would be required in practice to match their outstanding liabilities, nor should they be used as an anti-takeover or similar device. Furthermore an ESOT's deed should provide that any unvested shares held in the ESOT shall not be voted at shareholder meetings. The prior approval of shareholders should be obtained before 5% or more of a company's share capital at any one time may be held within ESOTs.

21.2 Where companies have provided for an ESOT to be used to meet scheme requirements, they should disclose the number of shares held by the ESOT in order to assist shareholders with their evaluation of the overall use of shares for remuneration purposes. The company should explain its strategy in this regard.

22. All-Employee Schemes

22.1 All-Employee schemes, such as SAYE schemes and Share Incentive Plans (SIPs) – (formerly known as AESOPs), should operate within an appropriate best practice framework. If newly issued shares are utilised, the overall dilution limits for share schemes should be complied with. Guidelines relating to timing of grants (except for pre-determined regular appropriation of shares under SIPs) apply.

Appendix A

The following are the minimum criteria that shareholders will expect to be satisfied in respect of any share incentive scheme adopting performance at point of grant instead of performance criteria governing the vesting of awards or exercise of options (See Paragraph 10.1).

- The scheme should be tailored to executives who are exposed to global remuneration practices and the approach should not be applied automatically to UK-based participants. Comparisons with overseas companies should take account of the different practices for setting remuneration, including pension provision, when compared with UK practices.

- Performance conditions covering the grant should refer to overall corporate performance as a reference, not just individual performance of the grantee.

- The basis of performance criteria should be fully disclosed and explained.

- Performance-linking at grant does not alter the requirement that the minimum period for exercise of options should be three years from the date of grant.

- The dilution limits set out in Section 20 are adhered to.

- Participants in schemes are expected by the Board to build up a significant and disclosed shareholding through retention of awards that vest. Holding share options is not a substitute for share ownership in meeting ownership targets.

- Disclosure concerning the scheme should comply with the highest standards relevant to the other jurisdictions in which the company operates e.g. those applied by the US Securities and Exchange Commission.

Appendix B

Note 1: Potential value of the award

Shareholders are likely to have regard to the potential value of the award assuming full vesting. This should be expressed on the basis that a conditional award is made of shares, or options over shares, with a face value, at current prices, equal to a given percentage of base salary. However the potential value will also be a function of share price at the time of vesting and of illustrative disclosures of potential outcomes may also be helpful. Full vesting of awards of higher potential value should require the achievement of commensurately greater performance.

Note 2: Expected value

The concept of expected value (EV) should be central to assessment of share incentive schemes. Essentially, EV will be the present value of the sum of all the various possible outcomes at vesting or exercise of awards. This will reflect the probabilities of achieving these outcomes and also the future value implicit in these outcomes. The calculation of the EV of share schemes is often complex and relies on a range of assumptions, and reliance on this concept by Remuneration Committees will require a sufficient measure of disclosure to enable shareholders to make informed judgments about such arrangements.

The nature of performance hurdles governing exercise is also crucial to calculations of EV and it must also be recognised that any facility for 'retesting' will also increase the EV of the award whereas in contrast if the exercise price is set at a premium to the share price at the outset, this will reduce the value of the EV of the instrument.

Institutional investors welcome efforts towards ensuring that accounting for share options and other share-based payment awarded under incentive schemes fully reflects the true cost to shareholders.

Appendix 11

ICSA GUIDANCE NOTE: TERMS OF REFERENCE – REMUNERATION COMMITTEE
(October 2003)

Following the publication of the Higgs Review[1] the Financial Reporting Council has indicated its intention of introducing the revised Combined Code with effect from 1 July 2003. This Guidance Note advises on best practice in light of the recommendations contained in the Higgs Review and has been redrafted using the provisions in the suggested code.

The Combined Code states as one of its principles that:

> *"Companies should establish a formal and transparent procedure for developing policy on executive remuneration and for fixing the remuneration packages of individual directors. No director should be involved in deciding his or her own remuneration".*[2]

As with most aspects of Corporate Governance, the above stated principle makes it clear that, not only should companies go through a formal process of considering executive remuneration, but also they must be seen to be doing so in a fair and thorough manner. It is, therefore, essential that the Remuneration Committee is properly constituted with a clear remit and identified authority.

The Combined Code recommends that the Remuneration Committee should consist of at least three independent[3] non-executive directors; larger companies may wish to increase the number. The Chairman should not be a member of the Committee but may be asked, as the Chief Executive may, to attend on occasion to assist in the discussions.

Although not a provision in the code, the Higgs review states as good practice in its Non-Code Recommendations, that the Company Secretary (or their nominee) should act as Secretary to the Committee. It is the Company Secretary's responsibility to ensure that the Board and its Committees are properly constituted and advised. There also needs to be a clear co-ordination between the main Board and the various Committees where the Company Secretary would normally act as a valued intermediary.

The frequency with which the Committee needs to meet will vary considerably from company to company and will no doubt change from time to time. It is, however, clear that it must meet at least once each year prior or close to the year-end; its purpose at this meeting should be to prepare the Remuneration Report which the Combined Code and now the Remuneration Report Regulations require to be submitted to shareholders with or as part of the company's Annual Report. The Remuneration Report must be put to the shareholders for approval at the AGM.[4]

---

1 *Review of the role and effectiveness of non-executive directors,* published January 2003.
2 Principles of Good Governance and Code of Best Practice,(The Combined Code), B.2 .
3 An Independent non-executive director is one that satisfies Combined Code Provision A.3.4.
4 *Directors' Remuneration Report Regulations 2002.*

The reporting requirements suggested by Higgs and expanded on in Schedule B to the Combined Code, means that the following has to be disclosed by the Board each year within the Annual Report:

- The Chairman and members of the committee need to be identified.

- The terms of reference need to be explained, to an extent that the role and authority is clearly demonstrated.

- The number of committee meetings and attendance level by members.

- The Company's policy with regard to both executive and non-executive pay.

- The information required under Schedule B and the Directors' Remuneration Report Regulations 2002.

The list of duties we have proposed are those contained within the Summary of Principal Duties Of the Remuneration Committee which ICSA helped compile for the Higgs Review and which we believe all Remuneration Committees should consider. Some companies may wish to add to this list and some smaller companies may need to modify it in other ways. The Chairman of the Committee should attend the Annual General Meeting (AGM) and be prepared to respond to any questions which may be raised by shareholders on the Committee's report or other matters within the Committee's area of responsibility.

These recommendations and explanations clearly show the need for there to be a guiding document and the provisions of the Combined Code also advocate terms of reference for a Remuneration Committee. This has led the ICSA to produce this Guidance Note proposing model terms of reference for a Remuneration Committee. The document draws on the experience of senior Company Secretaries and Best Practice as carried out in some of the country's leading companies.

References to 'The Committee' shall mean the Remuneration Committee.

References to 'The Board' shall mean the full Board of Directors.

The square brackets contain recommendations which are in line with Best Practice but which may need to be changed to suit the circumstances of the particular organisation.

1. Membership

1.1   The Committee shall comprise of at least [3] members, each of whom shall be appointed by The Board.

1.2   All members of The Committee shall be non-executive directors who are independent of management and free from any business or other relationship which could interfere with the exercise of their independent judgement.

1.3   The Board should appoint The Committee Chairman and determine the period for which they shall hold office. The Chairman of the company shall not be eligible to be appointed as Chairman of The Committee.

1.4   Care should be taken to minimise the risk of any conflict of interest that might be seen to give rise to an unacceptable influence. (It is recommended that, where possible, the Chairman and members of The Committee should be rotated on a regular basis.) No member of The Committee shall also be a member of both the Audit and Nomination Committee.[5]

2. Secretary

2.1 The Company Secretary or their nominee shall act as the Secretary of The Committee.

3. Quorum

3.1 The quorum necessary for the transaction of business shall be [2]. A duly convened meeting of The Committee at which a quorum is present shall be competent to exercise all or any of the authorities, powers and discretions vested in or exercisable by The Committee.

4. Meetings

4.1 The Committee shall meet [not less than once a year] [quarterly on the first Wednesday in each of January, April, July and October] and at such other times as the Chairman of The Committee shall require.[6]

5. Notice of Meetings

5.1 Meetings of The Committee shall be summoned by the Secretary of The Committee at the request of any member thereof.

5.2 Unless otherwise agreed, Notice of each meeting confirming the venue, time and date together with an agenda of items to be discussed, shall be forwarded to each member of The Committee, any other person required to attend and all other non-executive directors, no fewer than [5] working days prior to the date of the meeting.

5.3 The Chief Executive [and Personnel Director] shall have the right to address any meeting of The Committee; others may be called upon or shall be able to speak by prior arrangement with the Chairman of The Committee.

6. Minutes of Meetings

6.1 The Secretary shall minute the proceedings and resolutions of all Committee meetings, including the names of those present and in attendance.

6.2 Minutes of Committee meetings shall be circulated to all members of The Committee and to all members of The Board.

7. Annual General Meeting

7.1 The Chairman of The Committee shall attend the Annual General Meeting prepared to respond to any shareholder questions on The Committee's activities.

---

5 It is recognised that small companies who do not have sufficient NEDs may not always be able to comply with this rule. Although not stated in the Code, ICSA consider it best practice that no member of the Nomination Committee be a Member of the Remuneration Committee, so that no conflict of interest can arise following a new appointment.
6 The frequency and timing of meetings will differ according to the needs of the company. Meetings should be organised so that attendance is maximised (e.g. by timetabling them to coincide with Board meetings).

8. Duties

The Committee shall:

8.1   Determine and agree with The Board the framework or broad policy for the Remuneration of the Chief Executive, the Chairman of the company and such other members of the executive management as it is designated to consider.[7] The remuneration of non-executive directors shall be a matter for the executive members of the Board. No director or manager shall be involved in any decisions as to his or her own remuneration. In order to assure his independence, the Committee will also review and recommend to the Board the remuneration of the Company Secretary;

8.2   In determining such policy, take into account all factors which it deems necessary. The objective of such policy shall be to ensure that members of the executive management of the company are provided with appropriate incentives to encourage enhanced performance and are, in a fair and responsible manner, rewarded for their individual contributions to the success of the company. It shall also liase with the Nomination Committee to ensure that the remuneration of newly appointed executives is within the company's overall policy;[8]

8.3   Determine targets for any performance related pay schemes operated by the company and asking the Board, when appropriate, to seek shareholder approval for any long term incentive arrangements;[9]

8.4   Within the terms of the agreed policy, determine the total individual remuneration package of each executive director including, where appropriate, bonuses, incentive payments and share options;

8.5   Determine the policy for and scope of pension arrangements, service agreements for the executive director, termination payments and compensation commitments;

8.6   In determining such packages and arrangements, give due regard to the comments and recommendations of the Combined Code[10] as well as the UK Listing Authority's Listing Rules and associated guidance;

8.7   Review competitor companies but insure that automatic increases are not implemented, thereby avoiding the 'ratchet' effect;

8.8   Be aware of and oversee any major changes in employee benefit structures throughout the company or group;

---

7 Some companies require the Remuneration Committee to consider the packages of all executives at or above a specified level such as those reporting to a main Board Director whilst others require the Committee to deal with all packages above a certain figure.

8 Combined Code Provision B.1.10 specifically refers to termination provisions within a service contract, but the Higgs Review refers to an obligation to consider that all incentives are properly structured.

9 A long term incentive is defined as an arrangement, whereby a payment either in shares or in cash, is paid to an executive at least two years after he was invited into the scheme and is not based on that year's performance.

10 In particular Schedule A of the Combined Code which details Provisions on the Design of Performance-Related Remuneration.

8.9　Vet and authorise the reimbursement of any claims for expenses from the Chief Executive and Chairman of the company; [11]

8.10　Ensure that provisions regarding disclosure of remuneration including pensions, as listed in the Directors' Remuneration Report Regulations 2002, are fulfilled; and

8.11　Produce an annual report of The Committee's remuneration policy.

9. Authority

9.1　The Committee is authorised by The Board to seek any information it requires from any employee of the company in order to perform its duties.

9.2　In connection with its duties The Committee is required by The Board to select, set the terms of reference and appoint Remuneration Consultants, at the company's expense.

9.3　Although the Committee can seek the advice and assistance of any of the Company's executives, it needs to ensure that this role is clearly separated from their role within the business.

11 It is suggested that the more common arrangement is for the Chairman to vet and authorise the Chief Executive's expenses and for the Chairman of the Remuneration Committee to vet and authorise the Company Chairman's claim. Whilst this may be more appropriate where Remuneration Committees do not meet that frequently we believe that the recommended provision is preferable.

Appendix 12

ASSOCIATION OF BRITISH INSURERS AND
NATIONAL ASSOCIATION OF PENSION FUNDS:
JOINT STATEMENT ON BEST PRACTICE ON
EXECUTIVE CONTRACTS AND SEVERANCE
(December 2005)

1. Introduction

1.1 Institutional shareholders believe top executives of listed companies should be appropriately rewarded for the value they generate. However, they are also concerned to avoid situations where departing executives are rewarded for failure or under-performance. This is a matter of good governance, about which the ABI and NAPF have been concerned for many years.

1.2 It is unacceptable that failure, which detracts from the value of an enterprise and which can threaten the livelihood of employees, can result in large payments to its departing leaders. Executives, whose remuneration is already at a level which allows for the risk inherent in their role, should show leadership in aligning their financial interests with those of their shareholders.

1.3 Our two organisations, whose members are leading institutional investors in UK markets, are therefore publishing this statement of best practice, which sets out the expectations of shareholders that boards will give careful consideration to the risk that negotiation of inappropriate executive contracts can lead to situations where failure is rewarded.

1.4 If companies are to recruit executives of sufficient calibre, Boards must bear in mind the basic demands of the market. These require them to offer incoming executives a degree of protection against downside risk. Contract law also provides employees with certain rights that must be respected.

1.5 However, shareholders also believe it is the duty of Boards to develop and implement recruitment and remuneration policies which will prevent them being required to make payments that are not strictly merited. When companies recruit senior executives, they do so in a mood of optimism and expectation of success. They may therefore tend to overlook the consequences of failure, which is clearly inappropriate.

1.6 At the outset, Boards should calculate the potential cost of termination in monetary terms. This should cover all elements of the severance package, including any property liabilities the company may be required to assume on behalf of the departing executive. They must also consider and avoid the serious reputational risk of being obliged to make and disclose large payments to executives who have failed to perform.

1.7 Shareholders will hold Boards accountable for the design and implementation of appropriate contracts. The primary responsibility resides, however, with Remuneration Committees.

1.8 Remuneration Committees should have the leeway to design a policy appropriate to the needs and objectives of the company, but they must also have a clear understanding of their responsibility to negotiate suitable contracts and be able to justify severance payments to shareholders.

1.9 This statement provides a reference point, both to make companies aware of the reasonable expectations of shareholders and to inform voting decisions under the new legislation giving shareholders an annual vote on the remuneration report. We expect that this guidance will be reviewed periodically and refreshed as necessary to take account of changing market circumstances.

2. Basic Principles

2.1 The design of contracts should not commit companies to payment for failure. Shareholders expect Boards to pay attention to minimising this risk when drawing up contracts. They should bear in mind that it may be in the interest of incoming executives and their personal advisers to exaggerate their potential loss on dismissal. Boards should resist consequent pressure to concede overly generous severance conditions.

2.2 Choices made when the contract is agreed have an important bearing on subsequent developments. Companies should have a clear, considered policy on directors' contracts which should be clearly stated in the remuneration report. Boards should calculate and take account of all the material commitments which the company would face in the event of severance for failure or underperformance. The Nomination Committee needs to see through the process of appointment by working with the Remuneration Committee to ensure that the contract is fair to all parties.

2.3 Objectives set for executives by the Board should be clear. The more transparent the objectives, the easier it is to determine whether an executive has failed to perform and therefore to prevent payment for failure. Wherever possible, objectives against which performance will be measured should be made public.

2.4 It should be clearly understood that investors do not expect executives to be automatically entitled to cash or share-based payments other than basic pay. Bonuses should be cut or eliminated when individual performance is poor. From the outset, Boards should therefore establish a clear link between performance and bonus as well as other aspects of variable pay.

2.5 Compensation for risks run by senior executives is already implicit in the absolute level of remuneration. Boards should ensure that there is an appropriate balance between contractual protection and total remuneration and be able to justify their policies to shareholders. Shareholders prefer short contracts of one year or less, and Boards must be able to justify the length agreed. The one-year period provided for under the Combined Code best practice should thus not be seen as a floor. Shorter periods would be appropriate if other remuneration conditions would mean that a one-year contract period would lead to excessive severance payment.

2.6   In highly exceptional circumstances – for example, where a new chief executive is being recruited to a troubled company – a longer initial notice period may be appropriate. These cases should be justified to shareholders and the longer notice period should apply to the initial term only with reversion to best practice at the earliest opportunity.

2.7   Experience suggests that courts take account of some elements of variable pay, such as bonuses, when making awards to departing executives. This can be limited through the attachment of clear performance conditions to variable pay. Boards may also wish to specify that a proportion of the bonus is for retaining the executive and this should fall away in the event of severance. A remuneration policy that favours relatively low base pay and a higher proportion of variable pay is a good way of linking remuneration to performance.

3. Contract Setting

3.1   There is no standard form of contract that can apply in all circumstances. Companies have taken a number of different approaches to severance in the past. These include phased payments, liquidated damages, and reliance on mitigation. It is important that Boards consider the relative merits of different approaches as they apply to their own company's situation, follow their chosen approach consequentially and are able to justify it to shareholders.

3.2   A welcome recent innovation has been the use of **phased payments**, which involve continued payment, eg on a normal monthly basis to the departing executive for the outstanding term of his or her contract. Payments cease when and if the executive finds fresh employment. Shareholders believe this approach has considerable advantages, which deserve the active consideration of Boards, but this approach does need to be specifically provided for in the contract and specific reference made to the legal obligation to mitigate. It does not involve payment of large lump sums, which cannot be recovered. In many cases, executives will wish to seek further employment rather than remain idle till the monthly payments lapse. Allowing the contract to run off may also obviate the need for pension enhancement (see below).

3.3   The **liquidated damages** approach involves agreement at the outset on the amount that will be paid in the event of severance. It is clear from the beginning how much will be paid, but the amount cannot be varied to reflect under-performance. Shareholders do not believe the liquidated damages approach is generally desirable. Boards which adopt this should justify their decision, and should therefore consider a modified approach. This would involve reaching agreement in advance that, in the event of severance, the parties would go to arbitration to decide how much should be paid. This approach needs to take account of the likely cost of arbitration.

3.4   The concept of **mitigation** refers to the legal obligation on the part of the outgoing director to mitigate the loss incurred through severance, for example by seeking other employment and reducing the need for compensation. Where this is the sole approach, shareholders expect reassurance that the Board has taken steps to ensure that the full benefit is obtained. As with liquidated damages, boards need to have considered at the outset what the cost of severance would be under the proposed contract as well as the relative merits of arbitration as opposed to litigation.

3.5 An essential problem is that it is not normally possible for under-performance to be established as a ground for **summary dismissal** without compensation. Under the Employment Act 2002, however, a statutory disciplinary procedure will be implied into every employment contract, including those of executive directors. Boards should be aware of this and be prepared to use disciplinary procedures if warranted.

3.6 In the wake of this legislation contracts should also make clear that, if a director is dismissed in the wake of a disciplinary procedure, a shorter notice period than that given in the contract would apply. A reasonable period would be the statutory period, comprising one week for each year's service up to a maximum of 12 weeks. Without such a provision the full notice period would continue to apply even after dismissal following a disciplinary procedure.

3.7 Companies should also consider including in contracts a safeguard for more extreme cases, for example, that compensation would not be payable in case of dismissal for financial failure such as a very significant fall of the share price relative to the sector.

3.8 Other than in highly exceptional circumstances, such as the recruitment of a new chief executive of a troubled company, contracts should not provide additional protection in the form of compensation for severance as a result of **change of control**. Where exceptional circumstances apply, any additional protection should relate to the initial contract term only and not be a rolling provision.

3.9 Companies may consider other options, including a provision for **compensation to be paid by reference to shares** with the amount of shares set at the outset of employment. Where such an option is proposed it should, however, be clearly explained both as to purpose and to the details of its operation. Remuneration committees should satisfy themselves that it is workable and will yield advantages greater than the phased payment and other approaches outlined above. Compensation paid by reference to shares should be paid in cash rather than directly in shares to prevent unmerited windfall gains.

3.10 The use of **shareholding targets** for senior executives and directors is likely to be a powerful and therefore more effective means of aligning the financial interests of executives with those of shareholders.

4. Pension Arrangements and Other Remuneration Issues

4.1 Pension enhancements can represent a large element of severance pay and involve heavy cost to shareholders, the full extent of which may not be immediately evident. It is important that Boards state the full cost for pension enhancement at the earliest opportunity. Boards should not support enhanced pension payments without making themselves fully aware of the costs.

4.2 A large liability looms in the future where companies choose not to fund an enhanced pension liability but to pay it as it arises. In all cases, whether the pension is funded or not, Boards must disclose the cost, justify their choice to shareholders and demonstrate that they have chosen a route that involves the least overall cost to the company.

4.3   An important principle with regard to pensions is that Boards should distinguish between the amount that is a contractual entitlement and the amount of discretionary enhancement agreed as part of a severance package. Contracts should state clearly that the pension would not be enhanced in the event of early retirement unless the board was satisfied that the objectives set for the executive had been met or that the enhancement was merited. Shareholders are likely to question enhancement decisions when they are doubtful of the merit and, if not satisfied with the board's justification, they may vote against the remuneration report.

5. General Considerations and Conclusion

5.1   Boards should have a clear and explicit policy on contracts and on how Remuneration Committees will play a primary role. It should include calculation of the cost of severance at the time the contract is drawn up and an approach to implementation which ensures that all payments made on severance take account of performance in relation to objectives set for the departing executive by the board.

5.2   Companies should fulfil their legal obligations to make contracts readily available for shareholders to inspect, together with any side letters relating to severance terms and pension arrangements. Shareholders will take account of contracts and the way they are implemented in considering their vote on the remuneration report.

© Association of British Insurers/National Association of Pension Funds. Reproduced with permission.

Appendix 13

ICSA GUIDANCE NOTE: TERMS OF REFERENCE –
AUDIT COMMITTEE
(October 2003)

Following the publication of the Higgs Review and the Report of the Smith Group, the Financial Reporting Council has indicated its intention of introducing the revised Combined Code with effect from 1 July 2003. This Guidance Note advises on best practice in light of the Higgs review and has been drafted referring to the provisions in the suggested code.

The Combined Code states:

> 'The board should establish formal and transparent arrangements for considering how they should apply the financial reporting and internal control principles and for maintaining an appropriate relationship with the company's auditors'

The Combined Code goes on to state that the Audit Committee should have "written terms of reference which deal clearly with its authority and duties". Such statements express a clear need for an Audit Committee, the requirement for which is also supported by other influential organisations such as the Commonwealth Association for Corporate Governance and the International Corporate Governance Network.

As with most aspects of Corporate Governance, the above stated principle makes it clear that, not only should companies go through a formal process of considering its internal auditing and control procedures and evaluating its relationship with its external auditors, but it must be seen to be doing so in a fair and thorough manner. It is, therefore, essential that the Audit Committee is properly constituted with a clear remit and identified authority.

As regards the make up of the Committee, we have followed the Combined Code and recommend a minimum of three non-executive directors who should be clearly independent of management and, as far as possible, free from any conflicts of interest. Although it may seem obvious, we would, for example, suggest that members of the Committee should have no links with the external auditors. We have made specific recommendations that others may be required to assist the Committee from time to time, according to the particular items being considered and discussed.

Although not a provision in the Code, the Higgs Review, states as good practice, in its Non-Code Recommendations, the Company Secretary (or their nominee) should act as Secretary to the Committee. The Smith Report states that the Company Secretary should attend the Audit Committee. It is the Company Secretary's responsibility to ensure that the Board and its Committees are properly constituted and advised. There also needs to be a clear co-ordination between the main Board and the various Committees where the Company Secretary would normally act as a valued intermediary. In addition, although the responsibility for internal controls clearly remains with the Board as a whole, the Company Secretary would normally have the day-to-day task of reviewing the internal control procedures of the company and responsibility for drafting the governance report.

The frequency with which the Committee needs to meet will vary considerably from company to company and will no doubt change from time to time. As a general rule, most Audit Committees would be expected to meet quarterly, however, it is clear that it must meet at least three times each year, prior to the publication of financial statements, and again close to the year-end for the purpose of considering the relationship with the external auditors and to recommend whether or not they should be put forward for re-appointment at the next Annual General Meeting (AGM).

The list of duties we have proposed are those contained in the Smith Report which we believe all Audit Committees should consider. Some companies may wish to add to this list and some smaller companies may need to modify it in other ways.

The Audit Committee should compile a brief report for shareholders which should be included in the company's Annual Report, and will need to disclose the following:

- Role and main responsibilities of the Audit committee;

- Composition of committee, including relevant qualifications and experience; the appointment process; and any fees paid in respect of membership;

- Number of meetings and attendance levels;

- A description of the main activities of the year to:

    - Monitor the integrity of the financial statements;

    - Review the integrity of the internal financial control and risk management systems;

    - Review the independence of the external auditors, and the provision of non audit services;

    - Describe the oversight of the external audit process, and how its effectiveness was assessed;

    - Explain the recommendation to the Board on the appointment of auditors.

The Chairman of the Committee should attend the AGM prepared to respond to any questions that may be raised by shareholders on matters within the Committee's area of responsibility.

The above recommendations and explanations clearly show the need for there to be a guiding document. Furthermore, the provisions of the Combined Code also advocate terms of reference for an Audit Committee. This has led the ICSA to produce this Guidance Note proposing model terms of reference for an Audit Committee. The document draws on the experience of senior Company Secretaries and Best Practice as carried out in some of the country's leading companies.

Companies who have a US listing may need to amend these terms in light of the requirements of the recently introduced rules following the Sarbanes Oxley Act.

Whilst this Guidance Note is aimed primarily at the corporate sector, the doctrine of good governance, including the introduction of Audit Committees, is increasingly being recognised and adopted by other organisations particularly in the public and not for profit sectors. The principles underlying the content of this Guidance Note are applicable regardless of the size or type of organisation and we trust that it will be to be found useful across all sectors.

Reference to 'The Committee' shall mean The Audit Committee.

Reference to 'The Board' shall mean The Board of Directors.

The square brackets contain recommendations which are in line with Best Practice but which may need to be changed to suit the circumstances of the particular organisation.

1. Membership and attendance

1.1. The Committee shall be appointed by The Board, on the recommendation of the Nomination Committee, and shall comprise of a Chairman and at least [2] other members.

1.2. All members of The Committee shall be independent non-executive directors. The Chairman of the Board shall not be a member of The Committee. At least one member of The Committee should have recent relevant financial knowledge.

1.3. Care should be taken to minimise the risk of any conflict of interest that might be seen to give rise to an unacceptable influence. (It is recommended that, where possible, the Chairman and members of The Committee should be rotated on a regular basis.) No committee member shall also be a member of both the Nomination and Remuneration Committees.

1.4. The Board, on the recommendation of the Nomination Committee, shall appoint The Committee Chairman who shall be an independent non-executive director. In the absence of The Committee Chairman and/or an appointed deputy, the remaining members present shall elect one of their number present to chair the meeting.

1.5. The Committee may ask the Chairman, Chief Executive, Finance Director and any relevant senior management to attend meetings either regularly or by invitation, but the invitees have no right of attendance.

1.6. The Committee shall ask a representative of the external auditors and the head of internal audit to attend all meetings. The Committee should have at least one meeting, or part thereof, with the external auditor without management being present.

2. Secretary

2.1. The Company Secretary or their nominee shall act as the Secretary of The Committee.

3. Quorum

3.1. The quorum necessary for the transaction of business shall be [2]. A duly convened meeting of The Committee at which a quorum is present shall be competent to exercise all or any of the authorities, powers and discretions vested in or exercisable by The Committee.

4. Frequency of Meetings

4.1. The Committee shall meet [*not less than once a year*] [*quarterly on the first Wednesday in each of January, April, July and October*] and at such [*other*] times as the Chairman of The Committee shall require.

4.2. Meetings will be arranged to tie in with the publication of the company's financial statements, allowing at least [3] working days prior to a Board Meeting where accounts or financial statements are to be approved.

4.3. Meetings can be requested by the external or internal auditors if they consider one is necessary.

5. Notice of Meetings

5.1. Meetings of The Committee shall be summoned by the Secretary of The Committee at the request of any member thereof.

5.2. Unless otherwise agreed, Notice of each meeting confirming the venue, time and date together with an agenda of items to be discussed, shall be forwarded to each member of The Committee, any other person required to attend and all other non-executive directors, no fewer than [5] working days prior to the date of the meeting.

6. Minutes of Meetings

6.1. The Secretary shall minute the proceedings and resolutions of all meetings of The Committee, including recording the names of those present and in attendance.

6.2. The Secretary should ascertain, at the beginning of each meeting, the existence of any conflicts of interest and minute them accordingly.

6.3. Minutes of Committee meetings shall be circulated promptly to all members of The Committee and to the Chairman and all members of The Board.

7. Annual General Meeting

7.1. The Chairman of The Committee shall attend the Annual General Meeting prepared to respond to any shareholder questions on The Committee's activities.

8. Duties

8.1. Internal Control and Risk Assessment

8.1.1. The Committee shall keep under review the effectiveness of the company's financial reporting and internal control policies and procedures for the identification, assessment and reporting of risks.

8.2. Internal Audit

8.2.1. The Committee shall consider applications for the post of and [appoint]/ [approve the appointment of] the head of the internal audit function; any dismissal of the post holder should be considered by The Committee.

8.2.2. The Committee shall consider and approve the terms of reference of the internal audit function, and shall be advised of the planned programme of audits and the reason for any change or delay in the programme.

8.2.3. The Committee shall review the management of financial matters and focus upon the freedom allowed to the internal auditors.

8.2.4. The Committee shall review promptly all reports on the company from the internal auditors.

8.2.5. The Head of Internal Audit shall be given the right of direct access to the Chairman of The Committee.

8.3. External Audit

8.3.1. The Committee shall consider and make recommendations to The Board as regards the appointment and re-appointment of the company's external auditors, and shall ensure that key partners within the appointed firm are rotated from time to time.

8.3.2. The Committee shall meet with the external auditors at least twice each year, once at the planning stage, where the scope of the audit will be considered, and once post audit at the reporting stage, and shall ensure that any auditor's management letters and management's responses are reviewed.

8.3.3. The Committee shall keep under review the relationship with external auditors including (but not limited to):

8.3.3.1. the independence and objectivity of the external auditors;

8.3.3.2. the consideration of audit fees which should be paid as well as any other fees which are payable to auditors in respect of non-audit activities; and

8.3.3.3. discussions with the external auditors concerning such issues as compliance with accounting standards and any proposals which the external auditors have made vis-à-vis the company's internal auditing standards.

8.4. Financial Statements

8.4.1. The Committee shall keep under review the consistency of accounting policies both on a year to year basis and across the company/group.

8.4.2. The Committee shall review and challenge where necessary the company's financial statements taking into account:

8.4.2.1. decisions requiring a major element of judgement;

8.4.2.2. the extent to which the financial statements are affected by any unusual transactions;

8.4.2.3. the clarity of disclosures;

8.4.2.4. significant adjustments resulting from the audit;

8.4.2.5. the going concern assumption;

8.4.2.6. compliance with accounting standards;

8.4.2.7. compliance with stock exchange and other legal requirements; and

8.4.2.8.   reviewing the company's statement on internal control systems prior to endorsement by The Board and to review the policies and process for identifying and assessing business risks and the management of those risks by the company.

8.4.3.   The Committee shall review the annual financial statements of the pension funds where not reviewed by The Board as a whole.

8.5.   Reporting Responsibilities

8.5.1.   The Committee or its Chairman shall meet formally with the Board of Directors at least [*once*] a year to discuss such matters as the Annual Report and the relationship with the external auditors.

8.5.2.   In the light of its other duties, the Committee shall make whatever recommendations to The Board it deems appropriate and shall compile a report to shareholders to be included in the company's Annual Report and Accounts.

8.6.   Other Matters

8.6.1.   The Committee shall give due consideration to the requirements of the UK Listing Authority's Listing Rules.

8.6.2.   The Committee shall be responsible for co-ordination of the internal and external auditors.

8.6.3.   The Committee will review the company's procedures for handling allegations from whistleblowers.

8.6.4.   The Committee shall oversee any investigation of activities, which are within its terms of reference and act as a court of the last resort.

8.6.5.   The Committee should, on a regular basis, review its own performance, constitution and terms of reference to ensure it is operating at maximum effectiveness.

9. Authority

The Committee is authorised:

9.1.   to seek any information it requires from any employee of the company in order to perform its duties;

9.2.   to obtain, at the company's expense, outside legal or other professional advice on any matters within its terms of reference; and

9.3.   to call any member of staff to be questioned at a meeting of The Committee as and when required.

Appendix 14

COMBINED CODE OF CORPORATE GOVERNANCE:
SMITH GUIDANCE ON AUDIT COMMITTEES
(July 2003)

1. Introduction

1.1 This guidance is designed to assist company boards in making suitable arrangements for their audit committees, and to assist directors serving on audit committees in carrying out their role.

1.2 The paragraphs in bold are taken from the Combined Code (Section C3). Listed companies that do not comply with those provisions should include an explanation as to why they have not complied in the statement required by the Listing Rules.

1.3 Best practice requires that every board should consider in detail what arrangements for its audit committee are best suited for its particular circumstances. Audit committee arrangements need to be proportionate to the task, and will vary according to the size, complexity and risk profile of the company.

1.4 While all directors have a duty to act in the interests of the company the audit committee has a particular role, acting independently from the executive, to ensure that the interests of shareholders are properly protected in relation to financial reporting and internal control.

1.5 Nothing in the guidance should be interpreted as a departure from the principle of the unitary board. All directors remain equally responsible for the company's affairs as a matter of law. The audit committee, like other committees to which particular responsibilities are delegated (such as the remuneration committee), remains a committee of the board. Any disagreement within the board, including disagreement between the audit committee's members and the rest of the board, should be resolved at board level.

1.6 The Code provides that a separate section of the annual report should describe the work of the committee. This deliberately puts the spotlight on the audit committee and gives it an authority that it might otherwise lack. This is not incompatible with the principle of the unitary board.

1.7 The guidance contains recommendations about the conduct of the audit committee's relationship with the board, with the executive management and with internal and external auditors. However, the most important features of this relationship cannot be drafted as guidance or put into a code of practice: a frank, open working relationship and a high level of mutual respect are essential, particularly between the audit committee chairman and the board chairman, the chief executive and the finance director. The audit committee must be prepared to take a robust stand, and all parties must be prepared to make information freely available to the audit committee, to listen to their views and to talk through the issues openly.

1.8 In particular, the management is under an obligation to ensure the audit committee is kept properly informed, and should take the initiative in supplying information rather than waiting to be asked. The board should make it clear to all directors and staff that they must cooperate with the audit committee and provide it with any information it requires. In addition, executive board members will have regard to their common law duty to provide all directors, including those on the audit committee, with all the information they need to discharge their responsibilities as directors of the company.

1.9 Many of the core functions of audit committees set out in this guidance are expressed in terms of 'oversight', 'assessment' and 'review' of a particular function. It is not the duty of audit committees to carry out functions that properly belong to others, such as the company's management in the preparation of the financial statements or the auditors in the planning or conducting of audits. To do so could undermine the responsibility of management and auditors. Audit committees should, for example, satisfy themselves that there is a proper system and allocation of responsibilities for the day-to-day monitoring of financial controls but they should not seek to do the monitoring themselves.

1.10 However, the high-level oversight function may lead to detailed work. The audit committee must intervene if there are signs that something may be seriously amiss. For example, if the audit committee is uneasy about the explanations of management and auditors about a particular financial reporting policy decision, there may be no alternative but to grapple with the detail and perhaps to seek independent advice.

1.11 Under this guidance, audit committees have wide-ranging, time-consuming and sometimes intensive work to do. Companies need to make the necessary resources available. This includes suitable payment for the members of audit committees themselves. They – and particularly the audit committee chairman - bear a significant responsibility and they need to commit a significant extra amount of time to the job. Companies also need to make provision for induction and training for new audit committee members and continuing training as may be required.

1.12 This guidance applies to all companies to which the Code applies – i.e. UK listed companies. For groups, it will usually be necessary for the audit committee of the parent company to review issues that relate to particular subsidiaries or activities carried on by the group. Consequently, the board of a UK-listed parent company should ensure that there is adequate cooperation within the group (and with internal and external auditors of individual companies within the group) to enable the parent company audit committee to discharge its responsibilities effectively.

2. Establishment and role of the audit committee; membership, procedures and resources

Establishment and role

2.1 **The board should establish an audit committee of at least three, or in the case of smaller companies two, members.**

2.2 The main role and responsibilities of the audit committee should be set out in written terms of reference and should include: to monitor the integrity of the financial statements of the company and any formal announcements relating to the company's financial performance, reviewing significant financial reporting judgements contained in them; to review the company's internal financial controls and, unless expressly addressed by a separate board risk committee composed of independent directors or by the board itself, the company's internal control and risk management systems; to monitor and review the effectiveness of the company's internal audit function; to make recommendations to the board, for it to put to the shareholders for their approval in general meeting, in relation to the appointment of the external auditor and to approve the remuneration and terms of engagement of the external auditor; to review and monitor the external auditor's independence and objectivity and the effectiveness of the audit process, taking into consideration relevant UK professional and regulatory requirements; to develop and implement policy on the engagement of the external auditor to supply non-audit services, taking into account relevant ethical guidance regarding the provision of non-audit services by the external audit firm; and to report to the Board, identifying any matters in respect of which it considers that action or improvement is needed, and making recommendations as to the steps to be taken.

Membership and appointment

2.3 All members of the committee should be independent non-executive directors. The board should satisfy itself that at least one member of the audit committee has recent and relevant financial experience.

2.4 The chairman of the company should not be an audit committee member.

2.5 Appointments to the audit committee should be made by the board on the recommendation of the nomination committee (where there is one), in consultation with the audit committee chairman.

2.6 Appointments should be for a period of up to three years, extendable by no more than two additional three-year periods, so long as members continue to be independent.

Meetings of the audit committee

2.7 It is for the audit committee chairman, in consultation with the company secretary, to decide the frequency and timing of its meetings. There should be as many meetings as the audit committee's role and responsibilities require. It is recommended there should be not fewer than three meetings during the year, held to coincide with key dates within the financial reporting and audit cycle.[1] However, most audit committee chairmen will wish to call more frequent meetings.

2.8 No one other than the audit committee's chairman and members is entitled to be present at a meeting of the audit committee. It is for the audit committee to decide if non-members should attend for a particular meeting or a particular agenda item. It is to be expected that the external audit lead partner will be invited regularly to attend meetings as well as the finance director. Others may be invited to attend.

---

1 For example, when the audit plans (internal and external) are available for review and when interim statements, preliminary announcements and the full annual report are near completion.

2.9   Sufficient time should be allowed to enable the audit committee to undertake as full a discussion as may be required. A sufficient interval should be allowed between audit committee meetings and main board meetings to allow any work arising from the audit committee meeting to be carried out and reported to the board as appropriate.

2.10 The audit committee should, at least annually, meet the external and internal auditors, without management, to discuss matters relating to its remit and any issues arising from the audit.

2.11 Formal meetings of the audit committee are the heart of its work. However, they will rarely be sufficient. It is expected that the audit committee chairman, and to a lesser extent the other members, will wish to keep in touch on a continuing basis with the key people involved in the company's governance, including the board chairman, the chief executive, the finance director, the external audit lead partner and the head of internal audit.

Resources

2.12 The audit committee should be provided with sufficient resources to undertake its duties.

2.13 The audit committee should have access to the services of the company secretariat on all audit committee matters including: assisting the chairman in planning the audit committee's work, drawing up meeting agendas, maintenance of minutes, drafting of material about its activities for the annual report, collection and distribution of information and provision of any necessary practical support.

2.14 The company secretary should ensure that the audit committee receives information and papers in a timely manner to enable full and proper consideration to be given to the issues.

2.15 The board should make funds available to the audit committee to enable it to take independent legal, accounting or other advice when the audit committee reasonably believes it necessary to do so.

Remuneration

2.16 In addition to the remuneration paid to all non-executive directors, each company should consider the further remuneration that should be paid to members of the audit committee to recompense them for the additional responsibilities of membership. Consideration should be given to the time members are required to give to audit committee business, the skills they bring to bear and the onerous duties they take on, as well as the value of their work to the company. The level of remuneration paid to the members of the audit committee should take into account the level of fees paid to other members of the board. The chairman's responsibilities and time demands will generally be heavier than the other members of the audit committee and this should be reflected in his or her remuneration.

Skills, experience and training

2.17 It is desirable that the committee member whom the board considers to have recent and relevant financial experience should have a professional qualification from one of the professional accountancy bodies. The need for a degree of financial literacy among the other members will vary according to the nature of the company, but experience of corporate financial matters will normally be required. The availability of appropriate financial expertise will be particularly important where the company's activities involve specialised financial activities.

2.18 The company should provide an induction programme for new audit committee members. This should cover the role of the audit committee, including its terms of reference and expected time commitment by members; and an overview of the company's business, identifying the main business and financial dynamics and risks. It could also include meeting some of the company staff.

2.19 Training should also be provided to members of the audit committee on an ongoing and timely basis and should include an understanding of the principles of and developments in financial reporting and related company law. In appropriate cases, it may also include, for example, understanding financial statements, applicable accounting standards and recommended practice; the regulatory framework for the company's business; the role of internal and external auditing and risk management.

2.20 The induction programme and ongoing training may take various forms, including attendance at formal courses and conferences, internal company talks and seminars, and briefings by external advisers.

3. Relationship with the board

3.1 The role of the audit committee is for the board to decide and to the extent that the audit committee undertakes tasks on behalf of the board, the results should be reported to, and considered by, the board. In doing so it should identify any matters in respect of which it considers that action or improvement is needed, and make recommendations as to the steps to be taken.

3.2 The terms of reference should be tailored to the particular circumstances of the company.

3.3 The audit committee should review annually its terms of reference and its own effectiveness and recommend any necessary changes to the board.

3.4 The board should review the audit committee's effectiveness annually.

3.5 Where there is disagreement between the audit committee and the board, adequate time should be made available for discussion of the issue with a view to resolving the disagreement. Where any such disagreements cannot be resolved, the audit committee should have the right to report the issue to the shareholders as part of the report on its activities in the annual report.

4. Role and responsibilities

Financial reporting

4.1 The audit committee should review the significant financial reporting issues and judgements made in connection with the preparation of the company's financial statements, interim reports, preliminary announcements and related formal statements.

4.2   It is management's, not the audit committee's, responsibility to prepare complete and accurate financial statements and disclosures in accordance with financial reporting standards and applicable rules and regulations. However the audit committee should consider significant accounting policies, any changes to them and any significant estimates and judgements. The management should inform the audit committee of the methods used to account for significant or unusual transactions where the accounting treatment is open to different approaches. Taking into account the external auditor's view, the audit committee should consider whether the company has adopted appropriate accounting policies and, where necessary, made appropriate estimates and judgements. The audit committee should review the clarity and completeness of disclosures in the financial statements and consider whether the disclosures made are set properly in context.

4.3   Where, following its review, the audit committee is not satisfied with any aspect of the proposed financial reporting by the company, it shall report its views to the board.

4.4   The audit committee should review related information presented with the financial statements, including the operating and financial review, and corporate governance statements relating to the audit and to risk management. Similarly, where board approval is required for other statements containing financial information (for example, summary financial statements, significant financial returns to regulators and release of price sensitive information), whenever practicable (without being inconsistent with any requirement for prompt reporting under the Listing Rules) the audit committee should review such statements first.

Internal controls and risk management systems

4.5   The audit committee should review the company's internal financial controls (that is, the systems established to identify, assess, manage and monitor financial risks); and unless expressly addressed by a separate board risk committee comprised of independent directors or by the board itself, the company's internal control and risk management systems.

4.6   The company's management is responsible for the identification, assessment, management and monitoring of risk, for developing, operating and monitoring the system of internal control and for providing assurance to the board that it has done so. Except where the board or a risk committee is expressly responsible for reviewing the effectiveness of the internal control and risk management systems, the audit committee should receive reports from management on the effectiveness of the systems they have established and the conclusions of any testing carried out by internal and external auditors.

4.7   Except to the extent that this is expressly dealt with by the board or risk committee, the audit committee should review and approve the statements included in the annual report in relation to internal control and the management of risk.

Whistleblowing

4.8   The audit committee should review arrangements by which staff of the company may, in confidence, raise concerns about possible improprieties in matters of financial reporting or other matters. The audit committee's objective should be to

ensure that arrangements are in place for the proportionate and independent investigation of such matters and for appropriate follow-up action.

The internal audit process

4.9 The audit committee should monitor and review the effectiveness of the company's internal audit function. Where there is no internal audit function, the audit committee should consider annually whether there is a need for an internal audit function and make a recommendation to the board, and the reasons for the absence of such a function should be explained in the relevant section of the annual report.

4.10 The audit committee should review and approve the internal audit function's remit, having regard to the complementary roles of the internal and external audit functions. The audit committee should ensure that the function has the necessary resources and access to information to enable it to fulfil its mandate, and is equipped to perform in accordance with appropriate professional standards for internal auditors.[2]

4.11 The audit committee should approve the appointment or termination of appointment of the head of internal audit.

4.12 In its review of the work of the internal audit function, the audit committee should, inter alia:

- ensure that the internal auditor has direct access to the board chairman and to the audit committee and is accountable to the audit committee;
- review and assess the annual internal audit work plan;
- receive a report on the results of the internal auditors' work on a periodic basis;
- review and monitor management's responsiveness to the internal auditor's findings and recommendations;
- meet with the head of internal audit at least once a year without the presence of management; and
- monitor and assess the role and effectiveness of the internal audit function in the overall context of the company's risk management system.

The external audit process

4.13 The audit committee is the body responsible for overseeing the company's relations with the external auditor.

Appointment

4.14 The audit committee should have primary responsibility for making a recommendation on the appointment, reappointment and removal of the external auditors. If the board does not accept the audit committee's recommendation, it should include in the annual report, and in any papers recommending appointment or reappointment, a statement from the audit committee explaining its recommendation and should set out reasons why the board has taken a different position.

4.15 The audit committee's recommendation to the board should be based on the assessments referred to below. If the audit committee recommends considering the

---

2 Further guidance can be found in the Institute of Internal Auditors' Code of Ethics and the International Standards for the Professional Practice of Internal Auditing Standards.

selection of possible new appointees as external auditors, it should oversee the selection process.

4.16 The audit committee should assess annually the qualification, expertise and resources, and independence (see below) of the external auditors and the effectiveness of the audit process. The assessment should cover all aspects of the audit service provided by the audit firm, and include obtaining a report on the audit firm's own internal quality control procedures.

4.17 If the external auditor resigns, the audit committee should investigate the issues giving rise to such resignation and consider whether any action is required.

Terms and remuneration

4.18 The audit committee should approve the terms of engagement and the remuneration to be paid to the external auditor in respect of audit services provided.

4.19 The audit committee should review and agree the engagement letter issued by the external auditor at the start of each audit, ensuring that it has been updated to reflect changes in circumstances arising since the previous year. The scope of the external audit should be reviewed by the audit committee with the auditor. If the audit committee is not satisfied as to its adequacy it should arrange for additional work to be undertaken.

4.20 The audit committee should satisfy itself that the level of fee payable in respect of the audit services provided is appropriate and that an effective audit can be conducted for such a fee.

Independence, including the provision of non-audit services

4.21 The audit committee should have procedures to ensure the independence and objectivity of the external auditor annually, taking into consideration relevant UK professional and regulatory requirements. This assessment should involve a consideration of all relationships between the company and the audit firm (including the provision of non-audit services). The audit committee should consider whether, taken as a whole and having regard to the views, as appropriate, of the external auditor, management and internal audit, those relationships appear to impair the auditor's judgement or independence.

4.22 The audit committee should seek reassurance that the auditors and their staff have no family, financial, employment, investment or business relationship with the company (other than in the normal course of business). The audit committee should seek from the audit firm, on an annual basis, information about policies and processes for maintaining independence and monitoring compliance with relevant requirements, including current requirements regarding the rotation of audit partners and staff.

4.23 The audit committee should agree with the board the company's policy for the employment of former employees of the external auditor, paying particular attention to the policy regarding former employees of the audit firm who were part of the audit team and moved directly to the company. This should be drafted taking into account the relevant ethical guidelines governing the accounting profession. The audit committee should monitor application of the policy, including the number of former employees of the external auditor currently employed in senior positions in the company, and consider whether in the light of this there has been any impairment, or appearance of impairment, of the auditor's judgement or independence in respect of the audit.

4.24 The audit committee should monitor the external audit firm's compliance with applicable United Kingdom ethical guidance relating to the rotation of audit partners, the level of fees that the company pays in proportion to the overall fee income of the firm, office and partner, and other related regulatory requirements.

4.25 The audit committee should develop and recommend to the board the company's policy in relation to the provision of non-audit services by the auditor. The audit committee's objective should be to ensure that the provision of such services does not impair the external auditor's independence or objectivity. In this context, the audit committee should consider:
- whether the skills and experience of the audit firm make it a suitable supplier of the non audit service;
- whether there are safeguards in place to ensure that there is no threat to objectivity and independence in the conduct of the audit resulting from the provision of such services by the external auditor;
- the nature of the non-audit services, the related fee levels and the fee levels individually and in aggregate relative to the audit fee; and
- the criteria which govern the compensation of the individuals performing the audit.

4.26 The audit committee should set and apply a formal policy specifying the types of non-audit work:
- from which the external auditors are excluded;
- for which the external auditors can be engaged without referral to the audit committee; and
- for which a case-by-case decision is necessary.

In addition, the policy may set fee limits generally or for particular classes of work.

4.27 In the third category, if it is not practicable to give approval to individual items in advance, it may be appropriate to give a general pre-approval for certain classes for work, subject to a fee limit determined by the audit committee and ratified by the board. The subsequent provision of any service by the auditor should be ratified at the next meeting of the audit committee.

4.28 In determining the policy, the audit committee should take into account relevant ethical guidance regarding the provision of non-audit services by the external audit firm, and in principle should not agree to the auditor providing a service if, having regard to the ethical guidance, the result is that:
- the external auditor audits its own firm's work;
- the external auditor makes management decisions for the company;
- a mutuality of interest is created; or
- the external auditor is put in the role of advocate for the company.

The audit committee should satisfy itself that any safeguards required by ethical guidance are implemented.

4.29 The annual report should explain to shareholders how, if the auditor provides non-audit services, auditor objectivity and independence is safeguarded.

Annual audit cycle

4.30 At the start of each annual audit cycle, the audit committee should ensure that appropriate plans are in place for the audit.

4.31 The audit committee should consider whether the auditor's overall work plan, including planned levels of materiality, and proposed resources to execute the audit plan appears consistent with the scope of the audit engagement, having regard also to the seniority, expertise and experience of the audit team.

4.32 The audit committee should review, with the external auditors, the findings of their work. In the course of its review, the audit committee should:
   - discuss with the external auditor major issues that arose during the course of the audit and have subsequently been resolved and those issues that have been left unresolved;
   - review key accounting and audit judgements; and
   - review levels of errors identified during the audit, obtaining explanations from management and, where necessary the external auditors, as to why certain errors might remain unadjusted.

4.33 The audit committee should also review the audit representation letters before signature by management and give particular consideration to matters where representation has been requested that relate to non-standard issues.[3] The audit committee should consider whether the information provided is complete and appropriate based on its own knowledge.

4.34 As part of the ongoing monitoring process, the audit committee should review the management letter (or equivalent). The audit committee should review and monitor management's responsiveness to the external auditor's findings and recommendations.

4.35 At the end of the annual audit cycle, the audit committee should assess the effectiveness of the audit process. In the course of doing so, the audit committee should:
   - review whether the auditor has met the agreed audit plan and understand the reasons for any changes, including changes in perceived audit risks and the work undertaken by the external auditors to address those risks;
   - consider the robustness and perceptiveness of the auditors in their handling of the key accounting and audit judgements identified and in responding to questions from the audit committees, and in their commentary where appropriate on the systems of internal control;
   - obtain feedback about the conduct of the audit from key people involved, e.g. the finance director and the head of internal audit; and
   - review and monitor the content of the external auditor's management letter, in order to assess whether it is based on a good understanding of the company's business and establish whether recommendations have been acted upon and, if not, the reasons why they have not been acted upon.

---

3 Further guidance can by found in the Auditing Practices Board's Statement of Auditing Standard 440 'Management Representations'.

5. Communication with shareholders

5.1 The terms of reference of the audit committee, including its role and the authority delegated to it by the board, should be made available. A separate section in the annual report should describe the work of the committee in discharging those responsibilities.

5.2 The audit committee section should include, inter alia:
- a summary of the role of the audit committee;
- the names and qualifications of all members of the audit committee during the period;
- the number of audit committee meetings;
- a report on the way the audit committee has discharged its responsibilities; and
- the explanation provided for in paragraph 4.29 above.

5.3 The chairman of the audit committee should be present at the AGM to answer questions, through the chairman of the board, on the report on the audit committee's activities and matters within the scope of audit committee's responsibilities.

© Financial Reporting Council, 2003. Reproduced with permission.

Appendix 15

SMITH REPORT: OUTLINE REPORT TO SHAREHOLDERS ON THE ACTIVITIES OF THE AUDIT COMMITTEE

1. **Role of the audit committee**
   - Main responsibilities of the audit committee

2. **Composition of the audit committee**
   - Members and secretary – names and appointment/resignation dates
   - Appointment process
   - The relevant qualifications, expertise and experience of each member

3. **Resources**
   - Any dedicated resources available to the committee, internal or bought-in

4. **Meetings**
   - Number of meetings, and attendance

5. **Remuneration of the members of the audit committee**
   - Describe the specific policies in relation to the members of the audit committee (or cross refer to the Directors' Remuneration Report)

Main activities of the committee in the year to xxxx

6. **Financial statements**
   - Describe the activities carried out in order to monitor the integrity of the financial statements

7. **Internal financial control and risk management systems**
   - Describe the activities carried out in order to review the integrity of the company's internal financial control and risk management systems

8. **External auditors**
   - Describe the procedures adopted to review the independence of the external auditors, including disclosure of the policy on the provision of non-audit services and an explanation of how the policy protects auditor independence
   - Describe the oversight of the external audit process and confirm that an assessment of the effectiveness of the external audit was made
   - Explain the recommendation to the board on the appointment of the auditors and, if applicable, the process adopted to select the new auditor

9. **Internal audit function**
   - Confirm that a review of the plans and work of the department was carried out. If there is no function explain the committee's consideration of whether there is a need for an internal audit function in accordance with the recommendations of the Turnbull Report.

Appendix 16

FINANCIAL REPORTING COUNCIL: INTERNAL CONTROL – REVISED GUIDANCE FOR DIRECTORS ON THE COMBINED CODE
(October 2005)

PREFACE

Internal Control: Guidance for Directors on the Combined Code (The Turnbull guidance) was first issued in 1999.

In 2004, the Financial Reporting Council established the Turnbull Review Group to consider the impact of the guidance and the related disclosures and to determine whether the guidance needed to be updated.

In reviewing the impact of the guidance, our consultations revealed that it has very successfully gone a long way to meeting its original objectives. Boards and investors alike indicated that the guidance has contributed to a marked improvement in the overall standard of risk management and internal control since 1999.

Notably, the evidence gathered by the Review Group demonstrated that respondents considered that the substantial improvements in internal control instigated by application of the Turnbull guidance have been achieved without the need for detailed prescription as to how to implement the guidance.

The principles-based approach has required boards to think seriously about control issues and enabled them to apply the principles in a way that appropriately dealt with the circumstances of their business.

The evidence also supported the proposition that the companies which have derived most benefit from application of the guidance were those whose boards saw embedded risk management and internal control as an integral part of running the business.

Accordingly, the Review Group strongly endorsed retention of the flexible, principles-based approach of the original guidance and has made only a small number of changes.

This however does not mean that there is nothing new for boards to do or that some companies could not make more effective use of the guidance. Establishing an effective system of internal control is not a one-off exercise. No such system remains effective unless it develops to take account of new and emerging risks, control failures, market expectations or changes in the company's circumstances or business objectives. The Review Group reiterates the view of the vast majority of respondents in emphasising the importance of regular and systematic assessment of the risks facing the business and the value of embedding risk management and internal control systems within business processes. It is the board's responsibility to make sure this happens.

Boards should review whether they can make more of the communication opportunity of the internal control statement in the annual report. Investors consider the board's attitude towards risk management and internal control to be an important factor when making investment decisions about a company. Taken together with the Operating and Financial Review, the internal control statement provides an opportunity for the board to help shareholders understand the risk and control issues facing the company, and to explain how the company maintains a framework of internal controls to address these issues and how the board has reviewed the effectiveness of that framework.

It is in this spirit that directors need to exercise their responsibility to review on a continuing basis their application of the revised guidance.

Turnbull Review Group

October 2005

ONE – INTRODUCTION

The importance of internal control and risk management

1. A company's system of internal control has a key role in the management of risks that are significant to the fulfilment of its business objectives. A sound system of internal control contributes to safeguarding the shareholders' investment and the company's assets.

2. Internal control (as referred to in paragraph 19) facilitates the effectiveness and efficiency of operations, helps ensure the reliability of internal and external reporting and assists compliance with laws and regulations.

3. Effective financial controls, including the maintenance of proper accounting records, are an important element of internal control. They help ensure that the company is not unnecessarily exposed to avoidable financial risks and that financial information used within the business and for publication is reliable. They also contribute to the safeguarding of assets, including the prevention and detection of fraud.

4. A company's objectives, its internal organisation and the environment in which it operates are continually evolving and, as a result, the risks it faces are continually changing. A sound system of internal control therefore depends on a thorough and regular evaluation of the nature and extent of the risks to which the company is exposed. Since profits are, in part, the reward for successful risk-taking in business, the purpose of internal control is to help manage and control risk appropriately rather than to eliminate it.

Objectives of the guidance

5. This guidance is intended to:

   - reflect sound business practice whereby internal control is embedded in the business processes by which a company pursues its objectives;
   - remain relevant over time in the continually evolving business environment; and
   - enable each company to apply it in a manner which takes account of its particular circumstances.

The guidance requires directors to exercise judgement in reviewing how the company has implemented the requirements of the Combined Code relating to internal control and reporting to shareholders thereon.

6. The guidance is based on the adoption by a company's board of a risk-based approach to establishing a sound system of internal control and reviewing its effectiveness. This should be incorporated by the company within its normal management and governance processes. It should not be treated as a separate exercise undertaken to meet regulatory requirements.

Internal control requirements of the Combined Code

7. Principle C.2 of the Code states that 'The board should maintain a sound system of internal control to safeguard shareholders' investment and the company's assets'.

8. Provision C.2.1 states that 'The directors should, at least annually, conduct a review of the effectiveness of the group's system of internal control and should report to shareholders that they have done so. The review should cover all material controls, including financial, operational and compliance controls and risk management systems'.

9. Paragraph 9.8.6 of the UK Listing Authority's Listing Rules states that in the case of a listed company incorporated in the United Kingdom, the following items must be included in its annual report and accounts:

   • a statement of how the listed company has applied the principles set out in Section 1 of the Combined Code, in a manner that would enable shareholders to evaluate how the principles have been applied;
   • a statement as to whether the listed company has:
     – complied throughout the accounting period with all relevant provisions set out in Section 1 of the Combined Code; or
     – not complied throughout the accounting period with all relevant provisions set out in Section 1 of the Combined Code and if so, setting out:

       (i)   those provisions, if any, it has not complied with;
       (ii) in the case of provisions whose requirements are of a continuing nature, the period within which, if any, it did not comply with some or all of those provisions; and
       (iii) the company's reasons for non-compliance.

10. The Preamble to the Code makes it clear that there is no prescribed form or content for the statement setting out how the various principles in the Code have been applied. The intention is that companies should have a free hand to explain their governance policies in the light of the principles, including any special circumstances which have led to them adopting a particular approach.

11. The guidance in this document applies for accounting periods beginning on or after 1 January 2006, and should be followed by boards of listed companies in:

   • assessing how the company has applied Code Principle C.2;
   • implementing the requirements of Code Provision C.2.1; and
   • reporting on these matters to shareholders in the annual report and accounts.

12. For the purposes of this guidance, internal controls considered by the board should include all types of controls including those of an operational and compliance nature, as well as internal financial controls.

Groups of companies

13. Throughout this guidance, where reference is made to 'company' it should be taken, where applicable, as referring to the group of which the reporting company is the parent company. For groups of companies, the review of effectiveness of internal control and the report to the shareholders should be from the perspective of the group as a whole.

The Appendix

14. The Appendix to this document contains questions which boards may wish to consider in applying this guidance.

TWO – MAINTAINING A SOUND SYSTEM OF INTERNAL CONTROL

Responsibilities

15. The board of directors is responsible for the company's system of internal control. It should set appropriate policies on internal control and seek regular assurance that will enable it to satisfy itself that the system is functioning effectively. The board must further ensure that the system of internal control is effective in managing those risks in the manner which it has approved.

16. In determining its policies with regard to internal control, and thereby assessing what constitutes a sound system of internal control in the particular circumstances of the company, the board's deliberations should include consideration of the following factors:

- the nature and extent of the risks facing the company;
- the extent and categories of risk which it regards as acceptable for the company to bear;
- the likelihood of the risks concerned materialising;
- the company's ability to reduce the incidence and impact on the business of risks that do materialise; and
- the costs of operating particular controls relative to the benefit thereby obtained in managing the related risks.

17. It is the role of management to implement board policies on risk and control. In fulfilling its responsibilities management should identify and evaluate the risks faced by the company for consideration by the board and design, operate and monitor a suitable system of internal control which implements the policies adopted by the board.

18. All employees have some responsibility for internal control as part of their accountability for achieving objectives. They, collectively, should have the necessary knowledge, skills, information, and authority to establish, operate and monitor the system of internal control. This will require an understanding of the company, its objectives, the industries and markets in which it operates, and the risks it faces.

Elements of a sound system of internal control

19. An internal control system encompasses the policies, processes, tasks, behaviours and other aspects of a company that, taken together:

- facilitate its effective and efficient operation by enabling it to respond appropriately to significant business, operational, financial, compliance and other risks to achieving the company's objectives. This includes the safeguarding of assets from inappropriate use or from loss and fraud and ensuring that liabilities are identified and managed;

- help ensure the quality of internal and external reporting. This requires the maintenance of proper records and processes that generate a flow of timely, relevant and reliable information from within and outside the organisation;
- help ensure compliance with applicable laws and regulations, and also with internal policies with respect to the conduct of business.

20. A company's system of internal control will reflect its control environment which encompasses its organisational structure. The system will include:

- control activities;
- information and communications processes; and
- processes for monitoring the continuing effectiveness of the system of internal control.

21. The system of internal control should:

- be embedded in the operations of the company and form part of its culture;
- be capable of responding quickly to evolving risks to the business arising from factors within the company and to changes in the business environment; and
- include procedures for reporting immediately to appropriate levels of management any significant control failings or weaknesses that are identified together with details of corrective action being undertaken.

22. A sound system of internal control reduces, but cannot eliminate, the possibility of poor judgement in decision-making; human error; control processes being deliberately circumvented by employees and others; management overriding controls; and the occurrence of unforeseeable circumstances.

23. A sound system of internal control therefore provides reasonable, but not absolute, assurance that a company will not be hindered in achieving its business objectives, or in the orderly and legitimate conduct of its business, by circumstances which may reasonably be foreseen. A system of internal control cannot, however, provide protection with certainty against a company failing to meet its business objectives or all material errors, losses, fraud, or breaches of laws or regulations.

THREE – REVIEWING THE EFFECTIVENESS OF INTERNAL CONTROL

Responsibilities

24. Reviewing the effectiveness of internal control is an essential part of the board's responsibilities. The board will need to form its own view on effectiveness based on the information and assurances provided to it, exercising the standard of care generally applicable to directors in the exercise of their duties. Management is accountable to the board for monitoring the system of internal control and for providing assurance to the board that it has done so.

25. The role of board committees in the review process, including that of the audit committee, is for the board to decide and will depend upon factors such as the size and composition of the board; the scale, diversity and complexity of the company's operations; and the nature of the significant risks that the company faces. To the extent that designated board committees carry out, on behalf of the board, tasks that are attributed in this guidance document to the board, the results of the relevant committees' work should be reported to, and considered by, the board. The board takes responsibility for the disclosures on internal control in the annual report and accounts.

The process for reviewing effectiveness

26. Effective monitoring on a continuous basis is an essential component of a sound system of internal control. The board cannot, however, rely solely on the embedded monitoring processes within the company to discharge its responsibilities. It should regularly receive and review reports on internal control. In addition, the board should undertake an annual assessment for the purposes of making its public statement on internal control to ensure that it has considered all significant aspects of internal control for the company for the year under review and up to the date of approval of the annual report and accounts.

27. The board should define the process to be adopted for its review of the effectiveness of internal control. This should encompass both the scope and frequency of the reports it receives and reviews during the year, and also the process for its annual assessment, such that it will be provided with sound, appropriately documented, support for its statement on internal control in the company's annual report and accounts.

28. The reports from management to the board should, in relation to the areas covered by them, provide a balanced assessment of the significant risks and the effectiveness of the system of internal control in managing those risks. Any significant control failings or weaknesses identified should be discussed in the reports, including the impact that they have had, or may have, on the company and the actions being taken to rectify them. It is essential that there be openness of communication by management with the board on matters relating to risk and control.

29. When reviewing reports during the year, the board should:

- consider what are the significant risks and assess how they have been identified, evaluated and managed;
- assess the effectiveness of the related system of internal control in managing the significant risks, having regard in particular to any significant failings or weaknesses in internal control that have been reported;
- consider whether necessary actions are being taken promptly to remedy any significant failings or weaknesses; and
- consider whether the findings indicate a need for more extensive monitoring of the system of internal control.

30. Additionally, the board should undertake an annual assessment for the purpose of making its public statement on internal control. The assessment should consider issues dealt with in reports reviewed by it during the year together with any additional information necessary to ensure that the board has taken account of all significant aspects of internal control for the company for the year under review and up to the date of approval of the annual report and accounts.

31. The board's annual assessment should, in particular, consider:

- the changes since the last annual assessment in the nature and extent of significant risks, and the company's ability to respond to changes in its business and the external environment;
- the scope and quality of management's ongoing monitoring of risks and of the system of internal control, and, where applicable, the work of its internal audit function and other providers of assurance;
- the extent and frequency of the communication of the results of the monitoring to the

board (or board committee(s)) which enables it to build up a cumulative assessment of the state of control in the company and the effectiveness with which risk is being managed;

- the incidence of significant control failings or weaknesses that have been identified at any time during the period and the extent to which they have resulted in unforeseen outcomes or contingencies that have had, could have had, or may in the future have, a material impact on the company's financial performance or condition; and
- the effectiveness of the company's public reporting processes.

32. Should the board become aware at any time of a significant failing or weakness in internal control, it should determine how the failing or weakness arose and reassess the effectiveness of management's ongoing processes for designing, operating and monitoring the system of internal control.

FOUR – THE BOARD'S STATEMENT ON INTERNAL CONTROL

33. The annual report and accounts should include such meaningful, high-level information as the board considers necessary to assist shareholders' understanding of the main features of the company's risk management processes and system of internal control, and should not give a misleading impression.

34. In its narrative statement of how the company has applied Code Principle C.2, the board should, as a minimum, disclose that there is an ongoing process for identifying, evaluating and managing the significant risks faced by the company, that it has been in place for the year under review and up to the date of approval of the annual report and accounts, that it is regularly reviewed by the board and accords with the guidance in this document.

35. The disclosures relating to the application of Principle C.2 should include an acknowledgement by the board that it is responsible for the company's system of internal control and for reviewing its effectiveness. It should also explain that such a system is designed to manage rather than eliminate the risk of failure to achieve business objectives, and can only provide reasonable and not absolute assurance against material misstatement or loss.

36. In relation to Code Provision C.2.1, the board should summarise the process it (where applicable, through its committees) has applied in reviewing the effectiveness of the system of internal control and confirm that necessary actions have been or are being taken to remedy any significant failings or weaknesses identified from that review. It should also disclose the process it has applied to deal with material internal control aspects of any significant problems disclosed in the annual report and accounts.

37. Where a board cannot make one or more of the disclosures in paragraphs 34 and 36, it should state this fact and provide an explanation. The Listing Rules require the board to disclose if it has failed to conduct a review of the effectiveness of the company's system of internal control.

38. Where material joint ventures and associates have not been dealt with as part of the group for the purposes of applying this guidance, this should be disclosed.

FIVE – APPENDIX

Assessing the effectiveness of the company's risk and control processes

Some questions which the board may wish to consider and discuss with management when regularly reviewing reports on internal control and when carrying out its annual assessment are set out below.

The questions are not intended to be exhaustive and will need to be tailored to the particular circumstances of the company.

This Appendix should be read in conjunction with the guidance set out in this document.

Risk assessment

- Does the company have clear objectives and have they been communicated so as to provide effective direction to employees on risk assessment and control issues? For example, do objectives and related plans include measurable performance targets and indicators?
- Are the significant internal and external operational, financial, compliance and other risks identified and assessed on an ongoing basis? These are likely to include the principal risks identified in the Operating and Financial Review.
- Is there a clear understanding by management and others within the company of what risks are acceptable to the board?

Control environment and control activities

- Does the board have clear strategies for dealing with the significant risks that have been identified? Is there a policy on how to manage these risks?
- Do the company's culture, code of conduct, human resource policies and performance reward systems support the business objectives and risk management and internal control system?
- Does senior management demonstrate, through its actions as well as it policies, the necessary commitment to competence, integrity and fostering a climate of trust within the company?
- Are authority, responsibility and accountability defined clearly such that decisions are made and actions taken by the appropriate people? Are the decisions and actions of different parts of the company appropriately co-ordinated?
- Does the company communicate to its employees what is expected of them and the scope of their freedom to act? This may apply to areas such as customer relations; service levels for both internal and outsourced activities; health, safety and environmental protection; security of tangible and intangible assets; business continuity issues; expenditure matters; accounting; and financial and other reporting.
- Do people in the company (and in its providers of outsourced services) have the knowledge, skills and tools to support the achievement of the company's objectives and to manage effectively risks to their achievement?
- How are processes/controls adjusted to reflect new or changing risks, or operational deficiencies?

Information and communication

- Do management and the board receive timely, relevant and reliable reports on progress against business objectives and the related risks that provide them with the information, from inside and outside the company, needed for decision-making and management review purposes? This could include performance reports and indicators of change, together with qualitative information such as on customer satisfaction, employee attitudes etc.

- Are information needs and related information systems reassessed as objectives and related risks change or as reporting deficiencies are identified?
- Are periodic reporting procedures, including half-yearly and annual reporting, effective in communicating a balanced and understandable account of the company's position and prospects?
- Are there established channels of communication for individuals to report suspected breaches of law or regulations or other improprieties?

Monitoring

- Are there ongoing processes embedded within the company's overall business operations, and addressed by senior management, which monitor the effective application of the policies, processes and activities related to internal control and risk management? (Such processes may include control self-assessment, confirmation by personnel of compliance with policies and codes of conduct, internal audit reviews or other management reviews).
- Do these processes monitor the company's ability to re-evaluate risks and adjust controls effectively in response to changes in its objectives, its business, and its external environment?
- Are there effective follow-up procedures to ensure that appropriate change or action occurs in response to changes in risk and control assessments?
- Is there appropriate communication to the board (or board committees) on the effectiveness of the ongoing monitoring processes on risk and control matters? This should include reporting any significant failings or weaknesses on a timely basis.
- Are there specific arrangements for management monitoring and reporting to the board on risk and control matters of particular importance? These could include, for example, actual or suspected fraud and other illegal or irregular acts, or matters that could adversely affect the company's reputation or financial position.

Appendix 17

INSTITUTIONAL SHAREHOLDERS' COMMITTEE: THE RESPONSIBILITIES OF INSTITUTIONAL SHAREHOLDERS AND AGENTS – STATEMENT OF PRINCIPLES
(September 2005)

1. Introduction and scope

This Statement of Principles has been drawn up by the Institutional Shareholders' Committee.[1] It develops the principles set out in its 1991 statement 'The Responsibilities of Institutional Shareholders in the UK' and expands on the Combined Code on Corporate Governance of June 1998. It sets out best practice for institutional shareholders and/or agents in relation to their responsibilities in respect of investee companies in that they will:

- set out their policy on how they will discharge their responsibilities – clarifying the priorities attached to particular issues and when they will take action – see 2 below;

- monitor the performance of, and establish, where necessary, a regular dialogue with investee companies – see 3 below;

- intervene where necessary – see 4 below;

- evaluate the impact of their engagement – see 5 below; and

- report back to clients/beneficial owners – see 5 below.

In this statement the term 'institutional shareholder' includes pension funds, insurance companies, and investment trusts and other collective investment vehicles. Frequently, agents such as investment managers are appointed by institutional shareholders to invest on their behalf.

This statement covers the activities of both institutional shareholders and those that invest as agents, including reporting by the latter to their institutional shareholder clients. The actions described in this statement in general apply only in the case of UK listed companies. They can be applied to any such UK company, irrespective of market capitalisation, although institutional shareholders' and agents' policies may indicate de minimis limits for reasons of cost-effectiveness or practicability.

Institutional shareholders and agents should keep under review how far the principles in this statement can be applied to other equity investments.

---

1 In 1991 the members of the Institutional Shareholders' Committee were: the Association of British Insurers; the Association of Investment Trust Companies; the British Merchant Banking and Securities Houses Association; the National Association of Pension Funds; and the Unit Trust Association. In 2005, the members are: the Association of British Insurers; the Association of Investment Trust Companies; the National Association of Pension Funds; and the Investment Management Association.

The policies of engagement set out below do not constitute an obligation to micro-manage the affairs of investee companies, but rather relate to procedures designed to ensure that shareholders derive value from their investments by dealing effectively with concerns over under-performance. Nor do they preclude a decision to sell a holding, where this is the most effective response to such concerns.

Fulfilling fiduciary obligations to end-beneficiaries in accordance with the spirit of this statement may have implications for institutional shareholders' and agents' resources. They should devote appropriate resources, but these should be commensurate with the benefits for beneficiaries. The duty of institutional shareholders and agents is to the end beneficiaries and not to the wider public.

2. Setting out their policy on how they will discharge their responsibilities

Both institutional shareholders and agents will have a clear statement of their policy on engagement and on how they will discharge the responsibilities they assume. This policy statement will be a public document. The responsibilities addressed will include each of the matters set out below.

- How investee companies will be monitored. In order for monitoring to be effective, where necessary, an active dialogue may need to be entered into with the investee company's board and senior management.

- The policy for meeting with an investee company's board and senior management.

- How situations where institutional shareholders and/or agents have a conflict of interest will be minimised or dealt with.

- The strategy on intervention.

- An indication of the type of circumstances when further action will be taken and details of the types of action that may be taken.

- The policy on voting.

Agents and their institutional shareholder clients should agree by whom these responsibilities are to be discharged and the arrangements for agents reporting back.

3. Monitoring performance

Institutional shareholders and/or agents, either directly or through contracted research providers, will review Annual Reports and Accounts, other circulars, and general meeting resolutions. They may attend company meetings where they may raise questions about investee companies' affairs. Also investee companies will be monitored to determine when it is necessary to enter into an active dialogue with the investee company's board and senior management. This monitoring needs to be regular, and the process needs to be clearly communicable and checked periodically for its effectiveness. Monitoring may require sharing information with other shareholders or agents and agreeing a common course of action.

As part of this monitoring, institutional shareholders and/or agents will:

- seek to satisfy themselves, to the extent possible, that the investee company's board and sub-committee structures are effective, and that independent directors provide adequate oversight; and

- maintain a clear audit trail, for example, records of private meetings held with companies, of votes cast, and of reasons for voting against the investee company's management, for abstaining, or for voting with management in a contentious situation.

In summary, institutional shareholders and/or agents will endeavour to identify problems at an early stage to minimise any loss of shareholder value. If they have concerns and do not propose to sell their holdings, they will seek to ensure that the appropriate members of the investee company's board are made aware of them. It may not be sufficient just to inform the Chairman and/or Chief Executive. However, institutional shareholders and/or agents may not wish to be made insiders. Institutional shareholders and/or agents will expect investee companies and their advisers to ensure that information that could affect their ability to deal in the shares of the company concerned is not conveyed to them without their agreement.

4. Intervening when necessary

Institutional shareholders' primary duty is to those on whose behalf they invest, for example, the beneficiaries of a pension scheme or the policyholders in an insurance company, and they must act in their best financial interests. Similarly, agents must act in the best interests of their clients. Effective monitoring will enable institutional shareholders and/or agents to exercise their votes and, where necessary, intervene objectively and in an informed way. Where it would make intervention more effective, they should seek to engage with other shareholders. Many issues could give rise to concerns about shareholder value. Institutional shareholders and/or agents should set out the circumstances when they will actively intervene and how they propose to measure the effectiveness of doing so. Intervention should be considered by institutional shareholders and/or agents regardless of whether an active or passive investment policy is followed. In addition, being underweight is not, of itself, a reason for not intervening. Instances when institutional shareholders and/or agents may want to intervene include when they have concerns about:

- the company's strategy;

- the company's operational performance;

- the company's acquisition/disposal strategy;

- independent directors failing to hold executive management properly to account;

- internal controls failing;

- inadequate succession planning;

- an unjustifiable failure to comply with the Combined Code;

- inappropriate remuneration levels/incentive packages/severance packages; and

- the company's approach to corporate social responsibility.

If boards do not respond constructively when institutional shareholders and/or agents intervene, then institutional shareholders and/or agents will consider on a case-by-case basis whether to escalate their action, for example, by:

- holding additional meetings with management specifically to discuss concerns;

- expressing concern through the company's advisers;

- meeting with the Chairman, senior independent director, or with all independent directors;

- intervening jointly with other institutions on particular issues;

- making a public statement in advance of the AGM or an EGM;

- submitting resolutions at shareholders' meetings; and

- requisitioning an EGM, possibly to change the board.

Institutional shareholders and/or agents should vote all shares held directly or on behalf of clients wherever practicable to do so. They will not automatically support the board; if they have been unable to reach a satisfactory outcome through active dialogue then they will register an abstention or vote against the resolution. In both instances it is good practice to inform the company in advance of their intention and the reasons why.

5. Evaluating and reporting

Institutional shareholders and agents have a responsibility for monitoring and assessing the effectiveness of their engagement. Those that act as agents will regularly report to their clients details on how they have discharged their responsibilities. This should include a judgement on the impact and effectiveness of their engagement. Such reports will be likely to comprise both qualitative as well as quantitative information. The particular information reported, including the format in which details of how votes have been cast will be presented, will be a matter for agreement between agents and their principals as clients.

Transparency is an important feature of effective shareholder activism. Institutional shareholders and agents should not however be expected to make disclosures that might be counterproductive. Confidentiality in specific situations may well be crucial to achieving a positive outcome.

6. Conclusion

The Institutional Shareholders' Committee believes that adoption of these principles will significantly enhance how effectively institutional shareholders and/or agents discharge their responsibilities in relation to the companies in which they invest. To ensure that this is the case, the Institutional Shareholders' Committee will monitor the impact of this statement with a view to further reviewing and refreshing it, if needs be, in 2007 in the light of experience and market developments.

Appendix 18

ICSA GUIDANCE NOTE: DISCLOSING PROXY VOTES
(August 2004)

Following the publication of the Combined Code in 1998, it has become common practice for companies to disclose proxy instructions lodged 'for' and 'against' each resolution being considered on a show of hands at a General Meeting. For ease of explanation, this guide refers to 'proxy votes', but recognises that it is the proxy appointment that is lodged and that, in the event of a poll, the actual votes cast may differ. ICSA have always cautioned that the disclosure of 'proxy votes' should not be made prior to a vote by show of hands as this might be seen as an attempt to influence the vote.

It should be noted that the original version of the Combined Code required only that companies 'except where a poll is called, should indicate the level of proxies lodged on each resolution, and the balance for and against the resolution, after it has been dealt with on a show of hands'.[1] The Hampel Report went on to explain 'This will indicate publicly the proportion of total votes in respect of which proxies were lodged, and the weight of shareholder opinion revealed by those proxy votes. Publication is thus likely to encourage an increase in shareholder voting'.[2] The new Combined Code issued in July 2003, however, provides 'The company should count all proxy votes and, except where a poll is called, should indicate the level of proxies lodged on each resolution, *and the balance for and against the resolution and the number of abstentions*, after it has been dealt with on a show of hands'[3] (our emphasis) There is however some ambiguity as to what, in this context, is meant by 'abstentions' and no mention is made of disclosing similar details when a resolution is decided on a Poll.

A strict interpretation of this rule means that a reading-out of the figures or the display on a screen at a general meeting is sufficient to meet the requirements of the Combined Code. However, as mentioned below, this usually means that attendees cannot make a note of the figures and the information is not available to non-attendees. Although such an announcement satisfies the specific wording of the Combined Code, ICSA believes that only publication meets the underlying intention.

We also recommend that, when publishing such figures, it be made clear that the breakdown of proxy votes being provided gives the position as at a given point in time (usually 36–48 hours prior to the meeting). The point being that shareholders may have subsequently amended the instructions to their proxy or, having lodged a proxy form may have attended the meeting themselves and, having heard the debate, voted in person thus overriding the proxy appointment/instruction.

---

1 Combined Code (July 1998) Provision C.2.1.
2 Committee on Corporate Governance, Final report (January 1998), para. 5.14(b).
3 Combined Code (July 2003) Provision D.2.1.

Several companies project the balance of 'proxy votes' on to a screen immediately following a vote by show of hands but, as mentioned above, some investors have indicated that the information is not always displayed long enough for them to take note of the details. Some companies also publish the information on the company's website after the close of the meeting, a practice we strongly support.

Whether or not the 'proxy votes' are displayed or announced during the meeting, ICSA considers it Best Practice that companies provide a written summary of the 'proxy votes' to be available for shareholders to collect at the end of the meeting as they leave, specifically including and drawing attention to the caveats and notes mentioned above and below. We also recommend that the same information should be made available on the company's website for a reasonable period following the Meeting.

One of the reasons for publishing the 'proxy votes' is to encourage institutional shareholders into exercising the voting rights attached to their holdings. Notwithstanding the fact that an abstention is, by definition, not actually a vote at all many institutional shareholders would consider an instruction to their proxy to abstain from voting on a resolution as meeting the obligation to 'vote' their shares. ICSA has recommended that proxy forms, particularly electronic versions that cannot be altered by hand, should include a 'vote withheld' option.[4]

Another reason for publishing 'proxy votes', is to reassure shareholders that a vote taken on a show of hands has not produced a result at odds with the overall weight of shareholders' opinion.[5] As only votes 'for' and 'against' are taken into account when calculating whether or not a resolution has been passed, it is only necessary, for this purpose, to publish the proxy votes cast for and against each resolution. Where the Chairman has been appointed proxy with discretion as to how to vote it is suggested that the summary of proxy votes also includes a note to indicate how those votes have been cast (which will, presumably, normally be in favour of management).

Companies should, however, be aware that many investors and other 'interested parties' may also request details of abstentions or 'votes withheld' on the basis that these are considered to be a 'warning shot across the bows'.

The problem here though is being able to distinguish between those votes that have been deliberately withheld for the purpose of providing such a 'warning shot' and those where shareholders have, for whatever reason, simply not bothered to vote. Thus the new code requirement to disclose both votes 'for' and 'against' and 'abstentions' begs the question as to what is meant by an abstention.

We believe that providing such information without detailed clarification, which may not always be available, may actually be misleading. The 'vote withheld' facility is provided to enable those shareholders who have made a conscious decision not to vote either 'for' or 'against' a resolution to register that fact however, to have any effect, it is essential that, in such cases, shareholders inform the company as to the reasons for such a decision. There have, also, been reports that some institutional shareholders are incorrectly using this facility where they have not received any voting instructions at all thus contaminating the 'vote withheld' calculation with straightforward abstentions. We have therefore proposed a slightly different approach in the attached pro-forma which enables readers to make their own calculations.

---

4 See ICSA Guidance Note Proxy Instructions – Abstentions.
5 See Guidance Note on Polls and Proxies – The Chairman's Obligation.

It would also seem odd to disclose voting levels only for resolutions passed on a show of hands especially where only some resolutions were dealt with in this way. Following the Myners' report to the Shareholder Voting Working Group there has been a trend towards a greater use of polls. It is our recommendation therefore that voting figures should also be provided for resolutions decided on a poll so that information is made available for all the business of the Meeting.

A pro-forma disclosure notice is attached.

Proxy Appointment Disclosure: Specimen Pro Forma

The AGM of XYZ PLC was held on DD/MM/YYYY

Total number of shares in issue: 15,500,000. Proxy appointments were received from shareholders of 8,457,980 amounting to 54.6% of the issued share capital.

For resolutions decided on a show of hands, the following levels of proxy appointments and associated instructions were received prior to the meeting:

Resolution Number	For		Against		Chairman's discretion (note 1)		Total proxy votes cast
	Number of shares	% of total	Number of shares	% of total	Number of shares	% of total	
1	5,986,498	71.6	578,502	7.0	1,785,287	21.4	8,350,287
2	5,684,262	72.3	395,822	5.0	1,785,287	22.7	7,865,371
3	1,548,377	18.9	5,045,241	61.7	1,585,287	19.4	8,178,905

Notes to the disclosure

1. Where shareholders have appointed the Chairman of the meeting as their proxy with discretion as to voting those votes have been cast in favour of resolutions 1 and 2 but against resolution 3

2. It should be noted that the appointment of a proxy is not an unequivocally precise indicator of the way that the shareholder would have voted on a poll, it merely reflects their intention at the time the instruction was given. Voting instructions can be changed at any time prior to a poll being completed, and a shareholder having lodged a proxy appointment, is still entitled to attend the meeting and, having heard/participated in the debate, vote their shares themselves as they see fit.

Comparable information for those resolutions decided on a Poll is:

Resolution Number	For		Against		Total votes cast
	Number of shares	% of total	Number of shares	% of total	
4	8,598,221	86.1	1,389,246	13.9	9,987,467
5	8,325,188	83.4	1,662,279	16.6	9,980,467

Glossary

accountability: the requirement for a person in a position of authority to justify, explain and take responsibility for the exercise of his or her performance or actions. Accountability is owed to the person or persons from whom the authority is derived.

Accounting Standards Board (ASB): an operating body of the Financial Reporting Council which is responsible for making, amending and withdrawing accounting standards.

active fund: an investment fund whose objective is to outperform the market average by actively seeking out stocks that are forecast to provide superior total return.

agency problem: the potential for conflicts of interest which arise where an agent (in the context of this book, a director as manager of a company's business) acts and takes decisions on behalf of a principal (in the context of this book, a shareholder as part-owner of a company).

agent: a person authorised to carry out business transactions on behalf of another (the principal), who is thereby bound by such actions.

allotment: the issue of shares by a company.

American Depositary Receipt (ADR): a certificate representing a specified number of shares in a non-US company. The share certificates themselves are held by a US bank (known as a depositary bank) which issues the ADRs, then collects dividends and distributes them to ADR holders after converting them into dollars. The holders of ADRs normally have all the rights of normal shareholders, including voting rights. ADRs are tradable instruments in their own right.

analyst: a financial professional working for a bank, fund manager or broker, whose job is to study key industry sectors (e.g. retail, oil, pharmaceuticals), forecast the prospects for the companies operating in them, and make buy and sell recommendations in respect of their shares.

annual accounts: financial accounts prepared in fulfilment of the directors' duty to present audited accounts to shareholders in respect of each financial year. Annual accounts of limited companies must be filed with the Registrar of Companies.

annual general meeting (AGM): a general meeting of a company's shareholders, which must normally be held in each calendar year.

annual report: a narrative statement prepared in fulfilment of the directors' duty to report to shareholders on the performance of the company over the previous financial year and to disclose specified non-financial information. Annual reports of listed companies typically incorporate the annual accounts.

annual return: a form filed each year with the Registrar of Companies containing specified information about a company's directors, secretary, registered office, shareholders, share capital, etc.

anti-takeover defence: a measure designed to impede or prevent an unwelcome takeover, for example by increasing the prospective purchaser's costs by issuing new shares carrying severe redemption provisions.

Articles of Association: a constitutional document setting out the internal regulations of a company; unless modified or excluded by consent of the shareholders, the specimen Articles in Table A of CA 1985 currently have effect in public and private companies limited by shares.

Association of British Insurers (ABI): the trade association for the UK insurance industry, the members of which account for approximately 20 per cent of shares listed on the London Stock Exchange. The ABI recommends responsible voting within the framework of a considered corporate governance policy but does not make specific recommendations on how its members should vote at company general meetings.

audit: a process of independent systematic examination, especially of a company's financial accounts.

audit committee: a committee of the board of directors responsible for a range of audit-related issues, in particular the conduct of the external audit and the company's relationship with its external auditor. The 2003 Combined Code recommends that the audit committees of listed companies should consist of a least three (or, in the case of smaller companies, two) independent non-executive directors, at least one of whom should have recent and relevant financial experience.

audit independence: the ability of external auditors to exercise independent professional judgment without being influenced by the closeness of the relationship with the client company or by considerations of self-interest.

Auditing Practices Board (APB): an operating body of the Financial Reporting Council with responsibility for developing auditing and assurance standards, including ethical standards relating to the independence, objectivity and integrity of auditors, and monitoring their application.

audit report: a report to shareholders prepared by the company's external auditors on completion of the statutory audit and included in the company's published annual report and accounts.

auditors: *see* external auditors, internal auditors.

authorised share capital: the maximum amount of share capital (by nominal value and number of shares) that a company is permitted to issue. A company's authorised share capital is stated in its Memorandum of Association and can be increased only with the agreement of shareholders, normally (in the case of public companies) by ordinary resolution in a general meeting.

balance sheet: one of the main components of a company's accounts, the balance sheet provides a snapshot of the company's assets and liabilities on a specified date (usually the end of its financial year) and is thus an indicator of the financial health of the company.

beneficial owner: the individual who benefits from ownership of a share or other property registered in the name of another person or corporate body (for example, a nominee company, pension fund or other investment body).

board: the group of individuals elected by the shareholders of a company to manage its affairs.

'box-ticking': the adoption, by listed companies or their shareholders, of a slavish or unreflective approach to corporate governance in which companies' compliance with best practice is assessed on the basis of prescriptive rules rather than by reference to qualitative measures and outcomes.

Cadbury Code of Best Practice: a voluntary code of corporate governance applicable to UK listed companies based on the recommendations of the Committee on the Financial Aspects of Corporate Governance chaired by Sir Adrian Cadbury. The Cadbury Code was appended to the Listing Rules in 1993 and remained in effect until its replacement by the Combined Code of Corporate Governance in 1998.

case law: the principles and rules of law established by judicial decisions. Under this system the decision reached in a particular case creates a precedent – that is, it is regarded as exemplifying rules of broader application, which must be followed in subsequent cases, except by higher courts.

chairman: the director nominated by a company's board to chair its meetings and take the lead in discussions with shareholders. It is established best practice in the UK that the positions of chairman and chief executive officer (CEO) should not be held by the same person.

chief executive officer (CEO): the director (usually a full-time employee of the company) nominated by the board to lead the company's executive management team. It is established best practice in the UK that the positions of chief executive officer and chairman should not be held by the same person.

City Code (or Takeover Code): rules written and enforced by the Panel on Takeover and Mergers and governing the management and timing of takeover bids involving listed companies. The objective of the City Code is to ensure that high standards of integrity and fairness are maintained, and that shareholders in both the bidding and target company are treated equitably.

Combined Code of Corporate Governance: a voluntary code of corporate governance applicable to UK listed companies which are required by the Listing Rules to disclose whether they comply with the Code and to explain any areas of non-compliance. The original Code introduced in 1998 was replaced by a revised version in July 2003.

common law: a body of law based on custom and usage and decisions reached in previous cases. The principles and rules of common law derive from judgments and judicial opinions delivered in response to specific circumstances, not from written legislation.

company: an association of persons which, on incorporation, becomes a legal entity entirely separate from the individuals comprising its membership. In the Companies Act 1985 (CA 1985), 'company' is restricted to companies registered under that Act or previous Companies Acts.

company secretary: an officer of the company with statutory duties (e.g. to sign the annual return and accompanying documents) and charged with a range of duties relating to the company's statutory books and records, filing requirements, etc. Currently, every company must have a secretary who, in the case of a public company, must meet the qualification requirements laid down in the Companies Act.

comply or explain: the approach adopted in the UK to compliance by listed companies with best practice in corporate governance. Under this approach, successive codes of corporate governance have been appended to the Listing Rules, with a requirement on listed companies to disclose in their annual reports whether or not they have complied with Code recommendations and, to the extent that they have not, to give reasons for the areas of non-compliance. While the company is under no formal obligation to comply with best practice recommendations, the disclosure obligation ensures that its shareholders can monitor the extent of its compliance, consider the explanations provided by the directors for any areas of non-compliance and, if dissatisfied, express their concerns through their voting behaviour at the AGM.

concentration of ownership: a situation, prevalent in some economies, in which a large proportion of the shares in a listed company are held by a single shareholder or a small group of shareholders connected by family ties, cross-shareholdings or other mutual interests.

conflict of interest: a situation in which an individual or corporate body is in a position of trust which requires him/her/it to exercise judgment on behalf of others, but also has self-interests which interfere with the exercise of his/her/its independent judgment.

connected person: any person with whom a director is connected, including the spouse, child or stepchild of a director; or any business partner or company associated with a director in which he or she has 20 per cent of the equity share capital (CA 1985, s 346).

Co-ordinating Group on Audit and Accounting Issues (CGAA): a group established by the UK Government to review arrangements for audit and accountancy regulation following the collapse of Enron and other major US corporations. The CGAA produced its interim report in July 2002 and its final report in January 2003.

corporate social responsibility (CSR): the recognition by a company of its responsibilities to parties other than shareholders, usually including employees, customers, suppliers, local communities and the environment.

cross-directorship: a situation (also known as a 'board interlock') in which the boards of two or more listed companies have directors in common. Cross-directorships are considered to have a detrimental effect on corporate governance by impairing the independence of the directors concerned.

cross-shareholding: the holding of shares between two or more publicly listed companies that gives each company involved an equity stake in the other. This is prevalent in economies in insider systems, where cross-shareholdings reinforce concentration of ownership; and may also be employed as a means of preventing unsolicited takeovers.

de facto director: any person occupying the position of a director, even if his or her appointment or qualifications prove to be invalid.

debenture: a bond issued by a company to providers of long-term borrowing, whereby the company agrees to pay a fixed rate of interest ('coupon') to debenture holders each year until maturity, when the loan will be repaid. If the company fails to pay either the interest or the principal amount of the loan at maturity, debenture holders can force the company into liquidation and recover their money from a sale of its assets.

demutualisation: in the UK, the process by which building societies have converted from being mutual organisations owned by their members to profit-making companies which distribute profits to their shareholders.

Department of Trade and Industry (DTI): the UK Government department responsible for the administration of company law. The Companies Act confers certain powers on the Secretary of State for Trade and Industry.

director: an officer of a company responsible for determining policy, supervising the management of the company's business and exercising the powers of the company. Directors must generally carry out these responsibilities collectively as a board.

directors' report: a statement attached to the annual accounts containing certain information laid down in CA 1985.

distribution: the transfer of some or all of a company's assets (usually in cash) to its shareholders in proportion to their shareholdings, generally by way of dividend or on a winding-up.

dividend: the distribution of part of a company's earnings to shareholders, usually twice a year in the form of a main dividend and an interim dividend. The directors of a company have discretion as to the size of a dividend or whether to pay a dividend at all.

due diligence: a systematic investigation into a company's financial position, past performance, legal liabilities, etc. before a deal is done to ensure that no unexpected problems emerge afterwards. Due diligence is generally carried out by companies or their advisers before acquiring or merging with another company. The 2003 Combined Code of Corporate Governance recommends that prospective directors should also carry out a process of due diligence before joining the board of a company with which they have no prior involvement.

elective resolution: currently, a resolution, of which 21 days' notice must be given, requiring unanimous approval at a general meeting of a private company.

equity: the amount which shareholders own in a publicly quoted company. Equity is the risk-bearing part of the company's capital and contrasts with debt capital which is usually secured in some way and which has priority over shareholders if the company becomes insolvent and its assets are distributed. For most companies there are two types of equity: ordinary shares, which have voting rights, and preference shares, which do not. Owners of preference shares rank ahead of ordinary shareholders in a liquidation.

executive director: a member of a company's board of directors who is also an employee of the company.

'exit': the ability of shareholders to maintain, increase or dispose of their shareholdings in a company according to their opinion of the performance of the business and the quality of the directors.

external auditors: firms, or partners and staff of such firms, which provide financial audit (and often other consultancy) services to client companies, particularly in association with the statutory audit.

extraordinary general meeting (EGM): any general meeting of the company's members that is not an annual general meeting. An EGM is required to approve certain special resolutions, e.g. for a takeover or merger or break-up of the company. For such resolutions to be passed, 75 per cent of more of the shareholders have to vote for it.

extraordinary resolution: a resolution requiring a 75 per cent majority at a general meeting.

fiduciary duties: the duties of a trustee: the directors of a company are given their powers in trust by the company and therefore have fiduciary duties towards it, obliging them to act always in good faith and not to derive a personal profit from their position.

Financial Reporting Council (FRC): the UK independent regulator for corporate reporting and governance.

Financial Reporting Review Panel (FRRP): an operating body of the FRC which has responsibility for ensuring that the provision of financial information by public and large private companies complies with relevant accounting requirements.

FTSE 100: one of the Financial Times Stock Exchange indices designed to give investors an idea of the overall value and general movement of the stock market. The FTSE 100 is an index of the share prices of the 100 largest companies (by market capitalisation) in the UK and is updated throughout the trading day in real time.

fund manager: a financial professional employed by an investment trust, unit trust, pension fund or other investing institution to decide how its funds should be invested. Fund managers have considerable influence over the prices of company shares because of the large amounts of money for which they are responsible.

general meeting: a meeting of the company which all members (subject to any restrictions in the company's Articles) are entitled to attend.

Greenbury Code of Best Practice: a voluntary code of best practice on remuneration policy and the setting of individual directors' remuneration applicable to UK listed companies and based on the recommendations of the Study Group on Directors' Remuneration chaired by Sir Richard Greenbury. The Greenbury Code was appended to the Listing Rules in 1995 and remained in effect until its replacement by the Combined Code of Corporate Governance in 1998.

Hampel Committee: a Committee on Corporate Governance chaired by Sir Ronald Hampel and established in 1995 to review the implementation and effectiveness of the Cadbury Code of Corporate Governance and the Greenbury Code of Best Practice on directors' remuneration. In line with the Hampel Committee's findings, a Combined Code of Corporate Governance was appended to the Listing Rules in 1998.

Higgs Report: the report on the role and effectiveness of non-executive directors produced by Derek Higgs and published in January 2003.

hostile takeover: an unsolicited takeover not supported by the board of directors of the target company.

independence: in general terms, the state of being free from the influence of another individual or individuals and free from any conflict of interest. In the specific context of the 2003 Combined Code, an independent non-executive director is one who is independent in character and judgment and who has no relationships or circumstances which are likely to affect, or could appear to affect, his or her judgment. A non-executive director may be considered not to be independent if he or she has been an employee of the company or group within the last five years; has, or has had within the last three years, a material business relationship with the company either directly, or as a partner, shareholder, director or senior employee of a body that has such a relationship with the company; has received or receives additional remuneration from the company apart from a director's fee; participates in the company's share option or a performance-related pay scheme, or is a member of the company's pension scheme; has close family ties with any of the company's advisers, directors or senior employees; holds cross-directorships or has significant links with other directors through involvement in other companies or bodies; represents a significant shareholder; or has served on the board for more than nine years from the date of their first election.

insider dealing: share dealings by employees of a company or other individuals who use price-sensitive information not available to the market for personal gain or the gain of their associates. Insider dealing is a criminal offence under Part V of the Criminal Justice Act 1993.

insider trading: the term used in the US for the criminal offence known in the UK as insider dealing.

institutional shareholder: a financial institution, such as a pension fund or insurance company, which invests money in the share, bond and other financial markets on behalf of underlying investors and savers.

internal audit: employees of a company with responsibility for evaluating and providing assurance on the integrity and effectiveness of the company's system of internal controls.

investor relations: the process by which a company communicates with its shareholders and the wider investment community; used particularly in relation to the company's contacts with institutional shareholders and analysts.

issued share capital: the nominal value of the shares that a company has actually issued. The company's issued share capital must not exceed its authorised share capital.

keiretsu: in Japan, an alliance among suppliers and other companies that operate vertically and horizontally, centred on a bank or other financial institution.

limited company: a company in which the liability of members for the debts of the company is limited, either to the amount of share capital for which they have subscribed (a company limited by shares) or to a specific amount guaranteed in the event of a winding-up (a company limited by guarantee).

limited liability: a legal arrangement whereby the potential liability of members for the debts of a company is limited either to the nominal value of their shares (in the case of a company limited by shares) or to a specific amount guaranteed in the event of a winding-up (in the case of a company limited by guarantee). In either case, the personal assets of members are not at risk if the company becomes insolvent and is liquidated.

liquidation: the process by which a company ceases to trade and realises its assets for distribution to creditors and then shareholders. Also known as a 'winding-up'.

liquidity: in financial markets, the ease of dealing in a particular share or other financial instrument, measured by the readiness with which shares can be bought and sold without significantly affecting their price. Broadly speaking, liquidity is achieved where companies have large numbers of shares in issues and available for trading on stock markets in which there are many potential buyers and sellers. In contrast, markets tend to be illiquid where companies have few shares in issue and where there are few potential buyers and sellers.

listed company: in the UK, a company whose shares are listed by the United Kingdom Listing Authority (UKLA) and admitted for trading on the London Stock Exchange.

listing: the process by which a company's shares become tradable on a stock exchange.

listing particulars: details which a company is obliged to publish about itself and its securities before it can obtain a listing on a recognised stock exchange.

Listing Rules: rules published by the UKLA setting out the conditions for admission to listing and specifying the ongoing obligations of listed companies, particularly in respect of disclosure of information.

London Stock Exchange (LSE): the principal UK stock exchange.

majority shareholder(s): a shareholder, or alliance of shareholders, holding a majority of the voting shares in a company and so having a controlling interest over its affairs.

management board: in a two-tier board structure, a board comprising executive managers of the company and having responsibility for the operational performance of the business. A management board will typically be chaired by the chief executive officer and report to the company's supervisory board.

market abuse: a civil offence created by the Financial Services and Markets Act 2000 for which an individual can be fined by the FSA. Market abuse occurs when an individual distorts a market in investments, creates a false or misleading impression of the value or price of an investment, or otherwise misuses relevant information before it is published.

market capitalisation: the market value of a listed company, calculated by multiplying its current share price by the number of shares in issue.

median: the value of the middle item when all the items in a data set are arranged from lowest to highest: the median is the value halfway through the ordered data set, below and above which there lies an equal number of data values.

Memorandum of Association: a constitutional document stating the company's name, domicile, objects, limitations of liability (where applicable) and authorised share capital.

minority shareholders: shareholders whose combined shareholdings in a company are insufficient to enable them to influence the outcome of votes at a general meeting.

Model Code: a code for transactions in the securities of listed companies by directors, certain employees and persons connected with them. The Model Code is promulgated by the UKLA and incorporated within the Listing Rules.

Myners Report: a report of a review of institutional investment carried out on behalf of the UK government by Paul Myners and published in March 2001.

Nasdaq (US): the National Association of Securities Dealers Automated Quotations system – an electronic stock market established by the National Association of Securities Dealers.

National Association of Pension Funds (NAPF): an umbrella body representing 75 per cent of occupational pension funds in the UK, accounting for some 20 per cent of shares listed on the London Stock Exchange. Through its Voting Issues Service (VIS), the NAPF monitors the corporate governance practices of listed companies and makes recommendations to its members on the exercise of their voting powers at company general meetings.

New York Stock Exchange (NYSE): the largest stock exchange in the US.

nominal value: the 'face value' of a share, expressed as the proportion of the company's issued share capital represented by each of the shares in issue. The nominal value of a share defines the extent of the shareholder's liability to contribute to the company's debts at liquidation, but generally bears no relation to the share's market price.

nomination committee: a committee of the board of directors responsible for leading the process for board appointments. The 2003 Combined Code recommends that the nomination committees of listed companies should consist of non-executive directors, a majority of whom should be independent, and should be chaired by the chairman of the company or the senior independent director.

non-audit services: services other than the statutory audit performed by a firm of auditors on behalf of an audit client. From the point of view of corporate governance, there are concerns that the performance of non-audit services by an external auditor may compromise the auditor's objectivity and independence, particularly where the fees payable are substantial in relation to the statutory audit fee.

non-executive director (NED): a member of a company's board of directors who is not an employee of the company and who has no involvement in the day-to-day management of its operations.

OECD: the Organisation for Economic Co-operation and Development, the member countries of which are Australia, Austria, Belgium, Canada, Czech Republic, Denmark, Finland, France, Germany, Greece, Hungary, Iceland, Ireland, Italy, Japan, Korea, Luxembourg, the Netherlands, New Zealand, Mexico, Norway, Poland, Portugal, Spain, Sweden, Switzerland, Turkey, the UK and the US.

Official List: the main exchange of the London Stock Exchange whose members tend to be the larger quoted or listed companies.

Operating and Financial Review (OFR): a narrative statement intended to provide shareholders and other users with systematic and objective information on which to base their assessment of the business, including qualitative disclosures on the key dependencies of the business, the company's relationships with customers, suppliers and employees, and the factors and influences likely to affect future performance. Currently, preparation of an OFR is voluntary, but proposals for a mandatory OFR for major companies have been accepted by the UK Government.

ordinary resolution: a resolution proposed at a general meeting of shareholders, which may be carried by a simple majority of votes actually cast.

ordinary shares: the most common form of shares in a company, conferring on holders the right to share in the company's profits in proportion to their holdings and (with occasional exceptions) the right to vote at general meetings.

outside director (US): a member of a corporation's board of directors who is not an employee of the corporation and who has no involvement in the day-to-day management of its operations.

pension fund: a fund set up by a company, union, government entity or other organisation to invest the pension contributions of members and employees, and pay out pensions to those people when they reach retirement age. Pension funds accumulate huge pools of capital, which they invest in the stock markets. As a result, they exert considerable influence on the markets, and their decisions on which shares to hold in which sectors have a substantial impact on prices.

Pensions Investments Research Consultants Ltd (PIRC): a company which produces investment advice and voting recommendations for its clients, mainly local authority and other public sector pension funds. The PIRC is in some respects the most radical of the institutional investor bodies and is active in the public policy debate on issues of corporate governance and socially responsible investment.

preference shares: shares which give their holders the right to payment of a fixed dividend out of profits before the payment of an ordinary dividend or the preferential return of capital or both, but which do not usually carry voting rights.

price-sensitive information: information which, if made public, is likely to have a significant effect on the price of a company's securities. Such information must, in connection with a listed company, be reported via the London Stock Exchange so that it can be released to the market in a manner that is fair to all investors.

privatisation: in the UK, the sale of government-owned equity in nationalised industries or other commercial enterprises to private investors.

profit and loss account: a set of accounts, prepared annually, which depicts a company's trading performance. It is normally read in conjunction with the balance sheet and cash flow data.

profits warning: an announcement issued via the London Stock Exchange in circumstances where a listed company's directors expect its profits to be lower than forecast by analysts and other market participants. The warning is released to ensure that all investors have access to the news at the same time.

prospectus: a document published in accordance with the Listing Rules in the form of a notice, circular, investment advertisement or other invitation to the public to subscribe for or purchase a company's shares or debentures.

proxy: a person authorised by a shareholder to vote on his or her behalf at a general meeting.

Public Accounting Oversight Board (US): a regulatory body established under the terms of the Sarbanes-Oxley Act with responsibility for registration, inspection and discipline of public accounting firms, including the establishment of auditing, quality control, ethical, independence and other standards relating to the preparation of audit reports.

public company: a company which meets specified requirements as to its minimum share capital and which is registered as a public company. Only public companies are allowed to offer shares and debentures to the public.

Public Interest Disclosure Act 1998: UK legislation which protects from victimisation or discrimination workers who report known or suspected wrongdoings in their workplaces in relation to: criminal acts; failure to comply with legal duties (such as negligence or breach of contract); miscarriages of justice; danger to health and safety; damage to the environment; and deliberate cover-up of any of these.

quoted companies: for purposes of UK legislation and regulation, companies listed in any state of the European Economic Area (the EU plus Iceland, Norway and Liechtenstein) and on the NYSE and Nasdaq.

'rational apathy': an economic theory which states that, where share ownership in large publicly quoted companies is widely dispersed, it may not be worthwhile for individual shareholders to devote time, effort and resources to trying to change unacceptable management behaviour. Traditionally used by institutional investors to justify reluctance to exercise voting powers, the concept of rational apathy is increasingly being challenged by reference to the fiduciary duties of institutions to act responsibly on behalf of underlying beneficiaries.

registered office: the address at which legal documents may be served on the company and at which its statutory books are normally kept. The registered office need not be the company's place of business and may be changed freely so long as it remains in the company's country of origin.

Registrar of Companies: the official responsible for maintaining the company records filed under the requirements of the Companies Acts.

remuneration committee: a committee of the board of directors responsible for determining the company's remuneration policy and setting the remuneration of individual executive directors. The 2003 Combined Code recommends that the remuneration committees of listed companies should consist exclusively of independent non-executive directors.

resolution: a decision reached by a requisite majority of the shareholders of a company voting in person or by proxy at a general meeting of shareholders; in the case of a written resolution, a decision approved in writing by all shareholders.

rewards for failure: the perception, currently prevalent in the UK, that the severance terms paid to directors leaving their positions for reasons of underperformance fail to take account of poor performance and disappointing results for shareholders.

rights issue: an offer made by a listed company to its shareholders to enable them to buy new shares in the company at a discount to the market price. Existing shareholders are usually offered shares in proportion to their existing holding. Because the new shares are offered at a discount to the current market price, the rights have a value in themselves and can be sold separately.

risk management: the process of analysing a company's exposure to financial and non-financial risk and determining how best to handle such exposure.

Sarbanes-Oxley Act: US legislation adopted in the light of Enron and other major corporate failures. Significant provisions include measures intended to restore investor confidence in company financial reports, safeguard the integrity of the audit process and strengthen audit regulation.

Securities and Exchange Commission (SEC): the US federal agency empowered to regulate US financial markets in order to protect investors. All US quoted companies have to comply with SEC rules and regulations, including the filing of quarterly results statements.

senior independent director: the recognised senior member of the non-executive element on a company's board, other than the chairman.

shadow director: any person, including a corporate body such as a bank, in accordance with whose directions or instructions the other directors of the company are accustomed to act.

share: a unit of ownership of a company, representing a fraction of the share capital and usually conferring rights to participate in distributions. There may be several kinds of shares each carrying different rights. Shares are issued at a fixed nominal value, although the company may actually receive a larger amount, the excess representing share premium. Shareholders may not be required to subscribe the full amount immediately, in which case the shares are partly paid. The shareholders then await calls, which require them to pay further amounts until the shares are fully paid.

share capital: the proportion of the company's capital which is contributed by shareholders on the issue of ordinary shares and preference shares.

share option: an incentive given to company directors and employees in the form of an option to buy shares in the company at a fixed price at a defined future date.

share registrar: an organisation which maintains the register of shareholders on behalf of a client company. Registrars are generally responsible for the issue of share certificates, the despatch of company communications to shareholders and the processing of proxy voting returns and other shareholder responses.

shareholder: as defined by CA 1985, s 22, a member of a company limited by shares who has agreed to become a member of the company (whether by subscription to the Memorandum, by acquisition, by way of allotment or transfer or by transmission) and has been registered as such in the company's register of members.

Smith Report: the report and proposed guidance on audit committees by a group chaired by Sir Robert Smith and published by the Financial Reporting Council in January 2003.

socially responsible investing (SRI): an investment strategy that seeks to achieve a balance between financial returns and wider social benefits, usually by investing in companies which are judged to operate to appropriate standards of social, ethical and environmental responsibility.

special resolution: a resolution of which 21 clear days' notice must be given and which must be approved by 75 per cent of the votes cast in general meeting.

stakeholder: an individual or group with a direct interest in a company's performance or conduct, either because of a financial or non-financial investment in the company or because of the impact of the company's activities. Stakeholders may include shareholders, employees, customers, suppliers, competitors, local communities, government and regulators and proxies for the natural environment.

statute law: the body of law represented by legislation and thus occurring in authoritative written form. Statute law contrasts with common law, over which it takes precedence.

statutory audit: independent examination of, and expression of expert professional opinion on, the published financial statements of a company on behalf of its shareholders.

statutory books: a general term applied to the registers and minute books, etc. that a company is required by the Companies Act to maintain.

Summary Financial Statement (SFS): a short-form version of the annual report and accounts which UK listed companies are permitted by the Companies (Summary Financial Statement) Regulations 1995 to send to shareholders and other recipients who do not specifically elect to receive a copy of the full document. The minimum content of the SFS is specified in the Regulations.

supervisory board: in a two-tier board structure, a board comprising non-executive directors of the company and having responsibility for oversight of the management board.

sustainability: the ability of a community or society to develop a strategy of economic growth and development that continues to function indefinitely within the limits set by ecology and is beneficial to all stakeholders and the environment.

Table A: the specimen Articles of Association for a company limited by shares set out in Table A of the Companies (Tables A to F) Regulations 1985. Unless specifically modified or excluded, the Articles set out in the version of Table A in force at the time of a company's incorporation automatically apply.

takeover: the acquisition of one company by another, on either an agreed or a hostile basis. Strict rules apply in the UK to the conduct and timing of a takeover bid.

Takeover Code: *see* City Code.

Total Shareholder Return (TSR): a measure of the returns to shareholders over a defined period, increasingly used as the performance measure against which directors' rewards under performance-related remuneration arrangements are determined. TSR measures the percentage increase in the value of a given holding of the company's shares over a specified period, taking account of the increase or fall in the market share price of the company's shares over the period and assuming that all dividends received on the holding are reinvested in the company's shares.

tracker fund: an investment fund of which the objective is to achieve the same returns as a chosen share index by investing in all the companies in the index according to a market value weighting.

transparency: in the context of company reporting, the provision of information in a manner which ensures that the company's position and prospects can be assessed on the basis of complete, reliable and meaningful data; otherwise, the existence of clear and visible procedures for the making of decisions.

Turnbull Report: the report *Internal Control: Guidance for Directors on the Combined Code* produced by a working party chaired by Nigel Turnbull and published in September 1999 by the Institute of Chartered Accountants in England and Wales.

two-tier board: a board structure in which the management and supervisory functions of the board are formally separated and allocated between a management board of full-time executives and a supervisory board of part-time external directors. Two-tier boards are the norm in a small number of Continental European countries, notably Germany, the Netherlands, Denmark and Austria.

Tyson Report: the report on the recruitment and development of non-executive directors produced by a task force chaired by Laura D'Andrea Tyson and published in June 2003.

unitary board: the most common board structure worldwide, in which the management and supervisory functions of the board are discharged by a single body comprising both executive and non-executive directors.

United Kingdom Listing Authority (UKLA): the Financial Services Authority (FSA) in its capacity as the competent authority in the UK for the listing of company shares and other securities for trading on public stock exchanges. The UKLA promulgates and enforces the Listing Rules, which require companies, as a condition of listing, to prepare listing particulars and comply with ongoing disclosure obligations.

'voice': the ability of shareholders to exercise the voting powers attaching to shares to appoint and dismiss the directors and to give or withhold approval for proposals affecting their interests.

voting cap: a limit on the number of votes permitted to be cast by a shareholder or group of shareholders irrespective of the number of shares held. Voting caps may be used to secure for controlling shareholders voting powers in excess of their investment and are therefore considered to be detrimental to effective corporate governance.

voting rights: rights attaching to shares in a company which confer on their holder the entitlement to vote at general meetings of the company's shareholders.

whistleblower: an individual (usually an employee) who draws attention to concerns about suspected misconduct on the part of a colleague or superior or the organisation itself. Where no whistleblowing procedure has been established, a whistleblower may consider it necessary to raise concerns with a senior individual inside the company or with an external regulator or the media.

whistleblowing procedure: an internal procedure whereby employees with concerns about suspected misconduct on the part of a colleague or superior or the organisation itself can report them in confidence in the knowledge that they will not be subject to retaliatory action.

written resolution: a means by which a private company may obtain shareholder approval for a proposal without needing to convene a general meeting. To be passed, the written resolution must be signed by all members entitled to vote.

wrongful trading: a civil offence established in insolvency law which occurs where a company continues to trade when the directors are aware that the company had gone into (or would shortly go into) insolvent liquidation. A liquidator of the company can apply to the court for a director or shadow director to be held liable to contribute to the assets of the company.

Bibliography

ICSA Publications

Available from ICSA Publishing: www.icsapublishing.co.uk
Armour, D. (2002) *The ICSA Company Secretary's Checklists*, 4th edition
Armour, D. (2003) *The ICSA Company Secretary's Handbook*, 4th edition
Bruce, M. (2003) *The ICSA Directors' Guide*
Walmsley, K. *Company Secretarial Practice*

ICSA Best Practice Guides and Guidance Notes

Available from The Information Centre, ICSA, 16 Park Crescent, London W1B 1AH, UK.

The ICSA Policy Unit produces a range of Best Practice Guides and Guidance Notes to support company secretaries.

All relevant Guidance Notes are reproduced on the CSP CD-Rom. Copies are also available via the ICSA website at www.icsa.org.uk/news/guidance.php. This area of the site also offers an email alert service whereby users register to receive notification of any new Guidance Note published.

Appointment and Induction of Directors
Duties of the Company Secretary
Duties of the Company Secretary in Ireland
Electronic Communications with Shareholders
Establishing a Whistleblowing Procedure
Good Boardroom Practice: A Code for Directors and Company Secretaries
Guide to Best Practice at Annual General Meetings
Guide to the Statement of Compliance
Matters Reserved for the Board
Short Guide to the Retention of Documents
Specimen job description: the corporate governance role of the company
Terms of Reference of the Audit Committee
Terms of Reference of the Nominations Committee
Terms of Reference of the Remuneration Committee

Codes, guidelines and reports

Accounting Standards Board (2006) *Reporting Statement: Operating and Financial Review* (available at www.frc.org.uk/asb/publications)

Association of British Insurers (2001) *Disclosure Guidelines on Socially Responsible Investment* (available at www.ivis.co.uk)

Association of British Insurers (2005) *Principles and Guidelines on Executive Remuneration* (available at www.ivis.co.uk)

Association of British Insurers/National Association of Pension Funds (1999) *Statement on Responsible Voting* (available at www.ivis.co.uk)

Association of British Insurers/National Association of Pension Funds (2005) *Joint Statement of Best Practice on Executive Contracts and Severance* (available at www.ivis.co.uk)

Barclays plc (2004) *Board Governance: Role Profiles and Charter of Expectations* (available at www.investorrelations.barclays.co.uk)

Cadbury Committee on the Financial Aspects of Corporate Governance (1992) *Report of the Committee on the Financial Aspects of Corporate Governance: The Code of Best Practice*, Gee Publishing

Department of Trade and Industry (2003) *The Role and Effectiveness of Non-Executive Directors* (the Higgs Report) (available at www.dti.gov.uk)

Department of Trade and Industry (2004) *The Operating and Financial Review – Practical Guidance for Directors* (the Radcliffe Guidance) (available at www.dti.gov.uk)

Department of Trade and Industry (2005) *The UK approach to EU company law and corporate governance* (available at www.dti.gov.uk)

Edis-Bates Associates (2005) *Evaluating the Code: is board performance evaluation working?* (available at www.edisbates.co.uk)

Financial Reporting Council (2004) *The Turnbull Guidance as an evaluation framework for the purposes of Section 404(a) of the Sarbanes-Oxley Act* (available at www.frc.org.uk)

Financial Reporting Council (2005) *Internal Control: Revised guidance for directors of the Combined Code* (available at www.frc.org.uk)

Financial Reporting Council (2006) *Review of the 2003 Combined Code: Findings of the Review*

Financial Reporting Council (2006) *Review of the 2003 Combined Code: Consultation on possible changes to the Combined Code*

Good Corporation (2004) *The Good Corporation Standard* (available at www.goodcorporation.com)

Grant Thornton (2005) *4th FTSE350 Corporate Governance Review* (available at www.grant-thornton.co.uk)

Greenbury Study Group (1995) *Report on Directors' Remuneration*, Gee Publishing

Hampel Committee on Corporate Governance (1998) *Committee on Corporate Governance: Final Report*, Gee Publishing

HM Treasury (2001) *Institutional Investment in the UK: A Review* (the Myners Report) (available at www.hm-treasury.gov.uk)

HM Treasury (2004) *Myners Principles for Institutional Investment Decision Making – Review of Progress* (available at www.hm-treasury.gov.uk)

Institute of Chartered Accountants in England and Wales (2004) *Whistleblowing arrangements: Guidance for Audit Committees* (available at www.icaew.co.uk)

Institute of Risk Management (2002) *A Risk Management Standard* (available at www.theirm.org)

Institutional Shareholders' Committee (2005) *Responsibilities of Institutional Shareholders and Agents – Statement of Principles* (available at www. www.ivis.co.uk)

International Corporate Governance Network (2005) *Statement of Global Corporate Governance Principles* (available at www.icgn.org)

Myners, Paul (2004) *Review of the Impediments to Voting UK Shares – Report for the Shareholder Voting Working Party* (available at www.manifest.co.uk)

Myners, Paul (2005) *Review of the Impediments to Voting UK Shares: Progress One Year On – Report for the Shareholder Voting Working Party* (available at www.manifest.co.uk)

National Association of Pension Funds (2001) *Corporate Governance Policy* (available at www.ivis.co.uk)

Organisation for Economic Co-operation and Development (2004) *OECD Principles of Corporate Governance* (available at www.oecdbookshop.org)

Oxford Economic Research Associates (OXERA) (2006) *Competition and Choice in the UK Audit Market – Report for DTI and FRC* (available at www.frc.org.uk)

Pensions Investments Research Consultants Ltd (2003) *Shareholder Voting Guidelines* (available at www.pirc.co.uk)

Research Recommendations and Electronic Voting (RREV) (2005) *Board Effectiveness and Shareholder Engagement* (available at www.rrev.co.uk)

Research Recommendations and Electronic Voting (RREV) (2005) *Voting Review 2005* (available at www.rrev.co.uk)

RSM Robson Rhodes (2004) *Corporate Governance: A Practical Guide* (available at www.rsmi.co.uk)

Singh, V. (2004) *Diversity of FTSE100 Directors – Report for DTI* (available at www.dti.gov.uk)

Task Force on Human Capital Management (2003) *Accounting for People: Report to the DTI* (the Kingsmill Report) (available at www.accountingforpeople.gov.uk)

Additional reading

Bruce, M. *Rights and Duties of Directors*, 5th edition, Tolley

Cadbury, A. (2002) *Corporate Governance and Chairmanship: A Personal View*, Oxford University Press

Chambers, A (2003) *Corporate Governance Handbook*, Tolley

Charkham, J. and Simpson, A. (1999) *Fair Shares: The Future of Shareholder Power and Responsibility*, Oxford University Press

Charkham, Jonathan P. (1994) *Keeping Good Company: A Study of Accountability in Five Countries*, Clarendon Press

Cheffins, B. (1997) *Company Law: Theory, Structure and Operation*, Oxford University Press

Cowe, R. (2001) *Investing in Social Responsibility: Risks and Opportunities*, Association of British Insurers

Davies, Paul L. (ed.) (1997) *Gower's Principles of Modern Company Law*, 6th edition, Sweet & Maxwell

Department of Trade and Industry (2004) *Building Better Boards* (available at www.dti.gov.uk)

Dunne, P. (1997) *Running Board Meetings*, Kogan Page

Low Chee Keong (ed.) (2002) *Corporate Governance: An Asia-Pacific Critique*, Sweet & Maxwell Asia

Mallin, Christine A. (2004) *Corporate Governance*, Oxford University Press

Monks, A.G. and Minow, N. (2001) *Corporate Governance*, Blackwell

Parkinson, J.E. (1993) *Corporate Power and Responsibility*, Clarendon Press

Smith, Deborah (2002) *Demonstrating Corporate Values*, Institute of Business Ethics

Stiles, P. and Taylor, B. (2001) *Boards at Work*, Oxford University Press

Tricker, R.I. (1984) *Corporate Governance*, Gower

Wheeler, D. and Sillanpaa, M. (1997) *The Stakeholder Corporation*, Pitman Publishing
Zadek, S. Pruzan, P. and Evans, R. (1997) *Building Corporate Accountability*, Earthscan

Web resources

Association of British Insurers: www.abi.org.uk
Business for Social Responsibility: www.bsr.org
Business in the Community: www.bitc.org.uk
Council of Institutional Investors (US): www.cii.org
Department of Trade and Industry: www.dti.gov.uk
European Corporate Governance Institute: www.ecgi.org
Financial Reporting Council: www.frc.org.uk
Financial Services Authority: www.fsa.gov.uk
Global Corporate Governance Forum: www.gcgf.org
Institute for Business Ethics: www.ibe.org.uk
Institute of Chartered Secretaries and Administrators: www.icsa.org.uk
Institute of Directors: www.iod.co.uk
Institutional Voting Information Service: www.ivis.co.uk
International Corporate Governance Network: www.icgn.org
Investor Relations Society: www.ir-soc.org.uk
London Stock Exchange: www.londonstockexchange.com
National Association of Pension Funds: www.napf.co.uk
New York Stock Exchange: www.nyse.com
Organisation for Economic Co-operation and Development: www.oecd.org
Panel on Takeovers and Mergers: www.thetakeoverpanel.org.uk
Pensions Investments Research Consultants Limited: www.pirc.co.uk
Public Concern at Work (whistleblowing): www.pcaw.co.uk
US Securities and Exchange Commission: www.sec.gov

Index

Note: References in **bold** are to Appendices.

3i: independent directors training programme 84
accountability to shareholders 5, 15–16, 60, 96, 127–142, **217**; audit committee 156; internal control 172–173, **217**; nomination committee 102–103
Accountancy Investigation and Discipline Board 145
Accounting for People (2003): report of Task Force on Human Capital Management 140, 142
Accounting Standards Board (ASB) 5, 128, 145; Operating and Financial Review 131–135, 137–141
accounting standards: divergences between UK and US practices 30
Accounts Modernisation Directive (EU) 10, 45, 133, 135–136
activism, shareholder 37, 178–182
agency viii–ix, 18, 96–97, 108, 175
Ahold 29, 39
annual accounts *see* annual report and accounts
annual general meeting (AGM) 23, 190–204, **220**; advisory vote on remuneration policy 119, 120, 123–124; attendance 191; business 194–197; chairman's responsibilities 199–200, 201–203; Company Law Reform Bill proposals 192–193, 194, 195, 196–197, 198, 199, 200–201; Company Law Review recommendations 191; conduct 201–203; corporate representatives 197; frequency and timing 191–193; notice requirements 192, 193–194; questions 60, 201, 202, 203; quorum 203; receipt of annual report and accounts 127, 192, 193, 194, 195; *see also* General meeting; Proxies; Resolutions; Voting
annual report and accounts 15, 16, 127–142, **217**; accounts 5, 15, 21, 23; adequacy of narrative reporting 44–45; audit committee 154, 156; auditors' report 144; directors' remuneration 22, 23, 119–123; directors' report 7, 129–130, 134–136; directors' responsibility statement 143; internal control 172–173; Listing Rules requirements 130–131; nomination committee 102–103; receipt at AGM 127, 192, 193, 194, 195; social responsibility 45–47; *see also* business review; Operating and Financial Review; Summary Financial Statement
Arthur Andersen 25, 57, 147
Articles of Association 5, 13–14; delegation of authority 51, 60, 61; general meetings 193, 194, 195, 197,199, 201, 203; *see also* Memorandum of Association
ASB *see* Accounting Standards Board

Association of British Insurers (ABI) 37, 176, 178; disclosure guidelines on socially responsible investment 45, **225–228**; *Principles and Guidelines on Remuneration* 107, 112, 113, 115, 116, 117, 118–119, 122–123, **259–272**; (with NAPF): *Statement of Best Practice on Executive Contracts and Severance* 125, **278–282**
Association of Investment Trust Companies (AITC) 178
audit 143–159; Oxera report *Competition and Choice in the UK Audit Market* (2006) 148, 151
audit committee 19, 20, 21, 23–24, 25, 26, 143–159, **218–219**; access to information and resources 158–159; appointment, reappointment and removal of auditors 150–151; attendance of chairman at AGM 156, 201; auditor independence and objectivity 149–150; auditors' remuneration 151; compliance with Combined Code (2003) 157; delegated authority 60; integrity of financial statements 154, 155; internal control and risk management 153, 155, 163; membership 72, 85, 99, 100, 143, 157–158; non-audit work by external auditors 151; reporting to shareholders 156; Smith Review of role and effectiveness (2003) 26, 144, 156, 163, **300**; terms of reference 149, 153, **283–288**; whistleblowing 155–156, 165
Auditing Practices Board (APB) 145–148; Ethical Standards 147–148
auditors 5, 21, 143–144, **218–219**; APB Ethical Standards 146–147; appointment and reappointment 149–150; Companies (Disclosure of Auditor Remuneration) Regulations 2005 151; Company Law Reform Bill proposals 149; Eighth Company Law Directive (EU) 39; independence 7, 24, 146–150; limitation of liability 9, 148–149; non-audit services 147–148; regulation 7, 144, 145–148; removal 149; remuneration 149, 151; terms of engagement 149; *see also* Internal audit function
Australia/New Zealand Risk Management Standard (AS/NZ 4360:2004) 164
Balfour Beatty 196
Barclays plc ix, 123; directors' role profiles 78–79, 88–89, 102–103
BCCI 18
beneficial owners *see* ownership
Berle, A A and Means, C G 175
board: appointments 96–106, **212–213**; balance and independence 20, 65, 68–73, **210–211**; collective role 51–63, 65, 81, **209–210**; committees 55, 60–61; company secretary 88–90; composition 64–80, 99; delegation of authority 52, 55, 60–61;

diversity 96, 103–105; effectiveness 81–95; ICSA *Code of Good Boardroom Practice* 91, **252-253**; information requirements 81, 82, 87, **213**; internal control and risk management 160–173, **217**, **301–309**; key responsibilities 52–53; matters reserved for collective decision 53–56, 57, 86, 87, **209, 229–231**; meetings 85–88, 89, 90–92; operation 85–92; performance evaluation 82, 92–95, **214**; quorum 90; resolutions 91; setting values and standards 57–59; size 85; succession planning 96, 101; *see also* Audit committee; Chairman; Executive committee; Nomination committee; Remuneration committee

Board Effectiveness and Shareholder Engagement 2005 (RREV report) 72–73, 78, 86, 157

Board for Actuarial Standards 145

boards: two-tier 32–33

boards: unitary 51

box-ticking 19, 180, 182, **221**

BP 196

British Land 192

Building Better Boards (2004): DTI publication 84, 86, 87, 93–94, 105

business review 10, 27, 45, 133–136; DEFRA guidance on environmental KPIs 135–136

Cadbury Code of Best Practice 18, 19–22; audit committee 21, 144; auditors 21; board 20; chairman/CEO split 20, 74; company secretary 20; directors' remuneration 21, 119; induction of new directors 82; influence 31; institutional investors 185; internal control 21–22, 161; nomination committee 21, 100; non-executive directors 20–21, 68, 71; remuneration committee 108; reporting to shareholders 21

Cadbury Committee on the Financial Aspects of Corporate Governance 19–20, 144, 161

Cadbury Schweppes 123

Cadbury, Sir Adrian 191

capital maintenance 14–15

chairman: appointment 77, 101–102; contact with institutional investors 188; external directorships 101; general meetings 191, 199–200, 201–203; independence 75, 77, 99; membership of audit committee 99; membership of remuneration committee 75, 77, 109–110; performance appraisal 78, 93; remuneration 112; role 74–77, 87–89, 91; role separate from that of CEO 20, 23, 73–74, 99, **210**

chartered companies 3

Chartered Director qualification programme: Institute of Directors (IoD) 84, 105

chief executive officer (CEO): delegated authority 55; investor relations 187; role separate from that of chairman 20, 23, 73–74, 99, **210**

codes of corporate governance 18–27; European Corporate Governance Institute index of national and international codes 34

Combined Code of Best Practice (1998) 23–24; chairman/CEO split 23, 74; election and re-election of directors 23, 99; institutional investors 23; internal control 24, 161–162; nomination committee 100; non-executive directors 69, 71, 99

Combined Code of Corporate Governance (2003) 19,

26–27, **207–224**; audit committee 60, 156, 165, **218–219**; board 51–63, 81, 85, 92–93, **209–211**, 213–214; chairman 74–75, 77, 99, **210**; company secretary 89, **213**; directors' appointment 96, **212–213**; directors' induction and professional development 81, **213**; directors' remuneration 107, **215–217, 221–222**; disclosure of corporate governance arrangements **223, 224**; FRC review of implementation 26, 73, 93, 109, 110, 158, 182, 188; institutional investors 174, 179–180, 188, **219–221**; internal audit function 153, **219**; internal control and risk management 155, 161, 171, **217**; matters reserved for the board 53, **209**; nomination committee 60, 100–101, **212–213**; non-executive directors 69, 70–73, 111–112, **211**, **222–223**; remuneration committee 60, 109, **215–217**; senior independent director 78, **211**; *see also* Smith Review of role and effectiveness of audit committees

Committee of Sponsoring Organizations of the Treadway Commission (COSO): Enterprise Risk Management Framework 164

community interest companies (CICs) 7

Companies (Audit, Investigations and Community Enterprise) Act 2004 4, 7, 9, 67, 129, 145

Companies (Disclosure of Auditor Remuneration) Regulations 2005 151

Companies Act 1985 (CA 1985) 4–5, 51, 66–67, 97–98, 128–130, 198

Companies Act 1985 (Operating and Financial Review and Directors' Report etc) Regulations 2005 9, 44–45, 134–135, 137

Companies Act 1989 (CA 1989) 4–5

companies limited by guarantee 3

companies limited by shares 3

companies, types of 2–3, 7

Company Directors Disqualification Act 1986 (CDDA 1986) 4–6, 7, 66

company law 2–17; *see also* Company Law Reform Bill; Company Law Review

Company Law Action Plan (EU) 38, 39

Company Law Reform (White Paper, 2005) 9

Company Law Reform Bill 9–17, 26; annual general meetings 190–194; auditors' liability 149; disclosure of institutional investor voting 180; disclosure of proxy votes 200; DTI consultation on narrative reporting 137; elective resolutions 195; electronic communications 192–194; extraordinary resolutions 195; independent assessment of poll procedure 200; preliminary results announcement 193; rights of beneficial owners 194; shareholder resolutions 196; statutory derivative procedure 66; statutory statement of directors' duties 44, 163; year-end reporting timetable 192–193

Company Law Review (CLR) 8–9; annual general meeting 191; auditor liability 148–149; company reporting 43–44, 132, 192–193; corporate purpose 40–43; institutional investor voting 177, 180; Operating and Financial Review recommendation 44, 132–133; rights of beneficial owners 194; shareholder resolutions 196–197; statutory statement of directors' duties 44

company secretary 20, 81, 88–90, 158, 201–203, **213**;

ICSA specimen job description for corporate governance role 90–91

Competition and Choice in the UK Audit Market: Oxera report (2006) 148, 151

comply or explain 6, 18–19, 31, 34, 131, 180, 182, **207–208, 223–224**

Confederation of British Industry (CBI) 84, 108, 125

Convivium: opinion survey of independent NEDs 86, 87

Co-operative Insurance Society 180

Co-ordinating Group on Audit and Accounting Issues (CGAA) 26, 129, 144, 150

corporate culture 46–48, 52, 57–59, 62–63

Corporate Governance Review 2005: Grant Thornton report 157, 158

corporate governance: codes 18–27; European Corporate Governance Institute index of national and international codes 34; in insider systems of company ownership 33; in outsider systems of company ownership 30–31; international principles 35–37

corporate purpose: considered by Company Law Review 40, 42–43; enlightened shareholder value model 8, 13, 43–44; profit maximisation model 40–42; social welfare objective 42

COSO *see* Committee of Sponsoring Organizations of the Treadway Commission

Cranfield School of Management: board diversity study 105

customers: as stakeholders 8, 42, 127

Deloitte and Touche: Report on Impact of Directors' Remuneration Report Regulations 2002 (2005) 113, 121–122, 123–124

Department for the Environment, Food and Rural Affairs (DEFRA): guidelines on environmental KPIs for use in business reviews 135–136

Department of Labor (US) Interpretative Bulletin on ERISA 178, 181

Department of Trade and Industry (DTI) 3, 4, 84, 105, 113, 121, 123, 139, 148; *Building Better Boards* (2004) 84, 86–87, 93–95, 105; company investigations regime 7; consultation on narrative reporting 137; *Director and Auditor Liability* consultation paper (2003) 149; *Rewards for Failure* consultation paper (2003) 124–125

derivative action 8, 17, 66

Dey Report (Canada) 31

Director and Auditor Liability (2003): DTI consultation document 149

directors: appointment and reappointment 23, 96–97, **212–213**; attendance at board meetings 86, 100; disclosure of interests 15, 90; due diligence for 68; due diligence for directors: ICSA guidance note 68, **245–247**; duration of appointment 96, 102; election and re-election 23, **214**; external directorships 100–101; indemnification 67; independence 97; induction 81–83, **213**; induction of directors: ICSA guidance note 83, **248–251**; insurance 7–8, 67; insurance, directors' and officers': ICSA guidance note 67, **237–244**; legal obligations 4, 7, 15–16; liability 7–9, 13, 16–17, 66, **222–223**; loans 14; notice periods 124; offences 66; performance evaluation 81–82, 93–95; powers 13–14; professional development

23, 81–85, 105, **213**; proposed EU Directive on responsibilities 39; removal 96–99; reputational risk 67–68; responsibility for preparation of accounts 21, 143; retirement by rotation 98–99; service contracts 14, 22, 108, 124–125; substantial property transactions 14; *see also* Directors' duties; Directors' remuneration; Executive directors; Non-executive directors

directors' duties 65; acting fairly between shareholders 182, 184; breach 17, 66; duties of care and skill 12–13, 65, **222–223**; fiduciary 7, 12, 14, 65; proposed statutory statement of 8–9, 13, 40, 44, 65–66, 163

directors' remuneration 107–126, **215–217, 221–222**; ABI *Principles and Guidelines on Remuneration* 107, 112, 113, 115, 116, 117, 118–119, **259–272**; ABI/NAPF *Joint Statement of Best Practice on Executive Contracts and Severance* 125, **278–282**; DTI consultation paper *Rewards for Failure* (2003) 124–125; Greenbury Code of Best Practice 22, 108; *see also* Remuneration committee

Directors' Remuneration Report Regulations 2002 22, 112–113, 119–122; Deloitte and Touche report on impact (2005) 113, 121–122, 123–124

disclosure: ABI disclosure guidelines on socially responsible investment 45, **225–228**; auditors' remuneration 151; corporate governance arrangements **223–224**; directors' attendance at board meetings 86; directors' interests 4–5, 15; directors' remuneration 21, 112–113, 119–123; institutional investor voting 177, 179–180; internal control and risk management 164; proxy votes 200, **314–316**; proxy votes: ICSA guidance note on disclosing 200, **314–316**; remuneration committee 112–113; social, ethical and environmental (SEE) issues 40, 45, 132, **225–228**

diversity: of board 96, 104–105

dividends 5, 185, 195

due diligence for directors 68; ICSA guidance note 68, **245–247**

Edis-Bates Associates: research on board performance evaluation 93, 154

Eighth Company Law Directive (EU) 5, 26, 39, 157

electronic communications 9, 192, 193, 194; polling at general meetings 199–200; proxy appointment 198

employees: as stakeholders 8, 40, 42, 127; codes of ethics 48, 52, 57–59; codes of ethics in US Sarbanes-Oxley Act 34, 47

Employment Retirement Income Security Act 1974 (US): Department of Labor Interpretative Bulletin 178, 181

enlightened shareholder value model of corporate purpose 8, 13, 43–44

Enron viii, ix, 7, 9, 19, 24–26, 29, 33–34, 38, 40, 47–48, 52, 57, 69, 97, 128, 129, 143–144, 147, 150, 155, 165; *see also* Sarbanes-Oxley Act of 2002

Enterprise Act 2002 4, 7

Enterprise Risk Management Framework (COSO) 164

environment: as stakeholder 40–42; DEFRA guidance on environmental KPIs for use in business reviews 135–136

Environmental Protection Act 1990: directors' liabilities 66

Equitable Life 29
European Corporate Governance Forum (EU) 38
European Corporate Governance Institute 34
European Union (EU) 5; Accounts Modernisation
    Directive 10, 45, 133–135; Company Law Action
    Plan 38–39; Eighth Company Law Directive 5, 26,
    39, 157; Fourth Company Law Directive 163;
    Seventh Company Law Directive 5, 38, 163;
    Takeover Directive 11
executive committee 60; ICSA guidance note on terms
    of reference 60, **232–236**
executive directors 21, 55, 61, 65
exit: shareholders' power of 16, 175
filing requirements 16
financial reporting: adequacy 131
Financial Reporting Council (FRC) 5, 19, 24, 26, 73,
    75, 128–129, 145, 149; review of implementation
    of 2003 Combined Code 73, 75, 77, 93, 109, 110,
    158, 182, 188; review of Turnbull Guidance on
    internal control 24, 162, 163, 170–173; revised
    guidance on internal control 163–164, 168,
    171–173, **301–309**
Financial Reporting Review Panel (FRRP) 5, 7, 133,
    145
Financial Services and Markets Act 2000 (FSMA
    2000) 4, 5, 6, 66
Financial Services Authority (FSA) 5, 133, 187
Flint, Douglas 24, 162
Fourth Company Law Directive (EU) 26, 38, 163
fraudulent trading 66
FRC see Financial Reporting Council
free-rider problem 175
Friedman, Milton 41
Friends Provident 180
FRRP see Financial Reporting Review Panel
FTSE 100 cross-company mentoring programme 84
general meeting 14, 15, 51, 184, 190; appointment and
    removal of directors 96, 97, 99; extraordinary
    general meeting 98, 190; legal provisions 5; notice
    15; shareholder requisition 192; see also Annual
    general meeting; Resolutions
GlaxoSmithKline ix, 123
Global Corporate Governance Principles: International
    Corporate Governance Network (ICGN) 37
going concern 21
Grant Thornton: *Corporate Governance Review 2005*
    157, 158
Greenbury Code of Best Practice 22, 108, 113;
    directors' service contracts 22; disclosure on
    directors' remuneration 119; performance
    incentives 22; performance-related remuneration
    117; remuneration committee 22, 109;
    termination payments 22, 124
guarantee companies 3
Hampel Committee on Corporate Governance 23, 96,
    99, 161
Hermes 37, 182
Higgs Report on role and effectiveness of non-
    executive directors (2003) 26, 69, 70; board
    diversity 104–105; board performance evaluation
    92–93; chairman/CEO split 74; chairman's
    appointment 77; chairman's role 74–76; directors'
    liability 67; due diligence 68; independence of

NEDs 71; induction of new directors 82–83;
    institutional investors 187–188; nomination
    committee 100; professional development of
    directors 83–84; reappointment of directors 99;
    role of NEDs 70; senior independent director 78
human rights 41, 42
ICSA Code of Good Boardroom Practice 91, **252–253**
ICSA guidance notes: audit committee terms of
    reference 149, **283–288**; directors' and officers'
    insurance 67, **237–244**; disclosing proxy votes
    200, **314–316**; due diligence for directors 68,
    245–247; executive committee terms of reference
    60, **232–236**; induction of directors 83, **248–251**;
    matters reserved to the board 53, **229–231**;
    nomination committee terms of reference
    100–101, **254–258**; remuneration committee
    terms of reference 109–111, **273–277**
ICSA specimen job description for corporate
    governance role of company secretary 89–91
incorporation 2
indemnification: of directors 67
independence see Auditors; Chairman; Non-
    executive directors
index tracking see Institutional investors
induction: of directors 69, 81- 82; ICSA guidance note
    83, **248–251**
insider dealing 6
insider systems of company ownership 29, 31–33
Insight Investment 192
insolvency 66
Insolvency Act 1986 (IA 1986) 4, 7
Institute of Business Ethics 58–59
Institute of Chartered Accountants in England and
    Wales (ICAEW) 24; guidance for audit
    committees on whistleblowing arrangements 156;
    register of potential NEDs 105; Turnbull
    Guidance on internal control 162
Institute of Directors (IoD) 84, 86, 93; Chartered
    Director qualification 84, 105; Company
    Direction programme 84
Institute of Risk Management (IRM): Risk
    Management Standard 164
Institutional Investment in the United Kingdom
    (Myners Report, 2001) viii, 69, 177–178
institutional investors 23, 97, 98, 174 -189, **219–221**;
    activism 37; AGM attendance 191, 198; and
    NEDs 73, 188; Combined Code (2003)
    recommendations 179–180, **219–221**;
    concentration of ownership 177, 191; fiduciary
    duties 177–178; guidelines on directors'
    remuneration 107, 112, 113, 114–115, 117–119,
    122–124, 125, **259–272**, **278–282**; index tracking
    177; Myners Principles for Institutional
    Investment Decision-making 178, 180–181; UK
    representative bodies 176; voting 9, 38, 177,
    179–181, 191, 198, **221**
Institutional Shareholders' Committee (ISC) 176;
    *Statement of Principles on the Responsibilities of
    Institutional Shareholders and Agents* 176,
    178–181, **311–313**
insurance, directors' and officers' 67; ICSA guidance
    note 67, **237–244**
interim report 131, 154–155, 185

internal control 21–22, 24, 161; FRC revised guidance to directors on Combined Code 24, 163–164, 168, 171–173, **301–309**; *Internal Control: Guidance for Directors on the Combined Code* (Turnbull Report, 1999) 24, 162; Ruttemann Report (1994) 161

internal control and risk management 160–173, **217**; audit committee responsibilities 155; board's review of effectiveness 171–173; reporting to shareholders 172–173; risk register 169

International Corporate Governance Network (ICGN): *Global Corporate Governance Principles* 37

international principles of corporate governance 35–37

Investment Management Association (IMA) 176, 179, 182–184; *Relations with Investee Companies – guidance on good practice* 176, 182–184

Joint Statement of Best Practice on Executive Contracts and Severance (ABI/NAPF) 125, **278–282**

Kingsmill, Denise 140

Laxey Partners 98, 192

limitation of liability 3

limited companies 3

Listing Rules 6, 14, 15, 51, 117, 119, 130–131, 184, 192; admission to listing 6; continuing obligations 6, 185–187; Model Code 6; statement of compliance with Combined Code 6, 19, 131

local communities: as stakeholders 40, 42, 127

London Stock Exchange 19

maintenance of capital 14–15

management board: in two-tier board system 33

Manifest 176, 180

Marconi 52

market abuse 6

matters reserved for the board 53–56, 86–87, 89, 101, 111, **209**; ICSA guidance note 53, **229–231**

Maxwell viii, 18, 20

Memorandum of Association 5, 14; *see also* Articles of Association

MFI Furniture Group 124

Model Business Corporation Act (US) 30

Model Code 6

Modernising Company Law (White Paper, 2002) 9, 134

Morley Fund Management 192

Myners, Paul viii, 69, 177

Myners *Principles for Institutional Investment Decision-making* 178, 180–181

Myners Report (2002): *Institutional Investment in the United Kingdom* viii, 69, 177, 178

Nasdaq (US) 31, 34

National Association of Pension Funds (NAPF) 125, 176, 179; (with ABI): *Joint Statement of Best Practice on Executive Contracts and Severance* 125, **278–282**

New York Stock Exchange (NYSE) 31, 34

New Zealand: Australia/New Zealand Risk Management Standard (AS/NZ 4360:2004) 164

nomination committee 20–21, 77, 100–103, 201, **212–213**; delegated authority 60; frequency of meetings 101; ICSA guidance note on terms of reference 100–101, **254–258**; membership 72, 85,

100–101; reporting to shareholders 102–103; role 96, 101–102

nominee shareholders 9, 194

non-executive directors (NEDs) 19, 20–21, 23, 65, 69–73; and institutional investors 188; appointment 21, 69, 73, 99, 102; Convivium opinion survey 86, 87; effectiveness 69, 70; external directorships 101; Higgs Report on role and effectiveness (2003) 26, 69–70; ICAEW register of potential NEDs 105; independence 20–21, 38, 69–73, 99, 109, **211**; induction 69; liability **222–223**; non-independent NEDs 72, 73, 99; number 69, 72, 85; professional development 69, 83; remuneration 111–112; resignation statement 70; role 20, 21, 70; time commitments 102; Tyson Report on recruitment and development (2003) 84

North Atlantic Value 192

OECD *Principles of Corporate Governance* 35–37

Operating and Financial Review (OFR) 9, 10, 27, 134–141, 142; ASB statement of best practice 137–139; ASB voluntary reporting frameworks 131–132; Companies Act 1985 (Operating and Financial Review and Directors' Report etc) Regulations 2005 9, 44–45, 134–135; Company Law Review recommendation 44, 132–133

Operating and Financial Review Working Group: *Practical Guidance for Directors* (2004) 139–141

Organisation for Economic Cooperation and Development (OECD) 35; *Principles of Corporate Governance* 35–37

outsider systems of company ownership 28–31

ownership: beneficial owners 194; concentration of ownership by institutional investors 177, 191; insider systems 29–31; outsider systems 28–31; separation from control viii–ix, 18, 28–30, 108, 175

Oxera report: *Competition and Choice in the UK Audit Market* (2006) 148, 151

Parmalat 29, 39

pension funds *see* Institutional investors

Pensions Investment Research Consultants (PIRC) 37, 176

performance evaluation: of board, directors and committees 81–82, 92–95, **214**

performance incentives *see* Directors' remuneration

policies and procedures 62–63, 91–92, 167

Polly Peck 18

Practical Guidance for Directors (2004): report by Operating and Financial Review Working Group 139–141

preliminary results announcement 131, 154–155, 185, 192–193

price-sensitive information 6, 154–155, 185–187, 201

Principles and Guidelines on Remuneration: ABI guidelines 107, 112, 113, 115, 116, 117, 118–119, **259–272**

procedures *see* Policies and procedures

Professional Oversight Board for Accountancy (POBA) 145

profit maximisation model of corporate purpose 40–42

proxies 194, 197–198, 199–200; disclosure of proxy votes 200; electronic appointment 198; rights 198

proxy voting agencies: Manifest 176, 180; PIRC 176; RREV 72, 73, 86, 99, 100, 157, 176
Prudential 180
public companies 3
Public Company Accounting Oversight Board (US) 34
Public Concern at Work *see* Whistleblowing
Public Interest Disclosure Act 1998 (PIDA 1998) 166
Radcliffe, Rosemary 139
rational apathy 175, 177
Reckitt Benckiser 123
records: statutory requirements 16
registered companies 2–3
Registrar of Companies 4, 16
Relations with Investee Companies: Investment Management Association (IMA) guidance on good practice 176, 182–184
remuneration committee 20–22, 60, 99–100, 109–111, 119, **215–222**; attendance of chairman at AGM 119, 201; Cadbury Code recommendations 21, 108; delegated authority 60, 109; Greenbury Code recommendations 22, 109; ICSA guidance note on terms of reference 110, **273–277**; membership 72, 85, 99–100, 109; membership of board chairman 75, 77, 109, 111; remuneration consultants 112–113; remuneration of NEDs 111–112; reporting to shareholders 119; role 109, 110–111
Research, Recommendations and Electronic Voting (RREV) 176; *Board Effectiveness and Shareholder Engagement 2005* 72, 73, 78, 86, 157; *Voting Review 2005* 99, 100
resolutions: elective 195; extraordinary 195; of board 91; ordinary 97–98, 194–195; shareholder 9, 97–98, 195–197; special 194–195
returns: filing requirements 16
rewards for failure *see* Directors' remuneration
Rio Tinto 196
risk management 155, 160–161, 168–169; *see also* internal control and risk management
Risk Management Standard (Australia/New Zealand AS/NZ 4360:2004) 164
Risk Management Standard (Institute of Risk Management) 164
RSM Robson Rhodes 94
Ruttemann Report (1994) 22, 161
Sainsbury 124
Sarbanes-Oxley Act of 2002 (US) 34, 47, 155, 163, 165
Securities and Exchange Commission (US) 31
senior independent director 73, 77–79, 188, **211**
service contracts *see* Directors
Seventh Company Law Directive (EU) 5, 38, 163
shareholder powers and entitlements 5, 13, 16–17, 96–99, 150, 182, 184, 193–194; exit 16, 175; general meeting requisition 192; shareholder resolutions 195–197; voice 16, 175
shareholders: activism 37, 178; legal remedies 16–17, 66; proposed EU Directive on shareholders' rights 38
shares: allotment 5; variation of voting powers 5
Shell 196
short-termism 41

SkyePharma plc 98, 192
Smith, Adam ix
Smith, Sir Robert 144
Smith guidance on role and effectiveness of audit committees 26, 144, 150–159, 163, **300**
social, ethical and environmental (SEE) issues 40, 45
social responsibility 40, 43, 45–47; reporting frameworks 45–47
social welfare objective model of corporate purpose 42
socially responsible investment (SRI): ABI guidelines on disclosure 45, **225–228**
stakeholders 8, 40, 42, 127
Statement of Principles on the Responsibilities of Institutional Shareholders and Agents: Institutional Shareholders' Committee (ISC) 176, 179–181, **311–313**
statutory corporations 3
Summary Financial Statement (SFS) 132–133
supervisory board: in two-tier board system 32
suppliers: as stakeholders 8, 40, 42, 127
Table A 5, 51, 60, 61, 74, 98
takeover 14; Takeover Code 14; Takeover Directive (EU) 11
Task Force on Human Capital Management: *Accounting for People* (2003) 140, 142
termination payments *see* Directors' remuneration
Tesco ix, 123
Total Shareholder Return (TSR) 118–119
Turnbull Report: *Internal Control: Guidance for Directors on the Combined Code* (1999) 24, 161–162; FRC review of Turnbull guidance on internal control 24, 162–163, 170–173
two-tier boards 32–33
Tyson, Laura D'Andrea 84
Tyson Report on recruitment and development of NEDs (2003) 84, 104–105
unfair prejudice 17
unitary boards 51, 53
United Business Media 124
United Kingdom Listing Authority (UKLA) 5, 6
US Department of Labor Interpretative Bulletin on ERISA 178, 181
voice: shareholders' power of 16, 175
voting 197–201; by corporate representatives 197; by institutional investors 9, 177, 180–181, 191, 198, **221**; by poll 196–197, 199; by show of hands 199; in Articles 197–199; independent assessment of poll procedure 200–201; role of chairman 198, 199; *see also* Proxies
Voting Review 2005: Research, Recommendations and Electronic Voting (RREV) 99, 100
whistleblowing 48, 57, 165, 167; and Enron 155; in US Sarbanes-Oxley Act 34, 47; Public Concern at Work 167; role of audit committee 155–156, 165; UK statutory position 166
White Papers: *Company Law Reform* (2005) 9; *Modernising Company Law* (2002) 9, 134
WorldCom 7, 26, 29, 147
WPP 123
wrongful trading 7, 66
Wyevale Garden Centres plc 98
Xstrata 124